CAPITAL AND EMPLOYMENT

CAPITAL AND EMPLOYMENT

R. G. HAWTREY

LONGMANS, GREEN AND CO
LONDON • NEW YORK • TORONTO

LONGMANS GREEN AND CO LTD
6 & 7 CLIFFORD STREET LONDON W 1

ALSO AT MELBOURNE AND CAPE TOWN

LONGMANS GREEN AND CO INC
55 FIFTH AVENUE NEW YORK 3

LONGMANS GREEN AND CO
215 VICTORIA STREET TORONTO 1

ORIENT LONGMANS LTD
BOMBAY CALCUTTA MADRAS

First Published . . . 1937
Second Impression . . 1939
Second Edition . . . 1952

PRINTED IN GREAT BRITAIN AT
THE UNIVERSITY PRESS
ABERDEEN

PREFACE TO THE SECOND EDITION

THE first edition of this book appeared in 1937, far on in the disastrous depression of the nineteen-thirties. Along with *A Century of Bank Rate*, which followed it in 1938, it made a protest against the " deplorably prevalent tendency to disparage, distrust or ignore the bank rate tradition ",[1] and against the various proposals to do the work of monetary control by regulating the disbursements of the Government and public authorities, instead of relying on the short-term rate of interest and the influence of the banking system on the creation of credit. At that time the controversy was still in one sense academic, because the desirability of continuing a low bank rate when the world was suffering from extreme depression and unemployment was beyond dispute. But since the end of the Second World War, London and New York have continued the policy of low bank rate and cheap money, though the circumstances are just the contrary of those prevailing in the nineteen-thirties. Only with the change of Government in October, 1951, has British policy been modified.

The danger is no longer deflation and unemployment, but inflation and the degradation of money. The bank rate policy, with all that it implies in the regulation of the flow of money through the creation of credit, is not only the most effective instrument for keeping inflation in check, but is indispensable for that stabilisation of the purchasing power of the money unit by which both inflation and deflation are to be avoided.

In this new edition of *Capital and Employment* I have found numerous amendments and alterations desirable, and some material changes and additions. In particular, the criticism of Keynes's *General Theory of Employment, Interest and Money* has been largely re-written.

That criticism, as it appeared in the first edition, was the

---

[1] *A Century of Bank Rate*, pp. 263-4.

outcome of a prolonged correspondence with him, first in 1935 when he was still writing his book, and later when I was writing my criticism of it. In a letter of 31 August 1936, he expressed his intention of writing articles about some of the points I had raised, and he proceeded : " I am thinking of producing in the course of the next year or so what might be called *footnotes* to my previous book, dealing with various criticisms and particular points which want carrying further. Of course, in fact, the whole book needs re-writing and re-casting. But I am still not in a sufficiently changed state of mind as yet to be in the position to do that. On the other hand, I can deal with specific points."

This process of reconsideration was interrupted all too soon by Keynes's illness, and he did not carry his replies to criticisms very far. His recovery, incomplete as it was, saw him immersed in the affairs of the nation and the war.

There would have been something to be said for reproducing my criticism in this new edition unchanged, leaving it as it was when he and I had been corresponding about it. But it seemed much in need of revision. Not that I have seen reason to alter the main lines of criticism. But there are some aspects which the original version failed to bring out or at any rate to treat with sufficient thoroughness. It referred very perfunctorily to the relation of Keynes's " speculative motive " to securities repayable at a due date, and it overlooked altogether the importance in that connexion of the unspent depreciation allowances and reinvested profits of traders. It accepted Keynes's broad concepts of liquidity preference and liquidity premium without touching on the question of how they ought to be measured. Many other points in which elaboration or amendment was needed could be instanced. And I have been led to re-write the greater part of the criticism. In doing so I have felt that a closer study of what Keynes wrote, and of what is implied in it, was required than during his life-time, and I have found some corrections necessary in my former presentation of his views.

Professor Hayek and Mr. Harrod very kindly read the chapters criticising their respective works in the first edition, and helped me with their comments, and I have to thank them once again for their comments and suggestions on the passages in these chapters dealing with some of their subsequent works. But I do not claim any authority other than my own for the interpretations placed upon their views.

Certain portions of my book make some use of mathematical notation. Readers who do not find that form of expression helpful may omit the concluding section of Chapter I and the note at the end of Chapter IV without misgiving. Chapter IX employs some simple applications of the calculus derived from the book, Professor Pigou's *Theory of Unemployment*, which forms the subject of that chapter. For the rest I hope the mathematical expressions employed in Chapters VI, VII, VIII and X will be found simple enough not to form a stumbling block for anyone.

The greater part of Chapter VI is reproduced, with revision, from an article which appeared in the *Economic Journal* for December 1934. Chapter VIII, criticising Professor Pigou's *Theory of Unemployment*, appeared in *Economica* for May 1934, and has also been revised for re-publication. The concluding chapter, which examines the Experts' Report of December 1949 to the United Nations on *Measures for Full Employment*, is new. It appeared in Italian in the *Rivista di Politica Economica* for January 1951.

R. G. HAWTREY.

July, 1952.

CONTENTS

CHAPTER I

INTRODUCTION

IN recent years it has been a reproach to economists that they do not agree among themselves ; there is no authoritative body of doctrine to give guidance to public opinion and to public policy. It is no sufficient defence to say that there are matters in regard to which there is no material difference of opinion, so long as there are questions of vital and immediate practical moment of which that cannot be said.

Economists can best remove this reproach by criticising one another's theories. · That does not mean merely raising objections and giving reasons for dissent. What is wanted is intensive, sympathetic, constructive criticism. It has been my aim in this book to apply such criticism to certain current economic doctrines. I have endeavoured to avoid cheap or superficial debating points, and, so far as possible, to enter into the spirit of each theory criticised and to see it from the author's point of view. Where I have lapsed from this very desirable standard of controversy, I must ask pardon for human weakness.

Since the end of the First World War there has been observable a growing scepticism among economists in regard to the theory of credit regulation which was formerly generally accepted. It used to be taken for granted that the amount of borrowing from the banks would respond to changes in the short-term rate of interest, and that therefore it was practicable to regulate the quantity and the flow of money by appropriate adjustments of bank rate. No doubt the underlying complexities of the theory were insufficiently explored, and any economist on first becoming aware of the complexities might well be led to distrust the theory or even to repudiate it altogether.

But this is a department of economics which was not evolved *a priori*. It was based on practice, and the inadequacy of the theoretical arguments by which it has been supported in the past affords no sufficient reason for rejecting it.

The practice on which it is based goes back to 1832, when Horsley Palmer, the Governor of the Bank of England, advocated a rise of the rate of discount as a means of limiting transactions and causing a reduction of prices.[1] The limitation of the rate of discount to

---

[1] See " Evidence before the Committee of 1832 on the Bank of England Charter ", question 678.

1

5 per cent by the usury laws was removed in 1833, and in 1839 for the first time the Bank of England, in raising bank rate to 6 per cent, used its new power.

The rate of discount was essentially the rate applicable to borrowing for transactions in *commodities*. In the course of the nineteenth century the principle enunciated by Horsley Palmer came to be in some degree obscured, because bank loans and overdrafts gradually superseded bills of exchange for the financing of transactions in commodities, except those arising out of international trade. There was no longer so clear a boundary line between borrowing for the purchase of commodities and borrowing for capital outlay or for the purchase of securities. And the rates of interest on loans and overdrafts were adjusted to variations in bank rate even more automatically than the rates of discount on bills.

Writing in 1913 on the subject of the trade cycle, I became aware of the necessity of some analysis of the ultimate reactions of the short-term rate of interest on the dealers in commodities, by way of an explanation of the limitation of transactions, and the reduction of prices imputed in Horsley Palmer's theory to a rise in the rate. I dealt with the matter as follows :

" One of the special functions of a dealer is to keep a stock or ' working balance ' of the goods in which he deals. This is necessary to enable him to meet the varied needs of his customers without delay. Now a dealer borrows money to buy goods, and repays the money as the goods are sold. Consequently when his stocks are large his indebtedness to his banker will be correspondingly large. The extent of the stocks which he sees fit to keep will be based on experience, but can, of course, be varied within fairly wide limits without much risk of inconvenience. When the rate of interest goes up, he will be anxious to reduce his indebtedness, so far as he can without incurring serious inconvenience. He can reduce his indebtedness if he can reduce his stocks of goods, and he can reduce his stocks of goods by merely delaying replenishment when they are sold." [1]

At the time that reasoning seemed to me self-evident. And it still does. Yet economists seem strangely reluctant to accept it. The theories of the trade cycle and of trade depression and unemployment now in vogue obscure the distinction between the influence of the short-term rate of interest on borrowing for holding stocks of goods and that of the long-term rate on the raising of funds with a view to capital outlay. They even look for the influence of bank

[1] *Good and Bad Trade*, p. 62.

rate in its direct effects on long-term investment, and thereby deprive the bank rate policy of its principal theoretical basis. The effect of movements of the short-term rate of interest on the long-term rate is small,[1] and it is easy to show that as an instrument of credit regulation the long-term investment market is very intractable. Pessimistic conclusions result as to the possibility of guarding against monetary instability with all its disastrous consequences.

If bank rate does not meet the need, what is left ? The banking system supplies the community with money through lending : it lends to traders, to consumers and to the Government, and thus directs the flow of money into all channels. If the banks cannot regulate the borrowing of the traders and consumers effectively, there is still the Government. Nowadays governments have taken upon themselves greatly extended economic functions, so that the budget accounts for a substantial share of the entire flow of money. And monetary policy has fallen back on Government action ; the flow of money is to be regulated through an adjustable programme of public works or through budget deficits and surpluses.

Budget policy has nothing like the flexibility and power of quick action characteristic of credit policy under the guidance of bank rate. Yet the idea has grown up, both among economists and among governments and their experts and advisers, not merely that budget policy is the instrument by which the flow of money is to be regulated, but that by its use the problem of trade depression and unemployment has been successfully solved. Governments and political parties unquestioningly claim that " full employment " is a part of their policy. Full employment figures among the aims of the International Monetary Fund, the Economic and Social Council, and the Geneva Agreement on Tariffs and Trade, and it is invariably assumed that full employment can be assured by Government expenditure.

By contrast with the methods which were evolved and acted upon in the nineteenth century, and stood the test of experience up to 1914, the maintenance of employment by Government expenditure is an untried expedient.

When an economic expert makes practical recommendations, he passes from the theoretical plane to one in which quite different tests are necessary. In theoretical reasoning he may construct whatever hypothesis he thinks fit and proceed by deduction to general propositions as to human behaviour within the limits of the hypothesis. But as soon as he deals with a situation on the practical plane, he is

[1] See my *A Century of Bank Rate*, pp. 146 ff.

bound to take account, so far as possible, of *all* actual relevant circumstances. Omniscience being unattainable, we must in economic as in other decisions be content with an approximation in which we try to give due weight to each element of the situation. A hypothesis which excludes any element or gives it insufficient weight vitiates the result. For the purposes of theory, the result may have a sufficient resemblance to the truth, in that the train of reasoning contains all the requisite steps correctly set forth, and indeed all the various practical measures that might be called for may be separately formulated. But none the less the final conclusion may for practical purposes be fatally wrong, if a distortion of the facts at the beginning is reflected in the conclusions, and the worse is made to appear the better way.

Though the main purpose of this book is critical, Chapters II to IV are occupied with exposition rather than criticism. They set out certain portions of the theory of capital and interest to be used in the subsequent arguments. They have nevertheless a critical side, in that I have attempted to free the subject from the limitations of blackboard economics, and to bring the theoretical principles into as close relation as possible with practical facts and behaviour. One or two passages in Chapter III take the form of criticism, particularly on the subject of Profit (pp. 31-4), which has a bearing on several of the criticisms in later chapters (see pp. 168-72, 248-52, 257-62 and 286-7).

Chapter II treats of the theory of the period of production, which we owe to Jevons and Boehm-Bawerk. The fundamental principle that capital is to be expressed in terms of time is of great theoretical importance, but its practical application is subject to certain limitations, and it is by no means essential to the development of those aspects of the subject with which we are specially concerned. Chapter II is to be read in connexion with Chapter VIII, for Professor Hayek's *Prices and Production*, which is explained and criticised in that chapter, goes back to first principles and requires a clear understanding of the period of production and the structure of production.

Chapter V turns more definitely to the task of criticism. It deals with some of the prevalent ideas on the subject of the dependence of the trade cycle or of credit regulation on the long-term investment market.

Chapter VI is in the nature of a digression. It supplies an analytical background for the monetary theory employed in Chapters IV and V. It is occupied partly with a more rigorous definition of terms, and partly with setting out the arithmetical relations between them. These relations, simple in themselves, compose a whole too complex to be easily grasped without an algebraical notation.

The remainder of the book, Chapters VII to XI, consists of a series of criticisms of individual writers on economics. Of these, the first is a criticism of Keynes's *General Theory of Employment, Interest and Money*. That brilliant and famous work gave full scope to the fertility and acuteness of Keynes's mind. It was written with the express object " of persuading economists to re-examine critically certain of their basic assumptions ".

Foremost among the basic assumptions referred to was the classical doctrine of interest, that " investment represents the demand for investible resources and saving represents the supply, whilst the rate of interest is the ' price ' of investible resources at which the two are equated " (below, p. 157). Keynes challenged this position. He so *defined* investment as to make it identically equal to saving, and thereby to deprive the classical doctrine, as he formulated it, of significance. He supplied its place with his own theory that interest is compensation for forgoing liquidity.

One of his most important contributions to economics has been the introduction of the concept of liquidity into the theory of capital and interest. But the idea has its limitations. It supplements the classical doctrine of interest, but is far from superseding it.

Keynes's pronouncement that the rate of interest is a " highly conventional phenomenon " looks at first sight like mere scepticism or academic theorising. Not at all. It is a really significant modification of the theory itself.

My criticisms of Keynes's book form the subject of Chapter VII. There is no denying that they amount to a considerable divergence of view. All through them there runs my fundamental objection that the book fails to preserve the distinction between the long-term and short-term rates of interest.

In fact Keynes himself was, I think, responsible for the assumption that the holding of stocks of goods with borrowed money is not sensitive to the rate of interest. It was in his *Treatise on Money* (1930) that he argued the case (see below, pp. 108 and 186). In the *General Theory* it is tacitly assumed ; it is a postulate underlying his reasoning all through.

Professor Hayek, whose *Prices and Production* and *Profits, Interest and Investment* form the subject of Chapter VIII, does not by any means deny the susceptibility of working capital to the rate of interest. Rather he adopts the nineteenth-century assumption that all forms of borrowing must be more or less responsive to variations in the rate of interest. But he obscures the boundary line between working capital and instrumental capital, and so misses the special characteristics of the former. He is led to base his theory on the effects of a shortening of the period of production in throwing " specific " forms of capital, which are only adapted to a longer period of production, out of use.

Professor Pigou's *Theory of Unemployment* is not concerned with industrial fluctuations. They formed the subject of an earlier work which I criticised in my *Trade and Credit* (Chapter VIII). He is not one of those who doubt the response of borrowers to the rate of interest, whether they borrow for working capital or for fixed capital (see his *Industrial Fluctuations*, especially Chapters V to VII of Part II). But in his *Theory of Unemployment* he approaches his subject from the non-monetary or, as he calls it, the " real " standpoint. Much of my criticism is directed to showing the defects of that method of approach. It is not that the causes of unemployment which predominate in his theory do not exist. Much of his analysis is very relevant for example to technological unemployment. But such causes do not account for the *epidemics* of unemployment which are the real trouble.

Mr. Harrod's works, *The Trade Cycle* and *Towards a Dynamic Economics*, are largely concerned with what has come to be called the acceleration principle. The activity of the instrumental industries depends on the increment of capital equipment and the increment of capital equipment depends on the *rate of increase* in production by the industries which use the equipment. In itself this is a valid principle, but it is subject to limitations.

The concluding chapter is a criticism of the recent Report on *Measures for Full Employment* by five experts to the United Nations. The Report may be regarded as a summing up of the position taken at the present time by the predominant section of economic opinion. It illustrates both the astonishing extent to which the former well established instruments of monetary policy have fallen into neglect, and the pitifully inadequate expedients to which policy is thereby reduced.

CHAPTER II

THE PERIOD OF PRODUCTION AND THE STRUCTURE OF PRODUCTION

THE PERIOD OF PRODUCTION

THE idea that capital can be expressed in terms of time may be traced back to the early days of economics in the period of the Physiocrats. Quesnay describes both working capital and fixed capital as wealth " advanced " for the purposes of production. Faithful to Physiocratic principles, he interpreted wealth to mean the produce of the soil. The capitalist's vital function was to provide the essentials of life for the workmen and, so long as the subsistence theory of wages survived, this idea persisted.

Adam Smith, on the other hand, preferred the conception of capital as a " stock " of wealth, but the idea of an advance to cover the period, long or short, between productive activity and the appearance of the completed product remained familiar to the classical economists.

It was Jevons who first elaborated the idea of advances into that of a period of production.

His thesis was that, when the use of additional or more elaborate instruments permitted increased production from a given amount of human effort and natural resources, this meant essentially that producers had to wait longer for the final product. Capital was deprived of the status of an independent factor of production, and became nothing more than a lapse of time, which was a condition of more round-about methods of production where these were technically more efficient. There remained " land and labour ", or, more comprehensively, natural resources and human effort, as the only original factors of production.

The period of production is the average lapse of time intervening between the activities of the original factors of production and the fruition of their products by the consumers.

Jevons expressed the output of the community as a function, F, of the period of production, or, as he described it, of " the interval elapsing between the first exertion of labour and the enjoyment of the result ".[1] If the period of production be extended by an

---

[1] *Theory of Political Economy*, p. 248.

increment, t, the output, F, will be increased by an increment, f. This additional output is obtained at the cost of forgoing the original output, F, for the time, t. A sacrifice of wealth, tF, yields a return of f per unit of time ever after, and will have been worth while if the rate of interest does not exceed $\dfrac{f}{tF}$.[1] That expression therefore gives the equilibrium rate of interest. Jevons made the assumption (justified in a purely static theory) that under any given limitation people would choose the most economical methods of production, and therefore the rate of interest would be at the equilibrium rate.

Jevons did not express the entire stock of capital in terms of the period of production, but only the increment. Approaching the matter from another point of view, we might say that, if C is the total capital of the community, and I the total income, the ratio $\dfrac{C}{I}$, which may be regarded as measuring the intensity of capitalisation of the economic system, is a period of time. For C is wealth and I is wealth per unit of time. But we cannot place any simple interpretation on this period of time; we cannot identify it with the period of production. This is obvious from the mere fact that I fluctuates, and its changes, though they correspond to no changes in the period of production, nevertheless directly affect the ratio $\dfrac{C}{I}$.

And there are difficulties in the way of a direct computation of the total capital. The items composing it have to be valued in terms of a common unit in order to be aggregated together. Their first cost depends on the technological conditions prevailing at the times they were severally produced. Their present market value depends partly on the hypothetical cost of replacement, with allowance for depreciation, partly on their expected usefulness. In fact the best way to arrive at total capital is first to calculate the period of production.

We shall find that, in the particular case where C and I are both constant, the ratio $\dfrac{C}{I}$ (subject to certain corrections) is equal to the

---

[1] Jevons expressed this result in the notation of the differential calculus. Taking t to denote the period of production (not, as above, the *increment* of it) he found $\dfrac{1}{F}\dfrac{dF}{dt}$ as the expression for the rate of interest (*loc. cit.*, pp. 266-7).

period of production. That is only a particular case, and one not likely ever to occur in reality, but we can generalise it by introducing a " standard " period of production (below, p. 20).

INSTRUMENTS AND WORKING CAPITAL

Even if we conceive of the use of capital as essentially a device for utilising the technical advantages of a more prolonged period of production, we still find a place for the conception of capital as an accumulated stock of wealth. At any moment of the productive process those productive operations which are already past will have left their mark in some material objects which embody their contribution to the process as a whole. These material objects fall into two broad classes, instruments and working capital.

Working capital is composed partly of goods in process or in transit, partly of stocks of materials and intermediate products [1] awaiting use in manufacture, partly of stocks of goods awaiting sale. An instrument is a material object which is used in any productive process, but is distinguished from materials and intermediate products which when used in production are *used up*. If there is a stock of a commodity to be used as a material of manufacture, each successive portion taken from the stock for use ceases to be that commodity and becomes merged in the new product manufactured out of it. (Sometimes the material survives in the manufactured product, like the leather in the glove, but sometimes it is completely destroyed, like the fuel used in smelting or in generating power.)

On the other hand, the loss of value (if any) which the instrument suffers through use takes the form, not of the consumption of a separable portion of it in manufacture, but of *depreciation*. The cost of the final product includes the *whole* value of the materials used up in producing it, and of the processes applied to them, but only an *apportioned part* of the value of the instruments used. This apportioned part of depreciation is included, along with the cost of maintenance of the instruments, in the value of the processes to which the instruments contribute. Where the use of an instrument contributes to processes giving rise to more than one final product, the apportionment of its contribution among the joint products may involve arbitrary assumptions.

Depreciation should be so calculated that the whole value of the

---

[1] It is, I think, more convenient to use the term, intermediate products, for materials which have been carried by manufacturing process beyond the raw stage, than for producers' goods in the widest sense.

instrument is eventually included in the cost of the products to the production of which it has contributed. When the moment comes for the instrument to be discarded as worn out or obsolete, its value has fallen to nothing, yet immediately before that moment it was still an effective instrument complete in all its parts (though possibly developing defects and involving excessive expenditure on maintenance). If the depreciation allowance is correctly estimated, the moment at which the value of the instrument has been written down to nothing will coincide with the moment at which it is discarded. But in practice, of course, this cannot usually be accomplished with precision ; either, through caution, a larger depreciation allowance is fixed than is strictly necessary, and this results in the value being written down to nothing when the instrument still has some years of usefulness before it ; or an unexpected breakdown or premature obsolescence destroys its usefulness when the depreciation allowance has not sufficed to extinguish the whole value, and a residue has to be summarily wiped off the balance sheet.

As usually happens in the definitions employed by the social sciences, the boundary line between instruments and working capital is not absolutely clear. A sheep, regarded as a producer of wool, is an instrument ; regarded as a producer of mutton it is working capital. Yet an entire flock might be regarded as an instrument even for the production of mutton.[1]

These borderline cases are of little practical importance ; we can decide them as we please.

We have been confining our attention to producers' capital, but our account would be incomplete without some reference to consumers' capital. We may make the conception of capital co-extensive with that of wealth, whether in the hands of producers or in those of consumers. Logically we can hardly avoid including some goods in the hands of consumers, for the distinction between a house which is let and one which is owned by the occupier, who is the " consumer ", is merely accidental. We ought to include all houses. We may make the same distinction between instruments and working capital among the consumers' possessions as among the producers'. The " working capital " of the consumer will be composed of stocks of things, such as food, which are destroyed by the act of consumption, whereas he will have " instruments of consumption ", which will go on rendering him services for a period of time without being diminished otherwise than by wear.

---

[1] See Adam Smith, *Wealth of Nations*, Book II, Chapter I.

It will be observed that instruments of consumption are not precisely identical with durable consumers' goods. There are some commodities, such as fuel, cleaning materials or tinned foods, which are durable, in that they may be kept for a long time without deteriorating, but are not instruments, for they are destroyed in consumption.

For the purposes of our investigation it is not important to extend the conception of capital to include all the consumers' possessions. What we need is to define the moment when a commodity passes into consumption in an unambiguous and self-consistent way. We need not include any of the consumers' working capital. We can treat all the goods composing it as passing into consumption or reaching fruition when bought, without enquiring how soon they are destined to be actually consumed.

Instruments of consumption are more difficult. We can treat the consumption of a house as spread over its entire life, and its enjoyment for any limited space of time can be valued at the rent which is or might be paid for it. The purchaser of a house does in practice regard it as an investment, a source of income, even though he intends to occupy it and the income takes the form of living in it free of rent.

But for other instruments of consumption the case is not so clear. Even in the case of motor cars, where hiring is common, the private owner would not estimate the value of the car to himself in terms of its hiring value. For furniture, utensils, clothes, or ornaments such a method of valuation is even more unnatural. It will be best to regard all instruments of consumption except houses and landed property as passing into consumption when purchased by the consumer.

THE PERIOD OF PROCESS

It will be found convenient to distinguish two parts of the period of production of any commodity. One part, which we shall call the *period of process*, is the time occupied by the productive processes applied to the material composing the commodity itself, without regard to the time taken in the construction of the instruments used in those processes. It is the period of production as it would be if every instrument were treated as an original factor of production and if the only capital were working capital. The rest of the period of production is that which is composed of the respective ages and periods of production of the instruments used.

We may apply to the operations of the original factors of production in any interval of time the convenient term " input ". When we treat instrumental capital as a factor of production, we may call the operations of the original factors in conjunction with capital " mixed input ", and if we want to distinguish input in the former sense from mixed input we shall call it " pure input ".

The original factors of production have been described above as human effort and natural resources. Human effort is a wider expression than labour, and must be interpreted here as including enterprise. Enterprise contributes to production and so to the value of the product. It is an original factor of production, and its contribution is to be valued at the profit which constitutes its remuneration. If we count enterprise as a factor of production and include profit in costs, the result is to make the price of the product necessarily equal to its cost. For profit is the difference between selling value and cost.

On the other hand, in calculating mixed input during the period of process, we confine the contribution of an instrument to maintenance and depreciation, to the exclusion of interest. Interest is destined to appear at the end of the calculation as the gain effected by prolonging the period of production. Consequently, notwithstanding the inclusion of profit, prices and costs for the purposes of this calculation are not equal ; price exceeds cost by interest.

In computing the period of process of any commodity, we must ascertain the time that has elapsed from every operation by which the factors of production, including instruments, have contributed to the final product up to the moment of fruition when the final product reaches the consumer.

We have to calculate the period of process of current output. Current output will be taken to mean the final products placed in the hands of consumers averaged over a selected interval of time, which includes the moment designated as the " present ", and which is long enough for the output of each of the various commodities to form a significant total. We shall start with the period of process of a particular commodity. We can be content to calculate it for the total output of a productive unit, such as a factory, and assume it to be the same for every portion of the output of that productive unit. We need not inquire the precise age of every morsel of flour that goes to make a loaf of bread. We take the total output of the productive unit for the selected interval of time, and ask how long ago all the various economic activities which have gone to the making of it were applied. When we have found the answer in respect of every constituent of value (including all overhead charges except interest) we calculate the average and arrive at the period of process for that productive unit.

The period of process will depend to a great extent on the time for which materials, intermediate products and the final product have been *held in stock*, and in many cases mainly on this. Chance may therefore play a large part in the result.

For certain portions of current output the period of process is *nil*. For personal services, using neither materials nor instruments, not only the period of process but the whole period of production is *nil*. For an instrument of consumption, such as a house, the period of production is calculated in the same way as for an instrument of production; the period of process of the final product, the accommodation given, is the interval between completion and actual occupation, when it is, as it were, held in stock.

THE PERIOD OF PRODUCTION CALCULATED RETROSPECTIVELY

To arrive at the entire period of production of a commodity, we have to add to its period of process a further item representing the time that has elapsed since each of the activities of the original factors (labour, enterprise and natural resources) which have contributed to produce the instruments used in the production of the commodity. An instrument used in the output of a productive unit during a selected interval of time contributes to the value of the output its depreciation and maintenance for that interval. Maintenance is already included as an overhead charge in the calculation of the period of process of the commodity; it is only depreciation that brings the age of the instrument into calculation. For depreciation means a share of the first cost of the instrument.

The first cost of the instrument, however, must be interpreted to mean cost in terms of the original factors of production, that is, exclusive of interest previously accruing. This we may call the " input cost ". The depreciation allowance must be computed from the input cost taken in that sense, and will differ from the depreciation allowance reckoned in the ordinary way.

The instrument will itself be of a certain definite age at the beginning of the selected interval of time. If we go back to the time when the instrument was produced, we shall find that its period of production is composed of its period of process together with something more on account of the instruments employed in its production. In fact we have to construct a kind of family tree, giving the " ancestry " of the instruments employed in producing the commodity we started with, a family tree, however, in which the number of parents of any child is not limited to two, but may be one or several. An instrument which has been produced without the use of any pre-existing instrument at all will appear as having no parents.

This family tree may extend far into the remote past. But any instrument only figures in it in virtue of the depreciation allowance which it contributes to the value of the final product. That will be a small fraction, and each generation of instruments to which we pass means the application of another such fraction. Thus the family tree of instruments forms a highly convergent series.

Suppose, for example, that the depreciation of instruments used in the production of a commodity composes on an average one-tenth of the value of the commodity, that the average life of an instrument is twenty years, so that the average age of any instrument when employed in production may be assumed to be ten years, and that the period of process averages two years. With these assumptions we can estimate the period of production of a commodity of which the input cost is 100 units. In the first place the whole value of 100 is spread over the period of process, two years. Depreciation is ten units, and must be spread over a further period made up of the average life of the instruments employed, ten years, *plus* their period of process, two years. The depreciation of the next most recent generation of instruments amounts to one unit, and must be spread over the age and period of process of the preceding generation. The depreciation of the generation before that counts for a tenth of a unit and must be spread over the age and period of process of that generation, and so on.

Thus we get the series :

$$100 \times 2$$
$$+ \quad 10 \times 12$$
$$+ \quad 1 \times 12$$
$$+ \quad \tfrac{1}{10} \times 12$$
and so on.

This sums up to $333\tfrac{1}{3}$, making the period of production three years and four months. But the first three terms, representing what has been done within twenty-six years, account for 332, and the fourth (going back twelve years more) for $1\tfrac{1}{5}$ out of the remaining $1\tfrac{1}{3}$. All older generations taken together account for about half a day in the period of production.

Up to this point we have been calculating the period of production of a particular commodity, the output of a given productive unit. We have next to obtain the period of production of current output as defined above. For this purpose we proceed to average the periods of production of all the products composing current output (including consumable services, for which the period may be *nil*).

Let a be the pure input of the community as a whole a time t ago, and let k be the proportion of this input which contributes to the current output at the present time. Then the period of production of current output is equal to $\dfrac{\varSigma kat}{\varSigma ka}$ taken over all past time. The denominator, $\varSigma ka$, being the sum of all the contributions of the past activities of the original factors of production (including profit) to the value of current output, is equal to the input cost of current output.

In our calculation we have attributed to each instrument its actual age at the time it was used in a process contributing to the current output. This method may be defended as simply recording the facts. But it is open to objection in that it makes the period of production of a commodity to some extent a matter of chance. Flour ground in a new mill will be treated as having a shorter period of production than flour ground in an old mill of equal cost, and similar in all respects except age to the first. This is not what Jevons meant, and indeed for the purpose of calculating the period of production, he takes the age of the instrument to be equal to half its life, whatever its actual age at the moment of production may be.

When we arrive at the period of production for the entire economic system by calculating it for every consumable product and then taking an average, there may be little difference in the result between the method of taking the actual age of each instrument and that of taking half its life. But if there *is* any difference, the latter method gives us the result we seek. And circumstances can readily be imagined in which the difference would be material. In a rapidly expanding community (particularly one which is importing capital on a large scale) the average age of the instruments used is likely to be substantially below half their average life. The same would be true of a community in which a great amount of capital has been destroyed by a natural calamity or by war, or in which some very sweeping change in productive processes has made a great part of the pre-existing capital obsolete. In such cases, even if the total new capital outlay is not increased, the proportion of new capital equipment would soon be greater than is normal.

THE PERIOD OF PRODUCTION CALCULATED PROSPECTIVELY

Hitherto we have been estimating the period of production *retrospectively*, by examining the past history of the current output of consumable commodities. But we can equally well approach the problem from the other end, and estimate *prospectively* the average interval of time destined to elapse before the *current input* bears fruit in consumable goods. The fact that these two alternative methods of calculation do not in general give the same result is, I think, well recognised among the supporters of the period of production theory of capital.

An estimate based on the input of the present moment must be based not on facts, but only on forecasts of facts. Nevertheless, for theoretical purposes we can assume our forecasts to be exactly accurate. It is just as true that what will be will be as that what has been has been.

The pure input or current activities of the original factors may be divided into operations applied directly to the production of consumable goods and those applied to the production of instruments. For each operation of the former there will be an assignable interval of time at the end of which the consumable commodity to the production of which the operation contributes will reach fruition. This interval of time will sometimes be itself an average, for the operation of a moment may be applied to a quantity of material which is destined to enter into the composition of a number of different articles. And the fruition of instruments of consumption is spread over a period of time.

When we have averaged the intervals within which the input applied directly to the production of consumable goods will reach fruition, the result is nearly the equivalent of what we have already called the period of process. The weighting of the factors will not be exactly the same, but that is a matter of detail.

Next we turn to the activities applied to the production of instruments. First we take for each operation the interval up to the completion of the instrument which is being produced, and the average of these intervals gives the period of process of all the instruments in course of production.

The instruments can then be divided into those which will be used in the production of consumable goods and those which will be used in the production of other instruments. An instrument of the former kind will contribute to the value of the consumable goods it produces in the form of a depreciation allowance. To find its contribution to the value of each unit of its output, we divide its input cost by the number of units produced throughout its life. For the purpose of our calculation we are only concerned with so much of its input cost as is being incurred in the interval which we call the " present ". But the input that is being applied to instruments of a given kind should in general include all the stages of production. In practice depreciation is reckoned at so much per unit of time and is made, as nearly as may be, equal to the first cost divided by the life of the instrument. If the instrument is uniformly employed so that the same number of units of output come into every unit of time, the result is the same. But if it is sometimes idle or under-employed, it is theoretically better to apportion the depreciation allowance by units of output than by units of time.

An operation contributing to the production of the instrument will attain fruition after an interval composed of the time elapsing up to the completion of the instrument, *plus* the average time elapsing from its completion to the successive operations performed by the instrument throughout its life, *plus* the average time elapsing from each of those operations to the fruition of the consumable commodities to the production of which they contribute. The second of these three constituents is likely to be approximately equal to half the life of the instrument.

There remain those instruments in course of production which are destined for the production of further instruments. These further instruments of the second generation will themselves include some destined for the direct production of consumable goods, and others destined for the production of instruments of the third generation.

Thus the current operations of the original factors of production are to be divided into those directly applied to the production of consumable goods and those leading to the production of consumable goods after one, two, three, four, etc., generations of instruments. Each consumable commodity has its period of process, and each instrument has its period of process, and the period of production for an operation attaining fruition after n generations of instruments is attained by adding to their several periods of process the average interval from the completion of each instrument to each unit of its output throughout its life.[1]

In a prospective calculation the life of an instrument is still uncertain. But the depreciation allowance, which has to be

---

[1] For a more exact analysis of the retrospective and prospective expressions of the period of production, see the algebraical note below (pp. 24-8).

2

calculated as a matter of practical business, in order to arrive at the cost of the final product, presupposes an estimate of the life. It is in this calculation of cost that any error in the estimate of life is reflected. If the input cost of an instrument is c, its output per unit of time b and its life l units of time, the depreciation for each unit of output is $\frac{c}{lb}$. The average interval from the completion of the instrument to successive units of its output may be put at $\frac{1}{2}l$, and the contribution of the instrument to the period of production of the final product is $\frac{c}{lb} \times \frac{1}{2}l$, or $\frac{1}{2}\frac{c}{b}$. This is independent of l. The uncertainty of the life of the instrument cancels out against the consequent uncertainty of the depreciation allowance.

Professor F. H. Knight, as one of his objections to the whole theory of the period of production, has contended that " there is no such thing as an average durability of capital goods. Presence of a single infinite item makes the average infinite." [1] And Professor Hayek in his *Pure Theory of Capital* (1941) actually excludes " permanent " works from his definition of capital.

But the infinite items cause no difficulty. If the life l of an instrument of input cost c is very long, the share of cost, $\frac{c}{lb}$, attributable to each unit of output by way of depreciation allowance becomes very small, and the influence of the instrument on the period of production correspondingly slight. In any case a literally infinite duration is an absurdity which need not be considered.

THE STRUCTURE OF PRODUCTION

The purpose of extending the period of production is to enable producers to obtain the technical advantages of more highly capitalised production. The expression, Structure of Production, is used to mean the totality of productive processes employed by the community. A producer will aim at using the most technically efficient processes available, and his choice will be limited by the amount of capital he is in a position to employ. The power of lengthening the period of production gives producers a wider choice among possible structures of production.

[1] *Capitalist Production, Time and Rate of Return in Economic Essays in Honour of Gustav Cassel* (1933), p. 338.

To every process corresponds its appropriate capital equipment. Since the methods of production must conform to the capital equipment available, the nature of that equipment determines the processes and so determines the structure of production. It might likewise be said that the nature of the technical aptitudes and skill of the working population determine the methods of production. But there is no real conflict here, for in practice their technical aptitudes and skill and the capital equipment have grown up together and determined one another.

The principle that the structure of production is determined by the existing capital equipment and technical aptitudes must not be interpreted too rigidly. The existing factors of production can be directed to modifying the structure of production, and that possibility presupposes *some* freedom of choice in the manner of their application.

Whereas various structures of production may result in the same period of production, we want to be able to say that any one structure of production determines one and only one period of production. Otherwise the idea of an extension of the period of production being aimed at an improvement of the structure of production loses all significance.

But if we base the period of production, whether calculated retrospectively or prospectively, on the facts, we introduce an element of chance into the result.

The period of process depends partly on the vagaries of demand which modify the time for which materials, intermediate products and finished goods are kept in stock. The prospective calculation avoids the anomalies arising in the retrospective method from reckoning the age of the instruments, for the former method takes account of the average interval from the beginning of the instrument's activity to each unit of its output. But the life of an instrument itself depends on various chances, among others the contingency of obsolescence through new discoveries or inventions or other changes of circumstances.

And if an instrument is under-employed, a greater share of its input cost has to be allocated to each unit of output under the head of depreciation, and this also affects the final result.

A further complication arises from the purchasing power of money. If we value the operations of the original factors of production at the money they commanded at the time they were performed, we introduce an arbitrary and irrelevant element into the calculation. Wages may have changed, and economic rent, arising from differences of costs, should move up and down with wages. Profit is more variable still, since it responds to fluctuations in the price level which may not be reflected in wages.   To avoid adding together heterogeneous valuations of the services rendered by the factors of production, we must apply to them uniform rates of wages and, what is more difficult, uniform rates of profit.   That adjustment would carry us a long way from the recorded facts.

But there is a still more fundamental difficulty. When the calculation of the period of production is based on *data* extending over a long period of time, the structure of production is sure to change in the course of it.   Some of the instruments now employed in production were manufactured at a time when the structure of production was materially different from what it is now, and when we go on to earlier generations of instruments the differences are still greater.   Similarly, by the time some of the instruments now in course of production come into operation, the structure of production will have changed.   The period of production, whether calculated by the retrospective or by the prospective method will not correspond to one definite structure of production, but partly to that of the present time and partly to those of the past or the future as the case may be.

A STANDARD PERIOD OF PRODUCTION

Neither the retrospective calculation of the period of production, based on current output, nor the prospective calculation, based on current input, will serve our purpose.   What we want is rather the period of production appropriate to current *methods of production*. For every consumable commodity and for every instrument in supply at a given moment of time, there are methods of production in operation, with the appropriate capital equipment.   A consumable commodity is produced with the aid of certain instruments. We shall not ask how each of those instruments was actually produced in the past, but how it would be produced at the present time. Nor shall we ask what is destined to happen in the interval up to the time when the instruments now in course of production make their contribution to consumable products.   The instruments now in course of production are only to be taken into account as showing what methods of production are to be assumed for the *replacement* of the instruments in use.

Thus to every product entering into current output we attribute a hypothetical period of production corresponding to existing methods of production, and the weighted average of these hypo-thetical periods of production for the entire current output gives what may be called the " standard " period of production.

The standard period of production omits altogether so much of the current economic activity as is devoted to *extending* the period of production (that is to say, the deepening of capital see below, p. 31). This economic activity and the capital equipment used in association with it cannot be taken into account without involving a contradiction. Its contribution to the period of production is a lengthening, a *change* in virtue of which the period will no longer be that corresponding to current methods of production.

On the other hand, any changes which are already in progress, and have actually affected methods of production, must be allowed for. If a part of the output of a commodity is being produced by a new method and the rest by an old one, the period of production of each part must be calculated separately and the two must be combined in the final average.

Obviously the chance of an instrument's actual age must not be allowed to affect the standard period of production. As we have seen, the prospective method avoids this and averages the interval from the beginning of the instrument's life to every unit of its output. Substantially that is equivalent to Jevons's assumption that the age of the instrument may be deemed to be half its life. But the life of the instrument is not the only uncertain factor. Depreciation is provided with a view to replacement, and, when the time for replace-ment comes, technological progress and changes in the value of the money unit may make first cost quite inapplicable. Therefore the cost assumed ought to be derived not from actual first cost but from a hypothetical replacement cost—hypothetical because it is *present* replacement cost, while actual replacement is still in the *future*.

Depreciation has to provide not only for replacement but for loss of value through obsolescence, even when actual replacement will never occur. Much of the work done to clear, drain or level land, with a view to cultivation or to other forms of development, is done once for all. If the use of the land ceases to be remunerative and has to be abandoned, the work simply becomes derelict. In such a case there is no replacement, and the depreciation merely provides the owner with compensation for his loss. The life of the work is the period during which it remains *in use*. The calculation of input cost of, say, a Roman road becomes rather fanciful, but it is, of course, of purely theoretical interest. A road also raises in aggravated form the problem of apportionment of joint products ;

the apportionment of its maintenance and depreciation charges among all that use it is arbitrary indeed.

The input cost of current output is composed of that part of current input which is applied directly to the production of consumable goods, together with a proportion of the input cost of the instruments employed. If the first cost of any instrument is c, and its life is l, its contribution to productive activity in a unit of time

is $\dfrac{c}{l}$, provided it is fully employed. It may be under-employed, and

of the work it does a portion may not be applied towards current output (i.e. it may be applied towards extending the period of production of future output). We may assume its contribution

towards current output to be $q\dfrac{c}{l}$. This contribution will be deemed

to be of an age $\frac{1}{2}l$, and it will enter into the period of production as $\frac{1}{2}qc$. If the total input cost of current output is u, and the period of

process is s, the period of production will be $s + \dfrac{\Sigma\frac{1}{2}qc}{u}$. Now Σqc

is the amount of instrumental capital, reckoned in terms of input cost, used in the production of current output, and $\Sigma\frac{1}{2}qc$ may be interpreted as the depreciated value of this capital computed on an ideal basis.

If we thus transform that portion of the period of production which depends on the instrumental capital, we ought so far as possible to apply a corresponding method to the period of process, which depends on working capital.

There may be a discrepancy between mixed input and output, causing an increase or decrease in working capital. We can distinguish the mixed input which is applied to maintain working capital as fast as it is used up in further processes and in sales, from any excess which is applied to increasing working capital, in just the same way as we distinguish the production of instruments to make good depreciation from that which adds to the capital of the community. In place of an excess of mixed input there may be a deficiency, resulting in a diminution of working capital. And this may also occur in the case of instrumental capital, production being insufficient to cover depreciation.

And just as instrumental capital may be under-employed, so working capital may be in excess of requirements.

For the purposes of the standard period of production, we assume stocks of commodities to be " normal ". It may be difficult to say precisely what stocks are normal, but the standard period of production must not be made to depend on the chances by which the accumulation of stocks is determined.

When goods are bought for use in production or for sale, the average time they are held in stock will be equal to the average stock held, divided by the amount used or sold per unit of time. Similarly, the period of process is equal to the average amount of material in process divided by the amount processed per unit of time.

Thus, for the purposes of the standard period of production, input is analysed into the following:

(1) consumable services;

(2) conversion of materials into consumable products;

(3) capital replacements.

Capital outlay other than on replacements is excluded from the calculation. Replacements must not be confined to actual replacements; the whole provision for depreciation, whether actually being spent or not, must be included.

To every structure of production there corresponds one standard period of production, as we have defined it, and one only. A decision to instal additional capital in any industry may be regarded as a decision to alter its structure of production in such a way as to increase the standard period of production by a determinate amount.

Jevons's formula for the rate of interest makes output a definite function of the period of production. But it requires it to be so only for the purposes of the calculations of the people who have to decide to what extent they will increase the period of production through the accumulation of wealth. The formula is concerned with their *intentions ;* it is concerned with facts, past and future, only so far as their intentions are affected by them.

It is in the standard period of production that the best measure of their intentions is to be found. That expresses the conditions on which an improvement in the structure of production is to be obtained, divested of disturbing contingencies which cannot be foreseen.

At the same time there seems to be little advantage in seeking a measure in terms of the period of production at all. The practical points to be taken into consideration are always a capital outlay of a certain amount and a prospective yield or cost-saving capacity.

The fact that capital can, subject to certain reservations, be expressed in terms of a lapse of time is of theoretical interest and importance. Without it the theory of capital would undoubtedly be incomplete. When we treat the lapse of time as a factor of production, regulating the application of the advantages of protracted processes, we can link this lapse of time with the waiting to which economists have reduced the function of saving.

But when economists go beyond this and attempt to express the ordinary operations of the investment market in terms of the period of production, they are simply introducing unnecessary difficulties. When, instead of saying that a producer adds to the capital of his business, they say that he extends the period of production of his output, this form of expression is not only open to the objection that it is unfamiliar to the people who use capital and compile balance sheets, but it is open to theoretical objections too. It cannot be given precision except in the form of a standard period of production which is, after all, an abstraction not corresponding to any actual facts.

ALGEBRAICAL NOTE

A statement in algebraical notation will help to make the complexities of the period of production clearer. Suppose economic activity to begin at a zero time in the past, sufficiently distant for any elements of value that have survived from earlier input to be negligible. Assuming all the problems of apportionment, etc., to be satisfactorily solved, we call the input in successive equal intervals of time a_1, a_2 . . ., the input in the sth interval being a_s.

Suppose that the proportion of the input a_s in the sth interval contributing to the output in the $(s + r)$th interval is $k_s(r)$. Thus $k_s(o)a_s$ reaches fruition in output in the sth interval contemporaneously with the appearance of the input, a_s, $k_s(1)a_s$ in the $(s + 1)$th interval, and so on. The total proportion of a_s that has reached fruition up to the nth interval from zero is :

$$a_s(k_s(0) + k_s(1) + \ldots + k_s(n - s)) = a_s \sum_{r=0}^{r=n-s} k_s(r)$$

If $n - s$ is great enough for the whole of the input a_s to have reached fruition, $\sum_{r=0}^{r=n-s} k_s(r) = 1$. It may be that, to conform

rigorously to that condition, account must be taken of input embodied in hundreds or even thousands of years before in constructions, like Roman roads, which still make a contribution to output. But the share of such input attaching by way of depreciation allowance to any unit of output will be small in proportion to the length of life of the construction, and can be neglected.

To make the prospective calculation of the period of production from time, s, we average the period in which each element of the input, a_s, will reach fruition. An element equal to $k_s(r)a_s$ reaches fruition in a period equal to r intervals of time after the sth, and the average to a future mth interval is:

$$\frac{k_s(1) + 2k_s(2) + \ldots mk_s(m)}{k_s(0) + k_s(1) + k_s(2) \ldots + k_s(m)}$$

or

$$\frac{\sum\limits_{r=0}^{r=m} rk_s(r)}{\sum\limits_{r=0}^{r=m} k_s(r)}.$$

If m is assumed great enough to exhaust the effects of the current input the denominator is equal to unity. Therefore the period of production is $\sum\limits_{r=0}^{r=m} rk_s(r)$.

To make the retrospective calculation, we base our average on the *output* (or consumption) at the time n. This is composed of all the elements that are reaching fruition in the nth interval, that is:

$$k_1(n-1)a_1 + k_2(n-2)a_2 + k_3(n-3)a_3 + \ldots + k_n(0)a_n$$

or

$$\sum\limits_{s=1}^{s=n} k_s(n-s)a_s.$$

It should be noted that this expression gives the value not of the output in the nth interval but of all the elements of input contributing to the value of that output. The difference between the two consists of interest.

The period of production is:

$$\frac{\sum\limits_{s=1}^{s=n} (n-s)k_s(n-s)a_s}{\sum\limits_{s=1}^{s=n} k_s(n-s)a_s}.$$

(This is the same formula as on page 15 above, with $n-s$ written for t, $k_s(n-s)$ for k, and a_s for a.)

To get the value of output, including interest, which we assume to be at a uniform rate, i per unit, we multiply a_s by $(1+i)^{n-s}$, and we have:

$$\sum\limits_{s=1}^{s=n} (1+i)^{n-s}k_s(n-s)a_s.$$

Similarly, for the prospective calculation, the total output derived from the input at time s will be:

$$\sum_{r=0}^{r=m} (1+i)^r r k_s(r).$$

Of the input, a_s, in the sth interval, the portion which has reached fruition by the nth interval is $\sum_{r=0}^{r=n-s} k_s(r)a_s$. Consequently $a_s - \sum_{r=0}^{r=n-s} k_s(r)a_s$ has not reached fruition and is embodied in existing capital. The total accumulated capital at the nth interval embodies an input of

$$\sum_{s=1}^{s=n} (a_s - \sum_{r=0}^{r=n-s} k_s(r)a_s).$$

This expression gives the value of the total capital of the community *exclusive of accumulated interest*. The true value, inclusive of interest, is:

$$\sum_{s=1}^{s=n} (1+i)^{n-s} a_s (1 - \sum_{r=0}^{r=n-s} k_s(r)).$$

If the conditions of production and consumption were completely stereotyped, a_s being equal to a constant a, and $k_s(r)$ having the same value, k_r, for all values of s, the expression for the accumulated capital would become:

$$\sum_{s=1}^{s=n} (1 - \sum_{r=0}^{r=n-s} k_r)a$$

$$= na - a \sum_{s=1}^{s=n} \sum_{r=0}^{r=n-s} k_r$$

$$= na - a \sum_{r=0}^{r=n-1} (n-r)k_r$$

$$= na - na \sum_{r=0}^{r=n-1} k_r + a \sum_{r=0}^{r=n-1} rk_r.$$

Now $\sum_{r=0}^{r=n-1} k_r = 1$, so that the first two terms cancel out, and we are left with $a \sum_{r=0}^{r=n-1} rk_r$. If we divide by the constant input, a, we have the period of production calculated prospectively.

Moreover, with the assumptions made that $a_s = a$ and $k_s(r) = k_r$ for all values of s, we find that the period of production calculated retrospectively becomes equal to that calculated prospectively.

$$\text{For } \sum_{s=1}^{s=n} (n-s)k_s(n-s)a_s = a\sum_{s=1}^{s=n} (n-s)k_{n-s}$$

$$= a \sum_{r=0}^{r=n-1} rk_r$$

$$\sum_{s=1}^{s=n} k_s(n-s)a_s = a \sum_{s=1}^{s=n} k_{n-s}$$

$$= a \sum_{r=0}^{r=n-1} k_r$$

$$= a.$$

In effect this assumption of stereotyped conditions of production and consumption is equivalent to the assumptions embodied in our standard period of production. The standard period of production is simply the period of production of a stereotyped system so devised as to coincide momentarily with the actual structure of production, exclusive of new investment.

To express the analysis in the notation of the calculus, we must employ two independent time variables, s, the time at which the input is a, and r, the further time after which the proportion of that input which is reaching fruition is $k(s, r)$. The total proportion of the input at time, s, which has reached fruition at time, n, is

$$a\int_0^{n-s} k(s, r)dr.$$

If $n - s$ is great, $\int_0^{n-s} k(s, r)dr$ approximates to unity.

The prospective period of production is:

$$\int_0^m rk(s, r)dr$$

where m is great.

The retrospective period of production at time, n, is:

$$\frac{\int_0^n (n-s)k(s, n-s)a_s ds}{\int_0^n k(s, n-s)a_s ds}.$$

Accumulated capital in terms of input is:

$$\int_0^n a\,ds - \int_0^n \int_0^{n-s} k(s,\,r)a\,dr\,ds.$$

If we make a constant and $k(s,\,r)$ equal to $k(r)$, a function of r only, the prospective period of production becomes $\int_0^n rk(r)dr$, and the retrospective period of production

$$\frac{\int_0^n (n-s)k(n-s)ds}{\int_0^n k(n-s)ds} = \frac{\int_0^n rk(r)dr}{\int_0^n k(r)dr},$$

and, since the denominator is unity, the two are identical.

Accumulated capital becomes

$$na - a\int_0^n \int_0^{n-s} k(r)dr\,ds = a\int_0^n rk(r)dr.[1]$$

[1] If $\;K_s = \int_0^{n-s} k(r)dr,\; \dfrac{dK_s}{ds} = -\,k(n-s)\;$ and $\;K_n = 0,$

$$\frac{d}{ds}(sK_s) = K_s + s\frac{dK_s}{ds},$$

$$\left[sK_s\right]_0^n = \int_0^n K_s ds + \int_0^n s\frac{dK_s}{ds}ds,$$

$$\left[sK_s\right]_0^n = 0$$

$$\int_0^n K_s ds = \int_0^n \int_0^{n-s} k(r)dr\,ds, \quad \int_0^n s\frac{dK_s}{ds}ds = -\int_0^n sk(n-s)ds$$

$$= \int_0^n (n-r)k(r)dr$$

$$= n - \int_0^n rk(r)dr.$$

Therefore $\quad\quad\quad n - \int_0^n \int_0^{n-s} k(r)dr\,ds = \int_0^n rk(r)dr.$

CHAPTER III

INTEREST AND MARGINAL YIELD

JEVONS'S FORMULA

JEVONS, in his formula for expressing the rate of interest in terms of the marginal yield of capital, expressed the increment of capital in terms of an increment of the period of production. But it is not necessary to bring in the period of production at all.

What Jevons had in mind was evidently the *standard* period of production, which may be regarded as a multiplier relating the stock of capital (valued in terms of input) to current input. Current input is for this purpose a datum, a mathematical constant. We may simply say that if an increment, c, in the stock of capital yields an increment, f, in output, and if the highest available yields are invariably obtained, then the equilibrium rate of interest is $\frac{f}{c}$. In terms of the calculus, if C is the total stock of capital and F the total output of the community, the equilibrium rate of interest is $\frac{dF}{dC}$.

Jevons's theory of interest was static. His formula states the conditions of equilibrium. For that purpose the promoters of enterprises are assumed to have made the right decisions. Any decision which, within the limits of technological knowledge, is erroneous is a source of disequilibrium, for the means of correcting it are available, and a state of things liable to this correction is not one of equilibrium.

If the promoters have made perfectly right decisions, then theoretically all the capital equipment installed must have been such that, in the conditions obtaining at the time of installation, it was the most remunerative available.

The increment of capital postulated is not an actual growth or increment in time. It is a hypothetical departure from equilibrium, and may be compared to the hypothetical displacement of a system from equilibrium assumed in the principle of " virtual work " in Statics, the analogy of which Jevons referred to (*Theory of Political Economy*, Preface, p. vii).

In the following pages our task will be to explore the applications of Jevons's formula to a *dynamic* system, in which account has to be taken not only of equilibrium conditions, but of the movements and tendencies set up when equilibrium is disturbed. In the present chapter we shall direct attention to the motives by which capital outlay is actuated. Afterwards in Chapter IV we shall turn to the working of the investment market, through which the available resources are directed to capital outlay.

WIDENING AND DEEPENING OF CAPITAL

Were we to assume a stationary population and no technological progress, the rate of interest would fall continuously, and the rate of interest at any moment would be such that every form of capital equipment yielding more than that rate had already been installed, the actual rate of interest would thus represent the yield of the most remunerative forms of capital equipment not yet installed. It would be equal to the marginal yield of capital.

A growing population will require a proportional growth of capital to preserve the same structure of production and the same rate of interest. If we still assume no technological progress, any further growth of capital will require a fall in the rate of interest. If the growth of capital fails to keep pace with the growth of population, the rate of interest rises.

For this purpose it is rather the growth of active working population than of total population that has to be taken into account. An increase in the amount of employment tends to require a corresponding increase in capital equipment, though in practice under-employment of labour usually means under-employment of capital, and a trade revival may make considerable progress without requiring any appreciable capital outlay on extensions of capacity.

Against the tendency of the rate of interest to fall as the growth of capital fills in succession the more remunerative openings for investment, and leaves the less remunerative still to be filled, must be set the tendency of invention and discovery to disclose new and more remunerative openings. These may take the form either of new contrivances for saving costs or increasing output, or the development of new natural resources.

A static theory does not disregard change altogether. It treats change as pointing to a new equilibrium position, and infers *tendencies* to arise in the various quantities concerned to move into the new position. It is the function of a dynamic theory to investigate the actual path travelled by these quantities and their mutual relations during the transition.

The process by which the capital equipment of a community is increased may take two forms, a " widening " and a " deepening ". The widening of the capital equipment means the extension of productive capacity by the flotation of new enterprises, or the expansion of existing enterprises, without any change in the amount of capital employed for each unit of labour. The deepening means an increase in the amount of capital employed for each unit of labour.

The latter involves an increase in the period of production and a change in the structure of production. The former involves no change in either. It will be noted that the widening process will not account for any change in the rate of interest. It is in the deepening process that we must look for the forces making for the equilibrium expressed by Jevons's formula.

The proportion of capital employed to labour may also be altered through a change in the relative magnitude of different industries. When the more highly capitalised industries expand relatively to the less highly capitalised, the amount of capital required for a given amount of labour is increased. This effect may be called a " thickening " of capital.

PROFIT

The widening process is induced by the prospect not of interest, but of *profit*. The immediate motive of the extension of capacity of an industry is the opportunity of *selling* additional output. The promoter sees an expanding demand for his product, and judges that the expansion is sufficiently permanent to enable him to dispose of the output he plans without any sacrifice of price. For the purpose of calculating the period of production we treated profit itself as a cost. That was a fiction, which must now be dropped.

In the early days of the classical economists the theory of capital was apt to be vitiated by a confusion of interest with profit. Enterprise was in the hands of capitalists, and it was very natural to think of the reward of enterprise and the reward of capital as one. Undoubtedly passages can be quoted from Adam Smith and Ricardo showing a recognition of the distinction, but neither they nor their successors ever elaborated the theory of profit into a separate study.

Even in recent times theories of profit have often been unsatisfactory. The subject has been approached with the assumption that free competition *must* somehow always tend to allot a fair reward to every economic activity.   From that starting point economists have hoped to arrive at the conclusion that, after excluding interest and so much as may be regarded as a premium of insurance against loss of capital, the remainder of profit will only differ from the equivalent of a fair salary in consequence of some quasi-monopolistic advantage of the profit-maker.

As Marshall put it, " that share of the normal expenses of production of any commodity which is commonly classed as profits, is so controlled on every side by the action of the law of substitution, that it cannot long diverge from the normal supply price of the capital needed, added to the normal supply price of the ability and energy required for managing the business, and lastly the normal supply price of that organisation by which the appropriate business ability and the requisite capital are brought together " (*Principles*, 8th edition, pp. 605-6).

When Professor Cassel, after excluding remuneration of management and a premium against risk, comes to pure profit, he says that " there are, of course, no rules as to the extent of this kind of profit. It is not a normal thing, but a specific element of the individual business.   It is often an outcome of sheer accident " (*Theory of Social Economy*, p. 168).   " When the principle of cost is realised in an ideal way . . . there is no employer's profit of the kind we have described " (p. 170).

Now that is not the way the system works.   If competition limits the income of the profit-maker with reference to the standard of normal remuneration, that is because the man who actually makes the choice between trade and salaried employment has to compare the prospects of profit with the prospects of salary.   But profit is essentially a margin between selling price and costs (whether costs of purchase or costs of production) and is *a proportion of turnover*. The income from profit is proportional to turnover.   The choice between the prospects of profit and the prospects of salary is governed by an appropriate assumption in regard to turnover, and free competition tends to establish a common standard between incomes derived on the one hand from salaries and on the other from profit on a very modest turnover.   Beyond that free competition has *no* tendency to keep down the incomes derived from profit.[1]

Traders who are already in business and are not interested in any comparison between incomes from profits and incomes from other

[1] See my *Economic Problem*, Chapter V, and my address to Section F of the British Association on *The Nature of Profit* (*Economic Journal*, Sept. 1951).

sources, make strenuous efforts to increase their gains by enlarging their turnover, that is to say, by extending their sales. To some extent they do so at the expense of their competitors, but in a growing community there is also the opportunity to extend sales by exploiting new demand. When business is taken by one trader from another, there is not necessarily any extension of capital equipment. Sometimes the successful competitor will actually buy out the unsuccessful and use his plant, sometimes the former extends his plant, while the latter lets his decline through insufficient maintenance and renewals till it is finally closed down. But when new demand is to be exploited, an extension of capacity is required. It is in that extension of capacity, whether through the establishment of new enterprises or adding to the capital equipment of existing enterprises, that the widening of capital consists. The motive is the prospect of increased sales. The foundation of profit is selling power, and profit is so precious that the trader who sees his way to employ additional selling power will make strenuous efforts to do so.

The responsibility for selling a product is inseparable from the *ownership* of the product. The owner may employ someone else at a salary or fee to effect the sale, but he still claims the proceeds, and retains the residue if the sale is successful. If he assigns the *whole* residue to the other, the latter becomes in effect the owner. Profit, therefore, attaches to the ownership of the product sold.

It may be said, and with truth, that this selling power or " goodwill " is just that quasi-monopolistic advantage which permits an excess of profit over a fair reward of the economic activities of the trader. But this advantage is of the essence of profit, and to regard it as accounting for a departure from an assumed normal fair reward is an error. Profit is not so violent a departure from the principles of equitable distribution as Marx or Veblen, founding themselves on the Ricardian theory of a subsistence wage, made out. Nevertheless it is quite definitely an exception to the general principle of the equalisation of rates of remuneration through the labour market. There is here a congenital malformation of the individualist economic system.

Professor F. H. Knight, whose book, *Risk, Uncertainty and Profit*, is a most important contribution to the subject, would identify profit with the remuneration for *risk*, but for risk of a very special kind, " a unique uncertainty resulting from an exercise of ultimate responsibility which in its very nature cannot be insured nor capitalised nor salaried " (pp. 310-11). He who assumes this ultimate responsibility cannot divest himself of the risk, because that

3

which would have to be insured against is the exercise of his own volition. Professor Knight is led to stretch the meaning of profit, in that even the bond-holder, in virtue of his decision to lend, bears a share of the risk. That in itself, however, would not be a serious defect in the theory.

The foundation of the theory is Professor Knight's view, that, if uncertainty could be completely eliminated, profit would vanish with it. " With uncertainty entirely absent, every individual being in possession of perfect knowledge of the situation, there would be no occasion for anything of the nature of responsible management or control of productive activity. Even marketing operations in any realistic sense would not be found. The flow of raw materials and productive services through productive processes to the consumer would be entirely automatic " (p. 267).

The elimination of uncertainty is a hypothesis, and, if it is framed on these lines, it does indeed dispense with profit. If industry manages itself and goods sell themselves, no one will expect to make an income by undertaking to perform these services. If management and selling result from uncertainty then profit results from uncertainty.

But it is possible to modify the hypothesis so that, though uncertainty is eliminated, the services of selling and management are not. Suppose that every one who engages in trade knows precisely what his costs will be, at what price he will sell his product and how much he will sell at that price. Uncertainty will for our purposes be completely eliminated. A trader's sales will be " certain ", but only because the amount of effort and skill which he brings to his opportunities will be certain, and there may be great inequality in the amounts that different traders sell. Those who can foresee that they would not sell enough to yield an adequate income will never start ; they will choose some other occupation. Some, foreseeing a moderate but sufficient income, will enter trade or industry and *ex hypothesi* will realise their expectations. Others will foresee (and will realise) larger and larger incomes, possibly up to extravagantly large amounts. In fact, so long as the volume of sales depends on the skill, the efforts, and the opportunities of the traders, the characteristics of profit as we know it will remain.

THE DEEPENING OF CAPITAL

The promoter of a new enterprise, to produce the intended output, must provide appropriate productive power in the forms of labour and capital. And it is in deciding the relative contributions of labour and capital that the deepening process is given effect. To begin with, we will consider instrumental capital. Working capital we shall turn to presently (below, p. 45).

Certain kinds of capital equipment are essential. If the promoter is producing a commodity for which machinery is used, he will probably find that some portions of the usual machinery could only be dispensed with at the cost of a prohibitive increase in the amount of labour employed. The labour-saving or cost-saving capacity of an instrument may be thousands per cent per annum on its first cost. Such a machine is regarded as indispensable, for no manufacturer would attempt to do without it. Jevons instances the enormous additional labour that would be involved in digging without a spade.

But, besides this essential machinery, the promoter will have the choice of installing various labour-saving contrivances or employing additional labour. That is an application of Marshall's law of substitution. The question is which is the more economical method of production, and the answer is to be obtained from a comparison of the cost-saving capacity of the instrument with the rate of interest. The promoter has to calculate the first cost, life, and cost of maintenance of the instrument and the cost of the labour which would make the same contribution to the productive process. If the labour cost exceeds the maintenance and depreciation charges of the instrument by a sum exceeding the rate of interest on the first cost of the instrument, then the instrument will pay. Interest has to be calculated on the whole outstanding capital cost. It may be that little or no interest is actually paid on borrowed capital, but the resources of the proprietors or shareholders must be reckoned as earning interest at the market rate. The depreciation charges provide the means of replacing each portion of the equipment as it wears out, and, so long as replacement is duly effected, the enterprise is continued in existence as a going concern. The charge for interest is a permanency, so the rate to be assumed is the long-term rate prevailing in the investment market.

Now these calculations have to be made at the outset, when the enterprise is being equipped with capital. They are in the nature of estimates, and can only be approximate. They are particularly liable to error when they apply to any new departure. The natural course of the promoter is to instal precisely the same machinery as his neighbours and competitors are using and as he himself has hitherto used if he is already established in the industry.

A reduction in the rate of interest is a sign that the widening of capital is insufficient to use up the resources of the investment market. The investment market finds that its net sales of securities to investors exceed its purchases of new issues, and tries to elicit additional new flotations by raising the prices of securities, or in other words by reducing the rate of interest yielded. This condition of the market affords a double inducement to promoters; not only do they pay a lower rate of interest for any sums borrowed at long term, but the market absorbs new issues more readily; underwriting involves less risk than usual, and is more easily arranged.

MARGINAL YIELD

If the widening of capital equipment is insufficient to absorb the available flow of new savings, it is this favourable state of the investment market that ought to induce the deepening process and to restore equilibrium. In practice, however, even a big drop in the rate of interest might take a long time to induce manufacturers to adopt a piece of plant (other than a new invention, which for the moment we have ruled out) previously neglected on the ground that it would not pay. This especially applies to any instrument which has a relatively short life and consequently a high depreciation allowance, or to one with high maintenance costs. If the yearly maintenance and depreciation amount to, say, 20 per cent of the first cost of the instrument, and the estimated cost-saving capacity of the instrument is 25 per cent, the net yield of 5 per cent is an exceedingly doubtful quantity. If we allow a margin of error of 10 per cent both ways in the two estimates, the difference between them will lie between $\frac{1}{2}$ and $9\frac{1}{2}$. Since these limits are matters not of calculation but of judgment and estimate, the probability of the instrument paying for itself will not be very much affected by a fall in the rate of interest from $3\frac{1}{2}$ to 3 per cent.

It is evident that, for all kinds of capital goods for which maintenance and depreciation are large in comparison with net yield, the response of the deepening process is likely to be sluggish. But there are some capital goods for which maintenance and depreciation are moderate in comparison with net yield. In the extreme case, where an improvement may be expected to last for ever, to cost nothing for maintenance and never to lose its usefulness, interest represents the whole cost. In practice, however, it is never certain that such an improvement will not be superseded, and the prudent man will allow something by way of depreciation or sinking fund. Almost all forms of machinery involve fairly heavy depreciation charges. For buildings and works of construction they are often much less. This applies particularly to dwelling-houses. Instruments of consumption are a topic to which we will turn presently (see pp. 41-3).

If for the moment we confine ourselves to instruments of production (in which we include those used to assist any form of economic activity, production, transportation or distribution), we find that the yield or cost-saving capacity covers a very wide range. It is by no means to be taken for granted that the capital equipment of a particular industry includes *any* marginal item at all. It is quite likely that in a concern with £100,000 of fixed capital, £90,000 is such as to yield in cost-saving capacity over 50 per cent per annum, that the remaining £10,000 yields from 10 to 30 per cent, and that no other device known to man exists which if installed in that industry, would even yield zero (i.e. would cover depreciation and maintenance). Instruments near the margin need not necessarily be at all common in industry as a whole, and it is not even *certain* that they must exist anywhere.

On the other hand, the cost-saving capacity of an instrument is not a fixed quantity determined once and for all by its technical functions. It depends on the particular and local conditions of the concern in which it is to be installed. The first cost includes not only the actual cost of installation, but the cost of experience in its use and of changes of organisation and routine. Along with the first cost, the cost of maintenance, the cost of the labour which the instrument supersedes, above all the possibility of its not being employed up to capacity, these and other circumstances must all be taken into account. For example, a tractor, which, if used under the most favourable circumstances, would yield in net annual labour-saving efficiency 50 per cent of its first cost, may on a farm less suitable to its employment yield 20 or 10 or zero per cent. There are likely to be some farms for which the tractor is near to being an instrument of marginal yield.

This sort of case is common enough in all branches of industry to afford a presumption that there will always be marginal instruments of some kinds to be installed in some industries. But that does not mean that each separate class of instrument has a marginal member. Consider some highly specialised machine which has become essential in an industry, in that without it the cost of production would be increased by an amount equal to many hundreds per cent per annum on its first cost. Probably it will never be installed without a reasonable expectation that it will be fully employed. If it turns out that in no instance is it employed for less than two-thirds of the time for which it is available, then in the least favourable case it will still be yielding hundreds per cent per annum.

TECHNOLOGICAL IMPROVEMENTS

Technological improvements modify the problem by introducing a tendency towards deepening even without any lowering of the rate of interest. The rate of interest may actually have to be *raised* to prevent the deepening process from going too fast. Thus the deepening process does not depend exclusively on the inducement offered by a falling rate of interest for the installation of instruments with lower and lower yield. It requires to be regulated by a fluctuating rate of interest, rising when the deepening process is going too fast and falling when it is not going fast enough.

The introduction of a new contrivance or process constitutes an alteration of the structure of production. If it involves the displacement of a certain amount of labour by a new kind of instrument, without any considerable alteration in the plant already used, the improvement can be carried out as fast as the new instrument can be produced and installed. If the total resources available for capital extension be assumed unchanged, then new capital outlay must be curtailed in other directions. Theoretically this should be accomplished by a rise in the rate of interest making the instruments previously marginal unremunerative. In practice, however, a number of other reactions must be taken into account.[1]

A newly invented instrument may supersede an existing instrument or may involve modifications in the plant in conjunction with which it is to be employed. In that case, though it can be included without difficulty in the capital equipment of a new enterprise, it can only be installed in an existing enterprise at some sacrifice, unless the time at which the instruments to be superseded or modified will in any case require replacement is waited for. In practice the improvement would probably be carried out some time before the time of replacement that would have been otherwise adopted. As the instruments to be discarded get nearer and nearer the end of their normal life, the sacrifice of value involved in replacing them gets less and less.

The effect is to slow down the introduction of improvements. A very advantageous improvement may be introduced rapidly because

[1] We shall be dealing with the working of the investment market in the next chapter (below, pp. 55-8).

its increased cost-saving capacity will pay for an extensive premature scrapping of obsolescent plant. But where the saving is moderate, the normal replacements may be little if at all anticipated, and the introduction of the improvement may be spread over a period approximating to the normal life of the plant to be replaced. Replacement very often means the substitution for the discarded instrument of one of a substantially different pattern, and in calculations of depreciation some allowance for obsolescence is ordinarily made.

Technological progress is not confined to the invention of new processes and new kinds of instrumental goods. It includes also the invention of new consumable goods, and the establishment of new industries to produce them. That is part not of the deepening but of the widening process. If it occurred in a community without the former kind of invention, the new industries would have to draw away productive resources from the old. But when both kinds of invention proceed concurrently, the man-power displaced by new inventions in existing industries becomes available for widening, and can be used, directly or indirectly, for manning the new industries.

Up to a certain point cost-saving inventions in existing industries may meet with an elastic demand ; the charge to the consumer is reduced, but consumption increases more than in proportion, and the numbers employed in the industry (including those employed in producing the new kinds of instrumental goods) may actually be increased in spite of the displacement of labour. So long as this tendency exists, the deepening process is associated to some extent with the widening process. But for any product, as cost declines and output is increased, demand must *eventually* become inelastic, and cost-saving inventions do tend ultimately to displace labour. Even without cost-saving inventions, the deepening process is essentially a displacement of labour by instruments. If a community were perpetually growing richer through the elaboration and extension of its capital equipment, but without any new variety in the products, consumption would inevitably approach satiety. Satiety or glut is an ultimate possibility in any case by no means to be ignored, but the development of new products and new industries may make possible an indefinitely great improvement in material welfare before the problems of satiety arise.

We have seen that technological progress introduces a tendency towards deepening the capital equipment of the community without lowering the rate of interest. To imagine a well-defined boundary line separating those instruments which yield more than the market rate of interest from those which do not would be a misconception of the facts. We have already shown how uncertain and approximate the estimates of yield even of instruments already in use must often be; between the certainly unremunerative and the certainly remunerative is a broad zone of uncertainty, merging insensibly on the one side into the remunerative and on the other into the unremunerative.

With newly invented or untried instruments the uncertainty is still greater. The introduction of any new process or appliance is an adventure requiring initiative. Even when it has passed out of the hands of the scientist into those of the technical expert who proves its practical value, it may still have to wait a long time before it is actually brought into use, and even then a prolonged successful experience may be necessary to persuade industrialists generally to take advantage of it. Thus at any moment there is likely to be a vast accumulation of potentialities of remunerative investment waiting to be exploited, investment not merely remunerative but promising a yield far above the " margin " corresponding to the market rate of interest. If industrialists were prepared to take advantage of these opportunities systematically, and to embark upon the most remunerative first, the marginal yield might be pushed up ever so high and the deepening process correspondingly modified. The deterrent of a very high long-term rate of interest would be necessary to sift out the most remunerative openings and postpone the rest.

In practice this does not occur, because the majority of industrialists are content to proceed along well tried paths, and the minority, who show exceptional enterprise in trying new things, are so few and make such modest demands on the funds currently available for investment that no deterrent is needed to limit their activities.

The result is to make the deepening process all the more insensitive to the rate of interest. The sifting out of instruments of production of which the yield exceeds the rate of interest is a gradual or long-term process, and its effects in any short interval are likely to be slight. And even in the long run the strictly marginal instrument will not be attractive; if it yields nothing in excess of bare interest there is no inducement to use it.

In any case there tends to be an element of profit in the yield required from an instrument. So far as different industries offer alternative openings for those putting capital into new enterprises or extensions, the proportion of profit expected to the amount of capital needed will be taken into account. That does not mean that competition will make the ratio of normal profits to capital the same in all industries, but whenever deepening adds to the amount of capital needed for an enterprise, a yield something in excess of interest is likely to be required from the new instruments.

INSTRUMENTS OF CONSUMPTION

We have now reached the stage at which we must consider instruments of consumption, that is to say, durable consumers' goods, such that the process of consumption is prolonged over a considerable period, throughout which the instrument preserves its identity. Houses are the principal example. The description likewise covers the majority of ornaments and utensils, but the durable character is of less practical significance for things which are not normally hired or rented.

The theory regarding instruments of production, with which we have hitherto been occupied, requires some modification in its application to instruments of consumption. The decision to instal an instrument of production is ultimately governed by its cost-saving capacity, which, difficult though it may be to estimate with precision, is a matter of objective fact, expressible in pecuniary terms. It is a part of the decisions in regard to capital equipment and organisation generally, which are quite separate from the decision to start the enterprise in which the capital equipment is to be used. The purpose of the enterprise is to realise a profit on the sale of the output; the purpose of the capital equipment is to produce the output at the lowest possible cost.

But in the case of a house this distinction is not so clear. The house is itself an enterprise. If it is let to a tenant, the rent represents both interest and profit. Cost-saving capacity no longer enters into the calculation (except that labour-saving contrivances may be included for the benefit of the occupier). Of every feature embodied in the house the question to be decided is whether its value to a tenant will be such as to add to the rent that can be asked an amount sufficient to compensate for its capital cost.

Just as there are instruments of which the cost-saving capacity immeasurably exceeds the rate of interest, so there are features in a house of which the contribution to well-being immeasurably exceeds interest on their capital cost. No householder would do without glass in his windows in order to save five shillings a year from the rent. And when all the obviously desirable features have been provided for, there will remain marginal features, of which it is doubtful whether they will pay for themselves in rent. The utility of every feature of the house has to be conceived in the form of so much enjoyment per unit of time, and the marginal utility, that is to say, the utility of the least attractive feature, will tend to be equal to the market rate of interest *plus* profit on the capital value of the feature.

In the case of a productive enterprise the advantage of all those instruments of which the cost-saving capacity exceeds the rate of interest is passed on to the consumer of the product in a reduction of price. That is so because the cost of the instrument to the producer is no more than depreciation, maintenance and interest, and so long as all producers are free to acquire it and use it, competition will keep down prices to costs on this basis, *plus* normal profits. Thus cost-saving contrivances take effect in a kind of consumers' surplus. And similarly in the case of instruments of consumption, every constituent, however advantageous, figures in the rent for interest at the market rate, and the excess of its utility above the margin is a consumers' surplus.

In the cost of production of a commodity interest is rarely a large item. Even in the highly capitalised industries of the United States the capital employed in manufacturing hardly equals two years' net output,[1] and the total interest to be earned (including that which is merged in profits as well as that actually payable to creditors) would be substantially less than one-tenth of the net output. In the cost of transport interest is a more considerable part, but on the other hand it is a very small proportion of the costs of wholesale and retail dealing. Consequently, when the long-term rate of interest rises or falls, the effect of the change on the prices charged to consumers is very small.

But the effect on house rent is substantial, and there may result a considerable contraction or expansion of the demand for houses. When a feature of house construction and fittings is marginal, that means that it is marginal at a certain standard of living. People below a certain income will usually do without it. If the rate of interest falls and brings down rents, the feature becomes marginal at a lower level of income. Some features previously marginal at some income level may become in universal demand. Some features previously not adopted at all may be put on the market and taken advantage of by the very rich.

---

[1] Net output is the value of the manufacturing activity, and is arrived at by deducting from the selling value of the manufactured output the value of materials etc., used.

When we reckon the effect of a change in the rate of interest on the charge made to the consumer, Jevons's formula requires a little adaptation. We can distinguish two distinct ways in which the change in the rate of interest affects capital outlay and so modifies the period of production. By causing an advance or a retreat, as the case may be, of the marginal yield, it affects the deepening process. But it also alters the relative cost of production, and so the charge to the consumer, according to the proportion which interest bears to other constituents of costs for different products. The change in the relative demand for the various kinds of products, induces a corresponding change in the relative output, and there results a thickening of capital or the reverse : the widening process is modified in such a way as to increase or decrease the amount of capital employed for a given total output.

The adjustment of cost-saving capacity acts through the instruments used. It is a particular case of the principle of substitution : a more economical factor is substituted for a less economical in order to reduce costs to a minimum. The adjustment through the relative demand for the products involving more and less interest in their costs, takes effect not through the yield of *instruments*, but through the yield of *enterprises*.

From the preceding three sections it is evident that the adaptation of Jevons's formula to a dynamic system removes it a long way from its static simplicity. Not only is the marginal yield to which the long-term rate of interest is to be equated a matter of very uncertain estimates, but there are impediments in the way of the adjustment of the rate even to the expectations of yield which are held.

It is hardly going too far to say, that in the great majority of projects for capital outlay, the rate of interest regarded as an item of cost is an insignificant consideration. Nevertheless, as we shall see (below, pp. 80-90), the favourable or unfavourable state of the investment market exercises a decisive influence on the progress of capital outlay.

VALUE AND PRESENT VALUE

Irving Fisher, in his *Theory of Interest*, adopts the doctrine that " the price of any good is equal to the discounted value of its expected future service " (p. 325). " Past costs have no *direct* influence on value. Only indirectly do they enter to the extent that they have determined the existing supply of goods and have thus either raised or lowered the value of the services of these goods " (p. 16).

So far as this doctrine is applied to an enterprise, or to any object which yields a money income, it is quite tenable. The value of a house, regarded as an investment, is the discounted value of the rent to be received from it (*minus* so much as is to be reckoned not as interest but as profit). But that is not true of an instrument which does not itself yield an income but contributes as a means of production to the output of an enterprise. The yield or cost-saving capacity of an instrument may greatly exceed the market rate of interest, so that the present value of the services it is to yield, discounted at the market rate of interest, will greatly exceed the value of the instrument. It might be contended that the instrument could be hired for a sum corresponding to the rate of interest on its first cost, and that the services it renders must be assessed at their hiring value, because that is all that the market allows for them. But that is to derive the valuation of the services rendered from interest on the first cost of the instrument. It is just the reverse of Fisher's doctrine, that the value of the instrument is derived from the value of the services it renders.

Similarly, in the case of the constituent parts or features of a house or other instrument of consumption, the value of the services they render to the consumer may greatly exceed interest at the market rate on their first cost. Here the value of the services rendered is purely subjective, and we have no independent method of measuring it, but if we are reduced to valuing the services on the basis of interest on the first cost, we are deriving their value from the value of the constituent which renders them, not the value of the constituent from the value of the services.

Now it is undeniable that an instrument either of production or of consumption is valued only *for the sake* of the services it is to render. But, except in the case of the marginal instrument, the price of the instrument is not equal to the present value of the services. In other cases the present value of the services *exceeds* the price. It is true that the application of this principle to an instrument of consumption involves the elusive and rather unsatisfactory concept of consumers' surplus, depending on total utility. But the cost-saving capacity of an instrument of production is free from that complication ; it is a matter of objective fact, even though it has to be calculated hypothetically.

Fisher expresses the choice exercised between two alternative forms of investment in terms of the " rate of return over cost ", the limiting rate of interest which would make the two alternatives just equally attractive. If the actual rate is lower, the more highly capitalised will be chosen ; if it is higher, the less highly capitalised. If the alternatives are production of a given output with an instrument and production without it, then the true cost-saving capacity of the instrument must enter into the comparison. If the value of the instrument were reckoned as equal to the present value of the services rendered discounted at the existing rate of interest, the choice would have no meaning.

Fisher illustrates the principle of the rate of return over cost from the choice to be made among a number of alternative *enterprises*. But an enterprise offers not only interest on the capital to be employed, but *profit*. Profit will be affected by the state of the market for the final product, and this is likely to be the deciding consideration in the choice.

When an enterprise is chosen, the choice implies not only the rejection of alternative enterprises but also the selection of the particular degree of capitalisation decided on for that enterprise. The degree of capitalisation may be assumed to be such that the yield of the marginal instrument will be equal to the market rate of interest. And presumably that would have been so for any other enterprise that might have been chosen. Consequently, apart from differences of profit, the rate of return over cost in the comparison of any two alternatives would simply always be equal to the market rate of interest. With that assumption the choice between enterprises would be determined exclusively by profit. This is merely to say once again, that the rate of interest is determined by the deepening not by the widening of capital.

WORKING CAPITAL

Our examination of the relations of the rate of interest to capital outlay has been confined, up to this point, to instruments of production and instruments of consumption, and implicitly to the long-term rate of interest. To complete our survey, we must turn to working capital and the allied question of the short-term rate of interest.

We have to find how far the general principle, that the rate of interest tends to be equal to marginal yield, is applicable to working capital. And first we must enquire wherein the " yield " of working capital consists.

In every economic process applied to material objects there is a certain minimum amount of working capital, determined by the minimum time the process occupies. If a producer bought his materials from moment to moment as required, so that he held no stock of them at all, and if the partially finished product were passed on from each process instantaneously to the next and the completed product were sold the moment it appeared, his working capital would consist only of the articles actually undergoing change in the hands of his workpeople, and would be an absolute minimum. In practice the minimum must provide for a certain amount of materials and of the successive intermediate products, in stock at every stage, if only to avoid the risk of unforeseen delays and vexatious difficulties of organisation.

But the essential stocks could be kept very low if they could be replenished day by day to whatever extent might be necessary to replace the amount actually used. The various processes to be applied cannot be expected to keep pace with one another exactly, and, if no process is to be held up by delays or irregularities in the preceding process, there must be available for it an accumulated stock of the product of the preceding process. But the stocks held on this account would rarely exceed a few days' supply. The reason why a manufacturer will sometimes hold stocks equivalent to several weeks' or even months' use is the *convenience of buying* in larger quantities and at less frequent intervals than the exigencies of a minimum stock require. It is not merely that he can thereby make more favourable bargains and save something on transport and handling, but he can avoid the trouble of making unnecessarily frequent decisions. The price he pays for this convenience is the interest on the capital tied up in the stocks of goods held, together with the cost of storage. If he buys two months' supplies at a time, he will have an average of one months' supply in stock in excess of the necessary minimum. The necessary resources may be provided either out of the permanent capital of the concern or from temporary borrowing. In the former case, what is sacrificed is the interest that might be obtained by the temporary investment of the money used to purchase the goods. If this is no more than the interest on money on deposit or at call, it is a relatively low rate. But for that very reason it may be found preferable to rely on temporary borrowing to cover the fluctuating portion of working capital, rather than to raise permanent capital which for part of the time will not be earning full interest.

The cost in interest of holding stocks of goods tends therefore to be the short-term rate, the rate to be paid for a few weeks or months, whether in the form of discount on bills or in that of interest on bank advances or overdrafts.

The position of wholesale and retail dealers in commodities in regard to working capital is very similar to that of producers. The retail dealer must have sufficient stocks of all the principal varieties of goods he deals in to be able to suit his customers' tastes and to give them a choice. Theoretically he could keep his stocks at a bare minimum by replenishing them every day. But, like the manufacturer buying materials, the retailer will be led by considerations of convenience in buying to obtain relatively large quantities of each commodity at relatively long intervals. The same applies to the wholesale dealer, at any rate in manufactured products.

SEASONAL PRODUCTS

On the other hand, with agricultural products of a seasonal kind the problems of working capital are quite different. Where there is an annual crop, a year's supply becomes available in the short interval of harvesting, and dealers have to be found who are willing to hold it and to go on holding so much as remains unconsumed at any time during the ensuing twelve months. The circumstances differ from those of manufactured goods, which need not be produced till orders are actually given by purchasers. Agricultural producers, when they start ploughing, are in a state of great uncertainty both as to the prospective state of the market when the product comes to be sold, and as to the actual amount of the crop that the land will yield. An excess or deficiency of supply is ultimately corrected by a restriction or extension of cultivation, but the process is slow, and meanwhile the dealers in the product have to take charge of the supply, whatever it may be, and to provide for a suitable carry-over from each crop to the next. These uncertainties take practical shape in big and frequent fluctuations of prices, compared with which the charges for interest are relatively insignificant.

Three other causes contribute to widen the fluctuations in the prices of agricultural products. In the first place, their value in proportion to bulk being low, the cost of storage is high relatively to value. The natural or primary products sold by the farmer are usually the raw materials for subsequent processes, which go on adding to their value stage by stage, without adding to their bulk, till at last a completed consumable product appears of the value of which the sum originally received by the farmer represents only quite a small fraction. The cost of storage of grain, for example, is very considerable, relatively to its value. The charge for storing wheat may be put at 6d. a ton a week, or 26s. a year, say, 5 per cent of its value.

That makes the burden of holding the big seasonal stocks all the greater. The cost has to be paid for out of the difference between the traders' buying and selling prices. One who is faced with the prospect of paying high charges for storage, as well as interest, for a long time will arrive at the price he can afford to pay by deducting all those charges, as well as his profit, from the selling price he expects ultimately to realise. A contracting demand which threatens not only to reduce the future proceeds of sale but to prolong the period for which the goods will have to be held in stock, has a doubly unfavourable effect on price.

Secondly, in consequence of the primary product contributing so small a fraction to the price paid by the consumer, price concessions on the primary product have relatively little effect upon the consumers' demand. The demand for primary products being derived from the demand for the finished products is therefore very inelastic, or, in other words, large price fluctuations have little effect on the volume of sales.

Thirdly, prime costs form a relatively small part of the total costs of agricultural products, and the selling price has to fall a long way before the gross profit is entirely wiped out, so that a reduction of output will actually save a direct loss.

The result is that the markets in primary products are highly speculative. Dealers must be prepared for large gains and losses. They must study the conditions both of supply and of demand with a view to anticipating future movements. But it is not to be inferred that the cost of interest on stocks of primary products can be neglected. For the trader who holds a stock can eliminate the fluctuation of the market price by hedging: that is, he can compensate possible changes in the money value of the stock he holds by effecting a forward sale.

An organised market in a primary product performs two distinct services. On the one hand, for the trader who acquires a quantity of the product with a view to sale, it affords facilities for finding a buyer, and for exercising his skill, knowledge and business connexions to select a buyer whom the special characteristics of the particular material he has to dispose of will suit. On the other, there are expert dealers, who specialise in forecasting the movements of the market as a whole, and who, with that object, study all the influences likely to affect the supply of the product and the demand for it.

These latter are really professional speculators, and it is they who provide facilities for hedging. They deal in forward purchases and sales : contracts for delivery and payment at specified future dates. The prices they quote for future dates are linked with one another and with the spot price (for immediate delivery and payment) because a trader will not buy for a later date if he can do better by buying for an earlier date, and holding the goods bought in stock for the interval. The price at the later date therefore will not exceed the price at the earlier date by more than the cost of holding in stock (storage, interest, etc.). If the speculative dealers foresee a shortage at a future date, they will raise their forward price for that date, but will have to raise all the earlier prices (including the spot price) so far as is necessary to prevent the margins between them from exceeding the limit.

If interest and storage cost 1 per cent per month, and the price three months hence is expected to rise from 100 to 120, the spot price must rise to 117.

An anticipated fall of price is not so certainly reflected in a fall of the spot price. Traders will be unwilling to hold stocks of a commodity of which the price is expected to fall, and, so long as they have surplus stocks to spare, the spot price will follow the forward price downwards. But when they can no longer spare any more goods from stock, the link between spot price and forward price will be broken ; the latter may be lower, even far lower, than the former. That happens when there is a present scarcity of a seasonal product, along with the prospect of future abundance.[1]

The adjustment of the chain of prices which links the spot price to a future price is effected through the transactions of the speculative dealers, and is reflected in fluctuations of the stocks held by them. When the price anywhere in the chain is above or below what would accord with their forecasts, they correct the discrepancy by selling or buying on their own account. The result is that their purchases and sales do not correspond exactly with the demands for hedging from the traders who want to avoid speculating.

[1] It may also happen in a market where producers make a regular practice of selling their output forward some time before it is actually available, for there are then no immediate supplies not already contracted for to a forward buyer. The merchants who have bought forward, hold between them all the spot supplies and there is a continuous premium on spot supplies (a " backwardation ") which is in effect the merchant's " turn ", or the margin between buying price and selling price. It is the payment which the producer makes to the merchant for relieving him of uncertainty during the interval between the time when his output can be accurately foreseen and the time when it is available for delivery.

That is the case, I think, which Keynes had in mind when he said that " in normal conditions there is a backwardation " (*Treatise on Money*, Vol. II, p. 143).

4

The total stocks of the product are thus composed of those in the hands of speculative dealers, which are determined mainly by anticipations of price movements, and those in the hands of traders who by hedging exclude price movements from their calculations. The former may be little influenced by the rate of interest. For the latter on the contrary, in so far as they hold stocks with borrowed money, the rate of interest will not be a negligible item in the balancing of carrying costs against convenience.

A rise in the rate of interest may induce the non-speculative traders to delay their purchases. But, as the production of a seasonal product can only be affected after a long interval, the total stock to be carried remains undiminished. The speculative traders have to be induced to carry additional stocks, and the price falls.

MANUFACTURED PRODUCTS

Some, but not all, of the foregoing considerations apply to non-seasonal primary products and materials, such as minerals. The demand for them, being derived from the demand for the finished products in which they are used, is inelastic. They are subject to wide and frequent fluctuations of price, and organised markets with hedging facilities have come into being for some of them.

So long as production is not seasonal, however, it can be adjusted to demand. The manufacturer usually produces only in response to orders, that is to say, firm forward contracts with intending purchasers. He will to some extent try to attract orders, when business is dull, by making price concessions, and, if his overhead costs are high, these price concessions may occasionally be very considerable. But prime costs set a lower limit to the price he can accept, and he will in general refuse to accept any price which does not allow a tolerable margin above that lower limit.

If anything occurs to make traders less willing to hold stocks of a commodity, the effect will be felt in a curtailment of orders given to the producers of that commodity. The orders given will be something less than sufficient to replace the amount sold. The result will be in the case of manufactures and minerals a reduction of output. Only in the case of agricultural products will output persist for a relatively considerable time undiminished.

In either case the general principle that the marginal yield is equal to the rate of interest is fulfilled. But the rate of interest is the short-term rate of interest, and we have to interpret the marginal yield in the appropriate way. For speculative holdings of agricultural products the yield consists in the prospect of a rise of price ; dealers will not buy them except at a price low enough to afford the prospect of ultimate sale at a profit.

In the case of manufactured products the yield takes the form of *convenience* in buying and taking delivery. Sometimes there may be an anticipated variation of price. But where output depends not on natural conditions, but on human volition, variations of price are likely to be the result of changes in *demand*, which cannot usually be foreseen. Even when a change in demand is expected, it does not necessarily mean a change in price. Apart from a possible deficiency of raw materials, supply can, within limits, be adjusted to demand, and where raw materials are an important consideration the manufacturer can escape the risk by hedging ; he can make a forward purchase at the time he receives the order.

Thus in general the stock held of any manufactured or semi-manufactured commodity is the resultant of the yield of convenience on the one hand and the rate of interest and cost of storage on the other.

The cost of storage is often insignificant. Manufacturers and retail dealers have a certain amount of storage accommodation of their own, which is probably sufficient for the stocks corresponding to their maximum buying convenience. They would not involve themselves in hiring accommodation unless there were some strong reason for holding exceptional stocks (such as an anticipated shortage or rise of price). Wholesale dealers and merchants are more likely to resort to hiring, but even they would usually possess a considerable amount of accommodation of their own.

Moreover, even when hiring is resorted to, the cost of storing manufactured goods is for the most part small. A cubic yard of wheat at 10s. a bushel is worth only £10 10s. A cubic yard of manufactured goods ready for consumption would often be worth hundreds of pounds. Consequently, except for bulky articles, such as vehicles or furniture, the actual cost of space is likely to be small in comparison with the rate of interest. That does not apply of course to perishables, which either cannot be stored at all without rapid loss of value, or have to be preserved by costly devices such as refrigeration. And articles subject to changes of fashion or obsolescence are liable to losses of value on that account, which require stocks to be kept down to a minimum, at any rate at certain seasons.

But for the great majority of manufactured products a principal consideration in determining the practice of traders in regard to the intervals of buying, and so to the average stock held, will be the rate of interest, or rather the facility of borrowing. The stocks of finished manufactures are held for the most part by wholesale and retail dealers. Manufacturers are unwilling to produce for stock, and can usually deliver goods ordered as soon as they are ready.

The facility of borrowing does not depend exclusively on the rate of interest. Short-term lending is mainly in the hands of bankers, who regulate the amount they lend not only by their charges for interest but to some extent also directly. The stock of goods a trader is willing to hold will sometimes be limited not by the rate of interest he has to pay, but by the amount that his banker will allow him to borrow for the purpose.

LONG- AND SHORT-TERM LOANS

The simple formula enunciated by Jevons, that the equilibrium rate of interest is $\dfrac{f}{Ft}$, conceals complications. There is not a single unequivocal rate of interest, but there are different rates for different lengths of loans. In particular there is the outstanding distinction between the long-term and short-term rates. The increment, t, in the period of production may represent any of an indefinite variety of changes in the structure of production, some of which will make $\dfrac{f}{Ft}$ equal to the long-term rate of interest, others to the short-term rate, and yet others to combinations of the two.

The market fixes different rates of interest for different types of loan. But there is not necessarily any close correspondence between the period for which an industrialist borrows and the life of the plant which he instals. An enterprise is usually intended to be permanent. Syndicates formed for temporary ventures, to be wound up after a few years or even months, do not play any considerable part in the investment market.[1] An enterprise which is intended to carry on its operations permanently, or for an indefinite period into the future, will instal plant with a limited life, but the intention will be to replace the plant as it wears out or becomes obsolete, and to accumulate a depreciation fund for that purpose.

----

[1] A big construction contract is often paid for over a period of years, but that is a purely financial arrangement with no relation to the subsequent life of the works to be constructed (which are probably of a permanent character).

If the fund is used to pay for replacement, it is not available to pay off a loan. When the promoter of the enterprise borrows on bonds, debentures or mortgages, his calculations will be based on the assumption that the enterprise is permanent. If the loan raised has a due date for repayment, that will not be because there is any expectation that the enterprise will be wound up when the date arrives. The due date will be arranged for the convenience of the lender, and the intention will be either to provide a sinking fund to extinguish the loan when the due date arrives, or to raise a new loan to provide the money for paying off the old. A long-term loan of thirty or forty years, a medium-term loan running for five or ten years, or a mortgage continuing indefinitely, subject to six months' notice, may equally form part of the permanent capitalisation of the undertaking.

And a considerable part (or even the whole) of the working capital may be provided for by the permanent capitalisation. Some concerns prefer to be quite free from any dependence on bank loans, even if this involves some sacrifice of interest when they accumulate idle balances. And those which rely in the normal course on bank loans would not do so for the whole of their working capital. A usual practice is to cover from permanent capitalisation the minimum below which the working capital is never likely to fall, and to provide the fluctuating excess over this minimum from bank loans.

On the other hand, traders do from time to time find it convenient to raise bank loans for other purposes than working capital. They may use them, for example, to acquire or construct new plant, undertaking to pay them off in a year or two out of undistributed profits.

The trader who borrows for periods which do not correspond with the life of the capital on which the money raised is spent runs the risk of a change in the rate of interest. If he borrows for a short term of years to instal plant which is to last for a generation, he may have to pay a higher rate when he raises a second loan on the maturity of the first. Even if there is a fall in the rate of interest, it may be that, had he foreseen the fall, a different kind of capital installation would have been more appropriate. But in reality the decision as to the terms on which capital is to be raised is made on financial grounds (below, p. 57). The rate of interest assumed for the purpose of determining whether a particular installation will pay for itself is the rate prevailing in the market ; if the installation is to be permanent, the appropriate rate will be the long-term rate, whatever the period of the loan raised may happen to be.

If the appliance is expected to require replacement in a certain period of years, the depreciation allowance will be so calculated as to provide the requisite sum at the end of the period. A depreciation allowance is itself assumed to earn interest in the interval before it is needed to pay for replacement, whether it is actually invested in securities and accumulated, or is re-invested in the business itself. A change in the rate of interest will affect the rate of accumulation. A higher rate hastens the process, but a rise in the rate may also cause loss through a fall in the market price of securities previously acquired.

In planning capital equipment the only possible course is to assume for all purposes a rate of interest based on the existing market long-term rate. The cost of any appliance takes the form of a terminable annuity computed for the estimated life of the appliance at the assumed rate of interest. If a different rate of interest were taken, the change in the annuity would be less than in proportion to the change in the rate.

CHAPTER IV

CAPITAL AND EMPLOYMENT

THE INVESTMENT MARKET

CORRELATIVE to the theory which measures capital by the period of production is the view of saving as " waiting ". Both capital and saving are expressed in terms of time. Waiting is the service rendered by postponing or forgoing consumption, and placing resources at the disposal of those who seek to increase productivity at the cost of extending the period of production. The period of production cannot be extended up to the limit at which no gain of output can be obtained from any further extension, because the supply of waiting is limited. People insist on consuming a certain portion of their incomes without waiting, and the growth of their total accumulation is limited to the residue which they leave unconsumed. That residue, the excess of consumers' income [1] over consumption, is the aggregate *saving*.

The unconsumed residue will be represented in part by instruments of consumption and stocks of goods in the hands of consumers. For the rest, it may either be invested or held in cash. In this connexion, to " invest " money means to acquire with it rights in or over any income-yielding enterprise or institution. [2] Such rights, including as they do shares, bonds, debentures, and mortgages, we will call securities. We count governments and municipalities and other local authorities as income-yielding institutions for this purpose.

It is the function of the investment market to deal in securities. It buys new flotations, and both buys and sells existing securities. It buys securities from those who wish to *raise capital*, that is to say, to obtain money for capital purposes, and from those who wish to change their investments, and it sells securities to investors. The amount of investment in any interval of time is a net amount arrived at by subtracting the value of securities bought from investors from

---

[1] The " consumers' income " is simply the total of incomes, for an income can only belong to a physical person or consumer. The " consumers' outlay " is what is spent out of income, including investment (below, p. 132).

[2] This definition corresponds to ordinary usage, but differs from Keynes's definition of investment (below, pp. 157, 160, 166).

the value of those sold to them. This net amount of investment is made available through the market for those who are raising capital.

The purchase of instruments of consumption by the consumers, for example, of a house by the intending occupier, we will call *consumers' capital outlay*. It combines investment, the raising of capital and capital outlay all in one transaction. Investment as defined above excludes consumers' capital outlay, though it includes the acquisition of such instruments as a source of income through letting to consumers.

It is through the investment market that the long-term rate of interest is determined. We have already examined the conditions to be fulfilled by the rate of interest to maintain equilibrium. Equilibrium must mean equality between the net amount of investment and the openings offered to it in the form of capital raised. If the openings are not sufficient, the dealers in the market will find themselves selling more securities than they buy, and they will raise the prices of securities, or, in other words, lower the rate of interest. If the openings offered exceed the available funds, the dealers will be asked to buy more securities than they sell ; they will lower prices and so raise the rate. The results of an excess or deficiency of openings for investment are not materially altered by the fact that the funds entering the market are not necessarily placed directly in the new openings, but may be used to buy existing securities, for the sellers of the existing securities will have money to invest.

The resources seeking investment through the market will not be exactly equal to current savings. A portion of the savings, as we have seen, will be applied directly to the purchase of instruments of consumption by the intending consumers. And a further portion may be absorbed in cash balances. There may also, on the other hand, be a *reduction* of cash balances, the consumers' outlay exceeding the consumers' income, so that the funds seeking investment exceed current savings. And current savings may be still further supplemented by bank advances obtained by speculators or speculative investors to buy securities. The money so applied is included in " investment " as we have defined it. So long as it comes from individuals or consumers, we regard the net amount (after setting off the proceeds of sale of securities) as part of the consumers' outlay.[1] Stockjobbers and other professional dealers in the investment market may also hold part of the securities that form their stock-in-trade with borrowed money.

Any money borrowed from the banks for the holding of securities

[1] Below, p. 136.

is added to the inflow of resources into the investment market, any such money repaid is subtracted from it. Here we have a link between the long-term and short-term rates of interest. Another link is to be found in the power of the trader to choose between long-term and short-term borrowing for various purposes.

The raising of capital is not effected exclusively by means of new flotations. When traders supplement their capital resources by reinvesting undistributed profits, investment and the raising of capital are combined in a single act. And they often accumulate reserves of marketable securities, so that they can raise capital by selling these.

The types of securities they acquire will be determined by financial considerations. Finance is the art of providing the means of payment. The marketable securities which a concern holds are a substitute for cash, and they are destined ultimately to be turned into cash by being pledged or sold. If they were not so destined, they would not be needed for the business at all, but would constitute either a separate venture of dealing in securities, appropriate to the investment market, or surplus capital which could properly be distributed among the shareholders or proprietors by way of a capital reduction.

The securities will be so chosen as to mature at times calculated to suit the convenience of the concern, for example, when it needs cash for replacements or extensions of plant. And as forecasts of future needs of cash are extremely uncertain, the securities must be readily marketable. A great part of the demand for government securities is for the investment of the reserves and depreciation funds of industrial and commercial concerns. Medium-term securities, maturing in a few years, are particularly sought after, because they are not subject to any appreciable risk of capital loss on sale (below, p. 181). That is why they are quoted at prices allowing a relatively low yield, though higher than that allowed on time deposits. Governments take advantage of the traders' demand to borrow at a favourable rate on securities of this class.

A trader who sells securities is raising capital. When he buys securities he reverses the operation. The aggregate of capital raised is a net amount, the purchases of securities by traders being regarded as a negative raising of capital (below, p. 137).

A trader's holding of cash and marketable securities may be called his " free capital " : it is that part of his capital resources which is not tied up in the equipment and working capital of his business.

Free capital may be accumulated not only from reinvested profits, destined for extensions and improvements of plant, but from depreciation funds, destined for renewals and replacements.

Capital raised and depreciation allowances together constitute the resources available to traders for the purpose of installing instrumental goods. The capital installed is a gross total. Deduction from it of depreciation leaves the net total, *capital added*, for which capital raised is destined.

Capital added, together with the consumers' capital outlay, constitutes net capital outlay as a whole, or, as we shall usually call it, *capital outlay*. Capital outlay is not to be identified with the instrumental goods *produced ;* it is composed of the instrumental goods acquired for use. Those which have been produced, but still await sale to the users, form part of the working capital of the traders who hold them.

Traders raise capital for the purpose of installing instrumental goods in their enterprises. They also cover a part, or even in some cases the whole, of their needs for working capital. It is these operations that the market has to influence in order to attain equilibrium. Working capital plays only a subsidiary part in the long-term investment market, being more intimately related to short-term lending. The investment market determines the rate of interest at which capital is raised, and so the limits within which the cost-saving capacity of capital to be installed pays.

ABSORPTION AND RELEASE OF CASH

A sum added to a consumer's cash balance is a part of his saving. Not so a sum added to a trader's cash balance. We distinguish a trader from a consumer, even though trader and consumer may be the same individual. A trader is any one who carries on a business for profit. He may be an individual to whom the profit is income, and who in his capacity as the recipient of income is a consumer. Or, on the other hand, a trader may be a partnership or joint-stock company which earns profit for its members. It is they who are consumers, not the trading concern itself.

The important distinction is between the consumer's cash balance and the trader's cash balance. A trader's cash balance is included in his capital. If he increases his cash balance by transforming a part of his working capital from goods into cash, that is not saving. Savings, whether from his own income in the form of reinvested profits or from other people's incomes placed at his disposal through the investment market, may be invested in his concern, and an increase in capital may or may not be accompanied by an increase in the cash balance, but that does not affect the character of the saving.

In a community with an exclusively metallic currency and no banking system, an increase in cash balances would be simply an accumulation of the monetary metal, and would have no direct bearing on the resources of the investment market. But when cash balances take the form of bank deposits or of currency with a fiduciary backing, a relation is established between the amount of cash balances and the amount of short-term investment.

If we treat indebtedness to a bank as a negative cash balance, we may define anyone's net cash resources as the excess (positive or negative) of his cash balance over his indebtedness to his banker. When any one increases his net cash resources, we say that he absorbs cash ; when he decreases his net cash resources, we say that he releases cash. An absorption of cash is the result of an excess of receipts over disbursements, and a release of cash is the result of an excess of disbursements over receipts.

Since one man's receipts are another's disbursements and *vice versa*, it follows that there can never be a release or absorption of cash by the community as a whole. What one part releases or absorbs the rest absorbs or releases. But we must assign to the banks the function of releasing or absorbing cash in a special sense. When a bank creates a deposit by lending to a customer, the transaction, taken by itself, leaves the customer's net cash resources unchanged. Similarly when it increases or decreases its deposit liability by receiving or paying currency. It is when the bank goes outside the short-term investment market and acquires assets such as stock exchange securities, which are dealt in in the long-term investment market, that it releases cash, and when it sells such assets it absorbs cash. We make this distinction because the customers of the banks do in practice rely on bills and advances as the ready means of supplementing their cash, so that their net cash resources, as we define them, are a reality. In the long-term investment market the banks are merged in the general body of buyers and sellers, and their operations have no relation to the affairs of their customers. When a bank holds a marketable security on its own account, the debtor need not be aware of the fact.[1]

---

[1] Where a bank discounts a trade bill for a customer, the transaction is best regarded as an advance on the security of the indebtedness of the acceptor of the bill. In other cases bills may be more suitably treated as marketable securities.

If the amount of investment and of consumers' capital outlay is greater or less than the amount of savings, the consumers' outlay is greater or less than the consumers' income, and consumers are releasing or absorbing cash. If the amount of capital raised is greater or less than the amount of investment, the investment market is releasing or absorbing cash. If the amount of capital added is greater or less than the amount of capital raised, the traders engaged in these operations are releasing or absorbing cash. If there is neither release nor absorption of cash at any of these three stages, the capital added is equal to investment, and net capital outlay is equal to saving.[1]

Saving is the excess of the consumers' income over consumption. The consumers' income is equal to production.[2] Saving is therefore the excess of production over consumption. It follows that saving is equal to the increment of wealth in the form of material products. If saving differs from capital outlay, the difference must appear in an increase or decrease of stocks of goods.

The release and absorption of cash play a fundamental part in the process of monetary regulation. The banks can create additional money either by inducing their customers to borrow more or by themselves buying securities. In the former alternative the banks do not themselves release cash, but the customers do, since no one borrows money to hold it idle. They buy or produce something with it, and in so doing they release cash, and the people who receive the cash released will in their turn buy or produce something. Thus the release of cash evokes a continued further release. It means an increased acquisition of goods by traders, and so increased productive activity. Similarly an absorption of cash means a decreased acquisition of goods by traders and so decreased productive activity.

When banks themselves release cash by buying securities, the effect is to increase the net cash resources of the long-term investment market and to stimulate new flotations. New flotations are for the installation of capital, and so here also there is increased productive

---

[1] See below, p. 140. It should be mentioned that these propositions require to be qualified in that the release or absorption of cash by traders depends also on changes in their working capital, and the investment market may release or absorb cash in its dealings with the banks.

[2] See below, pp. 133-4. The consumers' income could be defined, alternatively, to include the unproductive or transfer incomes. But then the payment of the transfer incomes would have to be included in the consumers' outlay, along with the consumption and investment of those who pay them. The calculation of saving would be unaffected.

activity. And when the banks sell securities, productive activity is decreased.

GENERAL DEMAND, DISPOSALS AND EMPLOYMENT

Now productive activity generates incomes, and incomes generate demand. We will designate by the expression " general demand " the amount of money offered for products of all kinds by final purchasers. General demand is to be distinguished in some essential respects from the demand for a particular product. The demand for a particular product is not a single quantity, but takes the form of a mathematical *function*, or schedule, relating any possible value of the product in terms of other products to the quantity demanded at that value. And it is *relative ;* the quantity demanded is, in the ultimate analysis, the quantity demanded in exchange for other products. We can, if we please, introduce money and express the function in terms of price instead of exchange value, but money is no more than an intermediary in the calculation.

General demand, on the other hand, since it embraces all products, cannot be a relation of some products to others, and can only be expressed in money. And it is not a function, but a single total.

It is the total amount of money per unit of time offered for goods by final purchasers, that is to say, by those who buy consumable goods for consumption or instrumental goods for use. It corresponds closely, but does not coincide exactly, with *disposals* of these goods to final purchasers. The subject-matter of general demand is precisely the same as that of disposals. But, whereas disposals in any interval of time are composed of the actual transfers of ownership to final purchasers, general demand is composed of the spending or intention to spend manifested by the final purchasers in the market. For each commodity we compute the amount of disposals per unit of time which the current offers of money for it imply, whether those offers are made over the counter and satisfied on the spot, or are for future delivery, or remain temporarily unsatisfied because goods of the kind desired are not immediately forthcoming. We further make allowance for actual sales having exceeded or fallen short of the true demand because consumers have increased or diminished their stocks of goods. General demand is arrived at by making this calculation for all consumable goods and instrumental goods and adding the results together.

The distinction that we make between general demand and disposals is a fine one. General demand is simply disposals seen

from the point of view of the traders at a particular moment.   As
soon as we look back and ask what general demand *has been*, we can
no longer distinguish it from disposals.   Any demand which fails to
fructify in disposals withers away.

General demand, being limited to the demand from final purchasers, excludes all purchases of goods by traders with a view
either to resale or to use as ingredients in the production of goods
for sale.   A net addition to working capital, when made designedly,
is for the time being a real augmentation of demand.   It may be
called intermediate demand.   Intermediate demand is excluded from
general demand, which is thus composed of the demand from
consumers for goods for consumption, which we shall call " consumption demand ", together with the demand for instruments of
production or consumption for use as such.

General demand takes goods off the market; it is the source of
disposals.   Intermediate demand does not; the goods added to
traders' stocks still await final sale.   But for the moment intermediate demand is not less effective as a source of productive
activity.   It is productive activity that determines *employment*, and
productive activity is determined by the orders which producers
receive.

The orders may be given by the final purchasers themselves.
Personal services rendered direct from producer to consumer are
asked for by the consumer.   And capital outlay is ordered by the
intending user.   In these cases there is direct impact of general
demand upon the producers : production and disposal are equal
and simultaneous.

But so much of general demand as is directed to material products which are held in stock is felt in the first instance in sales from
stock; the demand is only transmitted to the producer through
orders given for the replenishment of the seller's stock.   Orders
given direct by consumer to producer for such products are relatively
insignificant.   If the orders given by a trader for the replenishment
of his stocks differ from his sales, the difference is just what we have
called intermediate demand.   So the orders received by producers,
upon which productive activity depends, reflect general demand
modified by intermediate demand, positive or negative.

When disposals differ from production, the difference appears in
an increment or decrement of stocks.   And, as the consumers'
income is equal to production, the same difference appears as an
absorption or release of cash.

The difference may start either with a change in disposals or with a change in the consumers' income. A change in disposals would arise from a release or absorption of cash either by consumers or by the investment market : consumers may increase or reduce consumption or investment ; the capital raised from the investment market may exceed the inflow of resources into the market or fall short of it.

A change in the consumers' income may arise from an absorption or release of cash by traders. The capital outlay they incur may diverge from the amount of capital raised, or the orders given to producers of consumable goods may diverge from the amount of sales.

THE VICIOUS CIRCLE

We have seen (above, pp. 31-3) that the primary motive of the widening of capital is the prospect of profit, or rather of selling additional output without any sacrifice of price or of profit. The widening is an extension of capacity in response to an extension of consumption demand.

Consequently if, for any cause, there is a fluctuation in consumption demand, there will be a corresponding fluctuation in the widening process. In any one industry the estimates of demand are almost entirely *empirical ;* the signal for an extension of capacity will be an actual increase in demand, not perhaps a mere casual increase, but an increase persistent enough to foreshadow an increase in price. The widening of capital is simply the sum total of all the extensions of capacity that occur in the particular industries. An increase in consumption demand makes the demand throughout industry greater than it would otherwise be, and, if persistent, calls for a general extension of capacity (unless there is already so high a degree of activity that there is no reserve of unemployed labour to man additional plant).

Similarly a decrease of consumption demand makes the demand in every industry less than it would otherwise be. Extensions of capacity that would otherwise be needed are dispensed with ; the widening of capital may even be entirely suspended. Thus at a time of low demand the widening process falls into arrears, and at a time of high demand arrears are overtaken. The reaction of widening to fluctuations in general demand is what is usually called the " acceleration principle ", Mr. Harrod's " Relation " (below, p. 276).

If traders could foresee future fluctuations of demand accurately, their arrangements would not be so dependent on the conditions of the present. But, except in the case of public utilities (below, pp. 69-70), they have no means of knowing whether a change in demand is temporary or permanent.

We may conceive of a community in which there are no fluctuations either in general demand as a whole or in consumption demand, that is to say, the flow of money through consumers' income and outlay and disposals just keeps pace with economic growth. Profits, then, will be always normal, and the widening of capital will likewise just keep pace with economic growth. If savings are more than sufficient to provide for widening, the excess will be available for deepening.

The widening is required to equip the actual working population with capital on the basis of the existing structure of production. The deepening means an increase in the capital equipment needed for a given population.

In practical life, however, fluctuations occur both in general demand and also in consumption demand. If, at a time when capital equipment is just adequate for the working population, there is a decline of consumption demand, the capital equipment will become redundant. So far as instrumental capital is concerned, it may be assumed provisionally that whatever savings come into the investment market will be applied to capital outlay, and that, if widening falls off or is suspended, they will be used up in deepening.

But the redundancy of working capital is not so easily disposed of. The widening process applies to working capital as well as to instrumental capital. When sales of a product increase, traders require proportionally larger stocks. When sales decrease, the stocks they need are proportionally less, and the widening of working capital is reversed: there is an actual narrowing. The immediate consequence of a decline of consumption demand is diminished sales, and increased stocks of unsold goods. For smaller sales smaller stocks are required, and the traders whose sales are diminished will seek to reduce their stocks by ordering from the producers something less than the amount of goods necessary to replace those sold. And producers, with output falling off, will seek to reduce their stocks of materials and intermediate products by ordering less of these than would be sufficient to replace what they use in production. There is a negative intermediate demand. Thus productive activity is reduced in a greater proportion than sales, and since general demand is generated by the consumers' income, and the consumers' income is generated by productive activity, there will be a further reduction of general demand and therefore presumably of consumption demand. This will react in the same way and a vicious circle will be set up ; declining demand causes declining activity, and declining activity causes declining demand. Declining activity means declining employment.

This process is, of course, spread over time. A trader's stock of any commodity is in a state of continual flux. His decision to buy is made every time his stock falls near what he regards as the minimum limit. When the sales of the commodity fall off, the first effect is to defer the time at which replenishment becomes necessary. A later effect, becoming operative in his first purchase after he is persuaded that the drop in sales is not merely casual and temporary, is the reduction of the amount purchased in proportion more or less to sales.

The former effect, the postponement, is felt immediately. If we suppose traders in all commodities to have made a practice of purchasing forty days' supply at a time, and to continue purchasing the same quantity in spite of a drop in sales of, say, one-ninth, then they will be buying forty-five days' supply instead of forty. The purchases which replace the stocks existing at the moment of the drop in sales will be spread evenly over forty-five days instead of forty, and forty-five days will remain the regular interval thereafter, so long as the quantities purchased and sold remain unchanged. That by itself accounts for a reduction of one-ninth in the orders given to producers. Even if the second effect did not operate at all, the vicious circle would still be set up, for the diminished orders to producers would result in a diminished consumers' income and a *further* drop in sales.

We have been assuming that the traders' purchases have been keeping pace with their sales. The negative intermediate demand occurs when they reduce the quantity purchased to forty days' supply. The reduction involves temporarily a further reduction of one-ninth in the orders given to producers, but only for one period of forty days. After that initial period, the reduction in the amount of each purchase will be compensated by the shortening of the interval between purchases. Nevertheless the falling off of orders during the forty days will have its due effect in accentuating the decline of sales, and aggravating the action of the vicious circle.

This reasoning still remains valid if we discard the hypothesis that all traders buy the same number of days' supply at a time. Each trader whose sales fall off will tend to postpone the date, whether near or far, at which he would otherwise have made his next purchase. Any trader is likely eventually to reduce the amount of each purchase more or less in proportion to his sales. And both

5

proceedings will cause a further falling off of productive activity, of consumers' income and of sales, which will produce the same effects over again cumulatively.

The time within which any influence, such as a credit restriction, on the stocks held will work its effect depends on the period of turnover of the stocks. If a commodity passes successively through the hands of several traders on its way from producer to consumer, the orders they give one another and therefore their stocks will all be affected *simultaneously*. Consequently, the period of turnover will be that corresponding to the individual trader's stock, not to the aggregate of stocks held by all the traders concerned. An article may be held by four traders in succession, each for forty days; it takes 160 days to pass through the hands of all, but the full effect of a decision by all four to hold larger or smaller stocks would be felt in forty days.

We have been assuming that a reduction in the consumers' income will be accompanied by an equal reduction in general demand, and a correction is necessary. Diminished incomes are likely to be associated with diminished cash holdings, and the consumers' outlay will therefore exceed the consumers' income. General demand to that extent exceeds output, and the potency of the vicious circle is diminished. This is a subject to which we return below (p. 72).

The vicious circle of deflation or depression might be explained in terms of the price level; when prices are expected to fall, traders are less inclined to buy or to produce goods, and the diminished activity aggravates the fall of prices and reinforces itself with cumulative effect. This reasoning requires the expected fall of prices to be general; it must cover a wide enough range of commodities to have a perceptible effect on activity and on the consumers' income. In practice the grounds for expecting a general fall of prices are simply an actual decline of demand and increase of unsold stocks of goods. These latter are the really operative causes. Nevertheless the expectation of a fall of prices may enter into the situation as a definite additional motive. A trader may on this ground cut down his purchases *more* than the reduction in his sales would warrant.

An expected fall of prices, however, as soon as the expectation is held by a considerable proportion of the traders concerned, tends to become actual. Each will be willing to make price concessions in order to increase his sales till the concessions bring down the price to the expected level.

A reduction of the prices charged to consumers in itself tends to increase the amount of sales, and so to stimulate activity. Such a reduction, if carried far enough, might be sufficient to break the vicious circle and reverse the whole process. But there is a limit to the price concessions that the retail dealers can afford to make ; they will insist on some margin of profit over the prices paid to manufacturers, and the manufacturers' price concessions will be limited by their costs, especially under the head of wages. In practice retailers are slow to make even the price reductions that the manufacturers' concessions would justify. And if they did adjust retail prices immediately and completely to the fall of demand, they would be saddling themselves with the entire loss, for if sales and output were undiminished, there would be no reason why manufacturers should reduce their prices at all. There is no way out by this door unless wages are reduced. If wages could be reduced as fast as consumption demand, and if retail prices were reduced *pari passu*, activity might be maintained undiminished.

This does not really conflict with the interpretation of the vicious circle of deflation as due to an expected fall of prices. The shrinkage of demand and accumulation of unsold goods give rise to the expectation of a fall of prices, but when the fall actually occurs the expectation is to that extent satisfied and discharged ; it ceases to be an expectation. The expectation applies not only to retail prices but to wholesale prices and the prices of materials and intermediate products. But the demand in the wholesale markets at all stages back to the primary products is derived from the consumption demand. It is the consumption demand which is the governing factor.

An expansion of consumption demand will tend to start a vicious circle of inflation. The immediate effect of the expansion is increased sales of consumable goods, and there follow increased orders to producers to replace the goods sold. As sales expand, existing stocks of goods become insufficient, the orders to producers tend therefore to exceed the equivalent of sales, and there is a positive intermediate demand. Increased production generates increased incomes, and increased incomes generate increased general demand.

The progress of an expansion of consumption demand, however, is not the exact counterpart and contrary of the progress of a contraction. Whereas costs set a limit to the fall of prices in the latter case, there is no similar limit to the rise of prices in the former. And whereas there is no limit (short of zero) to the reduction of output in the case of a falling demand, full employment sets a limit to the increase of output in the case of a rising demand.

As output approaches capacity in one industry after another, and forward orders accumulate, the prices charged by the producers are put up. Retail prices have to follow wholesale, not only because the retailers must have an adequate margin, but also because rising prices bring rising incomes to the producers and so generate increased general demand. Increased general demand involves increased consumption demand, and so an encroachment on stocks.

Just as the vicious circle of depression could be broken if retail prices were reduced fast enough, so could the vicious circle of inflation be broken if retail prices were raised fast enough. And there is not the same obstacle to the latter course as to the former. Retailers cannot be expected to cut prices so far as to destroy their profits, even to sell off redundant stocks,[1] and they will prefer to reduce stocks by reducing or postponing their orders for fresh supplies. But there is no obstacle to traders raising prices to defend their stocks against depletion. Retail prices follow wholesale prices. The retailers rely on the wholesalers to supply whatever stocks they want. It is therefore the wholesalers who feel the effect of a shortage of stocks. If they are to fulfil their responsibility for keeping the retailers supplied, they must take the initiative in raising the prices they charge. To bring about an increase in their stocks, the prices charged to consumers must be relatively higher than the prices paid to producers, so that the incomes of the producers will suffice to buy only a part of the total output, and there will be an unsold residue to be added to stocks.

If the vicious circle is to be broken, the producers' prices must be held down till stocks are replenished. But so long as wholesalers' stocks are short and their selling prices high, the pressure on producers' capacity will continue. Producers' prices are likely to rise. And in a state of full employment the demand for labour, along with rising retail prices, will cause wages to rise. It is only too likely that producers' prices will quickly follow the rise in wholesalers' prices, and the vicious circle will continue unbroken.

In treating of the vicious circle of inflation or deflation, we have been assuming that nothing is being done to interfere with the supply of money for traders' buying or producing operations. That assumption we shall presently withdraw (below, p. 76).

---

[1] They will, it is true, make somewhat bigger price concessions at their customary periodical sales, but that is chiefly to clear stocks of goods which are losing touch with fashion.

FLUCTUATIONS IN CAPITAL OUTLAY

It will have been observed that in the foregoing reasoning we have neglected fluctuations in the demand for instrumental goods, which fills the gap between general demand and consumption demand. We started by assuming that, if the widening of capital is insufficient to use up the current resources of the investment market, the available margin will be applied to deepening.

Fluctuations in productive activity cause fluctuations in consumers' income, in general demand and in consumption demand. But it is likely that the fluctuations in consumption demand will be smaller than the fluctuations in the consumers' income. In other words, the fluctuations in unconsumed income or saving will be relatively greater. The reason is that the fluctuations in the consumers' income fall predominantly on profits, and profits are the principal source of saving. And the fluctuations in saving are likely to be even greater than the fluctuations in profits, since the personal expenditure of the profit-makers will not be fully adjusted, at any rate for a time, to the changes in their incomes.

If we could regard the investment market as a perfectly contrived machine which would infallibly transform any given flow of savings into an equivalent demand for capital goods, and if the output of capital goods reacted as easily to demand as the output of consumption goods, we might describe the effects of fluctuations in general demand without any explicit reference to the division between consumption demand and the demand for capital goods. But in practice there are several complications to be allowed for.

We have seen how a contraction of demand checks the widening of capital. So far as instruments and fixed capital are concerned, there might theoretically be an almost complete suspension of new extensions, and if there were also some postponement of maintenance and renewals and some premature scrapping of redundant plant, the widening would actually become a negative quantity. In practice, however, this is unlikely to occur, for there will be some industries and some concerns which look forward beyond the momentary state of demand to future growth. A large part of the widening of capital takes the form of providing transport and public utilities for growing communities. In the provision of such services there is an element of local monopoly or economic rent in addition to interest and profit, and the promoters' calculations are less dependent on the conditions of the present and the immediate future. Often their charges will be subject to public regulation, and will be all the more secure for being limited to something less than what free exploitation might yield. Sometimes these enterprises are undertaken by public authorities with a view not to profit but to meeting an ascertained need, and the state of general demand is hardly taken into account at all.

If the fluctuations in capital outlay do not just keep pace with the fluctuations in the available resources of the investment market, it is for the market to correct the disparity by altering the prices of securities, and by applying the more summary methods which are at their disposal (below, pp. 84-5). But an expanding capital outlay may encounter a limit in another direction : it may strain the capacity of the industries which produce and instal instrumental goods. When these, the Instrumental Industries, receive orders in excess of their capacity, they raise the prices of their products, and, if satisfied that the excess demand is not merely transitory, they also take steps to increase their capacity. But an increase of capacity of the instrumental industries has to be supplied by the instrumental industries themselves, and, for the time being, increases the pressure upon them. A part of their existing capacity being diverted to that purpose, so much the less is left to meet the requirements of all the other industries. Thus if the resources of the investment market expand to such an extent that the corresponding capital outlay would exceed the capacity of the instrumental industries, the projects of capital outlay meet with the deterrent effect of rising prices and costs. And in so far as the demand for capital outlay is not sufficiently deterred thereby, the remaining excess over capacity is perforce deferred by delay in execution.

When the investment market fails to limit capital outlay, and its resources are being supplemented by a credit expansion, the limit imposed by the capacity of the instrumental industries and the rise in the prices they charge relieves the strain on the market. In fact a rise in the first cost of capital equipment out of proportion to the prospective prices of the goods in the production of which it is to be used diminishes its yield. The comparison of yield with the rate of interest is affected no less than by a rise in the rate.

In the case of a contraction of general demand there may be a more than proportionate contraction both of saving and of capital outlay, and the instrumental industries may be heavily underemployed. They will reduce their charges, and the favourable effect on future yield of capital equipment will tend to stimulate not only deepening but widening. For even when the immediate state of general demand does not seem to justify any widening, a substantial saving in first cost is a justification for providing for future needs.

THE LIQUIDATION OF WORKING CAPITAL

In the sphere of working capital, the widening process is likely not merely to be suspended by a contraction of general demand, but to be sharply *reversed*. For when sales and output are reduced, traders, as we have seen, seek to reduce their stocks in proportion. Dealers will sell off their stocks, and buy something less than the equivalent in quantity of what they have sold, and they will probably buy it at reduced prices. The difference between their purchases and sales they will receive in money, which goes either to pay off bank advances or to swell cash balances. In other words, they absorb cash. The same thing happens to manufacturers. They complete the orders on hand, and receive money for them at the prices which prevailed when the contracts for them were entered into. They then proceed to carry out the diminished orders corresponding to the diminished demand. Their current costs are on a smaller scale; even if rates of wages are undiminished, the quantity of labour to be paid for is less, and on materials there is likely to be a reduction of price as well as of quantity.

Producers of primary products and dealers in them sell smaller quantities at lower prices, and, if they fail to reduce output, they must use up their cash and probably borrow to finance their unsold surplus. Unlike the other traders they release cash. In general, however, primary products form but a small proportion of the total value of the community's output of material commodities, and so the accumulation of primary products will be no more than a moderate set-off against the reduction of working capital in other directions.[1]

There may be other traders who suffer a net outflow of cash. If price concessions on new business leave an insufficient margin to meet overhead expenses, their profits become a negative quantity, and the proceeds of past contracts may be insufficient to outweigh the current loss.

Among the whole body of traders, those who contracted, while demand was still favourable, to produce or deliver goods at high prices accumulate cash at the expense of those who contracted to buy. These latter, with sales slowed down in an unfavourable market, may have to raise cash from the banks. Moreover, the probability is that the group of traders, taken as a whole, will

---

[1] It is not necessary to enter into the complications arising in a country which is a big producer and exporter of primary products. The surplus is probably financed in part by foreign banks.

have sold a quantity of goods for cash. If so the cash must have come from the rest of the community. Since banks do not buy goods, it must have come from the consumers. Consumers whose incomes are diminished will draw upon their balances and hold less cash. Thereby consumption demand is supplemented. General demand exceeds the consumers' income. Only so can a net reduction of traders' working capital be brought about.

This release of cash by consumers affords some relief from the decline of demand. Even if the whole of the cash released is absorbed by the traders, at any rate the excess of working capital over requirements, to which the vicious circle is attributable, is diminished. And it is not to be assumed that traders will necessarily absorb cash to an amount equal to the entire proceeds of liquidation of superfluous working capital. The cash absorbed goes to increase their free capital, and, rather than hold idle balances, they may place a part in marketable securities. The money thus applied becomes available in the long-term investment market.

Up to this point we have made no assumption as to the action of the banks or as to the monetary policy by which they are guided. If we assume that, when the liquidation of working capital involves the repayment of bank advances, the banks seek to restore the total of their earning assets to what it was before, then they will do what they can to encourage borrowers to take increased advances. If, as is likely in the circumstances supposed, there is only a limited demand for advances, the banks will fill the gap by buying securities on the stock market. Medium-term securities are as suitable an asset for a bank as for a trader who is accumulating a reserve against future capital outlay. Here is a further addition to the resources of the investment market.

At a time of low demand, therefore, though the volume of current saving will be very much reduced, a great part of the proceeds of liquidation of redundant working capital will come into the investment market and will tend to stimulate capital outlay. But the widening of capital will have slackened, and the investment market can only absorb these new resources by intensifying the deepening process.

LIMITATIONS OF THE DEEPENING PROCESS

It might be supposed that the deepening process could always be stimulated to any desired degree independently of any check to the widening process, for the substitution of instruments for labour would be just as advantageous at any given rate of interest. But this is not true without qualification.

The advantages of installing new cost-saving instruments in any concern depend partly on the prospects of the concern itself. In an industry which is employed below capacity the individual concern is liable to be under-employed or temporarily closed or may even be in danger of being abandoned altogether. An instrument which would pay for itself handsomely if fully employed might incur a loss if only employed intermittently.

And it often happens that the application of the deepening process to any given concern is most conveniently associated with an extension of capacity. A new appliance, whether it is a " marginal " instrument or some new invention or improvement, may be such that for it the former scale of operations of the concern is not the most economical.

Thus in many ways the deepening process is interwoven with the widening process. So far as instruments of production are concerned, there may be a real temporary glut, such that *no* reduction of the long-term rate of interest can evoke a sufficient volume of capital outlay to use up the resources of the investment market.

In such conditions, however, relief may sometimes be found in the demand for instruments of consumption, and particularly for houses. Interest would account for nearly half the cost (including maintenance as well as rent) falling on the occupier of a house, and consequently a reduction of the long-term rate of interest by half would permit a reduction of that cost by a quarter. There would be a substantial encouragement to the production of new houses. But this depends on the amount of additional demand elicited by the reduction of rents. If the decline of consumption demand is very great, even a reduction of rents by, say, a quarter may fail to restore the demand for houses to normal.

Therefore we ought not to be surprised to see a temporary glut in the investment market in the event of a collapse of general demand. The proceeds of liquidation of working capital coming into the investment market call for a great intensification in the deepening process, at a time when the deepening process is itself much less responsive than usual. That means an absorption of cash by the investment market and an intensification of the vicious circle of deflation.

Nevertheless it should not be overlooked that the liquidation of working capital in itself tends to *relieve* the strain of declining demand. And in so far as the proceeds of liquidation, being passed on to the investment market, can be made to generate incomes through capital outlay, the relief is all the greater. The absorption of cash by the investment market only means that this relief is not as great as it might be.

Is the glut to be regarded as genuinely " temporary ", in the sense that it contains within itself a definite tendency towards a revival of the deepening process ? It is caused by a decline of general demand, and would be ended by a revival of general demand. But that is not an answer to the question, for it would be assuming the revival of general demand to proceed from some unspecified and extraneous cause.

The deepening process might really come to an end, so that there would not be any further possibility of increasing the productive power of a given working population by equipping them with more capital. But that is a different hypothesis altogether. Our assumption is that there remain plenty of remunerative openings to be exploited for increasing capital equipment in proportion to manpower, but that the suspension of the widening process has made them for the time being impracticable or at any rate unattractive.

It is possible to point, at any rate, to three forces at work to end the glut. In the first place, new invention is constantly adding to the unexploited openings, and there is no limit to their remunerativeness. There will probably be some that are attractive enough to induce new capital outlay even without any near prospect of additional demand for the product.

Secondly, even in the absence of new enterprises or extensions of output, the renewals and replacements that become due will give opportunities for changes in processes taking advantage of the favourable investment market to increase the amount of capital equipment used for a given output.

Thirdly, the decline of demand for instrumental goods will cause a fall of their prices relative to the cost of labour, and will thus give an additional stimulus to the adoption of labour-saving plant.

WORKING CAPITAL UNDER EXPANDING GENERAL DEMAND

In the case of an expansion of general demand we find substantially the reverse of the various tendencies arising from a contraction. The intensification of the widening process takes effect in working capital in a positive intermediate demand. Retail and wholesale dealers, finding their sales increase, give orders to the producers more than equivalent to their sales. Manufacturers order supplies of materials and intermediate products in excess of what they use. All alike must obtain the means of payment, and, unless they hold superfluous cash, must either borrow or sell securities. If the banks are unwilling to increase their earning assets, they must sell securities to make room for additional advances. Thus, when securities are sold either by traders or by banks, the resources of the investment market will be drawn on to provide additional working capital. There will be increased profits and therefore increased current savings, but as the widening process will also be intensified in the sphere of long-term investment it is probable (though not in theory certain) that the margin left available for the deepening process will be diminished. And experience shows that at a time of high demand the long-term rate of interest rises.

It is probable that the opportunities of profit will lead to speculative purchases of shares (particularly new issues) with borrowed money, and bank advances to extend productive capacity in anticipation of reinvested profits. Whenever the widening of capital outstrips the resources of the investment market that is apt to happen, because the widening process offers the prospect of profit as well as interest. And it must be remembered too that a part of the deepening process offers the big gains that may come from new inventions or improvements for the adoption of which active business provides favourable opportunities.

When the banks lend for these purposes, the investment market receives resources in excess of current savings. The production of new capital equipment is stimulated, and the consequent productive activity generates additional incomes and increased general demand. The working of the vicious circle of inflation is accentuated.

These additional bank advances to the investment market at a time of high demand may be regarded as the counterpart of the glut of capital at a time of low demand. In the former case the investment market releases cash, in the latter it absorbs cash.

But the parallel is not quite perfect. For at a time of low demand the market may find itself unable to induce sufficient capital outlay to use up its resources, however low the long-term rate of interest may be, whereas at a time of high demand it is always possible for the market to prevent capital outlay outstripping resources by raising the long-term rate of interest high enough, or (as is usual in practice) by directly discouraging or refusing new flotations. The excess of capital outlay over savings is due to the intrusion of the proceeds of bank advances arranged by speculators, speculative investors and promoters outside the group of professional dealers by whom prices are made, though the dealers themselves are not unlikely to be influenced by the same motives as the speculators, and to accentuate the receptiveness of the market by their willingness to extend the usual amount of their indebtedness to the banks.

CREDIT REGULATION AND WORKING CAPITAL

Up to this point we have been tracing the effects of variations in general demand without supposing any *positive* action on the part of the banks. We have already pointed out (above, p. 60) that the banks have the power of stimulating or checking productive activity and so increasing or decreasing general demand. They do so partly by inducing a release or absorption of cash by traders and partly by releasing or absorbing cash themselves.

The free working of the vicious circle of inflation or deflation presupposes that traders desiring to increase or decrease their stocks of commodities will not be deterred or prevented from releasing or absorbing the equivalent amount of cash. We have been assuming in effect that the banks acquiesce in these operations, and that they make up any resulting difference between their deposit liabilities and their earning assets by buying or selling securities.

But the banks need not by any means be content with playing this purely passive part. They have the power, on the one hand, of initiating a movement in general demand, and thereby themselves producing the effects we have described, or, on the other, of stopping such a movement when originated by some independent cause.

If the banks raise the short-term rate of interest, the holding of stocks of goods with borrowed money is made less attractive. A trader can reduce the amount so held by buying less at a time. If his previous practice in regard to the intervals at which he replenishes his stock of each sort of commodity that he holds has been determined by his convenience, then a revision of this practice will involve some sacrifice of convenience. But the sacrifice is very small. If he has been accustomed to order six weeks' supply of a commodity at a time, it will be very little additional trouble or expense to him to order three weeks' supply only. We may suppose a trader who sells £10,000 worth of goods a month, and who holds stocks to an average total value of £15,000, to provide £10,000 of this from his own capital and to borrow the remaining £5000. If he pays his banker 5 per cent the charge is £250 a year. If the charge is raised to 7½ per cent or £375 a year, he can probably reduce the average stock held without difficulty from £15,000 to, say, £13,000, and bring down the interest charge to £225 on the £3000 borrowed. To a trader with a turn-over of £120,000 a year and an income which may be put at 3 per cent or £3,600, a saving of £150 is by no means negligible. The increase in the interest charged causes a negative intermediate demand.

For a manufacturer the proportion of stocks of materials and intermediate products to his income would be less, but the calculation is not essentially different. .

It must be clearly understood that there is no question of curtailing in any way the scale of the trader's operations, either the sales of the dealer or the output of the manufacturer. The average purchases of either per unit of time over any considerable period will be just what sales or output may require ; it is only the amount of each periodical purchase and the intervals at which such purchases are made that we assume to be varied.

When the short-term rate of interest is raised, the dealers in commodities will order from the producers less than they sell to the consumers, and the producers will order less from the producers a stage further back than they use. There will be a general decline of demand in wholesale markets, a negative intermediate demand. That is different from our previous supposition of a decline of consumption demand (above, p. 64), but it produces the same consequence, a decline of productive activity and of the consumers' income. There results in due course a decline of consumption demand, and the vicious circle is joined.

In the case of a reduction of the short-term rate of interest an inducement will be afforded to traders to hold larger stocks than before and to accelerate their purchases. There is a positive intermediate demand, productive activity is stimulated, and there results an expansion of consumers' income, of general demand and of consumption demand. The vicious circle of inflation is joined.

It might perhaps be thought that so slight a matter as an additional charge at the rate of 2 or 3 per cent per annum would be easily counteracted by a fractional fall in the prices of the goods to be bought. If a trader who keeps his goods in stock for an average period of two months has to pay an additional 3 per cent per annum for interest, that is only a half of 1 per cent for the two months, and if he can buy the goods at a price of 99½ instead of 100, he is as well off as before. But the price concession gives him no inducement whatever to increase his purchases unless he has reason to expect that it will be temporary and that the price will have risen again before

the goods come to be sold.　It will be just as well worth while as
before for him to save interest by reducing his stock.　The fall of
price is simply a windfall to him, unless he passes it on to the consumer and so stimulates demand.　And if it is passed on to the
consumer there is no longer a price difference to compensate the
trader for the rise in the rate of interest.

It is similarly true that a fall in the rate of interest cannot be offset
by a rise of prices.　But a rise of prices is somewhat more likely to
be passed on to the consumer than a fall.

It should not be overlooked that the power of the banking system
to induce an acceleration or retardation of the purchase of goods by
traders does not extend over the whole field of working capital.　As
we have already seen, traders' stocks of perishable goods and of
goods exposed to rapid changes of fashion are in any case kept down
to a minimum and cannot be varied to any appreciable extent.　We
have also shown that speculative stocks of seasonal products are not
sensitive to the rate of interest, because neither output nor demand
can be quickly modified, and the large stocks to be carried are
therefore subject to big speculative changes of price.

But the exclusion of these categories leaves the greater part of
manufactured and semi-manufactured commodities fully susceptible
to the influence of credit conditions.　That does not mean, however,
that their response is invariably immediate.

At a time of activity many producers are likely to have forward
contracts covering their output for months ahead.　So long as they
are fulfilling these contracts, they will be kept busy, and the corresponding incomes will continue as a source of demand.　If the
greater part of industry is in this state, the effect of credit restriction
will at first be slight.　A few of the less fortunately placed producers
will find themselves under-employed, and some among the busy ones
will no longer ask a premium for early delivery.　Only when existing
orders have to some extent been worked through will any considerable reduction of activity appear.

A CREDIT DEADLOCK

When credit relaxation is resorted to to excite revival from
depression, there are also possible obstacles, but they are of a somewhat different, and on occasions a more formidable, character.　As
has been shown above (p. 64), at a time of low demand traders seek
to reduce their stocks of goods by cutting down their purchases
below their sales.　But if the sales fall off more quickly than they

expect, their stocks will not diminish as much as they intend. A trader who, following a not uncommon practice, has given a standing order for the delivery of certain quantities of a commodity at stated intervals, may find his stock actually increasing. Traders who are already encumbered with excessive stocks cannot be induced by any facilities that may be offered them for borrowing money to add to their stocks. And even those who have succeeded in reducing their stocks, but have suffered in the recent past from such miscalculations, will think much more of avoiding redundant stocks than of the minor advantages of buying convenience. Under such conditions, " cheap money ", or extremely low rates of short-term interest, may fail to evoke revival. And once cheap money has been applied and failed, much of its virtue will have disappeared. Any trader who has adapted his arrangements to it will do no more. Either he will have attained the maximum buying convenience, or, if he has not, he will have been deterred from buying by pessimistic estimates of demand, which cheap money by itself cannot dispel. A complete deadlock may result.

This failure of cheap money to stimulate revival is a much more serious gap in credit control than the failure of dear money to check activity. The latter amounts to no more than delay. It may indeed endanger the monetary standard, and desperate efforts to safeguard parity of the monetary unit may lead to so severe a credit restriction as to precipitate a financial crisis. But there is no question of dear money being completely ineffective. If a high rate of interest is insufficient to check activity, it can be raised higher, and it can be accompanied by an actual refusal to lend.

Cheap money, on the other hand, does in the extreme case of a deadlock become really ineffective. A deadlock is a rare occurrence, but unfortunately in the nineteen-thirties it came to plague the world, and raised problems which threatened the fabric of civilisation with destruction.

The credit deadlock, like the temporary glut in the investment market, is really a breakdown of the deepening process, for the intermediate demand evoked by cheap money represents a deepening of working capital. Both alike are attributable to a collapse of consumption demand. But there are distinctive circumstances in each. The credit deadlock, though mainly due to the same pessimism in regard to the decline of demand as the glut in the investment market, is further complicated by the fact that a *real* glut of working capital is always within easy reach ; it merely means that traders have already attained their maximum buying convenience. A powerful contributory cause of the glut in the investment market is the overflow of the proceeds of liquidation of working capital. This overflow is in itself a release of cash, and, so far as the investment market passes it on to be applied to capital outlay, it relieves the depression arising from the absorption of cash otherwise caused by the liquidation of working capital. The glut in the investment market diminishes the efficacy of this relief; some of the cash is absorbed by the investment market, and fails to generate incomes and demand through capital outlay. The credit deadlock, on the other hand, is wholly an aggravation of the vicious circle of deflation.

BORROWING BY THE INVESTMENT MARKET

Short-term borrowing is not exclusively for the purpose of buying and holding commodities. It is also resorted to for the purpose of buying and holding securities, constituting one of the links referred to above (p. 57) between the long-term and short-term investment markets. When the banks expand or contract credit, their lending for this purpose will probably be influenced in the same direction as their lending for the purchase of commodities. But the effects are in many respects different.

The consideration of convenience in buying and taking delivery is of no significance to the professional dealer in securities. The dealer is ready in any case both to buy and to sell every day. If he makes any material variation in his holding of any security, that is probably because he anticipates a rise or fall in its price. And in the case of a speculator the prospect of gain from a rise or fall of price is the sole motive.

The professional dealer is not wholly indifferent to the short-term rate of interest. If he can see no reason whatever to think a rise in the prices of securities more or less probable than a fall, then so long as the rate of interest he pays on bank advances is less than the yield of the securities he holds, he is making a gain; if it is greater, he is making a loss. It is often assumed that these gains or losses must have a substantial effect on the security markets, so that there will be a marked tendency for the long-term rate of interest to move up and down with the short-term rate. In reality there is little foundation for this view. The dealers in securities can never disregard the prospects of a rise or fall of prices. Different dealers have different views of those prospects, and it would only be very exceptionally that any considerable proportion of them would expect no movement at all. In general the quoted price of any security tends towards a level which divides equally the resources of those dealers who expect it to be higher and those who expect it to be lower in the near future. A price movement of 1 or 2 per cent over a period of, say, a fortnight or a few days would outweigh many times any probable rate of interest.[1]

The actual effect of the short-term rate of interest on the prices of long-term securities depends upon the time for which the short-term rate is *expected to continue*. Very often a movement of the short-term rate is known to be caused by quite transitory circumstances, so that there is no reason to expect that it will be either above or below its normal average after a few months or even, it may be, a few days. When the rate for one or three months is exceptionally low or exceptionally high, the quotation for six months will often be found to be an intermediate rate nearer the average. Sometimes the six months rate will be so calculated as to be compounded of a high or low rate for the first three months and just an average rate for the remaining three. Under these conditions the effect of the short-term rate on the long-term rate is very small. If the long-term rate starts at 4 per cent, and if that is likewise the normal short-term rate, a rise of the three months rate to 6 per cent, associated with a six months rate of 5, implies an expectation that the 6 per cent rate will not extend beyond three months. Conditions between long-term and short-term investments would be equalised by a fall of $\frac{1}{2}$ per cent (the equivalent of interest at 2 per cent for three months) in the price of the former. Sometimes, however, quotations for six-month or twelve-month loans or bills do not reflect any expectation of an appreciable return of the short-term rate to normal. Market conditions may be such that a continuance of high rates seems probable for a year or two. The quotation for six months for example may be the same, 6 per cent, as for three and people may think a short-term rate averaging not less than, say, $5\frac{1}{2}$ per cent is likely to prevail for two years. In that case a drop of 3 per cent in the price of a 4 per cent security would be necessary to equalise conditions. It would be very exceptional for dealers in the market to form any expectation at all as to the trend of short-term rates more than about two years ahead.

On the other hand, dealers' opinions are apt to be very empirical. Conditions which have obtained in markets for a year or two or even

---

[1] Exception must be made of the fancy rates that used to prevail at times of crisis for call loans on the New York Stock Exchange before the Federal Reserve System was established. In the periods of tension in 1928 and 1929, however, the rate never exceeded 30 per cent or $\frac{1}{12}$ of 1 per cent per diem.

a few months begin to acquire the character of normal, and to supply the basis of subsequent calculations. If a spell of dear money depresses the prices of securities, and is prolonged beyond expectation, the market is likely to take the depressed price as its standard and, in view of the continuance of dear money, to depress it still further. This process will continue progressively till at last the high short-term rate is reduced. By that time the market will have become accustomed to the recently prevailing prices and they may rise by very little, until some other force begins to work.

It must not be assumed, however, that a movement of the long-term and short-term rates of interest in the same direction is in general due to the influence of the latter on the former. Their common movement is more likely to be due to a common cause. Depression lowers both rates and activity raises both. And the long-term rate also influences the short-term rate, for wherever the choice between long-term and short-term lending or between long-term and short-term borrowing is open, the two rates are in competition.

The speculative element is very much more prominent in the investment market than in the commodity markets. In the commodity markets speculation is not very conspicuous except in primary products, or in products, such as refined metals, which are not far removed from the primary stage. In the investment market not only is every professional dealer in some degree a speculator, but there is apt to be a crowd of amateur speculators intruding into the market whenever there is a prospect of gain.

Those who acquire securities with borrowed money resemble in their motives rather the traders who assume commitments in seasonal products than the holders of stocks of manufactured goods. They are influenced by prospects of price movements in comparison with which the rate of interest counts for little.

We have seen that the equality of the long-term rate of interest and the marginal yield of instrumental goods can only be approximate. The cost-saving capacity even of a well-tried instrument depends not only on its technical efficiency but on the circumstances in which it is used. And the prospective yield of those which technological progress is perpetually bringing into use is usually far above the rate of interest, but is at the same time subject to a wide margin of uncertainty.

The fact is, that when the investment market seeks to check sales of securities and new flotations by lowering the prices of securities, the deterrent effect is felt hardly, if at all, through the rise in the rate of interest causing marginal installations to become unremunerative. In order to cause the *abandonment* of projects of capital outlay to any considerable total amount, a heavy drop in the prices of securities would be required. A fall of 3 per cent in the price of a 4 per cent security only raises the yield to $4\frac{1}{8}$ per cent. But quite a modest fall may suffice to secure *postponement*. If owing to an unfavourable condition of the market the prices of securities are temporarily depressed 3 per cent, the raising of capital, whether by a new flotation or by sales of reserve securities, becomes unattractive. Provided the stringency can be expected to pass in a few months, it will be prudent to wait. An alternative is to finance the project at the outset by short-term borrowing. But the same conditions which cause pressure in the investment market are likely to cause the short-term rate of interest to be high.

And, quite apart from the rate charged, short-term borrowing for the sinking of capital is imprudent, and will not be resorted to to an unlimited extent. The investment market works through trial and error, and error makes itself felt in an increase or decrease in short-term indebtedness. Dealers, speculators and speculative investors depend for their solvency on the marketability of the investments they hold. And they are not willing to increase their short-term indebtedness without limit, especially when the market is unfavourable. If for a time too much of the demand for securities has been financed by bank advances, the borrowers will reach their limits, and the demand for securities will fall off.

Traders who cannot raise capital for extensions or renewals on satisfactory terms, may likewise resort to bank advances. But for them also, temporary borrowing has its limits. Indeed it is even more unattractive for the trader than for the dealer or speculator in securities, for what he holds against his indebtedness is not a marketable security but a value sunk in his own business, which cannot be fully assessed by any one outside it, and can only be realised by a flotation in the market.[1] Therefore when the rate of interest fails to keep capital outlay within the resources of the investment market, the limits to which the financing, direct and indirect, of capital outlay by short-term lending is subject will prevent the disparity from going very far.

Borrowing short for lending or spending long in fact is imprudent, and the limit is put to it by the reluctance of lenders not less than of

[1] That does not apply to the trader who has adequate reserves of marketable securities, and prefers to obtain a bank advance in order to avoid selling the securities in an unfavourable market.

borrowers. Dealers and speculators are both amenable to the influence of bankers who may apply or withdraw direct pressure to restrict advances. Bankers are not compelled to lend, and they reserve to themselves the right to refuse to do so. When they wish to restrict credit, they are likely to discriminate against loans for speculative purposes, and speculation in securities is usually more easily identified than speculation in commodities.

When bankers restrict advances for the holding of securities, the effect is felt in forced sales and diminished purchases. The unfavourable market will discourage the raising of capital, but, till the effect is seen in a diminution of new flotations, the advances for the holding of securities *on the whole* cannot be considerably reduced. The diminished purchases by speculators with borrowed money mean diminished sales by professional dealers, and these latter may have to increase their borrowing by as much as that of the speculators is diminished. Pending the decrease of new flotations, the net effect will be confined to the money attracted, when the prices of securities fall, from investors who draw upon their balances to pick up bargains. (There may also be sales of securities *abroad*, but if the phase of credit is the same all over the financial world, this resource will not be available.)

The market is so organised as to be able to adjust new flotations to its resources with a reasonable approximation to precision. Issuing houses and promoters are careful to adjust their operations to the current resources of the market. As soon as symptoms of a strain appear, and new issues fail to be taken by investors, they become unwilling to make further ventures. New flotations thus get restricted by more summary methods than a rise in the rate of interest.

Nevertheless, if we regard the investment market as an instrument for regulating the amount of capital outlay, there is a substantial delay to be allowed for. New flotations need a considerable period of preparation, and cannot be immediately abandoned in face of an unfavourable market or quickly initiated when conditions are favourable. And even when the volume of new flotations has been successfully stimulated or checked, the resulting change in the amount of capital installed will only be felt after a further interval. The installation resulting from a flotation only begins after a further interval of preparation, and once begun will be spread over a time of some months and possibly several years.

On the other hand, when capital is raised not by new flotations, but by sales of securities from traders' free capital, no interval of preparation is required on the financial side, and the outlays involved, being for replacements or extensions of plant, will usually be on a smaller scale than for a new enterprise. For this kind of capital outlay the response to a favourable or unfavourable market will be quicker.

Whether the pressure be exercised by the limits on temporary borrowing, by the reluctance of issuing houses and underwriters, or by the loss on sales of reserve securities, the effect is felt almost entirely in the *postponement* of projects rather than in their abandonment. And the projects postponed will not be " marginal ". They will be those for which commitments have not gone too far, and for which postponement will not mean an irrevocable loss of opportunity.

They will include projects, under the head of widening, for new enterprises and capital extensions of which the yield, including profit as well as interest, far exceeds the rate of interest. Even those under the head of deepening include innovations of high yield. The strictly marginal instruments, of which the yield is so close to the rate of interest that they become unremunerative, are likely to be relatively few and unimportant—possibly non-existent.

Consequently Jevons's principle which equates the rate of interest to marginal yield has very little application to the short-period movements of practical life. The tendency for the capital resources of the community to be applied to those kinds of instrumental goods which offer the highest yields, and for those of inferior yield to drop out of use, works through experience in the long run. It is, as we saw above (pp. 29-30), a static principle, not to be employed, except under narrow limitations, in dynamic analysis. Under conditions of technological change, when new and untried forms of capital equipment are constantly being introduced, there is no moment at which the deepening process has settled down to a well defined standard of marginal yield.

PURCHASE OF SECURITIES BY BANKS

In addition to their power of permitting or refusing advances to speculators, the banks can also influence the investment market by themselves buying or selling securities. When a bank buys securities on its own account, it creates a deposit in favour of the seller. Thereby the net cash resources of the investment market are increased, and the market is in a position to take an equivalent amount of new securities. And when a bank sells securities, the net cash resources of the investment market are diminished, and the market is to that extent less able to take new securities.

The buying and selling of securities by the commercial banks must be distinguished from the open-market operations of the central bank. When the central bank buys or sells securities it increases or decreases not only its assets but also its liabilities, which compose the supply of currency and the reserves of the commercial banks. It is in the reserves that the immediate increase or decrease mainly appears. The effect of any variation in the reserves tends to be multiplied in the volume of credit. So long as the creation of credit by the commercial banks responds smoothly to the state of the reserves, the purchases and sales of securities by the central bank will be no more than a fraction of the increase or decrease in the volume of credit aimed at, and will have little effect on the investment market. And the central bank can attain its purpose by buying or selling bills of exchange, without affecting the investment market at all.

It is when the commercial banks find themselves unable to increase or decrease their advances to customers in proportion to the increase or decrease in their reserves that they resort to purchases or sales of securities to make up the difference. It is at such times that the purchases or sales are considerable enough to affect materially the volume of new flotations and the long-term rate of interest.

We have shown above (p. 72) that the difficulty in adjusting the volume of advances is especially likely to occur when traders' cash resources are swollen with the proceeds of liquidation of redundant working capital. It is then that the banks are led to buy large amounts of securities, and that, the widening process being retarded, the long-term rate of interest may fall very low without giving a sufficient stimulus to capital outlay.

REINVESTED PROFITS

We have defined investment to include the reinvestment of undistributed profits, for that means the acquisition, by those who derived their income from the profits, of additional pecuniary interests in the concern.

The reinvestment of undistributed profits is a matter which a trader must consider in close relation with depreciation. In view of the uncertainties in regard to the life of plant and to obsolescence, the prudent trader will create a reserve in addition to the depreciation allowance that he judges strictly necessary. And in an expanding business it will often be thought preferable to provide as far as possible for the requisite extensions of its capital equipment out of its own profits, rather than to raise capital by an issue of shares or debentures in the market from subscribers who will have to be convinced of the prospects of the business, and will require an inducement to venture their money.

But the convenient times for accumulating undistributed profits will not coincide with the convenient times for extending the capital equipment. The former process will be more or less continuous, but will be carried further at times of high profits, and will be slowed down or suspended or may even make way for drafts on reserves to pay dividends at less prosperous times. The extension of capital equipment will for the most part consist of relatively considerable operations at intervals of some years, and the cost of any one such operation would greatly exceed the surplus profits accruing while it is being carried out. The cost falls on the free capital, the margin of capital resources in excess of what has already been laid out in the installation of capital.

As we saw above (p. 57), the purchase of securities from a trader's free capital is a reversal of the raising of capital, entering into the total as a negative quantity. A trader may raise capital by the sale of securities previously held as well as by a new flotation, and the net amount of capital raised by industry will be the excess of its sales of securities, new and old, to the investment market over its purchases of securities.

The purchase of securities by traders out of undistributed profits does not differ materially in its effects from investment. But we do not include it in investment because the profits *have already been invested* when they were retained in the business. When a trader buys securities, he is putting back capital raised by him into the investment market ; he is undoing the raising of capital, but is not undoing the investment.

When he has occasion to undertake some extension of his capital equipment for which he is not prepared to provide the necessary funds by sales of securities, he may obtain a bank advance. In effect, so long as the advance is outstanding, a larger proportion of his working capital (and possibly even the whole) is met by borrowing.

The sum of a trader's working capital and his net cash resources we will call his circulating capital. Net cash resources, it will be remembered, may be a negative quantity. When capital added exceeds capital raised, the excess is provided at the expense of net cash resources and therefore of circulating capital.

Bank advances thus obtained for the installation of capital are to be reckoned as another method of supplementing the resources of the investment market by the creation of credit. In deciding whether to undertake an extension, a trader will be taking account of future prospects of profit in comparison with which the immediate cost of a bank advance is a trifle. But he may be influenced in choosing whether to proceed at once or to wait a little by the interest to be charged on the bank advance, and still more by the possibility of being embarrassed by a shortage of circulating capital at a time of credit stringency when bankers are unwilling to lend. Postponement is also possible in the case of replacements to be paid for out of depreciation funds, but not so easily as in the case of an extension.

In many respects a depreciation allowance involves the same considerations as reinvested profits. It is accumulated out of current receipts but not out of income, because the depreciation allowance is regarded as a cost to be deducted in arriving at income. If we give the name of gross profit to the margin remaining after deducting all costs other than depreciation, then the sum retained in the business out of gross profit is composed of depreciation *plus* reinvested net profits. The division of the reinvested gross profit into depreciation and reinvested net profit is a matter of judgment and estimate; it represents the best opinion the trader can form as to how much of the gross profit can be prudently treated as income, and this opinion may subsequently be liable to large corrections.

The accumulated gross profits are devoted partly to renewals and replacements which are a proper charge on the depreciation allowance, and partly to extensions which are counted as additional capital. But in practice renewals and replacements often include improvements which are in effect extensions.

The renewals and replacements, like the extensions, are likely to involve large outlays at long intervals, and the depreciation allowance, along with the reinvested net profits, will have to be accumulated in anticipation of such outlays.

In a community in which capital is growing the aggregate depreciation allowances will regularly exceed replacements, for the replacements are proportional to the capital installed years before.[1]

---

[1] Assume the life of plant to be a constant length of time n years, so that the capital in existence n years ago has all been scrapped. If c_r be the gross capital outlay in the year r, the capital in existence in the year n at cost is $\sum_{1}^{n} c_r$ and the annual depreciation is $\dfrac{1}{n} \sum_{1}^{n} c_r$. Replacements are c_0 and depreciation exceeds replacements by the average amount by which c_1 to c_n have exceeded c_0.

And there is no certainty that the excess will be either devoted to capital extensions or placed in securities. If it is not, it will go to increase net cash resources either by paying off bank advances or by increasing cash balances. There will, in fact, be an absorption of cash.

Depreciation differs from other costs of production in that it does not of itself generate incomes. Other costs are composed of wages, salaries, fees, interest and rent, and the net profit is the trader's income. These incomes are the source of general demand. The equilibrium of markets depends on general demand being sufficient to buy output. If all costs are composed of incomes and all incomes are either spent or invested, and if investment is equal to capital added, the equilibrium is secured. But if a part of costs does not generate any income, there is a deficiency of demand.

This applies equally to reinvested profits. If the reinvested profits are applied to increasing net cash resources, the result is an absorption of cash and a shortage of demand.

If the depreciation allowance is to earn interest (above, p. 54, any unspent balance must be placed in securities, and will then become available through the investment market for capital outlay. An unspent balance of reinvested profits may be similarly used. The capital outlay resulting will generate incomes. Yet at a time when the yield of securities is very low, it may seem hardly worth while to obtain it, and the free capital accumulated may be held in cash (below, pp. 158-60 and 173-80).

Some increase of net cash resources may be needed to provide for the natural growth of circulating capital. An addition to working capital constitutes an absorption of commodities and a release of cash. Provided the addition is made *designedly*, it is intermediate demand and is a real supplement to general demand, for the wealth added to working capital generates incomes when it is produced, and is then withheld from sale. Capital raised may be applied to such an increase in working capital instead of to the installation of instrumental capital without disturbing equilibrium. On the other hand, the appearance of an *undesigned* decrement or increment of working capital is a sign of disequilibrium; it is evidence of an excess or deficiency of total demand.

The absorption of cash, if it occurs, is not a question exclusively of unspent depreciation and reinvested profits ; it is rather the more general question of the relation between capital resources and cash resources. It is one of the tasks of those who regulate credit to see that the absorption of cash is not such as to cause a contraction of the flow of money. If the ordinary procedure of credit regulation does not induce a sufficient increase in bank advances, it may be necessary for the banks to buy securities. In the particular case where a disturbance of equilibrium arises from delay in placing unspent depreciation funds or undistributed profits, we can regard the banks as taking the place of the traders in buying securities from the investment market.

CHAPTER V

CAPITAL AND EMPLOYMENT (*continued*)

CAPITAL OUTLAY AND THE TRADE CYCLE

THAT fluctuations in industrial activity are associated with especially marked fluctuations in the activity of the industries producing instrumental goods has long been recognised as an empirical fact. And many economists have been led thereby to seek an explanation of the trade cycle in some movement originating in the investment market.

Now we know that the phenomena of the trade cycle, however they may be caused, include fluctuations in the consumers' income and in general demand. For activity invariably means both a higher price level and greater production, and depression means a lower price level and less production. The consumers' income, being compounded of production and prices, must exhibit the fluctuations of both super-imposed.

We have shown that such fluctuations in the consumers' income are bound to cause corresponding fluctuations both in the amount of savings and in the widening of capital. But even though we know that the fluctuations in capital outlay can be explained as effects, that does not of itself dispose of the possibility of their being *also* causes. The empirical correlation between the two sets of fluctuations does not tell us which is cause and which is effect. We are therefore bound to examine the hypothesis that it is the fluctuations in capital outlay that are the originating cause.

A disturbance might originate from the investment market either through a change in the amount of saving or through a change in the amount of capital outlay. The former is often assumed hypothetically for the purpose of illustrating the manner in which the market reacts, but I do not think industrial fluctuations have ever been attributed to spontaneous changes in the amount of saving.

Nevertheless the hypothesis has received so much prominence in discussions of the subject that it demands some consideration.

An increase in saving must be distinguished from an absorption of cash by consumers. The absorption of cash is not necessarily associated with any increase in saving. It may mean that people are choosing, for whatever reason, to accumulate a portion of a given amount of current savings in cash, and therefore to place less in investment and in instruments of consumption.

Whatever the motive, the absorption of cash by consumers must involve a curtailment either of consumption or of investment [1] or both. If consumption is curtailed and sales fall off, orders for new production of consumable goods are reduced and the vicious circle of deflation is started. If investment is curtailed, the investment market becomes less favourable to new flotations and to sales of securities, and after an interval there is a falling off in capital raised and in capital outlay. Here also, though by a slower process, there is a tendency towards a reduction of the consumers' income and of general demand.

An increase in saving may or may not be accompanied by an absorption of cash, which would have these consequences. Apart from that it would take effect in an increase in investment or in the purchase of instruments of consumption. The purchase of instruments of consumption, consumers' capital outlay, represents a diversion of demand from one object to another without any change in the total disposals, and need not have any important effects on productive activity as a whole.

The increase in investment, however, involves in the first instance an immediate reduction of consumption, and so of productive activity in the industries producing consumable goods, while the corresponding increase in the activity of the industries producing capital goods will not begin till the favourable investment market has stimulated capital outlay. Owing to the delay in the action of the investment market, there will be an interval during which the vicious circle of deflation may gain hold. It is then the investment market that absorbs cash instead of the consumers.

In practice any considerable increase or decrease in the volume of saving is usually the result of an increase or decrease in the consumers' income and particularly of that part which is derived from profit. Instead of being a cause of fluctuations when the stimulus to capital outlay is delayed, it is therefore a corrective, tending to moderate the extent of fluctuations attributable to other causes.

---

[1] Perhaps I should repeat that I am using the term investment to mean the purchase of securities or income-yielding rights, not in the sense adopted by Keynes (see below, p. 157).

SPECULATIVE PURCHASES OF SECURITIES

If anything occurs to give a sudden new stimulus to capital outlay, such as new inventions or discoveries disclosing profitable openings for investment, or even a mere psychological change in expectations for no very tangible reason,[1] investors and speculators may be attracted to the market and led to buy securities with borrowed money. This borrowed money, created by the banks, supplements the resources of the investment market as if it were additional saving, and induces additional productive activity in the industries producing capital goods. The same motives which lead some people to borrow money would lead others to draw on their cash balances to buy securities, and the borrowers may also be assumed to use up whatever surplus cash they have before resorting to borrowing. There thus tend to be both increased borrowing and increased velocity of circulation of money. There is a release of cash, which goes to pay for increased capital outlay, and so makes an addition to the consumers' income.

If capital outlay were outstripping the resources of the investment market, the dealers in the market would check it by reducing the prices of securities and discouraging new flotations. If speculative purchases of securities were swelling the resources of the investment market with the proceeds of bank advances, the dealers would raise the price of securities. But when the prospect of unusually remunerative capital outlay leads simultaneously to increased flotations and increased speculative borrowing to pay for them, the investment market does nothing to stop this twofold tendency.

Similarly, when the openings for capital outlay become for any reason less attractive, there may be a simultaneous decrease both of flotations and of speculative purchases. There is an absorption of cash and a decrease in the consumers' income, which the investment market of itself is not in a position to counteract.

Capital outlay may also be financed outside the investment market when traders pay for new plant by bank advances instead of raising capital from the market.

---

[1] We do not include an expansion of consumption demand among the possibilities, for at the present stage it is the manner in which such an expansion may be caused that we are considering.

CAPITAL OUTLAY AND DISPOSALS

Expansions and contractions of capital outlay which are thus induced, without any equivalent expansions and contractions of saving, cause expansions and contractions in the consumers' income and the flow of money.

For saving is the excess of the consumers' income over consumption, and disposals are composed of consumption and capital outlay. Consequently a difference between saving and capital outlay is a difference between consumers' income and disposals; the former difference is transformed into the latter simply by adding consumption to both its terms.

Consumers' income is equal to production, so a difference between consumers' income and disposals is a difference between production and disposals. When production exceeds disposals, there is an increment of traders' stocks of goods; when production falls short of disposals, there is a decrement.

These relations are not causal but arithmetical: they follow from the definitions of terms.[1] But the further step by which the increment or decrement of traders' stocks is followed by a decrease or increase of production, and therefore of the consumers' income, is causal. The effect is worked through the orders given to producers for goods to replace those sold.

Here then is a clear tendency to a monetary expansion or contraction. In so far as an excess of capital outlay over saving is financed from bank advances, the banks are in a position to check it. But they may fail to do so, especially when the expansion is effected through a more rapid circulation of money as well as through an actual increase in advances. What we have to consider is the argument that expansions and contractions of capital outlay would of themselves give rise to cyclical fluctuations without any positive action on the part of the banks.

At a time when the productive resources of the community are under-employed, the additional capital outlay will draw upon the unemployed labour and plant, and the resulting expansion of consumption demand can be met by an increase of output. Stocks therefore can be replenished. But when output reaches capacity and there is full employment, if the excess demand still continues, stocks can no longer be replenished and they cannot be drawn on indefinitely. The traders will defend their stocks, as we have shown (above, p. 68) by raising the prices charged to consumers. By

---

[1] See below, Chapter VI.

raising prices above replacement value, they gain an additional profit, and it is by *saving* this additional income and applying it to reinforce their working capital, that they preserve their stocks from depletion. So a fresh source of saving arises, in virtue of which the excess capital outlay may continue without further depletion of stocks.

The theories which explain the trade cycle through the occurrence of capital outlay in excess of saving have to show some inherent tendency for expansion to give place to contraction. Schumpeter looked for the explanation of the cycle in periodical outbursts of technological improvements, " innovations ". That innovations might acquire an approximately periodic character is not to be excluded from consideration (the periodicity of the cycle is itself not very rigid). What really rules out Schumpeter's explanation is that the major innovations which he had in mind, such as the introduction of railways, textile machinery, or the internal combustion engine, always extend over a period covering several cycles. When railway development was interrupted after the spurts in 1836-37 and 1842-45, the cause of the set-back is not to be looked for in a completion of the process!

He attached importance to the long-period cycles associated with Kondratieff, but they do not help towards an explanation of the typical trade cycle.

THE ACCELERATION PRINCIPLE

The acceleration principle often proves tempting (particularly for example to Mr. Harrod—see Chapter X, below). The widening of capital is induced by the need for extensions of productive capacity in response to expanding demand. The rate of progress of widening tends therefore to be proportional to the *rate of increase* in demand. When an expansion of demand calls for an increment of output beyond existing capacity, the widening required is the provision of the entire capital equipment appropriate to the additional output.

The acceleration principle tends to work by spurts. At a time of low demand, when industry is under-employed, there is little need of widening. When reviving demand brings the output of one industry after another up to capacity, extensions are required, and widening begins. In fact, when widening is suspended by deficiency of demand, the widening which is needed to keep pace with the growth of working population and normal economic progress falls into arrears, and, when demand revives, the overtaking of arrears entails an exceptional expansion of the widening process. The industries of which the productive capacity is being extended draw labour into employment, and, when capital equipment has been provided for the entire working population, the attainment of full employment signifies the completion of the arrears. The widening process then loses its exceptional impetus and relapses to normal. The shrinkage in capital outlay causes a shrinkage in demand ; the vicious circle of contraction is started.

This is, I think, in principle, the explanation offered by Professor J. R. Hicks in his *Contribution to the Theory of the Trade Cycle*. The fallacy lies in the undue emphasis laid on the " induced investment ", the portion of capital outlay which responds to the acceleration principle. Professor Hicks calls the residue of accumulation which does not so respond Autonomous Investment. It includes both the deepening of capital and so much of the widening as is continued without regard to transitory fluctuations of demand. And he identifies it with Mr. Harrod's long-range capital outlay (below, p. 290). In supposing this residue to be determined independently of the fluctuations of induced investment, he is leaving out of account the function of the investment market in equating the *aggregate* volume of capital outlay to its available resources.

When the acceleration principle stimulates widening, extensions of capacity take a larger share than usual of the resources of the investment market. With given resources, the immediate reaction of the market would be to restrict the raising of capital by making its terms less favourable. But it is expanding demand that sets the acceleration principle to work, and expanding demand presupposes an expanding consumers' income, which means not only increasing consumption but increasing saving. The resources of the investment market are therefore increased, and the increase may quite possibly be sufficient to provide for the additional widening without any restriction upon deepening. The investment market cannot be expected always to perform its equalising function with precision. When its resources increase or decrease, whether through a change in the volume of saving or through a change in cash movements for capital purposes, there may be some delay in the corresponding increase or decrease in capital raised. And other tendencies intervene to cause a disparity between saving and capital outlay. The liquidation of working capital during the phase of shrinking demand releases additional cash resources, and the reconstitution of working capital during the phase of expanding demand reabsorbs the cash resources. At one time the prices of securities may be so high and their yield so low that investors hang back (Keynes's

" speculative motive "—below, pp. 158-60 and 173) ; at another investments look attractive, and the inflow of funds into the investment market is hastened. Innovations, inventions or discoveries may at any time offer lucrative opportunities which tempt investors to anticipate their savings by borrowing. Expanding demand not only stimulates widening, but makes openings for deepening more attractive.

Taking such a variety of tendencies into account, we cannot associate any definite net effect with any particular phase of the cycle. But underlying all is the fundamental consideration that the phases referred to are phases in an expansion or contraction of the *flow of money*. And the supply of money to supplement the resources of the investment market is a matter which cannot be dissociated from the action of the banks in creating money for all the various needs of the community. If any of the vagaries of capital outlay and the investment market are allowed to influence the flow of money, that is a circumstance to which credit policy cannot be indifferent. The credit policy which prevailed during the nineteenth century ensured some limitation on the extent to which the resources of the investment market would be supplemented by bank advances. In the present century the strain of war finance, so long as it lasted, has thrown all such limitations aside. But given the limitations, it is approximately true that the volume of capital outlay has to conform to the volume of saving.

THE SCOPE OF DEEPENING

Nevertheless, when a monetary expansion culminates in full employment, and the volume of saving is swollen more than in proportion to the consumers' income, the special stimulus to widening is lost, and the investment market depends on an increase in deepening to use up its resources. May there not be a limit to the deepening process ?

That a failure of the deepening process may occur at a time of low demand we have already seen (above, pp. 73-4). When widening is almost entirely suspended, and many of the openings for deepening become for the time unattractive, the appearance of the proceeds of liquidation of working capital puts an exceptional strain on the deepening process. It may become temporarily impossible to find sufficient remunerative openings to use up the resources of the investment market.

But the case we are now considering is just the contrary. At a time of high demand, working capital is being built up and is

7

employing productive resources. Widening continues, and is only diminished in that, when full employment is reached, it is reduced to normal growth. And the expanding demand, which can no longer be met by abnormal widening and the absorption of un-employed labour, becomes an additional stimulus to deepening. For output can only be increased by labour-saving methods.

Undoubtedly there is a theoretical possibility that the deepening process might come to an end through the exhaustion of all openings for the use of labour-saving equipment. When every machine or contrivance by which labour can be saved not less than equivalent to its cost in upkeep and depreciation is already in full use, it may be that nothing the investment market can do will elicit sufficient capital outlay to use up its resources, even at a time of high demand. But this is mere speculation. It would not be possible to point to any moment, since the industrial revolution started nearly two centuries ago, when there were not numerous and important innova-tions in industry awaiting development, and promising big gains to whoever should exploit them.

Jevons's formula of marginal yield implies that in a given state of technological attainment all possible openings for capital outlay can be arranged in order of yield, and that the existing rate of interest makes a definite dividing line between those with higher and those with lower yield. If in the interval of time immediately following there are no new openings presented by technological progress, we may suppose the rate of interest to move downwards just so far as to make sufficient openings remunerative to use up the savings arising in the interval. The rate of interest is moved down just so far as to cut a slice of the right thickness off the sausage. If new openings are discovered with a yield above the market rate of interest, the slice can be made thinner, or no slice at all may be required. Some-times the rate of interest will be actually raised, and we have to imagine the slice becoming a negative quantity.

If the facts conformed to this scheme, the rate of interest might gradually progress down the sausage till the end is reached and glut supervenes and lasts possibly for ever, possibly only till technological progress reveals new openings, and a few negative slices bring back a positive rate of interest and a reincarnation of the sausage.

But the reality is very different. As we saw in Chapter III (pp. 36-43), the yield of any given instrument can only be estimated very approximately; a wide margin is usually allowed even for a well-tried instrument, and a still wider for an innovation. The introduction of a new instrument is a slow and gradual process.

The result of all this caution and imperfect knowledge is that at any moment in addition to those forms of capital equipment which have been left on one side because they yield less than the market rate of interest, there are innumerable others yielding more and sometimes far more, which have not yet materialised or have come only into very limited use. The deepening process is like a mine with enormous ore reserves in sight. So long as that is so, a true glut of capital will not occur.

That does not mean that a true glut is a contingency that can be wholly neglected. Though it has never yet occurred, and so has nothing to do with the trade cycle, there is no essential reason why it should not occur some day, and if it does it will give rise to some baffling problems.[1]

It follows therefore that, apart from the special case of a temporary glut of capital caused by extreme depression, we can assume that the investment market will succeed in finding an outlet in capital outlay for all the resources it receives ; and there need not be an absorption or release of cash by the market on any important scale.

A SPURT OF CAPITAL OUTLAY

It seems clear that the acceleration principle by itself does not explain why a spurt of capital outlay should be followed by a reaction. But there remains an argument which still deserves to be considered. At the end of the last chapter we saw that there is one item in the cost of a product which does not of itself generate income, the depreciation allowance. And it was there shown that, in a community in which capital is growing, the aggregate provision for depreciation exceeds current replacements, so that there is an unspent balance accruing to the traders' free capital. Likewise, after a sudden spurt of capital outlay, however caused, there is an addition of an appropriate proportion to the provision for depreciation, so that when the new capital comes into production, the price of each unit of product has to cover the charge for depreciation, and exceeds by that amount the incomes generated in producing it. Therefore the productive process does not automatically give rise to new demand equivalent to the new supply.

That is the element of truth in the Social Credit theory of Major C. H. Douglas, and recognition is due to his efforts in urging it, though it must be admitted that he habitually overstated the case.

[1] See my *Trade Depression and the Way Out*, Chapter VII (second edition).

He supposed that the deficiency of demand was not confined to the charge for depreciation, but extended to the entire burden of over-head costs.   Overhead costs, apart from depreciation, are currently disbursed, and generate incomes.[1]

And as to depreciation, we have already seen that, in so far as the provision is unspent, and is added to the traders' free capital, any part of the free capital in excess of the convenient cash holding is likely to be invested.   If the money passes into the investment market, it becomes available for capital outlay.

More capital outlay !   Is that not simply postponing the trouble and aggravating it?   No.   The new depreciation allowance in respect of the spurt of capital outlay constitutes a permanent addition to the gross amount currently available for capital outlay. When it begins, it is a small offset to the effects of the cessation of the spurt.   There is no need to refer here to the question of the openings for deepening coming to an end.

Can it be assumed that traders will promptly invest their free capital?   Even if they only delay doing so, there will be some absorption of cash and shortage of demand.   But a spurt of capital outlay has other after effects which must be taken into account.   If the capital outlay has been applied to equipping industries which supply stock-held products, the additional supply when it emerges will require additional stocks ;   there will be a positive intermediate demand, which should be more then sufficient to outweigh the small fraction of the proceeds of sale of the product corresponding to depreciation.

A part of the capital outlay, it is true, may be destined for the supply of immaterial products, which cannot be accumulated in stock, the services rendered to consumers by transport, housing, public utilities, entertainment, etc.   But much of the capital installed for these purposes consists of very durable constructions, carrying only small depreciation allowances.

We have been considering a spurt of capital outlay in itself, without regard to the circumstances in which it occurs.   If it is accompanied by no equivalent increase in savings, the excess of capital outlay results in an equal depletion of stocks, with an infla-tionary effect far transcending the contrary influence of the deprecia-tion allowance.   If the capital outlay is covered by savings, then the temporary expansion of outlay must be matched by a temporary expansion of saving.   That situation is characteristic of the climax

[1] In the first edition of this book a chapter was devoted to disentangling Major Douglas's arguments.

of cyclical activity. Expanding demand might theoretically reach a state of full employment, with prices in due relation to wages, and profits no more than normal. But in practice the rise of wages lags behind the rise of prices, profit margins rise above normal, and savings increase more than in proportion to profits. If wages never caught up, the increase in capital outlay would not be a mere spurt, and the increase in saving would not be temporary; both would continue.

With wages below the economic level, and profits correspondingly high, employers will seek to extend output by employing more labour. There will be a state not merely of full employment but of over-employment—a scarcity of labour. If traders delay investing the growing depreciation allowances, and their absorption of cash occasions a deficiency of demand, the effect is merely to moderate this state of over-employment. The set-back would reduce the excessive profit margins without diminishing productive activity.

But it is much more likely that the employers' competition in the labour market will bring about a rise of wages, which will put an end to the excessive profits and the exceptional savings and capital outlay. Disposals then remain unaffected, consumption taking the place of an equivalent amount of capital outlay. Increased consumption calls for increased stocks and an intermediate demand. And in any case, at the climax of activity, after a period of expanding demand, there is sure to be a substantial shortage of stocks and a positive intermediate demand. The credit restriction and dear money characteristic of that phase are the means resorted to to counteract this intermediate demand.

CREDIT REGULATION AND FLUCTUATIONS OF CAPITAL OUTLAY

Theories of the trade cycle must be distinguished from theories of trade depressions. The former aim at discovering some cause or set of causes *of a periodical character*, which include a phase of depression among their effects. The latter are interested in any causes of depression, whether periodical or not. Any investigation of the trade cycle ought to be directed to the economic conditions of the times in which the cycle is known actually to have prevailed, that is to say, the hundred and fifty years ending with 1914. The problem is to find in the economic circumstances of those years an adequate explanation of the periodical recurrence of depressions. The question is one of fact, but it presupposes some solution of the more general problem of the character and causes of the state of trade depression in itself.

As to that, there is in reality less room for differences of opinion than in theories of the trade cycle. A depression is essentially a deficiency of demand. If there is a deficiency of demand, there must be depression; if there is no deficiency of demand, there cannot be depression. Deficiency of demand means deficiency relative to costs, and more particularly relative to wages. No one has ever tried to prove the contrary of these propositions, and all theories of trade depressions will be found implicitly to assume them. A theory which involved a depression occurring in conditions of adequate demand would be self-destructive. The theories which trace depression to a decline of investment are none the less bound to show that the decline of investment brings about a decline of demand. But they fail to prove that this particular cause of a decline of demand has any unique importance. A decline of bank advances for speculative holdings of securities means an absorption of cash by those who repay the advances. An excess of investment over capital raised by industry means an absorption of cash by the investment market. In either case the absorption of cash, like any other absorption of cash however caused, tends to cause a decline of the consumers' income and of general demand.

But, as we have seen, the banks are in a position to counteract either an absorption or a release of cash, and to prevent a contraction or expansion of demand. The responsibility for doing so or for neglecting to do so rests upon them, for their intervention is not merely a hypothetical possibility but is closely related to their well recognised functions in the regulation of credit.

If the banks be assumed to limit their advances by reference to a proportion of cash reserves to deposits, any additional demand for advances will react upon their credit policy, and they will forthwith take steps to deter borrowers in whatever degree may be necessary. In so far as the release of cash takes the form of a depletion of existing balances instead of borrowed money, this direct reaction on credit policy does not occur. But credit policy, even according to nineteenth century traditions, is by no means governed exclusively by cash proportions. An international metallic standard is fundamentally a foreign exchange standard; any tendency of general demand to expand or contract is reflected in an unfavourable or favourable tendency of the foreign exchanges, and a contraction or expansion of credit is required to correct it. In nineteenth century practice it might happen that gold was lost or gained in considerable amounts in the interval before the appropriate credit measures had become effective, and the consequent change in reserves would be acquiesced in in preference to continuing the credit measures after the undesirable tendency had been corrected.

Under that system an expansion of general demand occurring through a release of cash, even without any visible expansion of credit, would nevertheless be met by a restriction of credit, if it caused an adverse exchange position and a loss of gold.

A release or absorption of cash by the investment market is one possible cause of an expansion or contraction of the consumers' income. It is the task of the banking system, in regulating credit, to prevent *any* such cause from disturbing the operation of the prescribed monetary policy, whatever it may be. If a release of cash occurs at a time when monetary policy requires an expansion of general demand, the banks will acquiesce in it. If it occurs at a time when monetary policy is against such an expansion, the banks will intervene to counteract it. And similarly in case of an absorption of cash and a contraction of general demand.

If an expansion or contraction of general demand starts, and the banks take no steps to correct it, the movement is liable to be amplified by the operation of the vicious circle. Therefore a relatively small release or absorption of cash by the investment market might start a big expansion or contraction. But that is equally true of *any* release or absorption of cash in whatever part of the community it occurs. Absorptions and releases of cash are likely to be constantly occurring, and there is no special significance in those which happen to originate in the investment market. If an excess capital outlay involves a resort to bank advances, the banks are in a position to exercise control. Though those who borrow to acquire and hold securities are insensitive to the rate charged them, a banker can, if he chooses, *refuse* to lend for those purposes. The mobilisation of idle cash balances to buy securities cannot be checked by the banks, but it is a less dangerous tendency because more limited than the use of bank advances. And to meet the generally inflationary tendency, whether due to a mobilisation of cash or to borrowing being insufficiently checked, the banks can resort to a restriction of credit in other directions. They can raise rates against traders seeking to borrow for the purchase of commodities.

SENSITIVENESS OF WORKING CAPITAL TO CREDIT
REGULATION

When a release or absorption of cash originates in the investment market, the same corrective is appropriate as for a release or absorption of cash originating in any other way. The treatment to be applied depends on the sensitiveness of working capital to credit regulation, and much of the plausibility of the theories which attribute the trade cycle to fluctuations of capital outlay arises from the assumption, express or implied, that working capital does not possess this sensitiveness, and the corollary that credit regulation has to operate through the long-term investment market.

Keynes (below, pp. 108 and 186) was positively of opinion that borrowing for the purchase of commodities and holding them in stock is insensitive to the short-term rate of interest, but other economists are to be found who simply take it for granted without arguing or even explicitly raising the question at all.

Now, if credit regulation did have to act through long-term investment, its efficacy would be very seriously circumscribed. Not only are speculators who hold securities with borrowed money almost indifferent to the rate of interest exacted from them, but the response of capital outlay to the state of the market (on which the effect depends) is necessarily extremely tardy, on account of the long period of preparation, both financial and technical, which nearly always intervenes between the first initiation of a project and the start upon the installation of the capital equipment for it. It is very natural that the economists who believe that the efficacy of credit regulation depends on its influence on the long-term investment market should be very sceptical of its power to do anything worth mentioning at all. Such a view gives too much support to that dangerous repudiation of responsibility in which those entrusted with the direction of credit regulation and monetary policy take refuge when they are confronted with the magnitude of the consequences attendant on the decisions they have to take.

When bank rate was first adopted as the primary instrument of credit regulation more than a hundred years ago, no one had any doubt that it operated through working capital. It was the rate for the *discounting of bills* by the Bank of England in its capacity of lender of last resort, and the bills were drawn to finance purchases of commodities, not only in international trade, but at that time also in domestic trade.[1] Half a century elapsed before economists

[1] See my *A Century of Bank Rate*, pp. 4-8.

appreciated the significance of this practice. It was Marshall, in his evidence before the Gold and Silver Commission in 1888, who first introduced bank rate into economic theory. He attributed the operation of the discount rate to its effect on " speculators ", who, he supposed, were encouraged by easy borrowing to buy and hold commodities for a rise. He does not seem to have entertained the idea of anyone other than a speculator holding commodities with borrowed money. And he assumed too easily that speculators would be amenable to the pressure of the short-term rate of interest.

Wicksell may be regarded as the interpreter of the theory of credit regulation to Continental economists. After quoting Tooke's pronouncement on the insensibility of speculators to the rate of interest, Wicksell pointed out that speculation is exceptional, and that " it is not the exceptions which have to be taken into consideration but the ordinary regular and recurrent transactions " (*Interest and Prices*, p. 90). This was a step forward, but Wicksell unfortunately looked for the influence of the rate of interest on any business in its effect upon the profits of the business *as a whole*, instead of upon the limited field of the purchase of commodities and the stocks to be held. Since a fall in the rate of discount from 4 to 3 per cent would reduce the cost of a three-months' bill by no more than $\frac{1}{4}$ per cent, and such a change would be " too small to exert more than a very diminutive influence on the structure of prices ", he concluded that " it is a necessary condition that the easier terms of short-term lending shall have persisted sufficiently long to influence the long-term rate " (p. 92). In the case where raw materials or labour will be employed for one, two, three or more years before the finished product emerges, a fall of 1 per cent in the rate of interest will be responsible for a rise in the current prices of these raw materials and services of 1, 2, 3 or more per cent. And " where the investment is to all intents and purposes being undertaken ' for eternity ', as in the case of such things as buildings, railways, and durable machinery, the possible rise in price is considerably greater " (pp. 91-2). A concern that can issue debentures at 3 per cent instead of at 4 per cent could afford to pay almost $33\frac{1}{3}$ per cent more for its requirements.

The implication is that the installation of instruments or fixed capital is more susceptible to the influence of the rate of interest than an addition to working capital, because the rate of interest makes far more difference to an instrument of which the yield has to be discounted over a long period of years than to a consignment of merchandise which has to be discounted over a period of a few months only.   That would be so if the long-term and the short-term rates of interest *were equal.*

But when the short-term rate, as we are supposing, is moved up or down, the effect on the long-term rate is quite small.   It depends as we saw (above, p. 81), on the period for which people expect the short-term rate to continue at the level to which it has been moved. When we said that the dealers in the investment market would not form any expectation as to the short-term rate of interest more than two years ahead, we were allowing a liberal limit.   More often the expectation would not extend beyond a few months.

Past experience shows the fluctuations of the long-term rate (apart from the special disturbance of wars) to have been very slight. In the half century up to 1914 there was only one occasion when the yield of Consols diverged by as much as $\frac{1}{4}$ per cent from the seven years' moving average.[1]   That was in 1866, the year of the Overend and Gurney crisis, when the bank rate remained at 10 per cent for three months.   The lowest price of Consols was 84, giving a yield of 3·57 per cent, while the seven years' moving average, with 1866 as centre, was a price of 91·43, giving a yield of 3·28 per cent.   This half century was a period when bank rate was varying between 2 and 10 per cent, and even after the earlier years of very dear money, between 2 and 7.   In the earlier part of the nineteenth century the fluctuations of the yield of Consols were somewhat greater, but the divergence from the seven-year moving average only exceeded $\frac{1}{2}$ per cent on two or three occasions.   In fact the variations of the long-term rate of interest are of a different order of magnitude from those of the short-term rate.   Nor can the movements of the former be regarded as exclusively or even mainly caused by movements of the latter.   The influence of the short-term rate on the long-term rate is exercised through the various forms of short-term borrowing for the purchase of securities or for capital outlay.   This borrowing is only one of the factors contributing to determine the long-term rate of interest.

Wicksell, however, did not rely wholly on the long-term rate as the means of regulating the purchasing power of money.   He maintained that even the " diminutive influence " of the short-term rate must have its due effect.

" A fall in the rate of interest ", he said, " even though it is casual and temporary, will bring about a perfectly *definite* rise of prices ",

----

[1] For the years 1880-9, when the 3 per cents reached par and were prevented from rising higher by their liability to conversion, we can calculate the yield from the 2½ per cent annuities.

and its influence will be *cumulative* (pp. 94-5). And he adduced various ingenious arguments to show that a tendency initially very small might be indefinitely amplified. The process need not even be very slow. " The upward movement of prices will in some measure ' create its own draught '. When prices have been rising for some time *entrepreneurs* will begin to reckon on the basis . . . of a further rise of prices " (p. 96).

That a price movement, once begun, tends to be amplified owing to the inherent instability of credit we have already shown (above, pp. 64-8). But it is not necessary to invoke that principle in order to explain the reaction of the price level to the short-term rate of interest. An item of cost that is negligible in an enterprise as a whole may be substantial in relation to a limited section of its activity. An increase of postage charges is not likely to make all the difference between the flotation of an enterprise and its abandonment, but it may cause a substantial reduction in the number of letters and circulars despatched. Similarly, an increase in the rate of interest on bank advances will not result in a contract that would otherwise have been accepted being refused, but it may materially affect the buying programme for the replenishment of stocks.

Traders decide for the sake of a very trivial saving to restrict and delay their purchases of commodities, and it is something of a paradox that the decision so lightly made by one trader may have a potent and possibly a calamitous effect on another. Yet this is no more irrational than the far-reaching effect of people's decisions in regard to their cash balances. A cash balance is a working balance, the precise amount of which at any moment is governed by decisions very lightly made, decisions as to the moment of making or obtaining payment, as to the amount which it is convenient to invest at a time, or as to the amount to be raised by borrowing or by a sale of securities in case of a shortage of cash. But none the less the variations of cash balances play a fundamental part in monetary affairs. A change in velocity of circulation is simply the resultant of innumerable individual decisions regarding cash balances.

A trader's stock of a commodity is a working balance. Indeed when he procures a fresh supply to replenish it, he is at the same time releasing cash. His net cash resources and working capital together constitute his circulating capital, which provides him at the same time with a working balance of money and a working balance of each commodity that he uses in his business. With a given circulating capital, a release or absorption of cash necessarily means a net increase or decrease in working capital.

Keynes argued in his *Treatise on Money* that the volume of investment in working capital and stocks of goods is not sensitive to the short-term rate of interest, chiefly on the ground that variations in the rate of interest are small in comparison with carrying costs and with expectations of price changes.

As regards carrying costs, I offered (in my *Art of Central Banking*, p. 368) some criticisms of Keynes's arguments. He maintained that " a fluctuation of 1 or 2 per cent in bank rate will represent so small a part of the total carrying charges that it is not reasonable to assign to the *expense* of high bank rate a preponderating influence on the minds of dealers in stocks " (*Treatise*, Vol. II, p. 146). Yet of carrying costs, *including* interest, he observed : " they seldom cost altogether less than 6 per cent per annum, and 10 per cent per annum may be regarded as a normal figure " (*ibid.*, p. 136). A fluctuation of 1 or 2 per cent is not a negligible proportion of a total of 6 or 10. But bank rate would sometimes advance by gradual stages from 2 per cent to 7 or more, and fall by rapid stages from 7 to 2. The operation of minimum rates might somewhat reduce the range of variation for overdrafts, but not below 3 or $3\frac{1}{2}$, and something has to be allowed for the increased willingness of bankers to lend at the minimum rate, when competing rates, such as the discount on bills, have fallen very low.

Keynes illustrated the effect of carrying costs on market price from the case of redundant stocks of copper in 1921-2 (*ibid.*, pp. 139-40). If traders expected that the absorption of the stocks would take two years, and looked forward to a normal price of $14\frac{1}{2}$ cents a pound, the market price would abate two years' carrying costs. If carrying costs were 10 per cent they would offer something over $11\frac{1}{2}$ cents. But in fact the carrying costs of copper, apart from interest, are very slight. And Keynes, when he reverted to the same illustration in the *General Theory of Employment, Interest and Money* (pp. 70-1), said that the present value of a ton of surplus copper would be " equal to the greatest of the values obtainable by subtracting from the estimated future value at any given date of a ton of copper the interest cost and current supplementary cost on a ton of copper between that date and the present ". Interest at any rate deserved mention.

For primary products and other specially bulky goods, and also for perishable goods and those subject to rapid changes of fashion, the cost of storage or the loss through storage may be a serious matter. But for the wide range of manufactured goods outside these categories the cost of storage is, as we have seen (above, p. 51), often insignificant. And of course it is not necessary for a restriction or relaxation of credit to react on stocks of commodities of *all* kinds ; it is quite enough that it should react on the greater part or even a substantial part of them.

With regard to expectations of price changes, it is true that agricultural products and minerals are subject to wide price fluctuations, the prospect of which is likely greatly to outweigh any changes in the rate of interest in the mind of a trader who proposes to buy a supply with borrowed money. But, as we have seen (above, p. 50), to a holder who has eliminated the price risk by hedging, the rate of interest may be quite a consideration.

The prices of manufactured products are in general much more affected by conditions of demand than by conditions of supply. In some instances (such as cotton yarn) the raw material forms a substantial proportion of the value of the manufactured product, but here also traders who buy such products can usually rid themselves of that part of the price risk by hedging, through a forward sale of the material concerned.

In general, the output of a manufactured commodity is adjusted to the demand, with relatively little change of price, except where demand unexpectedly outstrips the capacity of the industry, and a temporary extra profit or quasi-rent is secured by those who can meet the demand in the interval before capacity is extended. Such price changes originate in changes of demand. But there is usually little or no positive ground for forecasting any definite change in demand.[1] The data on which traders base their judgment are simply the *existing* intensity of demand and *existing* stocks. There may be a disposition among some traders to think that a tendency that has affected the demand for a commodity in the recent past will continue, or among others to think that it is merely temporary and will be reversed. On balance there is not likely to be any very marked expectation of a change of demand. Demand, it should be understood, means demand from final purchasers. In the case of an intermediate product traders can always assume that, when the demand has failed to adjust itself to the demand for the finished product, it will do so sooner or later.

Producers take time to adjust the prices they quote to a change in demand. But when the state of demand portends a rise or fall of price, wholesale dealers will enlarge or restrict their orders, and thus

---

[1] A definite change in tastes, habits or methods of production such as foreshadows a substantial change in demand is an exceptional event in the history of any one commodity.

put pressure on the producers to hasten the change of price. When demand is shrinking, prime cost will put a limit to the price concessions a manufacturer can make. But if there is a prospect of prime cost being diminished by a reduction of wages, the dealers may still hold up orders, and thereby indirectly put pressure on the work people to accept the reduction.

Thus it is really only where price and demand are visibly out of harmony that an expectation of a change of price can be said to exist. The want of harmony becomes manifest in an undue increment or decrement of stocks. That is the real basis of an expectation of a price movement in the case of a manufactured product. And we can at once see that such an occurrence may have a very powerful effect on the working of the rate of interest. This is simply the vicious circle of expansion or contraction over again. A movement in general demand tends to be amplified, and as it gathers impetus more and more drastic measures of credit regulation are required to reverse it.

BANK RATE

If the movement is one of expansion, it is always possible to stop it by a sufficiently severe credit restriction, unless the inflationary virus has been introduced into the fiscal system and meets every restrictive measure with a flood of fresh paper currency. If bank rate is not high enough, it can be raised higher. By selling securities in the market, the central bank can make bank rate effective ; it can compel the other banks to borrow from it in order to keep up their own supplies of currency. If the banks cannot keep the advances they allow their customers within the limits which they desire under these conditions, they will refuse to lend.

Banks are not as a rule very desirous of exercising the power, which they necessarily reserve to themselves, of refusing to lend. Any one bank that refuses accommodation risks the loss of offended customers. It will only be done in a systematic manner when the entire banking system is exposed to severe pressure, and every banker takes courage to refuse because he knows his competitors are compelled to do the same.

At times of more moderate credit restriction there are likely to be refusals of a selective character. Bankers sometimes say that in such conditions they refuse advances for speculative purposes, while allowing them for legitimate trade. A restrictive policy so limited would have some effect, in that it would put out of action a speculative demand which would otherwise tend to raise the prices of the commodities or securities concerned. But the commodities which are subject to speculation are for the most part such that output does not easily respond to a rise of price or an increase in demand. And capital outlay only responds very tardily to the influences affecting investment. So long as output and capital outlay are not affected, the calling in of advances made to speculators probably results in new advances being made to those (presumably " legitimate traders") to whom the speculators sell.

Thus the refusal to lend so limited would only have a very tardy effect, and the bankers must rely primarily on the short-term rate of interest as the instrument of credit control. The short-term rate has an insignificant effect upon the speculator, but it *does* influence the " legitimate trader " in those commodities which do not attract the speculator and for which price changes do not usually have to be anticipated.

If the rate is being raised to check a condition of expanding general demand, undoubtedly allowance must be made for the effect of increasing sales and diminishing stocks on the outlook even of the legitimate trader. Even if a trader in a commodity does not expect this growth of demand to outstrip productive capacity and lead to a rise of price, he will still want to increase his stock in proportion to his sales. The rise in the short-term rate of interest must be sufficient to offset this motive. How great the rise must be is evidently an empirical question. So far as the London discount market is concerned, bank rates of 8, 9 or 10 per cent were seen from time to time in the period from the passage of the Bank Charter Act of 1844 till the crisis of 1873, but since then bank rate has never exceeded 7 per cent (except in the abnormal circumstances of the week from 31 July to 6 August 1914).[1] That means rates of $7\frac{1}{2}$ to $8\frac{1}{2}$ per cent on bank advances and overdrafts.

In 1880, 1890, and 1900 the culminating activity of the trade cycle was checked without the rate rising above 6 per cent, and in 1912 and 1913 it did not rise above 5 per cent.

Were such rates sufficient to break the vicious circle of expansion, and was 7 per cent sufficient to check the impetus of the high state of activity in 1906 and 1907? Further, had 7 per cent the power to check the tremendous current of the post-war inflation in 1920?

It may be urged that it was not really the direct operation of dear money that had so potent an effect, but a psychological reaction.

[1] Bank rate was raised to 8 per cent on 31 July and 10 per cent on 1 August, but there followed the bank holidays, and when the banks re-opened on 7 August the rate was 6 per cent.

Traders looked upon a rise of bank rate as a sign that demand was going to decline and prices to fall, and it was this expectation rather than the direct pressure of the rate that caused the check to expansion.

There is probably some truth in this. The circumstance that the top levels of bank rate were noticeably lower after 1873 than before suggests that traders were becoming more amenable to this treatment.

In the course of English history the principle has become established that the House of Commons can compel the resignation of any Government which it dislikes by refusing to vote money, and can insist on having the Government which it prefers by getting rid of any other Government in this manner. But once the principle was established it was unnecessary to go through the complicated procedure of refusing to vote money; a simple vote of want of confidence is accepted by the Government as sufficient indication of the intention to apply the decisive constitutional sanctions.

Similarly, when it was recognised that the Bank of England would put up bank rate to 10 per cent (or higher if need be) to check a credit expansion, traders became accustomed to accept the warning of a 7, or 6, or even a 5 per cent rate, and to curtail their operations without any greater pressure.

If, however, at any time people were to become so sceptical of the Bank's power to curb an expansion that they took no notice of 6 or 7 per cent, the Bank could go up to 10 per cent, or indeed to 12 or 15 or higher.

And it is not to be inferred that, because the top rates of 6 or 7 per cent have been assisted by expectations, they have in themselves had no other efficacy than that of a signal. Even a moderate rise in the short-term rate of interest is a new factor, for what it is worth, in the calculations of every trader who considers buying goods with borrowed money. The psychological reactions may be helpful but are not essential to the power of bank rate.

That there are limits to the possibility of evoking an expansion of general demand by reducing the bank rate we have already shown. The reduction of the rate is to be regarded rather as the lifting of a check upon movement than as giving a positive stimulus. Cheap money is *one* of the conditions of revival, but may not be enough by itself.

In the period from 1866 to 1914 the active phase of the trade cycle was regularly accompanied by a rising bank rate, which rose to a maximum (usually 6 or 7 per cent) when the strain of the demand for currency upon the world's gold reserves was felt. The maximum rate was arrived at by trial and error ; it was the rate which proved sufficient to reverse the expansive tendency (at the cost sometimes of financial crises). This reversal once definitely achieved, it was the invariable practice to reduce bank rate *rapidly*. The transition from dear money to cheap money occupied only a few weeks, and usually some tendency towards revival was manifested within a few months.[1] So long as that procedure was adhered to, the credit deadlock did not occur. Even in the years of exceptionally cheap money, following the American crisis of 1893, though the price level did not begin to rise till 1897, the revival of activity was making slow but steady progress. If the transition to cheap money is unduly delayed, there is a danger that at no one moment will there be a sufficient stimulus to overcome the vicious circle of deflation, and that when the transition is complete and short-term rates have fallen to a minimum, the vicious circle will still be dominant.

When we assume that the high bank rate has done its work, that means that it has successfully overcome the vicious circle of expansion and started the vicious circle of deflation. In order to break the latter, it is essential to infuse into the traders a sufficiently concentrated tendency to increase their purchases. At a time when their purchases are still adapted to the restrictive tendencies of a high bank rate, a *sudden* transition to a low bank rate will have this effect. If the transition is delayed and spread over a longer interval, its power at any one time may be insufficient, and the vicious circle of deflation will go on gathering impetus till it becomes irresistible.

Possible though it is to stop this by taking prompt measures to relax credit in time, far better would it be to regulate credit at all times in such a way that neither of the two vicious circles ever gets a serious hold. In quiet conditions credit responds easily to moderate upward and downward movements of bank rate. If these movements were always initiated *in time*, the conditions need never be other than quiet in a monetary sense.

Critics of the traditional bank rate policy apply hypothetical tests to it, asking what would happen if it had to cope with some especially violent disturbance. That it could cope with an expansion even of formidable dimensions we have found reason to suppose, though admittedly a very severe depression may be beyond its control. But this is not really to the point. For the bank rate policy was, in fact, so applied as to *avoid* this contingency till recent

---

[1] There were occasions when a recrudescence of crisis conditions, as in 1878 and 1884, delayed the beginning of revival (see my *Gold Standard in Theory and Practice*, fifth edition, p. 108).

8

years. We had more violent disturbances in the years 1919-39 because the former practices were departed from. If the efficacy of bank rate as an instrument of credit regulation is such as I have argued it to be, it could be so applied as to smooth out fluctuations much more effectively than it was in the nineteenth century.

But if bank rate is to be used, it must be relatively high at a time of activity. If it is already at a minimum at a moment when for any reason activity is falling off, and there is a threat of depression, it cannot be put lower, and its power of stimulating activity is nullified.

THE TRADE CYCLE

Seen in the light of the foregoing theory, the trade cycles of the nineteenth century need not present a puzzle. There was an international banking system centred in London, based on a metallic standard (at first bimetallic and subsequently gold). Credit restriction and credit relaxation alternated according to the state of the available metallic reserves.

At a time when the metallic reserves of the world were ample, the banking system relaxed credit and encouraged borrowers. The result was a gradual enlargement of general demand, marked by increased productive activity and rising prices in the greater part of the world. If a set-back occurred anywhere, it soon corrected itself, for the banks would not desist from their efforts to encourage borrowers so long as they had ample reserves. The enlargement of general demand was resumed. It only encountered a real obstacle when the growing need for currency began to weaken the reserve position of the banks.

The active phase of the trade cycle was invariably brought to an end by a shortage of metallic reserves, which led the banks to apply measures of credit restriction. Those measures were intensified till the expansive tendency was visibly reversed, and the signs of declining general demand, falling prices and falling productive activity, were clearly discernible. That once achieved there was a rapid transition to cheap money and a gradual initiation of revival.

The clue to the cyclical or periodical character of the process is the slowness of the movements of currency by which banking policy was guided. The increase of the balances of currency in the hands of the people lagged far behind the conditions of activity which caused it, and the expansive process was allowed to go beyond the point ultimately consistent with available reserves before restriction was made effective. The restrictive measures were applied too late, and there was an interval before they took effect. The pressure, thus overdue, had to be intensified and it usually happened that the transition from activity to depression was suddenly hastened by the outbreak of a financial crisis. Indeed the problem of the trade cycle was long regarded as the problem of periodical financial crises rather than of alternations of activity and depression.

The return of currency from circulation, like its outflow, was gradual. The early stages of a depression were usually marked by a sudden transition to credit relaxation and very cheap money, which we may interpret as the symptoms of an extensive liquidation of working capital. Gold reserves presently became redundant and eventually the systematic bias of the banks to credit expansion started revival.

The experience of the nineteen-thirties has shown how prolonged the depression might be if a credit deadlock were allowed to develop. It is probable that on some occasions in the past, when revival was exceptionally slow, the vicious circle of deflation came near to a state of deadlock. But in no case was the length of the cycle from crest to crest prolonged beyond ten or eleven years.

The trade cycle is a monetary phenomenon because general demand is itself a monetary phenomenon. The phases of the trade cycle were marked by action on the part of the monetary authorities. The Bank of England issued currency against discounted bills. When the Bank lowered its discount rate, it was trying to issue more currency through this channel and its ultimate purpose in doing so was to enlarge general demand. The progress of revival signified its success.

Eventually the gold reserve began to run short and the Bank reversed its policy. It raised bank rate, and tried thereby to withdraw currency and compress general demand. The appearance of depression once again signified its success.

DEFICITS AND PUBLIC WORKS

Those who deny the sensitiveness of working capital to bank rate do not in general claim any high degree of sensitiveness for long-term investment. They are more inclined to a general scepticism in regard to all the traditional methods of monetary control through credit policy, and they recommend some such expedient as a large excess of Government expenditure over revenue to put new money into circulation and set it in motion.

And it is quite evident that a system of credit control acting exclusively through the long-term investment market and capital outlay without the aid of Government expenditure would be extremely ineffective. We have referred more than once to the relatively long interval between any movement in the investment market and its effects, and also to the insensitiveness of the speculator or speculative investor to credit regulation through the short-term rate of interest. Indeed the influence of the banks on the long-term investment market is not to be looked for in their control of the short-term rate of interest, so much as in their direct action on the resources of the market, whether through allowing or refusing advances to speculators or through buying or selling securities on their own account.

And even when the banks do not rely on the rate of interest but employ these methods, the response of capital outlay to the favourable or unfavourable state of the investment market is bound to be long delayed, and the field of economic activity that can be influenced is relatively very restricted. And in an extreme case there may be a temporary glut, so that there is not merely a tardy response of capital outlay but apparently for the time being no response at all.

A temporary glut of capital occurs when a shrinkage of general demand has made the widening of capital unattractive, and deepening fails for the time being to fill the gap. The investment market fails to use up its resources and absorbs cash. If a relaxation of credit induces an intermediate demand and an expansion of the flow of money, the resulting revival of capital outlay will take time.

It is under such conditions that Government expenditure offers a way of escape. It may be that public works demand as long a time of preparation as private enterprises, but the Government expenditure need not necessarily take the form of public works. The Government may borrow for current expenses, for example at a time when depression has caused the yield of revenue to shrink and the budget expenditure to be increased by unemployment relief.

The temporary glut of capital may be accompanied by a credit deadlock : there may be such an accumulation of unsold goods that a relaxation of credit fails to evoke a positive intermediate demand. In that contingency an excess of Government expenditure over revenue may be the only available expedient for reviving demand. The Government can meet a deficit by drawing on the idle resources of the investment market or can raise funds from the banks. The incomes generated in the hands of those whom the Government employs, together with the spending power of those who pay less in taxation, become the source of additional demand.

Experience has not afforded much confirmation of this thesis, except where the Government expenditure has been on the vast scale called for by war or by the preparation for imminent war. The deficits which raised the national debt of the United States from $17,000 million in 1930 to $47,000 million in 1939, and which in some years reached $4,000 million, were in themselves a very minor contribution towards making good a shortage in the consumers' income, which exceeded $40,000 million. And when signs of revival did appear, in 1933 and 1937, wages were raised and the increase of costs caused a set-back.

On the other hand, Hitler's immense expenditure on armaments in the years 1937-9 was accompanied by a rigid control of wages, and extinguished unemployment in Germany.

Supporters of the policy of deficits or public works argue that, even if the direct addition to the consumers' income is small, it may be a means of " priming the pump " or " setting the ball rolling ". In any given structure of incomes the proportion of consumption to saving will be a determinate ratio, corresponding to Keynes's " multiplier ". If the existing amount of capital outlay is insufficient to use up the savings corresponding to the existing consumers' income, there is disequilibrium. The consumers' income must shrink till savings no longer exceed capital outlay. If additional capital outlay is introduced by the Government the requisite shrinkage of the consumer's income is proportionately less or may be avoided altogether. If people save one-tenth of their incomes, an increase in capital outlay may mean a tenfold increase in the consumers' income.

This reasoning is valid only on the assumption that capital outlay is insufficient to use up current savings. If that is so, there will be an absorption of cash, either by the investment market or by industry or by consumers, equal to the difference, and this absorption of cash will cause a continual fall of consumers' income and of general demand till savings have been sufficiently reduced to be no more than equal to capital outlay. In the state of equilibrium so reached the consumers' income will be related to savings and therefore to capital outlay by the multiplier, and any addition to capital outlay permits a corresponding addition to the consumers' outlay.

But the deepening process, if it is normally operative, will adjust the amount of capital outlay to whatever the amount of savings may be. And, so long as that is so, no artificial addition to capital outlay is called for.

When there is a temporary glut in the investment market, the deepening process fails to keep pace with the resources which the market offers. But that occurs not because depression diminishes capital outlay, for it is likely to diminish savings to an equal extent, but because the resources of the investment market are supplemented by the proceeds of liquidation of redundant working capital. If the deepening process made its normal response, there would be a substantial excess of capital outlay over savings.

The true function, therefore, of the capital outlay undertaken by the Government is not to fill a gap between capital outlay and savings, but to bring about a release of cash. If it is sufficient to outweigh the general tendency to absorb cash, it will " set the ball rolling ". The general tendency to absorb cash is the resultant of a number of different forces, the chief among which are presumably the original contraction of general demand, and the amplification of that contraction by the vicious circle of deflation. It may or may not be successfully reversed, but, if it is, the consequent increase in the consumers' income and in consumption will not be related to the Government's capital outlay by the " multiplier ". Once the corner is turned and general demand begins to expand, the widening process will be resumed, savings will increase, and the deepening process will become operative and will fill any gap that there may be between savings and the widening process.

Thus the question is how big the capital outlay must be to over-come the absorption of cash. If it is insufficient to do so, it will merely delay the progress of depression without breaking the vicious circle. If it is sufficient, it will bring into operation more powerful forces making for recovery, which will soon make its own continuance unnecessary.

The intervention of the Government with its public works, or other capital outlay, is a device for injecting money into the economic system. It is only called for at all on the assumption that the banking system cannot perform the necessary service.

Under modern conditions it is the function of the banks to irrigate the economic system with money. They inject money into the system by inducing a positive intermediate demand and causing a release of cash, or draw off money from it by inducing a negative intermediate demand and causing an absorption of cash. The purpose is to enlarge or to compress the flow of money.

If, when cash is released, the result is only to transfer goods which already exist from one set of traders to another, nothing is accomplished. The sellers absorb as much cash as the buyers release. To modify the consumers' income, the buying must take the form of increased orders to producers for increased productive activity (or for production at higher prices).

The banks have to irrigate two fields of very different sizes. One field, that reached through the channel of bank advances for working capital, consists of the whole range of production of material commodities other than capital installations. All such commodities, with insignificant exceptions, are destined to be sold to traders to form part of their stocks.

The other field, that reached through the channel of the investment market, consists of capital outlay.

Not only is the former field incomparably greater in extent than the latter, but the pressure of the rate of interest, light though it may be, is exerted more directly. The whole effect of any increase or decrease of the pressure is felt within the period in which traders turn over their stocks.

Capital outlay is a narrow field, in which the response is slow. Even when what is needed is a check to a credit expansion which is being directly caused by speculative borrowing, it is by no means certain that the check can be applied by a refusal to lend. A concerted refusal to lend is difficult to bring about. Banks are unwilling to offend their customers, and, unless the refusal to lend is universally enforced, the banks that do not apply it will reap a rich harvest at the expense of those that do. And even a universally observed refusal to lend to speculators may quite possibly result in an equal amount of credit being allowed to apparently legitimate borrowers, who make it available through one channel or another for speculation.

It may well be that in such a case the direct pressure on the investment market and the speculators must be supplemented by pressure on the wider field of borrowing for working capital.

REDUNDANT MONEY AND THE INFLATIONARY GAP

The idea that Government expenditure is the principal factor in monetary inflation and deflation is in part the outcome of the experience of wartime and post-war financial conditions in the present century. The inflationary effects of war finance are obvious to everyone, and, when the war effort comes to an end, the need for reducing Government expenditure and raising revenue to cover it is seen to be essential to checking the inflation.

When wartime expenditure far exceeds whatever revenue can be raised, the excess has to be met by borrowing. Government loans compete with the raising of capital by industry, and strain the resources of the investment market. If the resources of the investment market are insufficient, the deficiency constitutes an " inflationary gap ".

It was Sir Kingsley Wood's financial statement of 1941 that first formulated the budgetary problem of avoiding inflation in terms of the " gap ". He reckoned that towards a deficit of nearly £2,100 million, savings and unspent depreciation, along with external resources, and some other funds, would provide £1,600 million. The " potentially dangerous gap " was " of the order of £500 million ". Towards filling the gap, he imposed additional taxes to yield £150 million, and for the rest he relied on measures for stimulating additional saving.

The inflationary gap became the dominant consideration in wartime budgets, but the budgets failed to fill it. The savings required to cover the enormous deficits were found through controls. Imports of food and materials were almost entirely in Government hands, and other imports were restricted by licensing. Manufacturers, being dependent on the Government for their materials, were required to conform to directions; priority had to be given to the requirements of the war effort and to exports, so that spending on consumption at home was kept down. Capital outlay was closely controlled, not only through the supplies of materials, but through licensing and the control of capital issues.

By these controls supplies to home markets were severely curtailed, and the price controls limited the prices at which the supplies could be sold. The objects on which it was possible to spend, and the prices at which they could be bought being thus restricted, the total amount of private spending was effectively limited. The excess of the incomes, swollen by Government spending, over the total of private spending provided the requisite savings.

The money unspent was not all placed in war loans. But in so far as it was not so placed it remained in the form of bank balances and currency, and the banks held equivalent assets in Treasury bills, Treasury deposit receipts or medium-term Government securities. So the whole, whether lent to the Government or not, was at the Government's disposal.

Then was not the gap filled? The controls themselves prevented an inordinate rise of prices. But the *potentiality* of inflation persisted unsubdued. For along with the growing stock of redundant money, arrears of spending were accumulating. Replacements, renewals and repairs had to be postponed for want of labour and materials, and plant and property were deteriorating. Traders' stocks of goods were depleted, and one form which the restriction of spending took was shop shortages ; people found that things they wanted to buy were nowhere to be had.

Year by year during the war the budget was accompanied by a White Paper setting out an " Analysis of the Sources of War Finance and an Estimate of the National Income and Expenditure ". The analysis revealed a residue of expenditure uncovered by income, and mainly representing arrears of renewals and upkeep, and depletion of stocks. This was the gap, and it was cumulative : the total gap outstanding at the end was the aggregate of the preceding annual gaps.

The statistics did not bring out the full extent of the yearly addition to the gap. In the five years 1940-4 aggregate capital formation at home was estimated at £941 million, and aggregate provision required for depreciation and maintenance at £2,470 million (Cmd. 7099 of 1947). The latter figure, being based on income tax allowances, took little account of rising costs. And arrears were accumulating not only of replacements but of indispensable improvements, which industrial concerns provide for by accumulating reserves additional to the depreciation allowances. Nor did the White Papers make any separate estimate of the reduction of stocks, which is the most direct source of inflation. At the end of the war the accumulated inflationary gap took shape not only in a mass of redundant money, amounting to several thousands of millions, but in these immense arrears of spending, which threatened to transform the money into active demand.

The strain of war finance did not entirely subside till 1947, but in the latter part of 1946 it was eased by the American and Canadian loans. The budget of 1947 provided a surplus, and according to the doctrine of the gap, a budget surplus should be a safeguard against inflation. But no possible budget surplus could extinguish more than a small fraction of the redundant money.

In the philosophy of the gap the presence of the redundant money was left out of account. The persistence of inflationary pressure, which was only too obvious, was accepted fatalistically. It may be that the aggregate surpluses of the years 1947-8 to 1950-1, along with the proceeds of the American and Canadian loans, and the American aid under the European Recovery Programme, ought to have sufficed to extinguish the redundant money, or at any rate to reduce it within manageable limits. But the Government's own heavy capital disbursements used up much of these resources, and so much as went to extinguish the Government indebtedness to the banks was replaced by bank advances to customers. The total of bank deposits actually increased : less than no progress was made towards getting rid of the redundant money.

All the time, up to the change of Government in October 1951, the use of bank rate to restrain a monetary expansion was deliberately rejected. Under the disastrous conditions of depression and unemployment that prevailed in the nineteen-thirties, bank rate had been kept at its traditional minimum of 2 per cent, and market rates of discount had been no more than nominal. In the post-war years, when the dangers were *just the contrary*, the same conditions of extremely cheap money were adhered to. The urge to spend was unchecked by any consideration of insufficiency of cash resources or of the cost of raising cash, and the strain on the controls was so much the greater.

The rate of interest, it may be said, is not the only means by which banks can deter borrowers. They have the power of directly refusing to lend or limiting the amount that a customer may be permitted to borrow. During the post-war years it has been the practice of the Treasury to request the banks to restrict their advances to customers, and especially to refuse advances for the speculative holding of securities or commodities. In October 1949, after the devaluation of the pound, they were specifically exhorted, in their policy regarding credit facilities, to " use every endeavour to ensure that inflationary pressures are held in check ".

But experience has shown, not for the first time, that restrictive measures of this kind are no substitute for dear money. So long as advances " in the ordinary course of business " were unrestricted, the flow of orders from dealers to producers would continue unrestrained by financial considerations.

Much of the urge to spend was by way of capital outlay, especially arrears of replacements and upkeep. The unspent depreciation funds and undistributed profits went to swell free capital, and investment of the money in Government securities was the only alternative to holding it idle. The Government could therefore command an apparently inexhaustible market for its securities at any price it chose to name, and prices rose so high that the yield of Consols was brought down to $2\frac{1}{2}$ per cent towards the end of 1946. The Government's power over the price depended on the controls by which the demands on the investment market for capital outlay were restricted. It was no one's business to measure the demands thus determined against the resources accruing to the market from savings, and, when in the course of 1947 the demands expanded beyond the accruing resources, the prices of securities began to drop. That did not mean that a competitive rate of interest had been established, but only that the effect of the controls was less narrowly restrictive.

The rise in the long-term rate of interest was substantial. But a rise in the long-term rate is no substitute for a rise in the short-term rate, the dear money of tradition.

It is not to be supposed that a spell of dear money would have been sufficient by itself to remedy the post-war monetary troubles. It may be that rationing and price controls were anyhow necessary to secure an adequate flow of savings. Heroic measures might have been required to extinguish the redundant money. And all would have been in vain so long as inflation was in progress in the United States, and the pound was tied to the dollar by a fixed rate of exchange (to say nothing of devaluation).

The assumption of office by the Conservative Government in October 1951 was immediately followed by a change of policy. Bank rate, having been unchanged at 2 per cent for twelve years, was raised to $2\frac{1}{2}$ per cent, and four months later (March 1952) to 4. These were very tentative measures ; 4 per cent has not in the past been reckoned as " dear money ". The rise of bank rate was accompanied by a more rigorous concerted credit restriction. If the restriction goes so far as to refuse overdrafts to traders purchasing goods in the course of business to replenish their stocks, it may be more effective than in the past. At the time of writing (July 1952) it is not possible to judge what results are to be expected from the change of policy.

To the principle of the desirability of stability in the wealth-value of money it is nearly always possible to obtain ready assent, alike from economists, from bankers and from those concerned in public policy. But to obtain concurrence in practical measures for the application of the principle is not so easy.

We have seen (above, pp. 64-8) how any departure from stability is apt to start a vicious circle of expansion or contraction with indefinitely amplifying effects. If stability is to be secured, *prompt measures* are necessary to counteract any incipient lapse before the vicious circle is joined. It is the special virtue of bank rate that it can be promptly applied ; it can be altered not merely at a week's but at an hour's notice. And the rate imposed, the pressure applied, can be delicately adjusted to the circumstances of the moment. We shall be returning to these considerations in our concluding chapter.

THE AMERICAN STOCK MARKET SPECULATION OF 1926-9

The real explanation of the great Stock Market speculation in the United States, which culminated in 1929, was the belated discovery that the prices of stocks and shares had not been adequately adjusted to the enormous change in the value of money. The national income (and therefore general demand) had more than doubled since 1914, and, if the price level had not doubled, that was only because technological progress had steadily reduced real costs ; the economic activity which received a national income more than doubled in terms of monetary units produced 40 or 50 per cent more goods than in 1914.

It was not the business of the monetary authorities to prevent this adjustment of value. A complete elimination of speculative borrowing would still have left the buyers and sellers of securities to act on their opinions of what prices ought to be and their opinions would not necessarily have differed much from those of the speculators.

What brought the speculation to an end in October 1929, was not the high rates of interest charged on call money or any other deterrent on speculative borrowing. The speculators were sublimely indifferent to such obstacles. It was the industrial activity which showed signs of slackening in the summer of 1929. That meant that general demand was declining. If bank rate policy has any meaning, the purpose of the measures of credit restriction systematically applied from July 1928 to November 1929, can only have been to cause a decline in general demand. Only after this slackening of activity had been in progress for several months did the Stock Market speculation collapse.

Moreover, it is significant that whereas the industrial recession gained momentum in the last months of 1929 and throughout 1930, there was at first a *recovery* in the Stock Market, which continued till April 1930. Thereafter the rapidly growing industrial depression dragged down the Stock Market. By 1932 the national income had fallen by more than half in comparison with 1929, and the index of industrial share prices which had touched 216 in September 1929 and was still as high as 170 in April 1930, had fallen to 32.

This course of events points to the conclusion that it was the state of industrial activity that was affected by the measures of credit restriction, and that the Stock Market speculation was eventually affected by the decline of industrial activity. That does not mean that the industrial activity was wholly cause and the Stock Market speculation wholly effect. The speculation was the cause of the creation of a certain amount of credit, which was added to the resources of the Stock Market, and was reflected in an expansion of new flotations and capital outlay. It may well be that if the credit restriction had been less severe, a dangerous inflation would have started. But the inflationary tendency was counteracted by the restrictive measures not in the investment market, where it had its source, but in the sphere of industry and commerce where its impact was to be felt.

The Stock Market speculation was without doubt a lamentable exhibition of cupidity. But when a market has to correct mistaken estimates of value on a large scale, great opportunities of gain are inevitably offered to those who are in a position to deal in it, and it is hardly fair to blame them if they get excited. When it is the Stock Market that is involved, the outside public are free to deal. In the end, the over-valuation of shares at its most extravagant height was not more absurd than the under-valuation in, say, 1923, when the index was 66·6 and no trace of the speculative fury had appeared, and the irrationality of either is thrown into the shade by the state of the market in 1932, when the index fell to 32.

All these vagaries may have been deplorable, but the idea that the speculation was a serious economic danger in itself, apart from the tendency to inflation, is a delusion. It is often contended that every boom is inevitably followed by a slump. If by a boom is meant an *excessive* rise in the prices of shares, it is undoubtedly likely to be followed by a fall, and may be followed, though by no means necessarily, by an excessive fall. But boom and slump alike in the stock exchange are local disorders. They are not necessarily connected with the states of industrial activity and depression by which the economic life of the world is so profoundly affected. The confusion between them is one more of the errors arising from the attempts to find the causation of trade depressions in the long-term investment market.

TECHNOLOGICAL UNEMPLOYMENT

Hitherto we have referred to technological progress primarily in relation to the deepening of capital, and to the problems of obsolescence and depreciation. It has another aspect, to which we have made passing reference, that which is commonly called technological unemployment.

Technological unemployment is a subject which extends somewhat beyond the strict limits covered by Capital and Employment, for, besides the displacement of labour by new instruments, it includes the displacement of labour from industries or processes which have been superseded for other reasons than the appearance of such instruments. But even displacements of the latter kind are not wholly unrelated to the capital market; they are almost inevitably accompanied by some displacement of old capital by new, the installation of which is a part of the activities of the investment market.

When a new labour-saving device is introduced into industry, the immediate effect is to dispense with a number of workpeople, whose incomes thereupon cease to accrue. On the other hand, the saving of cost will presumably be reflected in the price charged to the consumers of the product affected. The reduction of price, if substantial, will result in increased sales. If the demand for the product is elastic, and sales increase more than in proportion to the reduction of price, there may on balance be an increase in the amount of labour employed in the industry as a whole.

It cannot be taken for granted, however, that the amount of labour employed on the product is in exact proportion to the price charged to the consumer. The price must cover interest and depreciation and the proportion constituting profit, being composed of the margins secured by traders at all stages of production and sale, will not be always constant. The ultimate effect of a change in methods of production may be either to increase or to decrease this proportion, but the immediate effect is likely to be to increase it. The reduction of price to the limit permitted by the saving of cost will be arrived at gradually. If a considerable extension of capacity becomes necessary, it may take many years. Every fresh extension results in an experimental reduction of price, and only after the market has been tested will a further extension be embarked upon.

In the case where the demand for the product is inelastic there is a definite reduction of employment. It may be that the new process requires the installation of new instruments, the production of which *for a time* will employ more labour than the old process itself. But it would be a mistake to conclude that the demand for labour would be made up in this way even temporarily. For the new instruments are paid for through the investment market; they use up part of the resources available for the deepening of capital, and leave so much less of those resources for deepening in other directions. Only if the new process offers such attractive prospects of gain that it evokes speculative borrowing, and supplements the resources of the investment market with a creation of credit, will additional employment be given.

When unemployment is caused by a displacement of labour, there is no immediate disequilibrium. The aggregate output of the community and the consumers' income are *both reduced*, and there is not necessarily any inequality between output and general demand. Theoretically there is a disequilibrium in that there is an excess supply of labour in the market, which should result in a reduction of wages till it is absorbed, and under some social conditions this tendency would be a practical reality. But in the kind of community that interests us it may be practically inoperative.

If the new process is to add anything to the resources of the community, the labour displaced must be given employment in other industries. The demand for the products of these other industries must begin to expand. Some positive action is required to start the movement, to stimulate demand *before* it is increased by the spending power of the re-employed workmen.

This can be brought about by a suitable measure of credit relaxation, inducing traders to hasten and increase their purchases of goods for stock. That will enable industry to take on additional labour.

But that is not a complete solution, for the problem is twofold. Not only must there be an adequate demand for labour, but the openings offered must be such that the workpeople are able to fill them. If the workpeople are too specialised, they may be unable to take the work offered in industries strange to them. This is a difficulty which does not arise from a contraction in general demand as such, causing unemployment more or less in all branches of industry; it is especially characteristic of the unemployment arising from a dislocation of industry, a change calling for a transfer of productive resources from one set of industries to another. We cannot easily generalise about it, for the adaptability of labour to new occupations and its willingness to move into them will depend on circumstances. But it may be mentioned that recent experience goes to show that the transfer of labour into new occupations is by no means so difficult as it has sometimes been represented to be. In the course of each of the two World Wars an enormous amount of skilled and semi-skilled labour was rapidly made available for the purposes of war industries. Even under more normal conditions every new industry and in great part any industry that is rapidly expanding must be supplied with labour by transfer from other industries. The prevalent belief that there are great obstacles in the way of the adaptation of workpeople to new occupations has been based on the experience of times of depression, when there has been little demand for additional labour even in the more prosperous industries. But evidently we cannot infer from such experience that there will be any great difficulty in absorbing labour at a time of normal activity, when the most active industries require a rapid influx of new workpeople.

If there really are insurmountable obstacles to the absorption of the displaced labour, an attempt to eliminate unemployment by way of an enlargement of general demand will fail. Prices and profits will rise in industry generally, and the additional demand for labour, which is intended to absorb the surplus, is likely soon to spend itself in raising wages. When wages have risen in proportion to prices, there is no longer any additional demand for labour.

On the other hand, if the displaced labour is able and willing to enter new industries, it is essential that an enlargement of general demand be started. It is futile to adopt schemes for making the unemployed workpeople competent and willing to enter new occupations, if the way to an increase in the total amount of employment in the community is barred, and every man who is found employment merely displaces someone else.

Given a sufficient expansion of demand, one other thing is necessary to give the displaced labour employment in other industries, that is capital equipment. In other words, in so far as spare capacity does not already exist, there must be a widening of capital. A shortage of capital equipment may itself be a cause of unemployment. The production of additional capital equipment would give employment, but even that requires spare capacity and adaptability of labour.

The importance of technological unemployment ought not to be exaggerated. The introduction of new instruments, new processes and new industries is usually gradual, and the amount of labour in course of being displaced at any one time is not likely to be very great. Industry is always finding employment both for young people growing up and for numerous older workpeople who pass into new or expanding industries. It is not certain that this tendency will not be sufficient by itself to maintain the normal demand for labour.

Technological unemployment diminishes the consumers' income, but the diminution is not caused by an absorption of cash. There probably will be some absorption of cash by the industry affected, for producers will finish off contracts at the former price, and the change to the new labour-saving process is not likely to be so sudden as to involve the retail dealers in loss. But this absorption of cash

is a consequence of the reduction of incomes, and is not essel
to it.

MARX'S RESERVE ARMY OF LABOUR

Marx's explanation of unemployment and the trade cycle was really based upon technological unemployment. Marx accepted Ricardo's conception of working capital as a store of wage-goods and materials, accumulated in advance of a productive operation, to be gradually drawn upon during the productive process, so that the whole value of this store would be embodied in the final product. The value of the final product has to replace the value of the materials and a portion of the value of the instrumental capital used, representing depreciation. These compose what Marx called the constant capital. The wage-goods, " the subsistence fund of the labourers ", he called the variable capital.

The variable capital of an entire community was the wage-fund of the classical economists. Marx poured scorn on the wage-fund as an explanation of the rate of wages. But he did not escape from the principle that the variable capital constituted the *demand for labour*.

The variable capital was variable because the value that it contributed to the product exceeded the value of the labour applied in production. The excess was the " surplus ", upon which Marx's doctrine of exploitation rested.

The contradiction which he held to be inherent in Capitalism consisted in the inordinate tendency of the capitalists to accumulate out of their surplus, and Marx was confronted with the paradox that a growth of capital, so long as the relative proportions of its variable and constant constituents remained unchanged, meant a growing demand for labour, and a consequent rise of wages. Ricardo, pursuing the same line of reasoning, had reached the conclusion that the rise of wages would so encroach on profits that accumulation would be discouraged, and eventually be brought to a dead stop. An indefinite shrinkage of the surplus would strike at the foundations of Marx's doctrines, both of exploitation of labour and of excessive accumulation.

Ricardo himself had provided Marx with a ready answer. The tendency of profits to fall " is happily checked at repeated intervals by the improvements in machinery connected with the production of necessaries, as well as by discoveries in the science of agriculture, which enable us to relinquish a portion of labour before required " (*Principles*, Chapter VI).

9

Accumulation, so long as it is limited to the widening of capital, increases the demand for labour in proportion. But, in so far as there is deepening, it does not.

In Marx's phraseology, if accumulation is devoted to the constant constituent of capital, and the variable constituent remains unchanged, there is no increase in the demand for labour.

By adopting labour-saving devices, the capitalists could counteract the effect of accumulation in increasing the demand for labour and raising wages. They could create a reserve army of unemployed, the equivalent of a surplus population competing in the labour market, and driven perhaps to accept a subsistence wage.

Marx attributed the " violent fluctuations " of the trade cycle to an alternation of widening and deepening. An excess of widening would absorb the reserve army of unemployed, and raise wages ; deepening would then supervene, and carry the saving of labour to such a pitch as to reconstitute the reserve army.

This would be no explanation of the fluctuations unless there were a tendency for deepening to overshoot the mark, and to continue for a considerable time after the demand for labour had fallen off, and before a renewal of widening had set in. Widening, however, claims priority over deepening, for, while the marginal deepening yields only interest, widening yields the profit attaching to additional output. Indeed, according to Marx, only the variable capital can yield surplus. Therefore capitalists must be expected to take immediate advantage of any opportunity of expanding it. They would promptly absorb the surplus labour, and no reserve would ever be formed.

It is true that Marx's theory, as elaborated in the third volume of *Capital*, makes the power of competition distribute the surplus among the capitalists in proportion to their total capital. If that occurred automatically and immediately, deepening would earn profit no less than widening. A capitalist would not apply his accumulations to the substitution of plant for labour unless the saving were sufficient to yield him the market rate of profit on the capital cost of the plant.

There would thus be no preference for widening over deepening. They would proceed concurrently. If deepening went too far, and widening failed to provide employment for the displaced labour, the total surplus would shrink and the rate of profit (or interest) would fall. At the same time the labour market would be eased, and wages would tend to fall. On both counts deepening would become less attractive. Accumulation would therefore have to take the form of

widening. Marx never gave any reason why there should be delay in the absorption of the reserve army. It is " for its own varying needs in the way of self-expansion " that " capital creates an ever-ready supply of human material fit for exploitation ". But why should capital hesitate to exploit the human material ? Only full employment yields the maximum surplus, and it is not clear why on Marx's assumptions there should ever be anything less than full employment, except of course for the frictional unemployment inseparable from any structural change in the productive system. Structural changes are bound to cause some displacement of labour and some intervals of idleness even in a collectivist community.

Evidently a balance has to be reached between the two parts of accumulation, the widening which increases the demand for labour and the deepening which increases the supply of labour.

If widening is pushed too far, it forces up wages, and reduces and ultimately extinguishes the profit margin. Widening therefore will stop at the point where it still secures a " normal " profit margin, and the residue of accumulation will then be applied to deepening. If deepening is carried too far, wages will fall relatively to prices, the cost-saving capacity of labour-saving plant will be diminished, and profit-margins will increase.

The governing factor is thus the *normal rate of profit*, the terms on which capitalists in general are willing to exploit productive resources. Marx assumes competition to prevail among capitalists, but as we have seen (above, pp. 32-3) the prevalence of a normal rate of profit is consistent with competition.

Interest enters into the matter only as the means of selecting among the various projects of deepening. The amount applicable to deepening is the residue of accumulation after meeting the prior claims of widening.

Marx emphatically repudiated the theory of the economists who regarded " the expansion and the contraction of credit as the causes of the vicissitudes of the industrial cycle, when really the movements of credit are nothing more than symptoms of the phases of the industrial cycle ". But he failed to prove his alternative explanation.

CHAPTER VI

MONETARY ANALYSIS AND THE INVESTMENT MARKET

CONSUMERS' INCOME AND OUTLAY

IN the propositions of economics an algebraical notation has the advantage of a precision which cannot always be attained by the literary contrivances of language. That is so, not merely because the same symbol must always represent unequivocally the same idea, but also because, to justify the simple relations of *plus* and *minus*, we are compelled to settle a number of questions of definition which could otherwise be left open.

The purpose of this chapter is to provide an analytical background for the two preceding chapters. But it contains no subtle or abstruse mathematical calculations. It is devoted to elucidating the mutual relations of a number of variables employed in monetary theory, but the relations are of the simplest, and the primary interest is in adapting the definitions of the variables to these simple relations.

Consumers' income I define to be the total income of the community expressed in monetary units. Consumers' outlay is the total expenditure *out of income*, including expenditure on investment.

Consumers' cash balances are those balances (of currency and bank credit) which are fed from income.

If all income were paid into these balances and they were fed from no other source, the consumers' outlay could be simply identified with the disbursements from them. But in practice there are some incomes which are not paid in cash; for example, wages paid in kind, and profits which are not drawn out of a business but are treated as income reinvested in it. In such cases we regard a single act as combining the receipt and expenditure of income.

And consumers' cash balances are also fed by some receipts other than income, such as the proceeds of sale of securities or property, gifts, bequests, etc. These I call *extraneous receipts*, and the consumers' outlay in any interval of time is arrived at by deducting from the total disbursements out of the consumers' cash balances the extraneous receipts in that interval.

Traders' cash balances are the balances held for business purposes. They comprise, in fact, all the currency and bank credit

132

outstanding, other than the consumers' cash balances. A trader is anyone who incurs costs in the course of his business. His costs are met from his cash balance, and his receipts are credited to it. His income is the net profit which, in so far as it is not reinvested in the business, he draws out and places in the private cash balance belonging to him in his capacity as consumer.

The definition of a trader as one who incurs costs in his business must not be pressed too far. We can treat minor occupational expenses, which do not justify the maintenance of a separate business cash balance, as " extraneous outlay " or negative income. There may be people who keep no separate business balances, but who nevertheless incur costs on so considerable a scale that they must be classed as traders. In such cases the undivided cash balances are best regarded as exclusively business balances, so that the holders of them are deemed to keep their private balances always at zero, and their consumers' outlay always to be equal to their consumers' income (including reinvested profits).

The cash balance of any trading concern is a part of its capital, and payments from the balance are not payments out of income; they merely change so much capital from one form into another. Accordingly they are not part of the consumers' outlay.

When either a trader or a consumer becomes indebted to a bank, the indebtedness is to be treated as a negative cash balance. The excess (positive or negative) of the cash balances of any group of people over their indebtedness to the banks we call their net cash resources.

$$
\begin{aligned}
&\text{Let selling value of output} &&= A, \\
&\text{disposals for consumption or use} &&= A', \\
&\text{consumers' income} &&= B, \\
&\text{consumers' outlay} &&= B', \\
&\text{traders' cash balances} &&= C, \\
&\text{consumers' cash balances} &&= C', \\
&\text{traders' indebtedness to banks} &&= D, \\
&\text{consumers' indebtedness to banks} &&= D', \\
&\text{traders' net cash resources} &&= C - D = M, \\
&\text{consumers' net cash resources} &&= C' - D' = M'.
\end{aligned}
$$

Output here comprises every kind of economic activity. From such economic activity incomes are derived. Apart from the simple case of personal service rendered direct from producer to consumer without the intervention of any trader, incomes take the form either of costs (such as wages, salaries, interest or rent) or of profits. One trader's payments for intermediate products or materials are the receipts of another, and consequently they cannot ultimately be regarded as costs. The same applies to such payments when included in what we have called extraneous outlay. These are not included in disposals but their value is covered by the proceeds of sale of the commodities in the production of which they have been used. But we cannot draw the simple conclusion that $A = B$, for there is one category of costs by which incomes are not generated; that is depreciation. The selling value of output has to provide a margin sufficient to cover, over and above all other costs, the continuing loss of value of capital through the approach of the time when it must be discarded on account of wear, obsolescence or any other cause, and will have to be replaced.

If the necessary allowance for depreciation be K', we have $B = A - K'$.

There are, it is true, some incomes which correspond to no current output, such as interest on the unproductive national debt, and various gratuitous pensions and benefits. These are best treated not as incomes at all, but as extraneous receipts. We regard the Government as a " trader " supplying law, order, administration and military force to the community, and receiving payment in the form of taxation. We can regard these transfer incomes as part of the cost of Government, or, perhaps preferably in the case of the gratuitous pensions and benefits, we can regard them not as incomes at all but as extraneous receipts. The taxes paid to the Government are included, in their entirety, in the consumers' outlay, but a part of that section of outlay is for providing these extraneous receipts and not for meeting the cost of Government properly so called.

Similarly we regard any charitable institution which incurs costs as a " trader ". Contributions from its subscribers are included in consumers' outlay, and the salaries and wages received from it are included in consumers' income. The sums received by its beneficiaries are not income but extraneous receipts.

WORKING CAPITAL AND INVESTMENT

In any interval of time, t, let C, C', D, D', M, M', be increased by c, c', d, d', m, m' (any of which may be negative quantities).

Then $(B - B')t$, the excess of consumers' income over consumers' outlay, is equal to $c' - d'$ or m', the increase in consumers' net cash resources.

$(A - A')t$, the excess of output over disposals, is the addition made to working capital, that is to say, goods destined for sale and not yet sold, whether in course of production, in transit or in stock, together with materials or intermediate products that are to be used up in the processes of production.

Let the working capital in monetary units be E, and let the increment of working capital in the interval, t, be e, so that E becomes $E + e$, and

$$(A - A')t = e.$$

Disposals, it will be remembered, are sales to final purchasers. In the case of a consumable product the final purchaser is he who acquires it for consumption. In the case of an instrument the final purchaser is he who acquires it for use as an instrument. We regard people who consume or use their own products as " final purchasers " from themsleves.

Disposals include consumers' capital outlay. When a house is sold for the purchaser's occupation, we regard the purchaser as undertaking capital outlay without the intervention of the investment market, and we exclude the transaction from our definition of investment [1] (above, p. 56). Consumers' capital outlay and consumption together we will call direct outlay, so that consumers' outlay is equal to direct outlay *plus* investment.

Direct outlay, together with traders' gross capital outlay, makes up disposals. Traders' gross capital outlay includes, besides the purchase and installation of instrumental goods, every outlay properly chargeable to capital account : the technical fees to engineers, architects and others, for planning the installations ; the " invisible " capital charges on flotations, underwriting commissions, etc. ; even some outlays on the creation of goodwill, though it is not easy to define the limitations of this last item.

All this expenditure, being met from the traders' capital resources, is not a part of the consumers' outlay. The traders' capital resources are fed from the investment market by the raising of capital, and the investment market in turn is fed by investment, which is included in the consumers' outlay. Investment includes reinvested profits, in which investment and the raising of capital are both merged.

We shall find it convenient to distinguish the capital resources of the investment market from those of the other traders. The characteristic of the former is that they are employed exclusively in

---

[1] Investment here is what I have called Market Investment in my *Currency and Credit* (fourth edition, p. 63).

buying and selling securities. The rest of the traders' capital we shall refer to under the heading of Industry, a term here given an extended meaning to cover all those forms of economic activity that use instruments of production.[1]

Since the investment market's capital is invested only in securities and not in capital goods, the resources of the traders who are the final purchasers of capital goods are to be found exclusively in Industry. Industry raises capital by selling securities to the investment market, and the investment market sells securities to investors, thus serving as a channel between the investors who save and the traders who incur capital outlay.

Investment includes not only the purchase of securities in the usual sense of stocks, shares, debentures, bonds and mortgages, but the acquisition of any rights or interests in trading concerns or income-yielding enterprises. Undistributed profits of any concern count as income reinvested in it by the shareholders or proprietors. Life insurance premiums count as income invested in the assets held by the insurance companies.

Since the private investor not only buys securities but also sells them, investment will be a net amount, the excess of securities purchased over those sold. The speculative investor, who obtains a bank advance in order to take what he regards as a favourable opportunity to buy securities, we regard as anticipating income. Perhaps we should treat the pure speculator, who obtains an advance to buy securities for the express purpose of selling them at a profit, as a " trader ", and include him in the investment market; but, alternatively, we can, if we choose, treat his purchases as investments out of income, and the proceeds of his sales and of the loans from his broker as extraneous receipts to be deducted from these disbursements in arriving at the consumers' outlay.

Let consumption . . . . $= G$
direct outlay . . . . $= H$
investment . . . . $= I$
traders' gross capital outlay . $= K$

Then $H + I$ = consumers' outlay, B'
$H + K$ = disposals, A'
$H - G$ = consumers' capital outlay
$K - K'$ = traders' net capital outlay (capital added)
$K - K' + H - G$ = net capital outlay.

---

[1] It even covers the capital assets other than securities and cash held by the investment market itself, e.g. office accommodation and furniture.

CAPITAL RAISED

We will denote by I' the capital raised by industry. Capital raised is to include not only the new issues and existing securities sold to the investment market, but also reinvested profits, which are likewise included in investment, though they do not pass through the market. Capital raised is, like investment, a net amount, securities purchased or redeemed by traders being set off against those sold. When a trader gives credit to a customer he is regarded as buying a " security ", the customer's debt. It will be observed that, for the purposes of the idea of capital raised, we regard a trader's capital as comprising his instrumental capital, his working capital and his cash, but not his securities. The securities represent so much of his free capital as he is not using in his own business.

The investment market receives I and disburses I', and there results a change in its net cash resources equal to the difference between I and I'. But this does not cover all the transactions of the investment market, for securities may be bought and sold not only by traders and consumers, but by banks. When a bank lends to a trader, D and C are increased by equal amounts, and there is no change in the traders' net cash resources, $C - D$, or M. But when a bank buys securities, the investment market is credited with the proceeds, and C is increased, while, since there is no corresponding increase in traders' indebtedness, D, there is an equal increase in M.[1]

This increase in M takes the form of an increase in the net cash resources of the investment market. In view of the prevalent practice of carrying securities with borrowed money, the net cash resources of the investment market are likely to be a negative quantity. We will denote by F the *net indebtedness* of the investment market to the banks, so that the market's net cash resources are $- F$. Since the net cash resources of all traders are M, those of industry, being all traders other than the investment market, are $M + F$.

If S be the securities held by banks, and if F and S become $F + f$ and $S + s$ in time, t, then :

$$(I' - I)t = f + s.$$

[1] Alternatively, D is decreased, and there is no corresponding decrease in C. The indebtedness, D and D', to be deducted from cash balances to arrive at net cash resources is *short-term* indebtedness. In drawing the line between it and the securities to be included in S, we count bills in the former and mortgages in the latter. The distinction is more defensible on practical than on theoretical grounds.

DEPRECIATION

The traders procure the means of paying for their gross capital outlay partly by raising capital to the amount, I', and partly by intercepting a portion, K', of the proceeds of sale of goods in the form of a depreciation allowance. The total amount at the disposal of industry for gross capital outlay we will denote by J. $J = I' + K'$.

If (in this context) we give the name gross profits to the excess of selling value of output over all costs other than depreciation, then gross profits are equal to net profits *plus* depreciation. If R be gross profits reinvested, and R' be net profits reinvested, we have :

$$R = R' + K'.$$

The net profits reinvested appear in both investment and capital raised. If we deduct this common portion from both, we find $I - R' =$ securities sold by the investment market to investors, and $I' - R' =$ securities bought from industry. Also $I' - R' = J - R$, and $B - R' = A - R$.

The depreciation allowance appropriate to any concern is a matter of opinion ; it depends on estimates of the remaining life of each piece of plant. The time within which plant will be worn out is uncertain enough, while the chances of premature obsolescence or accidental destruction are incalculable.[1] Consequently the division of R into the parts R' and K', or of J into the parts I' and K', is not a matter of objective fact.

The same applies to the division of K into depreciation and capital added. Except for actual replacements of plant which is being scrapped, there is nothing to distinguish capital goods that are paid for out of depreciation from capital goods that are paid for out of capital raised.

Depreciation is to be regarded not as paying for an identifiable section of capital goods, but rather as a debit or lien attaching to the output of capital goods as a whole. Only the excess of the capital goods remaining after this debit has been discharged is available to satisfy the demand represented by investment.

The depreciation allowance of a concern may simply be re-invested in the concern itself, increasing its assets (or diminishing its liabilities). It is then indistinguishable from capital raised by the concern through net profits reinvested. Or it may be invested in

---

[1] Depreciation includes insurance against fire, shipwreck, etc. The chances of loss can, of course, be estimated *approximately* for the purposes of insurance premiums.

securities acquired by the concern for the purpose. In that case the money is being made available through the investment market for the capital requirements of other traders.

If the depreciation allowance is miscalculated, the result is a compensating error in the net profits reinvested. If the depreciation allowance exceeds the gross profits reinvested, the net profits reinvested are a negative quantity, and appear as such in I and also in I'. The capital raised by the concern is a negative quantity in the sense that its capital assets have been reduced and its share capital ought to be written down.

We may call output, *minus* depreciation, net output, and disposals *minus* depreciation, net disposals. Then net output is equal to consumers' income, and net disposals are equal to direct outlay, *plus* capital added. $(A - K' = B, \quad A' - K' = H + K - K'.)$ We might have employed net output and net disposals instead of output and disposals in our equations. That would have meant treating the capital goods sold to traders, to the amount required to make good depreciation, not as a part of output at all, but as a part of the cost of production of net output. Depreciation would then, like other costs, generate incomes through the production of these capital goods.

Or we might have defined consumers' income to mean *income distributed*, excluding from it the net profits reinvested. Income distributed $= B - R' = A - R$. The corresponding outlay, investment and capital raised would be $B' - R'$, $I - R'$ and $I' - R'$ or $J - R$.

But the equations as we have framed them are nearer to the facts. In dealing with consumers' income or with investment, we must take account of depreciation in spite of all its uncertainties, for it governs people's beliefs as to what they can legitimately regard as income or as an acquisition of capital, and it is essential to the definition of capital added. But in dealing with output and disposals, any such departure from a purely objective measure is unnecessary and therefore undesirable.

So much of the sum, J, available to industry for the purchase of capital goods as is not spent is added to the other capital resources of industry. These other capital resources, which are composed of working capital and net cash resources, we will call circulating capital, and denote by L. If l be the increment of L in time, t, then :

$$(J - K)t = l,$$
$$L = E + M + F,$$
$$l = e + m + f.$$

ABSORPTION AND RELEASE OF CASH

Whereas one part, H, of the consumers' outlay finds its destination immediately in an equal amount of purchases of goods, the remainder, I, follows a more devious path. It travels first into the investment market, whence, modified by the change of net cash resources, $f + s$, it emerges as I', the capital raised by industry. I' then joins forces with K', the depreciation allowance, to make a total, J, and finally, after an increment (or decrement) of the circulating capital of industry, l, has been provided, a sum, K, is spent on capital goods.

$$H + K = A',$$
$$H + I = B'.$$

Therefore, $\qquad\qquad B' - A' = I - K$

and, since $\qquad\qquad K' = J - I',$
$$(B' - A' + K')t = (J - K)t + (I - I')t$$
$$= l - f - s.$$

Thus $(B' - A' + K')t$, the excess of consumers' outlay over net disposals, or the portion of the consumers' outlay which fails to materialise in demand, is composed of $(I - I')t$, the difference between capital raised and investment, and $(J - K)t$, the difference between capital raised and capital added.

We may regard the net cash resources of various groups, the circulating capital, and the working capital as pools, and consumers' income and outlay, output and disposals, investment, capital raised and capital added as streams connecting the pools together.

The change of level in any pool in the interval of time, t, is the difference between the inflow and the outflow. When the disbursements of any group of people exceed their receipts, they release cash ; when their receipts exceed their disbursements, they absorb cash. There may be a release or an absorption of cash at any of the pools.

For consumers an absorption of cash is the difference between consumers' income and consumers' outlay.

An absorption $\qquad\qquad m' = (B - B')t$;

a release, $\qquad\qquad -m' = (B' - B)t.$

For the investment market, f is the release of cash, while the release of cash through the purchase of securities by the banks is s, and
$$f + s = (I' - I)t.$$

The release of cash by the banks and the investment market is the excess of capital raised over investment.

For industry the release of cash is composed of $A - A'$, the excess of output over disposals, together with $K - J$, the excess of capital added over capital raised.

$$(A - A')t + (K - J)t = e - l.$$

That is to say, the release of cash is the excess of the increment of working capital, e, over the increment of circulating capital, l. Circulating capital is the provision made by industry for working capital and cash, and whatever is not used for working capital is added to cash.

The release of cash by industry may be arrived at in another way. For the receipts of industry are composed of direct outlay, H, and capital raised, I', while disbursements $= B$. The release of cash is $(B - H - I')t$ or $(B - B' + I - I')t$. In fact the release of cash by industry is necessarily equal to the absorption of cash by the consumers, the investment market and the banks, or $m' - f - s$.

Since $\qquad\qquad A - B = K' = J - I'$

and $\qquad\qquad B' - I = H = A' - K,$

$$(A - A') - (B - B') + (I' - I) - (J - K) = 0,$$

or $\qquad\qquad e - m' + f + s - l = 0.$

Thus $\qquad\qquad B - B' + I - I' = A - A' + K - J,$

and $\qquad\qquad e - l = m' - f - s.$

For traders in the aggregate a release of cash $= -m = e - l + f$. This is equal to the absorption of cash by consumers and banks or $m' - s$.

Finally, the release of cash by the banks is equal to the absorption of cash by consumers and traders together, or $s = m + m'$.

We can express the equations in terms of net output and net disposals by making $K' = 0$, so that $A = B$, $K =$ capital added, and $J = I'$.

SECURITIES AND NEW FLOTATIONS

Again, we can give the equations a different form if we denote all the securities held by traders, both in industry and in the investment market, by U, and the new flotations by N. We will call the circulating capital of all traders V, so that $V = E + M = L - F$. If u and v be the increments of U and V in time t, then:

$$(N - I)t = u + s,$$
$$(N - K + K')t = u + v,$$
$$(I - K + K')t = v - s.$$

Capital raised is a more significant factor than new flotations, and therefore this alternative form of the equations is less useful than that which employs J and I'.

Since $F =$ the securities held by the investment market against bank advances, $U - F =$ those held by traders (including the investment market) with their own capital.

$$(N - I')t = u - f.$$

The increment, u, must include any gain or loss of value of the securities composing U, either when the gain or loss is realised in an actual sale, or alternatively whenever the market prices of securities change.[1]   If we choose the latter alternative, the gain is added to reinvested profits, R' (or the loss is deducted from them), and each of the quantities A, A', B, B', I, I', J and H is increased by the same amount.   The profit on the securities is treated as remuneration for the " service " of dealing in them, and that service is included (along with such charges as brokers' commission) in H, the value of goods and services sold direct to consumers.   When a trader realises a profit on securities sold to the investment market, his operations are an " intermediate product ", leading up to the finished product, the services rendered by the investment market to consumers.

When new money is invested in the investment market itself, e.g. to increase the capital of stock jobbers or investment companies (whether through an issue of securities to investors or the reinvestment of profits), this is included in I.   The immediate effect is to reduce F, the net indebtedness of the investment market, but, if the sum so made available is invested in securities, F remains unchanged and I' is increased.   Thus investment in the investment market has precisely the same effect as investment in industry.

Investment in new banking capital has in the first instance the same effects as a sale of securities by the banks ; the banks absorb cash to the amount of the investment.   But if the banks put their new capital in securities, the absorption of cash is undone, and here also the result is equivalent to an investment in industry.

This applies equally to the case where the new banking capital takes the form of reinvested profits.   When a bank receives income from interest and other sources it absorbs cash.   When it incurs costs on salaries, etc., or when it distributes dividends, it releases

---

[1] We only take account of the gain or loss on securities *held by traders*.   We do not include in income either the gain or loss on securities held by investors (consumers) or on the fixed capital in the hands of traders, represented by those securities.

cash. Banks sometimes create hidden reserves by excluding from their declared profits the profit from appreciation of securities. If they took credit for the appreciation, their accounts would show it as reinvested profits, increasing the value of the securities in their balance sheets by the appropriate amount.

To allow for these cases, we must define S as the result of deducting the capital, surplus and undivided profits of the banks from their holding of securities and their physical capital (buildings, etc.).

When a trading concern incurs a loss on its trading operations, that counts as negative income or extraneous outlay to its proprietors. Even if profits distributed are *nil*, the reinvested net profit, R', is a negative quantity. When a non-profit-making concern on a mutual or charitable basis incurs a loss, that is negative income to its subscribers. The loss in either case may be met from balances or temporary borrowing, occasioning a release of cash, or it may be covered by capital raised, e.g. through a sale of securities or borrowing otherwise than from banks.

The Government and other public bodies with powers of taxation resemble mutual trading concerns. A deficit is negative income to the taxpayers ; it is so to the taxpayers *as a body*, for the share of any one taxpayer in it is a matter of hypothesis. A government differs from other traders in that it can take special powers to release cash without limit through inflationary legislation.

THE FOREIGN EXCHANGE MARKET

In our analysis we have not as yet taken any account of foreign trade or the foreign exchange market. Exporters and people who become creditors abroad receive payment from the foreign exchange market ; importers and people who become debtors abroad make payment to it. The market acquires the credits abroad of the former, and assumes the liabilities abroad of the latter.

Those who receive payment from the foreign exchange market find their net cash resources increased, and are in a position to release cash ; those who make payment to the market find their net cash resources reduced, and will have to absorb cash. There will on balance probably be a release or absorption of cash, and this will reflect the position of the foreign exchange market itself, which will be releasing or absorbing cash according as its disbursements at home exceed or fall short of its receipts. When the market acquires a net credit abroad it releases cash at home ; when it assumes a net debit abroad it absorbs cash at home.

Exports and other operations ending in sales abroad generate incomes just like any other economic activities. But the goods, services or securities sold abroad are diverted from the consumers' outlay, so that a gap is created between the consumers' outlay and the supply of objects upon which it may be spent. The gap is filled by the goods, services and securities acquired from abroad. If, as is in general the case, the gap is not exactly filled, the excess or deficiency corresponds to the absorption or release of cash by the foreign exchange market.

The foreign exchange market is composed mainly of banks. It plays much the same part in our analysis as the purchase and sale of securities by banks. In fact securities and foreign exchange are simply two classes of bank assets not included in D and D', the indebtedness of traders and consumers.

There is this difference, however, that whereas the purchase or sale of securities by the banks affects in the first instance only the investment market, the purchase or sale of foreign exchange may affect any class of traders, or indeed consumers, for consumers may have dealings abroad without the intervention of any traders in their own country.

A release of cash by the foreign exchange market in a country implies a favourable balance of payments, while an absorption of cash implies an unfavourable balance. The significance of either movement is in practice to be found much more in the reaction on the credit system than in the direct effects upon consumers' income and outlay. An absorption of cash by the foreign exchange market represents a loss of monetary reserves and has to be corrected either by a restriction of credit, or by a depreciation of the currency. And a release of cash by the foreign exchange market will be corrected by the contrary measures.

The purchase of *anything* by a bank releases cash, and the sale of anything absorbs cash. Securities and foreign exchange are the principal classes of things bought and sold by banks, but there are others. For example, a bank releases cash by buying gold from a mine and absorbs cash by selling gold to a jeweller. A mint must be regarded as the equivalent of a bank ; when it issues coin to a trader, it releases cash. In practice, however, a mint usually coins for a bank, and in that case the release of cash has already been effected by the bank in buying the bullion. The passage of specie from banks to customers and from customers to banks does not affect net cash resources.

In interpreting our equations we must bear in mind that $m + m'$

is not precisely equal to s, and that account should be taken of the banks' purchases of things other than the securities and capital assets included in s. But we need not complicate the equations by introducing additional terms symbolising this possibility at each stage.

Hitherto we have been considering what may occur in an interval of time, t, of *any* length. The output and sales of goods, the consumers' income and outlay, investment, capital raised and capital added are all expressed in terms of *value*. Each has a definite money value during the interval, and gives rise to a significant average. The value of output in the interval t is At; and A is the average output per unit of time during the interval. Similarly the quantities A', B, B', H, I, J, K, K', are all averages per unit of time.

As soon as we take account of price levels, or seek to make quantitative comparisons of output, disposals, working capital, etc., we can no longer trust to this simple method of averaging. But we can take an interval of time short enough for variations in prices to be small, so that the price level can be legitimately averaged, and we can thus arrive at a price level, P. We can then put:

$$A = PX,\ A' = PX',$$
$$E = PW,$$
$$e = Pw.$$

X, X', W and w are quantities of wealth, and
$$(X - X')t = w.$$

When we put $A = PX$ and $A' = PX'$, we assume the same price level to be applicable to output and disposals. It is the price level of *finished products* that is appropriate to both. Finished products include both the goods and services bought by consumers and the capital goods bought by traders.

But whereas disposals are themselves composed of finished goods, each priced in an actual transaction, output is composed of costs and profits. The costs consist of wages, salaries, interest and rent, together with depreciation. The profits are a balancing factor, filling the gap between these costs and the selling value of the products.

Costs and profits are thus the ingredients composing between them the prices of the finished products. In a given state of the market each ingredient has its price. Profit is the price of the

10

services of the trader who takes the initiative and the responsibility in producing and selling.

The products may not be in the same proportion in output as in disposals. Not only may the proportion of any product in the total output differ from the proportion of the same product in the total disposals, but the various intermediate processes leading up to the production and sale of some product may not be in due proportion to one another. The production of materials or intermediate products may be overtaking or falling behind the sales of the finished product.

Here we have the familiar problem of weighting. To compare two aggregates of products quantitatively, we value each aggregate in terms of a basic price list, the unit of quantity of any product being that represented by the unit of value at its basic price. But if we compare output and disposals by this method, valuing the items in each at basic prices, we shall find that, owing to the differences of weighting, $\dfrac{A}{X}$ and $\dfrac{A'}{X'}$ are not exactly equal; in other words, the current price levels of output and disposals are different, although all the individual current prices are the same for both.

A difference of price level so arising would have no significance, and the preferable course will be to apply one and the same price level to output and disposals, and to derive our quantitative measurements from the equations $A = PX$ and $A' = PX'$. All the prices of intermediate products and processes have ultimately to be paid out of the proceeds of disposals, and they are fixed with reference to the prices at which those proceeds are reckoned. We make P the price level of disposals, and we *define* X and X' as $\dfrac{A}{P}$ and $\dfrac{A'}{P}$.

Similarly we define W as $\dfrac{E}{P}$. That means that in calculating E we must value working capital at market prices, and we must count any profit from its appreciation as income. If we took any other course, if, for example, we valued it at cost, the resulting price level at a time of fluctuating prices would have no relation to economic conditions; it would be an affair of balance sheets. The pricing of any commodity would depend upon the date at which the stocks of it happened to have been acquired. We should have to distinguish from which consignment of wool each fibre in the cloth came, or from which consignment of ore each particle in a steel plate.

When the price level rises from P to $P + p$, the holders of working capital make an additional profit equal to pW[1]. This we treat as part of the consumers' income at the actual moment when the rise of price occurs in the market. If it is not drawn out in cash, the corresponding consumers' outlay takes the form of profit reinvested to the same amount. (If prices fall instead of rise, p is negative, and incomes are diminished by the loss.)

We count the gain from a rise in the price level of working capital as income, but not that from a rise in the price level of fixed capital. This is justifiable, because working capital is composed of goods destined *for sale*, and fixed capital is already in the hands of the final purchasers who have acquired it *for use*. Working capital includes capital goods in course of production or in stock, which have not yet been bought for use.

When the price level of fixed capital rises, that is in itself no gain to the enterprise; on the contrary it means a rise in the cost of replacement, which is a liability. The gain, if any, accrues, in the price of the output in the production of which the fixed capital is to be used. If the rise in the money value of the fixed capital reflects a fall in the wealth-value of the money unit, then, in so far as the provision for depreciation is held in the form of free capital, cash or securities, there is in effect an actual loss. It is a matter of chance whether the free capital is counterbalanced by indebtedness, short-term or long-term.

Since P is the price level of finished products, it is unaffected by variations in the prices of intermediate products. We have already observed that output may include an excess or deficiency of any intermediate product. If we were forming an index number of the prices of all the items composing output, we should have to include all intermediate products which were in excess in relation to the output of the corresponding finished products, and to count as " negatively " weighted those which were in deficiency. But as we are applying to output the index number, P, derived from disposals, we avoid all such calculations. The intermediate products are treated as if the sum included on account of them in A represented a typical selection of finished products of equal value (positive or negative).

In so far as the intermediate products produced are neither more nor less than the quantity required in the simultaneous output of the finished products, any excess or deficiency of price of the former

---

[1] It is true that, if working capital is to be maintained, the goods sold will have to be replaced at the higher price. But the profit is none the less real, even if it has to be reinvested to maintain capital.

merely causes a deficiency or excess of profits of the traders producing
or dealing in the latter, without affecting the price level at all.

The price level of disposals covers finished capital goods as well
as consumable goods.   It would not be easy to arrive at a satisfactory price index of capital goods.   Capital goods include some
standardised products, tools, machines, vehicles, etc., to which
definite prices could be assigned, but in many cases the finished
products would be big constructional undertakings no two of which
are alike.   The actual prices paid in such cases offer no basis of
comparison, and it is probably best to assume the price level to
comprise, in place of them, the prices of the intermediate products
and operations employed in construction, together with contractors'
profits of appropriate amount.

Of these problems of price levels and index numbers there is no
perfect solution.   The actual facts to be analysed *concern particular
products*.   The traders interested in any one product encounter
quite definite prices, stocks, output, sales, etc., and their behaviour
is determined by these conditions.   It is only when we try to find
arithmetical expressions for the *summation* of the facts and the
resulting behaviour that we are confronted with these anomalies and
contradictions.

CREDIT REGULATION

The receipts and disbursements of the entire community are
equal to one another.   Therefore, when any section of it absorbs or
releases cash, the remainder must necessarily be releasing or absorbing cash to a precisely equal amount.   When consumers absorb cash
(unless the banks buy securities), traders necessarily release cash, and
the mere fact of the absorption or release of cash does not in itself
throw light on the tendencies at work.   All depends on the character
of the originating disturbance.   If it starts with an absorption of
cash, the release of cash in the rest of the community induces a
tendency on their part to absorb cash to make good the loss, and so
the absorptive tendency spreads with cumulative force.   And, on
the contrary, when it starts with a release, the consequent absorption
is itself an inducement to a further release.

Credit regulation consists essentially in devices for inducing a
release or absorption of cash.   A measure of credit relaxation is
directed to making traders willing to hold diminished net cash
resources.   They borrow more from the banks, D is increased, and
C is increased by an equal amount.   If their net cash resources are
to be diminished, there must be a release of cash.   So long as

traders merely buy existing goods from one another that does not occur, the seller absorbing cash as fast as the buyer releases it. The release of cash occurs when there is an increase in production which will generate an increase in consumers' income.

Assume that initially $B' = B$, $I' = I$, $J = K = I + K'$, and that the release of cash increases the consumers' income from B to $B + b$. Depreciation, K', may be assumed to remain unchanged, and the increase in output is therefore b. There will follow, almost immediately, an increase, b', in consumers' outlay.

These changes in the consumers' income and outlay take effect when the orders for increased production begin to be executed. They are discontinuous, in the sense, not of being literally instantaneous, but of being completed in a relatively short time, within which changes in M and M' will be so small as to be negligible. The changes in D and C may be discontinuous, but in the first instance they cancel out and do not affect M. The decrease in M only occurs gradually, as the increased consumers' income, $B + b$, causes an outflow from the cash balance, C. And meanwhile the consumers' outlay will have increased to $B + b'$.

If we suppose the traders to have intended a release of cash at the rate of b per unit of time, they will have been disappointed, for the release amounts only to $b - b'$. In fact they will be in a position to release a further amount, b', without going beyond their intentions.

Meanwhile consumers are absorbing cash at the rate of $b - b'$. The increase in the consumers' income from B to $B + b$ makes the consumers' cash balances, C', and their net cash resources, M', inadequate. The purpose of the absorption of cash is to strengthen them, and it will continue till the due proportion between cash and incomes has been restored.

As the traders accelerate their release of cash, the consumers' income will be further enlarged, and the consumers' absorption of cash will likewise be increased.

Thus b, b', and $b - b'$, will go on growing till the consumers' net cash resources, $M' + m'$, are in due proportion to the consumers' income, $B + b$, and the traders' net cash resources have been diminished to the desired extent. It should be mentioned that, inasmuch as the traders' transactions are expanded, they will not in the end want so considerable a diminution of net cash resources as they originally aimed at.

A restriction of credit will lead traders to absorb cash with a view to increasing their net cash resources. The consumers' income will be reduced to $B - b$, and consumers' outlay to $B - b'$.

Consumers' net cash resources will be reduced by $b - b'$ per unit of time.

In these tendencies we have the causal sequence which is the true foundation of the quantity theory of money. Anyone whose cash balance is redundant will release cash; anyone whose cash balance is insufficient will absorb cash. If, in the community as a whole, cash balances are redundant, there will be a predominant tendency to release cash, and the consumers' income and outlay will be enlarged; if cash balances are insufficient, there will be a predominant tendency to absorb cash, and the consumers' income and outlay will be compressed.

Any change in consumers' income is, of course, associated with a corresponding change in the money value of output, for $B = A - K'$. And any change in the money value of output is compounded of the change in the price level and the quantitative change in output, for $A = PX$.

The quantity theory, as usually enunciated, is concerned not with the net cash resources, $M + M'$, but with the aggregate cash balances, $C + C'$. So far as the behaviour of individuals is concerned, the two are identical in those cases where it is not the practice to rely on bank advances to reinforce balances. That applies to the great majority of consumers' balances, bank advances being obtained only occasionally for exceptional purposes. There are also a considerable number of traders who avoid depending on their bankers for accommodation.

On the other hand, for the trader who is a regular borrower the cash balance has only a secondary significance. He can rely on bank advances to meet those big payments for which cash in hand would otherwise be necessary, and may so calculate the advances that he will never have a large idle balance, or he may obtain overdraft facilities, so that his cash balance is always *nil*; the difference is one of form rather than of substance.

It is the people whose net cash resources are negative who respond to the restriction or relaxation of credit, while those whose net cash resources are positive respond to fluctuations in the supply of money.

CREDIT REGULATION AND INVESTMENT

The increase, b', we have assumed in the consumers' outlay is composed of h, direct outlay, and i, investment. The former goes direct to industry, increasing its net cash resources and decreasing working capital. The additional investment goes in the first instance to the investment market, decreasing its indebtedness. The investment market becomes more favourable to new flotations, and after the lapse of an interval of time there will be increases, i' in capital raised and k in capital added.

The effects on the investment market are complex. The original relaxation of credit may have encouraged borrowing by speculators and speculative investors. Though this kind of borrowing is not sensitive to the rate of interest, the banks may cause it to increase by relaxing their restraints upon it. The effect is already reflected in i, the additional investment. It may be mentioned that this portion of b' does not depend, like h, on a prior increase in the consumers' income, but may come into existence contemporaneously with the relaxation of credit.

The removal of restraints on speculative borrowing may make the dealers in the investment market more willing to borrow. But their willingness cannot take effect unless industry is induced to raise more capital and so to provide them with more securities.

These facilities for speculative borrowing, added to the increase in investment directly due to the increase in the consumers' income, make the investment market favourable to the raising of capital. But it is only when the increase, i', in the raising of capital actually materialises that the favourable market is anything more than a potentiality. Till then the speculators and investors can only obtain more securities by buying them from the dealers' holdings. The dealers, however willing to borrow, find their indebtedness decreasing.

It is this state of the investment market that induces industry to increase the extension of capital and for that purpose to raise more capital. An additional motive tending in the same direction is the expansion of consumption demand, which may call for an extension of capacity.

The increase, k, in capital added may not be exactly equal to the increase, i', in capital raised. The difference appears as an increase or decrease in circulating capital. If working capital is a given quantity, an increase in circulating capital means an absorption of cash by industry, a decrease means a release.

Disposals have increased by $h + k$, while output has increased by b. Working capital increases by $b - h - k$ per unit of time. Circulating capital increases by $i' - k$. The absorption of cash by industry is $i' + h - b$, or the release is $b - h - i'$. In fact the absorption of cash by consumers is $b - b'$ or $b - h - i$, and the absorption of cash by the investment market is $i - i'$. Since we are assuming no absorption or release of cash by the banks, the release of cash by industry must be the sum of these two or $b - h - i'$.

In the early stages, when i' and k are both zero, the release of cash by industry and the increase of working capital are each equal to $b - h$.

If in place of a relaxation of credit there is a restriction, we simply change the signs of b, b', h, i, i' and k. Instead of increases they become decreases.

The disturbance may originate not in industry but in the investment market. There may for example be an increase in saving.

If consumption is G, saving is $B - G$, and is composed of the following:

(1) Absorption of cash by consumers, $B - B'$;
(2) Investment, I;
(3) Consumers' capital outlay, $H - G$.

Since $B' = I + H$ these three together are equal to $B - G$.

It may be pointed out that, as the consumers' income is equal to net output, saving is equal to net output *minus* consumption, or in other words to the increment of wealth. In fact the saving $B - G$ is equal to $A - K' - G$, and this latter is composed of:

(1) Addition to working capital, $A - A'$;
(2) Capital added, $K - K'$;
(3) Consumers' capital outlay, $H - G$.

The two latter constitute capital outlay, $A' - K' - G$, and the difference between saving and capital outlay is the change $A - A'$ or $A' - A$ in working capital. The condition of equilibrium is that this be equal to intermediate demand.

An increase in saving may appear in any of the three constituents, consumers' cash balances, investment, or consumers' capital outlay. An absorption of cash by consumers, however, is not necessarily connected with an increase in saving. The desire to correct a deficiency of cash may arise from an increase in cash transactions, or from various and possibly obscure causes, a distrust of investments, an expectation of social disorders, perhaps a mere change of habits. To represent it in our notation we should make b initially zero and b' negative.

Consumers' capital outlay, which is a form of saving, merely diverts productive activity from one object to another. It alters the composition of H, A and B without altering their magnitude (except perhaps as the result of some transitional dislocation).

There remains the case of an increase in investment. We assume b and b' initially zero, and h initially equal to *minus i*. There is an immediate decrease in disposals by i. The increase in investment would permit of capital raised and capital added each being increased by i. But there will be a long delay before this can occur. The increases i' and k which actually occur in capital raised and capital added will start at zero and will remain for a long time less than i.

Meanwhile, so long as the consumers' outlay remains unchanged, disposals are reduced by $i - k$, and working capital is increased by unsold goods to that amount. In fact we are assuming no release or absorption of cash by consumers, and the absorption of cash by the investment market to the amount $i - i'$ must be offset by an equal release of cash by industry. This release of cash by industry is caused by an excess of output over disposals.

It must not be assumed that any excess whatever of output over disposals is a sterile accumulation of unsold goods. There may be an equivalent intermediate demand. Traders may be induced by relaxation of credit deliberately to increase their working capital by means of bank advances, or they may devote a part of the capital raised by effecting such an increase without incurring indebtedness. When that happens, the increase in stocks of goods awaiting sale is no embarrassment, and no disturbance of the equilibrium of markets ensues.

On the other hand, an *undesigned* increase of working capital, an unforeseen accumulation of unsold stocks, is a signal for a restriction of output and for a reduction of prices. Output and prices alike have to be adjusted to demand, and the adjustment can only be effected by the method of trial and error. The equilibrium price of any product is ascertained empirically by varying the price whenever disposals exceed output or output exceeds disposals. Output tends to be expanded whenever unsold stocks are inconveniently depleted, or to be contracted whenever they become redundant.

When there is an absorption of cash by the investment market, there results an undesigned excess of output over disposals, and the negative intermediate demand then leads to a reduction of both output and prices.

Keynes in his *Treatise on Money* regards an access of saving as abortive when it results in a fall of the price level, and consequent losses to traders. It is equally abortive when it results in a reduction

of output. And even when output and prices are both undiminished, saving that results in no other increment of wealth than an
undesigned accumulation of unsold goods may likewise be called
abortive.

These results are attributable not to saving as such but to the
absorption of cash by the investment market. Precisely similar
results would follow from an absorption of cash, however caused,
whether in the investment market, in industry or among consumers.
Saving only causes an absorption of cash by the investment market
so long as the capital added does not expand to a corresponding
extent.

The increase in investment will make the investment market
favourable to new issues and to sellers of securities, but some time
must elapse before these favourable conditions bear fruit in actual
new enterprises. And meanwhile the access of saving will have been
causing a diminution of activity and a decline of prices.

In the case where an absorption of cash originates in a restriction
of credit, the negative intermediate demand causes a reduction of
output and therefore of consumers' income. If, as is probable,
consumers' outlay falls by something less than consumers' income,
there will be an excess of disposals over output and an actual
reduction in working capital. But there is none the less an undesigned *excess* of working capital, because the credit restriction itself
has made traders revise their views of the amount of working capital
they wish to hold.

It is when they proceed to meet this situation with a further
reduction of output that the vicious circle of deflation sets in. The
reduction of output means a reduction of consumers' income and a
further shrinkage of disposals. It only accomplishes a reduction of
working capital equal to the difference between the contraction
of output and the contraction of disposals. And meanwhile the
reduction in the volume of transactions itself involves a reduction of
the amount of working capital required.

The twelve quantities, A, A', B, B', H, I, I', J, K, K', R, R'
represent seven independent variables, since they are related by the
five equations :

$$A - B = J - I' = R - R' = K',$$
$$A' - K = B' - I = H.$$

Depreciation, K', is determined by the actual circumstances of
the capital equipment employed. The other six variables are determined by the behaviour of the several groups of people. Output

and consumers' income are determined by the traders and others engaged in economic activity. Reinvested profits (gross and net) are determined by the traders. The remainder of the consumers' income is dealt with by the consumers, who determine the amount of H, their purchases of goods, and $I - R'$, their purchases of securities. Capital raised and capital added are in the hands of the traders.

NOTE

Throughout the foregoing we have been concerned only with finite intervals of time. And we cannot regard the quantities involved as " continuous " in a rigorous mathematical sense. If we scrutinise the behaviour, for example, of C', the total of consumers' cash balances, we shall find that it is subject to very numerous *discontinuous* increases and decreases in the shape of payments and receipts. If we suppose our intervals of time to be subdivided without limit, we shall eventually find that some of them contain no increases or decreases at all, while others, however short they may be, always contain finite increases or decreases.

It may perhaps be said that at any rate the *earning* of income is a continuous process. The payment of income is effected discontinuously at intervals, but in any interval income is accruing continuously in the form of a debt due from employer to employee, or of the growing value of goods destined for sale. But even if that is applicable to all incomes, so that B may be regarded as a continuous variable, B' and A', I, J, and K are in any case discontinuous.

Nevertheless the infinite subdivision of time applied to economic variables has very little significance. We can quite legitimately eschew pedantry and assume the existence of continuous mathematical functions which behave over any considerable interval of time for all practical purposes in the same way as the actual functions. And if we make that assumption we can restate our equations in terms of the calculus.

Thus :

$$B - B' = \frac{dC'}{dt} - \frac{dD'}{dt} = \frac{dM'}{dt},$$

$$\int (B - B')dt = M' - M'_0,$$

$$X - X' = \frac{dW}{dt},$$

$$\int (X - X')dt = W - W_0,$$

$$A - A' = \frac{dE}{dt},$$

$$\int (A - A')dt = E - E_0,$$

$$I' - I = \frac{dS}{dt} + \frac{dF}{dt},$$

$$J - K = \frac{dL}{dt},$$

$$\frac{dM}{dt} + \frac{dM'}{dt} = \frac{dS}{dt}.$$

CHAPTER VII

KEYNES'S " GENERAL THEORY OF EMPLOYMENT, INTEREST AND MONEY "

INTEREST AND THE CLASSICAL THEORY

KEYNES places the emphasis on the prefix *General* in the title of his book. Thereby he wished to contrast his arguments and conclusions with those of the " Classical " theory, which he regarded as applicable to a special case only and not to the general case.

His thesis will be best approached as a revision of the classical theory of interest. That is a topic which is not reached till nearly halfway through the book, but it furnishes the clue to much that is otherwise obscure in the earlier chapters, and a criticism of Keynes's position can start most conveniently with an exposition of his divergence from the classical theory of interest.

According to the classical theory, " investment represents the demand for investible resources, and saving represents the supply, whilst the rate of interest is the ' Price ' of investible resources at which the two are equated. Just as the price of a commodity is necessarily fixed at that point where the demand for it is equal to the supply, so the rate of interest necessarily comes to rest under the play of market forces at the point where the amount of investment at that rate of interest is equal to the amount of saving at that rate " (p. 175).

Keynes, however, did not use the term " investment " in its usual sense of " the purchase of a capital asset of any kind out of income " (p. 75). He defined current investment in a period to mean " the current addition to the value of the capital equipment, which has resulted from the productive activity of the period ". " Equipment " here included working capital as well as instrumental capital, so that " investment " simply meant the excess of production over consumption.

To examine the carefully reasoned chapter which Keynes devoted to his definition of income would be a digression. The upshot is a definition which conforms to generally accepted usage in making income, net or gross, equal to production, net or gross. Saving, being the excess of income over consumption, is therefore equal to the excess of production over consumption. In other words, saving is *identically* equal to investment, and Keynes's definitions

157

made nonsense of a theory which explained the rate of interest as that which equalises saving and investment. He accordingly discarded the classical theory, and concluded that the rate of interest must be given " from some other source " (p. 181).

The classical theory made interest the reward of saving. Keynes contended that it could not be " a return to saving or waiting as such, for if a man hoards his savings in cash, he earns no interest, though he saves just as much as before " (p. 167).

LIQUIDITY PREFERENCE

According to him, the rate of interest is to be regarded not as the reward of abstaining from consumption or of " waiting ", but as the reward of *forgoing liquidity*. By tying up their savings in investments people forgo liquidity, and the extent to which they are willing to do so will depend on the rate of interest. Anyone's " liquidity preference " is a function relating the amount of his resources which he will wish to retain in the form of money to different sets of circumstances, and among those circumstances will be the rate of interest. Consequently the rate of interest can be regarded as a function of the surplus cash remaining after the other motives for holding cash have been satisfied. The supply of money determines the rate of interest, and the rate of interest so determined governs the volume of capital outlay.

" If the rate of interest were lower, i.e. if the reward for parting with cash were diminished, the aggregate amount of cash which the public would wish to hold would exceed the supply, and if the rate of interest were raised, there would be a surplus of cash which no one would be willing to hold " (p. 167).

The motives, other than the rate of interest, for holding cash, Keynes analyses into three, the Income-motive, the Business-motive and the Precautionary-motive. The first two cover the need of cash to meet current transactions and the third is concerned with " contingencies requiring sudden expenditure ", and with " unforeseen opportunities of advantageous purchases " (p. 196). With these three motives he contrasts the " Speculative motive ", which determines the surplus cash with reference to the rate of interest.

If the total supply of money (bank deposits, *plus* currency) be M, this can be divided into two parts, one, M_1, required to satisfy the three former motives, the income-motive, the business-motive and the precautionary-motive, and the other, M_2, representing the surplus required to satisfy the speculative motive. The former depends on the economic activity and especially on the aggregate income of the community, and the latter depends on the rate of interest. Keynes points out that the motives determining M_1 and M_2 are not wholly independent, but " it is a safe first approximation to regard the amounts of these two sets of cash-holdings as being largely independent of one another " (p. 199). Accordingly, if Y be the total income of the community and r be the rate of interest, he expresses M_1 as a function of the former, L_1 (Y), and M_2 as a function of the latter, L_2 (r).

If monetary policy determines M, and the national income determines M_1, the rate of interest must accommodate itself to the residue, M_2, and the rate so determined will govern the volume of investment. The volume of investment is *effect*, and the rate of interest is *cause*. That is so because the rate of interest, being already determined by monetary policy, cannot be determined, as the classical school would have it, by the action of the investment market in equating saving and capital outlay.

It is rather inconvenient that Keynes has no name for either M_1 or M_2. The meaning given in the *Treatise on Money* to the expression " savings deposits " very nearly coincides with that of M_2 as now defined. But Keynes modified the definition of savings deposits so as to cover balances held for the precautionary motive (p. 195), which in the *Treatise* came under income-deposits and business-deposits (*Treatise*, p. 35). He uses the expression, " transactions motive ", to include the income-motive and the business-motive, but not the precautionary-motive.

I shall call M_1 active balances and M_2 idle balances.

Since Keynes so defines investment and saving that they are *necessarily and invariably equal*, their equality cannot depend on the rate of interest. Variations in other factors must be consistent with the equality of investment and saving. To a given total of incomes, Y, there corresponds a total of consumption, C, determined by the " propensity to consume ". Saving is $Y - C$, and investment, which is determined by the rate of interest, must be equal to $Y - C$. If the rate of interest determined by M, M_1 and M_2 is not such as to secure this result, then Y will be so adjusted as to attain it.

The process of adjustment will involve certain repercussions, since a change in Y will involve a change in M_1, and so in M_2 and in the rate of interest. And there may be psychological changes modifying liquidity preferences, the propensity to consume, and the relation between capital outlay and the rate of interest. But, subject to these and similar qualifications, the broad principle is that the supply of money in excess of active balances determines the rate of interest, the rate of interest determines the volume of investment and therefore of saving, and the national income must accommodate itself to the volume of saving in conformity with the propensity to consume. With a given level of money wages, the amount of employment is determined by the national income, and therefore this train of causation determines the volume of employment.

A state of equilibrium is attained in which there may be considerable unemployment. In the view of the classical school unemployment is essentially a sign of disequilibrium. If that is not so, and if it is consistent with a state of equilibrium, then chronic unemployment is possible.

ACTIVE AND PASSIVE INVESTMENT

This train of reasoning all proceeded from the definitions which made saving and investment " necessarily equal in amount, being, for the community as a whole, merely different aspects of the same thing " (p. 74). If we call the excess of production over consumption *accumulation*, then saving is accumulation seen from the standpoint of those who so determine their consumption as to be less than their incomes ; [1] investment is accumulation seen from the standpoint of the holders of items of unconsumed wealth. The identity of saving and investment may be compared to the identity of the two sides of an account.

Identity so established does not prove anything. The idea that a tendency for saving and investment so defined to become different has to be counteracted by an expansion or contraction of the total of incomes is an absurdity; such a tendency cannot strain the economic system ; it can only strain Keynes's vocabulary.

Nevertheless there is a sense in which saving and investment, suitably interpreted, while not identical, do tend to equality. Investment is the increment of unconsumed wealth, and every item of unconsumed wealth must be held by some one. If the rate of interest determines the volume of investment, that is because the prospective yield of an item of unconsumed wealth or a capital asset (" an " investment) supplies an " inducement to invest ", and the inducement must outweigh the rate of interest if the acquisition of the capital asset is to be worth while.

---

[1] Due account of course being taken of " negative " savings, where consumption exceeds income.

The inducement only applies to those items of unconsumed wealth that are *voluntarily* acquired in the expectation that they will be remunerative, if not in terms of money at any rate in terms of convenience. We may distinguish the acquisition of such items as " designed " or " active " investment.

Now the total increment of unconsumed wealth is identically equal to the total of saving. If active investment falls short of saving, then there must be a portion of the increment of unconsumed wealth which is not acquired voluntarily in the expectation of its being remunerative. This will be an involuntary accumulation of unsold goods. Such an accumulation, being part of the increment of unconsumed wealth, is included in Keynes's definition of investment; it may be called " undesigned " or " passive " investment. Passive investment may be a negative quantity; that is to say, active investment may exceed saving, and the excess will be represented by an undesigned disinvestment or decrement of stocks of unsold goods.

Thus active investment and saving may be unequal. If they are, the resulting undesigned increment or decrement of unsold goods will be a source of disequilibrium, leading to a decrease or an increase in productive activity and possibly also in the price level.

The distinction between accumulation and active investment does not differ very materially from that between *ex post* and *ex ante* investment, adopted by Professors Myrdal, Ohlin and others of the Swedish School. Professor Ohlin explains *ex ante* saving and investment to be " planned " or " expected " saving and investment.[1] In any interval of time *ex post* saving and investment are both equal to actual accumulation, but at the beginning of the interval *ex ante* saving and investment may differ from one another.

I am not disposed to accept this phraseology, for there are difficulties in the conception of an *aggregate* of plans or expectations at a selected moment of time. The plans and expectations are states of mind of individuals. Their forecasts are of varying degrees of incompleteness and uncertainty, and extend to varying future periods of time.

Whereas *ex ante* investment is defined with reference to forecasts, active investment is defined with reference to the inducement to invest. The term " active " is a quality distinguishing each act of investment when it is made. Substantially all capital outlay as defined above (p. 58) is active investment, and the distinction only has to be applied to the accumulation of stocks. If an increment

---

[1] See *The Problem of Employment Stabilisation* (1950), pp. 113-15.

11

(or decrement) of stocks is not acceptable, it is to be classed as passive accumulation. But even so it is not necessary that the respective aggregates of active and passive accumulation should be *measurable*. When a trader orders either more or less goods than would be needed to replace his sales, the difference is an ascertainable fact. It is the outward sign of his stocks being too low or too high but the extent of their divergence from the acceptable level is a matter of conjecture. The amount he orders is only one of the factors determining the stocks he will be holding when he receives delivery of the goods, and when the time comes to give another order he can reconsider the position.

Keynes referred (pp. 75-6) to a suggestion of my own, that he should exclude from his definition of investment " undesigned increments (or decrements) in the stock of unsold goods ". My suggestion was rather that he should distinguish what I now call active investment from accumulation or investment as a whole.

He conceded that, in the case of consumption goods, changes in stocks of unsold goods play an important part in the decisions of entrepreneurs concerning their scale of output. " But ", he went on, " I see no object in excluding the play of other factors on their decisions ; and I prefer therefore to emphasise the total change in effective demand and not merely that part of the change which reflects the increase or decrease of unsold stocks in the previous period ".

Effective demand, as used by him, means " expected " proceeds of output (p. 55). In the case of stock-held consumption goods the proceeds to which expectations are directed are the proceeds of sales to consumers. The scale of output decided on by the entrepreneurs will depend on the orders they get from the traders who hold goods in stock for sale to the consumers. It will not be exactly equal to the actual sales to consumers, nor even to the sales expected in the immediate future, for the traders must allow for such increment or decrement of stocks held as may be appropriate to the sales antici-pated and the output contemplated. In so far as any increment or decrement of stocks is acceptable, it reflects the operation of " effective demand " as defined by Keynes. Any divergence from what is acceptable represents a discrepancy between output and his " effective demand ". His reference to " other factors " is irrele-vant, for passive investment takes *all* factors into account ; the inter-mediate demand, positive or negative, engendered by an unaccept-able state of stocks, whatever the cause, faithfully reflects the " total change in effective demand ".

That refers to consumption goods. " In the case of fixed capital ", Keynes wrote, " the increase or decrease of unused capacity corresponds to the increase or decrease in unsold stocks in its effect on decisions to produce."

But the parallel is not just. For, whereas the order for consumption goods is in general given by a trader who holds a stock destined for sale, the order for fixed capital is usually given direct by the prospective user to the producer or constructor. We have seen (above, p. 95) that the existence of unused capacity reacts upon the widening of capital, and therefore on the production of capital equipment. But the reduction of productive activity is caused directly, without any intervening disparity between output and disposals, for the sale by the producer to the user is itself a " disposal ". That is why all capital outlay counts as active investment. The accumulation of stocks of materials and intermediate products destined to be absorbed in capital outlay is not included in capital outlay except in so far as it is paid for in advance by the ultimate user of the completed capital goods.

The distinction between active investment and accumulation or investment as a whole is essential to Keynes's argument. For example, we are told that " to justify any given amount of employment there must be an amount of current investment sufficient to absorb the excess of total output over what the community chooses to consume when employment is at the given level. For unless there is this amount of investment, the receipts of the entrepreneurs will be less than is required to induce them to offer the given amount of employment " (p. 27).

Investment, as defined by Keynes, is simply a name for " the excess of total output over what the community chooses to consume ". Consequently the condition of the given amount of employment, so stated, is always identically fulfilled and is therefore nugatory. To be significant, it must be formulated differently; it is the *active* investment that must be sufficient to absorb the excess output.

" Income ", he says, " depends on investment in such fashion that, when investment changes, income must necessarily change in just that degree which is necessary to make the change in saving equal to the change in investment " (p. 184). If we adopt his own definitions, and make both investment and saving signify accumulation, then we find this to mean, " when accumulation changes, income must change in just that degree which is necessary to make the change in accumulation equal to the change in accumulation ".

To make sense of it, we must introduce active investment, which can differ from saving. If the originating cause of the change is to be found in " the inducement to invest ", this takes effect in active investment, and in the first instance passive investment or disinvestment emerges to preserve the identity of saving and investment. At no moment can there be any difference between saving and investment to be corrected by a change in income. It is the passive investment or disinvestment that is the source of disequilibrium and the cause of change. The change in income must continue till saving and active investment are equal.

THE MULTIPLIER

Keynes examines the relation between investment and income in his tenth chapter on the Marginal Propensity to Consume. Let Y be income and I investment (expressed for this purpose in terms of wage units) then, if $\frac{dY}{dI} = k$, k is the " investment multiplier ", and $1 - \frac{1}{k}$ is the " marginal propensity to consume ". If C is consumption, $1 - \frac{1}{k} = \frac{dC}{dY}$. " When there is an increment of aggregate investment, income will increase by an amount which is k times [1] the increment of investment " (p. 115).

" If the consumption psychology of the community is such that they will choose to consume, e.g. nine-tenths of an increment of income, then the multiplier k is ten, and the total employment caused by (e.g.) increased public works will be ten times the primary employment provided by the public works themselves, assuming no reduction of investment in other directions " (pp. 116-17).

" This only sums up in a formula what should by now be obvious to the reader on general grounds. An increment of investment in terms of wage units cannot occur unless the public are prepared to increase their savings in terms of wage units." That is to say, it is the decisions to save that determine the action of the multiplier.

The public works are additional *active* investment; in themselves they do not increase accumulation at all, for if there is no offsetting reduction of active investment, they give rise to an equivalent passive

---

[1] Since k is not constant for all values of Y and I, it would be more accurate to say that the increase in income is $\int k \, dI$.

disinvestment. Active investment and passive disinvestment are necessarily together equal to saving, or accumulation. Clearly what brings about an expansion in income is the existence of passive disinvestment, an undesigned diminution of stocks of goods.

As Keynes explains it, the effort of the public " to consume a part of their increased incomes will stimulate output until the new level (and distribution) of incomes provides a margin of saving sufficient to correspond to the increased investment ".

When, however, he went on to say that the stimulation of output of consumption-goods would not keep pace with the expansion of demand unless the full effect of the additional capital outlay were foreseen, he was forsaking the purely static approach to which he had till then confined himself. If not foreseen, it " only produces its full effect on employment over a period of time " (p. 122). Meanwhile there will be an excess demand for consumption goods. A temporary equilibrium will be brought about " partly by high prices causing a postponement of consumption, partly by a redistribution of income in favour of the saving classes as an effect of the increased profits resulting from the higher prices, and partly by the higher prices causing a depletion of stocks " (pp. 123-4).

Here is a recognition of the occurrence of passive disinvestment, but not, I think, a correct account of the sequence of events. For a rise of prices to consumers does not follow immediately on an unforeseen expansion of demand. The first impact is felt in sales from stock at existing prices. And the sales from stock result in increased orders to producers and increased production and employment, even though there may be no rise of prices.

If a rise of prices does eventually occur, the consumers' income is correspondingly increased, so that the rise need not cause any postponement or restriction of consumption. A revival of profits will indeed mean a " redistribution of income in favour of the saving classes ", but, unless the rise of prices is such as to raise profit margins above normal, this will not involve any temporary depression of the propensity to consume.

The propensity to consume and the multiplier determine accumulation *immediately* : they designate the states of mind of which the accumulation is the outward symptom at the moment. These states of mind constitute the propensity to save, while the states of mind which constitute the inducement to invest are reflected in active investment. When the two fail to correspond, passive investment or disinvestment appears, and can only be eliminated by an adjustment occupying time.

The actual sequence of events is that the additional active investment generates additional incomes; so far as the additional incomes are consumed, stocks of goods are drawn upon; further productive activity, entered upon to reconstitute the diminished stocks, generates still more incomes; and the expansion of incomes continues progressively till sufficient savings have been generated to offset the increase in active investment, and passive disinvestment no longer occurs.

The introduction of the distinction between active and passive investment is not inconsistent with Keynes's main theory. But it carries with it the important consequence that the adjustment of income by which saving and active investment are made equal *takes time*. The recognition of transitional periods when such processes of adjustment are at work is the characteristic of a dynamic theory. Keynes's theory resembles the classical theory in being static.

At no time during the interval while this sequence is occurring can there be any discrepancy to be corrected between saving and investment as defined by Keynes. The distinction between accumulation and active investment is essential to a dynamic treatment of the multiplier. The occurrence of passive investment or disinvestment, being a cause of disequilibrium, is alien to a static theory. The theory of the multiplier is static, and Keynes only introduced the depletion of stocks in the passage quoted above because he had been diverted to a dynamic approach.

MARGINAL EFFICIENCY OF CAPITAL

Investment, as defined by Keynes, is the excess of production over consumption. But it is not the producer as such that invests; it is he who *procures* production with a view to retaining the product for use. The distinction is clear in the case of instrumental goods: it is the purchaser, not the producer, who is the investor. The sale of an existing investment is a negative investment or disinvestment.

In the case of working capital it would seem to follow that a purchase of goods for stock is investment, and a sale of goods from stock is disinvestment.

Keynes's treatment of the inducement to invest depends on what he calls the Marginal Efficiency of Capital. This part of the subject he introduces thus in Chapter XI:

" When a man buys an investment or capital-asset, he purchases the right to the series of prospective returns which he expects to obtain from selling its output, after deducting the running expenses

of obtaining that output, during the life of the asset. This series of
annuities . . . it is convenient to call the *prospective yield* of the
investment " (p. 135). If " an investment " includes a purchase of
goods for stock, its " prospective yield " is not very happily described as a " series of annuities ". That is a point we shall return
to (below, pp. 184-7).

Keynes proceeds to define " the marginal efficiency of capital as
being equal to that rate of discount which would make the present
value of the series of annuities given by the returns expected from
the capital-asset during its life just equal to its supply price. This
gives us the marginal efficiencies of particular types of capital-assets.
The greatest of these marginal efficiencies can then be regarded as
the marginal efficiency of capital in general. "

The marginal efficiency of any given type of capital will diminish
as investment in it is increased, partly because its prospective yield
will fall, partly because its supply price will rise. Keynes infers that
" we can build up a schedule showing by how much investment in
it will have to increase . . . in order that its marginal efficiency
should fall to any given figure ". The totality of these schedules
for all types of capital constitutes the investment demand-schedule
or the schedule of the marginal efficiency of capital.

" The actual rate of current investment will be pushed to the
point where there is no longer any class of capital-asset of which the
marginal efficiency exceeds the current rate of interest. In other
words the rate of investment will be pushed to the point on the
investment demand schedule where the marginal efficiency of capital
in general is equal to the market rate of interest. "

Keynes expresses the belief that his definition of the marginal
efficiency of capital " is fairly close to what Marshall intended to
mean by the term " (p. 139), and he quotes the passage from *Principles* (eighth edition, pp. 519-20), in which Marshall explains the
operation of different rates of interest in excluding machinery of
inferior yields from the plant of a hypothetical hat-making concern.

In this passage Marshall explains how the machines used in the
hypothetical concern have varying yields. There will be an essential
minimum of circulating and fixed capital, and " though competition
prevents anything more than the ordinary trade profit being got by
the use of this necessary capital ; yet the loss of it would be so
injurious that those in the trade would have been willing to pay 50
per cent on it, if they could not have got the use of it on easier
terms ". Thus the yield or cost-saving capacity of this essential
capital exceeds 50 per cent. Marshall supposes other items of

capital equipment to yield 20 per cent, 10 per cent or less, down to that " which it is only just worth while to employ ", because its yield is equal to the market rate of interest, assumed to be 3 per cent. It is only the last to which he gives the name of " marginal utility ".

Marshall in this passage expresses the yield of each item in terms of the additional output obtained by the use of it. The argument remains substantially the same if yield is expressed in terms of labour-saving or cost-saving capacity. So stated it becomes an illustration of the principle of substitution. The rate of interest affects the producer's choice between two alternative agents of production, labour and capital.

Keynes defines marginal efficiency to be that rate of discount which would make the present value of the yield of a capital asset equal to its supply price. How would he apply this calculation to Marshall's 50-per-cent-yielding plant ? To say that its marginal efficiency would be 50 per cent is to deprive the term " marginal " of all meaning.

ENTERPRISES AND INSTRUMENTS

Keynes was not thinking of the principle of substitution or of the cost-saving capacity of the separate instrument. He was thinking of the yield not of the separate pieces of capital equipment but of the *enterprise* which uses them. He identified marginal efficiency with Irving Fisher's rate of return over cost (p. 140), which departed from Marshall's marginal yield in just the same way (above, pp. 43-8). Keynes's definition of prospective yield of an investment is based on the returns expected " from selling its output ". The selling of output is the function of an enterprise.

It may be said that each piece of capital equipment or instrument makes its contribution to the selling value of the output, and that its prospective yield might be derived from this contribution. But selling value is composed of costs *plus* profit, and it is as an item in costs that an instrument contributes to it. Its contribution is arrived at (along with maintenance and depreciation) simply by taking interest at the market rate on its first cost. If the yield of a capital asset is *defined* to be equal to the market rate of interest, the whole theory of marginal efficiency becomes nugatory.

We cannot identify the contribution of an instrument to selling value with its cost-saving capacity. Its cost-saving capacity may be a hundred times the market rate of interest. The contribution of a spade used in digging potatoes to the selling value of the potatoes is

minute ; a shilling or two a year might cover interest and depreciation. But its cost-saving capacity, measured by the cost of cultiva-
ting the potatoes without a spade, may be many times their whole
selling value.

Prospective yield is the excess of proceeds of sale over the
" running expenses " of obtaining the output (p. 135). If running
expenses include all costs except interest, the yield of an enterprise
is composed of interest *plus* profit.

Keynes saw the foregoing passage in draft in 1936, and com-
mented : " My intention was to include the profit in the prospective
yield, but not in the definition of marginal efficiency. That is to
say, if the marginal efficiency is 5 per cent, the value of the capital is
not equal to the prospective yield discounted at 5 per cent, but at
such excess over 5 per cent as is appropriate to the type of business ".

He intended therefore to include profit, in the form of an appropriate additional percentage, in " running expenses ". If his
definition of marginal efficiency is to be significant, this appropriate
percentage must be determined independently of the rate of interest.
In the *Treatise on Money*, Keynes treated " the normal remuneration
of the entrepreneur " as part of the cost of production, and defined
the normal as that rate of remuneration which leaves the entrepreneurs " under no motive either to increase or decrease their scale
of operations " (*Treatise*, Vol. I, p. 125). In the *General Theory*
(pp. 60-1) he discarded the definition adopted in the *Treatise*, and
offered no alternative definition of normal profit to take its place.
But if an enterpreneur's margin " appropriate to the type of business ", which is to be included in running expenses, is identified with
his actual profit, " the excess of the value of his finished output . . .
over his prime cost " (p. 53), the calculation of marginal efficiency
becomes nugatory. Yield is interest *plus* actual profit, and, if
actual profit is treated as a cost, what is left is simply interest. If
normal profit is treated as a cost, the difference between marginal
efficiency and interest is the difference between actual profit and
normal profit.[1] Investment is said to be pushed to the point
" where there is no longer any class of capital asset of which the
marginal efficiency exceeds the rate of interest ", and that will be the
point at which profit does not exceed whatever margin is to be
included in current expenses for the normal remuneration of the
entrepreneur.

---

[1] In the following pages I assume that normal profit, however defined, is to
be treated as a cost. In the first edition of this book I assumed actual profit to
be included in marginal efficiency ; that means making normal profit zero.

Marginal efficiency is still attributed to the enterprise and not to the instrument. Where then is there any room for deepening ? Keynes, in his comments of 1936, wrote : " I have not thought it relevant to make a distinction between the widening of capital and its deepening, but I was not conscious of having excluded the deepening process. Everything I have said is intended to embrace both."

He dealt with deepening or the lengthening of the period of production in his sixteenth chapter, on the Nature of Capital. " If the rate of interest were zero, there would be an optimum interval for any given article between the average date of input and the date of consumption. . . . If, however, the rate of interest exceeds zero, a new element of cost is introduced, which increases with the length of the process, so that the optimum interval will be shortened " (p. 216). That is the pure doctrine of Jevons and Boehm Bawerk. The rate of interest limits deepening, because the " new element of cost " has to be set against the saving to be secured by it. Deepening saves costs by substituting plant for labour in the production of a given output. The saving is the difference between the cost of upkeep, depreciation and interest and the current cost of the labour dispensed with.

If the new plant is marginal, the net saving is small, but where it embodies technological improvements or inventions, the saving may be considerable. But either way the deepening is not part of the process of pushing current investment to the point " where there is no longer any class of capital asset of which the marginal efficiency exceeds the current rate of interest ". The pushing is done by the widening of capital. The deepening, if it affects marginal efficiency at all, *increases* it by diminishing costs. An additional supply of the product is then needed to bring down the price in due relation to costs, and so to reduce the profit margin to normal. In other words further widening is needed to counteract the effect of deepening on marginal efficiency.

Keynes's intention to embrace deepening as well as widening in his analysis was not carried out. Deepening enters into the reckoning, not as part of the process of carrying investment to the limit at which marginal efficiency does not exceed the rate of interest, but as a factor *retarding* this process. He could treat deepening as a relatively minor affair, because his reasoning all through is governed by the assumption of " a given situation of technique " (pp. 24, 28, 245). The deepening process is limited to marginal instruments, and the tendency of technological improvements to raise marginal efficiency is excluded from consideration. This assumption is

departed from for a moment (p. 141), but only in order to say that
the expectation of " inventions and new technique " *diminishes*
marginal efficiency because capital equipment may have " to compete
in the course of its life with the output from equipment produced . . .
by an improved technique ".

It is this assumption of unchanging technique that justifies
Keynes's repeated insistence on the tendency of marginal efficiency
to fall.   And upon it therefore depends the importance he attributed
to the speculative motive, which obstructs the fall in the rate of
interest required for full employment.

The doctrine of marginal efficiency is an adaptation of that of
saving and investment as expounded in the *Treatise on Money*, with
a suitable revision of the conception of the normal remuneration of
the entrepreneur " appropriate to the type of business ".

The expression " excess of investment over saving ", as used in
the *Treatise*, really means " excess of prices over costs ", or, as costs
are defined to include normal profit, it means excess of profit over
normal.   It is this excess, so far as it is foreseen, that is an inducement to increased productive activity.   In Keynes's later phraseology
it will be in the marginal efficiency of capital that the expectation of
excess profits is to be found.

Profit is the inducement for a widening of capital equipment.
But that does not mean that the extension of capital equipment is
adjusted simply to a varying *rate* of profit.   In general the inducement for such extension is an anticipated expansion of demand ; the
promoter sees his way to sell the additional output.   Profit enters
into the calculation, in the first place, because the expectation of
selling means the expectation of selling without any special price
concessions, and therefore at a normal rate of profit, and secondly,
because, when the extension of capacity lags behind the expansion
of demand, there is likely to be, for the time, a rise of price and
therefore of the rate of profit.   The rise of price and the rise of the
rate of profit, however, do not necessarily occur.   It may be that
an expansion of demand can be met from stocks in the interval while
capacity is being extended.

It was a defect of the theory contained in the *Treatise on Money*
that an excess of investment over saving was defined to mean an
actual excess of prices over costs, and the case where an expansion
of demand evokes increased output without any intervening rise of
prices and profits was not taken into account.   The theory of
marginal efficiency is open to a similar objection.   An expansion
of demand may evoke increased active investment without any

change in marginal efficiency (which depends on the yield actually anticipated). This, however, is a minor detail.

Keynes's definition of marginal efficiency, since it makes prospective yield dependent on the sale of output, does not in terms apply to public works destined for gratuitous use or enjoyment by the public. He recognised " a growing class of investments entered upon by, or at the risk of, public authorities, which are frankly influenced in making the investment by a general presumption of there being prospective social advantages . . . without seeking to be satisfied that the mathematical expectation of the yield is at least equal to the current rate of interest—though the rate which the public authority has to pay may still play a decisive part in determining the scale of investment operations which it can afford " (pp. 163-4). And the State " is in a position to calculate the marginal efficiency of capital-goods on long views and on the basis of the general social advantage " (p. 164).

There is thus a class of capital flotations which are not governed by prospects of profit. Investment under this head would still be more or less responsive to the rate of interest. Though some of the expenditure is on necessary undertakings which will not be cut down to any great extent whatever the cost of borrowing may be, some, though desirable, is of a type for which the community would be disposed to count the cost. Also a rise in the rate of interest, which is expected to be temporary, will cause the postponement of projects, and a temporary fall will cause them to be hastened.

But the main part of Keynes's theory of marginal efficiency is concerned with profit-making enterprises. What is the relation of marginal efficiency to the rate of interest in these cases?

With a given rate of interest, widening will be pushed to the point at which profits are normal and no more than normal, or, in other words, at which the output of consumer goods meets an equivalent demand at a remunerative price. If the resulting capital outlay is more than current savings can provide for, and widening falls behind, the output of consumer goods fails to meet the demand, and rising prices yield excess profits. Marginal efficiency then exceeds interest. The excess can be corrected by a rise in the rate of interest : a rate can be found which will offset the high yield of capital, and will thus so reduce the inducement to invest that capital outlay will just keep within the limit imposed by current savings. If the rate of interest is not raised, active investment exceeds saving, passive disinvestment depletes stocks, prices rise and " a state of true inflation will be produced " (p. 202).

Widening may exceed saving in a new country in course of development, or in a poor country where the growth of population is outstripping resources.   But it is more likely to fall substantially short of saving, and that is the case that more especially interested Keynes.   If there is no deepening, passive investment occurs, and the deficiency of disposals causes a fall of prices ; marginal efficiency falls below the rate of interest.   But if the rate of interest is determined by liquidity preference, there is no certainty that it will be reduced to the extent required to revive investment.   The speculative motive may intervene to keep the rate too high for equilibrium in a condition of full employment.

IDLE BALANCES AND THE RATE OF INTEREST

We can now resume consideration of liquidity preference and the speculative motive.

Our next step will be to examine the relation between idle balances and the rate of interest, expressed by the equation $M_2 = L_2(r)$.

" Given that the rate of interest is never negative, why should anyone prefer to hold his wealth in a form which yields little or no interest to holding it in a form which yields interest ? " (p. 168).

Keynes answers that a necessary condition is the existence of *uncertainty* as to the future of the rate of interest.   Since the rate of interest may rise, " there is a risk of a loss being incurred in purchasing a long-term debt and subsequently turning it into cash, as compared with holding cash.   The actuarial profit or mathematical expectation of gain . . . must be sufficient to compensate for the risk of disappointment " (p. 169).   The implication is that the risk of disappointment is something *additional* to the risk of pecuniary loss itself.

If the actual long-term rate of interest is r, and a man estimates the risk of loss on a long-term debt, arising from a future rise in the rate, at the equivalent of b (expressed as a rate per annum), then he will regard the net yield of the investment as equivalent to $r - b$. " What matters is not the *absolute* level of r but the degree of its divergence from what is considered a fairly *safe* level of r, having regard to those calculations of probability which are being relied on " (p. 201).   The greater the fall of r below the safe rate, the greater is the risk of loss, b.   As r diminishes, b increases, and there will be a certain stage at which b exceeds r, and the net yield of the investment is turned into a loss.

Keynes seeks to illustrate this principle in the following passage :
" every fall in *r* reduces the current earnings from illiquidity, which
are available as a sort of insurance premium to offset the risk of loss
on capital account, by an amount equal to the difference between
the *squares* of the old rate of interest and the new.[1] For example,
if the rate of interest on a long-term debt is 4 per cent, it is preferable
to sacrifice liquidity unless on a balance of probabilities it is feared
that the long-term rate of interest may rise faster than by 4 per cent
of itself per annum, i.e. by an amount greater than 0·16 per cent per
annum." A nervous investor, who is not sure he has not made a
mistake in sacrificing liquidity for the sake of interest, has the
alternative of accumulating the interest he receives as a reserve fund.
If he receives 4 per cent, the first year's interest will offset a loss of
4 per cent of his capital, or 0·16 per cent per annum, or (more
accurately) a reduction of his capital from twenty-five years' purchase to twenty-four. Keynes's 0·16 per cent, however, becomes
quite wrong for subsequent years. For each year, the investor can
afford to lose from his capital one year's purchase of the interest.
Thus, if compound interest be neglected, the limiting rate to which
the market rate of interest can rise without his being a loser is $\dfrac{100}{23}$
in two years, $\dfrac{100}{22}$ in three, $\dfrac{100}{21}$ in four and so on, up to 100 per cent
in twenty-four years. In twenty-five years he will have received in
interest a sum equal to the whole of his original capital.[2]

If the interest is subject to income tax, the time within which he
secures himself against a given capital loss is proportionally longer.
If the tax reduces his interest from 4 per cent to 3 it takes him
sixteen months to offset a capital loss of a year's purchase.

With a rate of interest of *r* per unit (or 100 *r* per cent) *n* years'
interest will be sufficient to offset a fall in capital value from $\dfrac{1}{r}$ years'
purchase to $\dfrac{1}{r} - n$. The limiting rate of interest after *n* years is
therefore $\dfrac{r}{1 - rn}$ per unit. If the interest received is reduced by

---

[1] I have no idea what this means.
[2] There is no need to complicate the calculation by supposing the interest to
be accumulated at compound interest.

taxation from r to $\dfrac{r}{m}$, mn years' interest will be needed to offset the

fall in capital value of $\dfrac{1}{r} - n$, and the limiting rate of interest after

n years is $\dfrac{r}{1 - r\,mn}$.

Though Keynes's calculation requires amendment, that does not altogether invalidate his conclusion. " If ", he says, " the rate of interest is already as low as 2 per cent, the running yield will only offset a rise in it of as little as 0·04 per cent per annum. This, indeed, is perhaps the chief obstacle to a fall in the rate of interest to a very low level. Unless reasons are believed to exist why future experience will be very different from past experience, a long-term rate of interest of (say) 2 per cent leaves more to fear than to hope, and offers, at the same time, a running yield which is only sufficient to offset a very small measure of fear " (p. 202).

The following is, I think, a more rigorous statement of the point. If we suppose an investor to look forward five years, then, when he buys a 4 per cent security, he knows that after five years he will not have actually lost so long as the security has fallen no further than from twenty-five years' purchase to twenty years'. He is safe-guarded against a rise of the market rate of long-term interest up to ·5 per cent. But if the market rate is 2 per cent and he buys a security with that yield, he is only safeguarded within five years against a fall in capital value from fifty to forty-five years' purchase, that is to say, a rise of the rate to $2\frac{2}{9}$ per cent. If we take a ten-year limit, the 4 per cent security is safeguarded against a rise to $6\frac{2}{3}$ per cent, the 2 per cent security only against a rise to $2\frac{1}{2}$ per cent. Nevertheless it should not be overlooked that when the alternative to investment is a time deposit in a bank (which Keynes includes in " money "), this difference is a good deal reduced. If the deposit interest, for example, is expected to average $1\frac{1}{2}$ per cent below the yield of the investment, the gain over ten years through investing will be 15 per cent. If the investment is made at 4 per cent, that is $3\frac{3}{4}$ years' purchase and insures against a rise in the rate of interest to 4·7 per cent. If it is made at 2 per cent, $7\frac{1}{2}$ years' purchase insures against a rise in the rate to 2·35 per cent. In particular cases the comparison becomes complicated. There is no fixed relation between the average short-term rate and the long-term rate, and expectations regarding the short-term rate depend on circumstances. Such expectations, when they extend beyond a few months, are extremely conjectural. The short-term rate also may *exceed* the long-term rate. And the rate of taxation varies and cannot be exactly forecast.

The foregoing examples are confined to securities with no due date of payment, practically perpetual annuities. Repayment at a due date makes a considerable difference, especially if the date is no more than five or ten years distant.

For a long-term security, compound interest has to be taken into account. Suppose the rate of interest to be r per unit, so that the present value of a per annum in perpetuity is $\frac{a}{r}$. The present value of a bond for $\frac{a}{r}$ payable in n years and with interest at a per annum is $\frac{a}{r}$, so long as the market rate of interest is r. But, if the market rate of interest changes to r', it becomes

$$\frac{a}{r'}\left(1 - \frac{1}{(1 + r')^n}\right) + \frac{a}{r(1 + r')^n},$$

or,

$$\frac{a}{r'} + a\left(\frac{1}{r} - \frac{1}{r'}\right)\frac{1}{(1 + r')^n}.$$

If r' is greater than r, the loss in capital value is

$$a\left(\frac{1}{r} - \frac{1}{r'}\right)\left(1 - \frac{1}{(1 + r')^r}\right).$$

For a moderate term of years $\frac{1}{(1 + r')^n}$ is not much less than 1, and the above expression is substantially less than $a\left(\frac{1}{r} - \frac{1}{r'}\right)$. For a security repayable at a due date the effect of income tax is not the same as for a perpetual annuity. For, when it falls below par, the holder can count on a capital gain when it is paid off at maturity. Unless the income tax is supplemented by a capital gains tax, the market price will allow for the advantage of this gain being free of taxation. The rate at which the market discounts the future capital payment will be the rate of interest *net of tax*.

Consequently in the foregoing formula a, r and r' are all to be taken net of tax.

The following table compares the capital loss arising from a rise in the interest received on a £100 bond from 4 per cent to 5 and from 2 per cent to $2\frac{1}{2}$:

Term of bond years	Rise from 4 to 5	Rise from 2 to $2\frac{1}{2}$
5	4·23	2·32
10	7·72	4·38
30	15·37	10·46
Perpetuity . . .	20·0	20·0

The term of years has to be reckoned from the time at which the bond has to be realised up to its maturity. If it is thirty years, the loss on a 4 per cent bond will be insured against when four years' interest has been received before it is sold. For a 2 per cent bond, five years' interest would nearly suffice. If the uninvested money obtains time deposit interest $1\frac{1}{2}$ per cent below the long-term rate, the period of holding before sale would have to be ten years for the 4 per cent bond and seven years for the 2 per cent. But if the money is likely to be needed within a moderate term of years, a five- or ten-year bond would be more suitable. If compound interest be neglected, interest at r per unit on a ten-year bond which has to be realised n years before maturity would insure against the capital loss due to a rise in the rate to r', where

$$(10 - n)r = n(r' - r)$$
$$r' = \frac{10r}{n}$$

If r is 4 per cent, two years' holding insures against a rise to 5 per cent, or $3\frac{1}{3}$ years against 6 per cent. If r is 2 per cent, two years' holding insures against $2\frac{1}{2}$ per cent, or six against 5 per cent.

EXPECTATIONS AS TO THE RATE OF INTEREST

The hopes and fears referred to in the foregoing quotation (p. 175) are subject to the condition, " unless reasons are believed to exist why future experience will be very different from past experience ". That is interpreted to mean that, if a rate of interest of r per cent has prevailed in the past, a similar rate is likely to prevail in the future. But is it not equally possible that, when the actual rate of interest falls, the standard of a " fairly safe rate of interest " will fall with it ? When the rate of interest has been falling, some people may be found to argue that, if past experience is a guide, the rate *will continue to fall*.

12

Keynes says that the rate of interest is a highly psychological or rather a highly conventional phenomenon. " Its actual value is largely governed by the prevailing view as to what its value is expected to be " (p. 203). " The long-term market rate of interest will depend, not only on the current policy of the monetary authority, but also on market expectations concerning its future policy " (p. 202).

" When M_1 is increasing faster than M, the rate of interest will rise, and *vice versa*. But it may fluctuate for decades about a level which is chronically too high for full employment—particularly if it is the prevailing opinion that the rate of interest is self-adjusting, so that the level established by convention is thought to be rooted in objective grounds much stronger than convention " (p. 204).

The assumption here is that the monetary authority regulates the rate of interest through the idle balances, $M - M_1$ or M_2, and that the function $L_2 (r)$ is derived from expectations of what the monetary authority intends to do. But the monetary authority only determines the rate of interest through M_2 in virtue of the relation $M_2 = L_2 (r)$. Is not this a circular argument ? People expect the rate of interest to be r because they expect the monetary authority to make idle balances equal to M_2, but if we ask why r corresponds to M_2, we find that people's practice in regard to holding idle balances is governed by their expectation that the rate of interest will be r. If there is a universal expectation that the monetary authority will keep M_2 at such a level that the rate of interest will be 5 per cent, then 5 per cent will be the safe rate of interest, and will correspond to the value $M_2 = 0$. If the monetary authority fulfils the expectation, it will do so by keeping M_2 zero. It may, however, prefer to make the rate 4 per cent. If so, it will proceed to create additional money, and, as M_2 grows, the rate of interest falls. Eventually an equilibrium position is reached in which M_2 has the value appropriate to a rate of interest of 4 per cent.

Perhaps the monetary authority and the public might continue at cross purposes for an indefinite period, the function $L_2 (r)$ merely measuring the miscalculation by the public of the intentions of the monetary authority. Are we to suppose that that state of things is probable or even possible ? It would seem much more likely that the *expectations of the public would be modified* in consequence of the action of the monetary authority. Of this possibility Keynes makes a rather grudging admission. " Precisely because the convention is not rooted in secure knowledge, it will not be always unduly resistant to a modest measure of persistence and consistency of purpose by the monetary authority " (p. 204).

But surely it is a mistake to introduce any expectation as to the policy of the monetary authority into those beliefs of the public regarding the rate of interest, on which the function $L_2(r)$ depends. For the public do not in fact think that the monetary authority has power to determine the long-term rate of interest, nor does the monetary authority know itself to possess that power. It assumes indeed a decisive power over the short-term rate of interest, and this is recognised to have some reaction upon the long-term rate. But the power which Keynes attributed to it of determining the rate of interest *through its control of the amount of idle balances* had never been thought of by any one before.

How then is a view as to the rate of interest ever started ? Some view or convention is presupposed in the very conception of the function $L_2(r)$. The only possible answer seems to be that the view or convention is *empirical ;* it is simply based on past experience. But then what is it that shapes this experience ? At any moment in the past there will have been a conventional rate of interest, but the actual market rate may depart from the conventional rate. If the conventional rate undergoes changes, and if those changes are purely empirical in origin, they must be attributed to the departures of the actual rate from the conventional rate.

The classical theory of interest assumes that those with savings to place will be content to receive whatever yield capital goods will bring them, and that they will not withhold part of their resources from the investment market merely because, as the openings for profitable investment get filled, this yield becomes low. If the actual yield is influenced by the marginal efficiency of capital, and in turn influences the function $L_2(r)$, we get an approximation to the classical theory. We are told that there may be " changes in the liquidity function itself, due to a change in the news which causes revision of expectations " (p. 198). Does this mean a revision of expectations regarding marginal efficiency ?

Keynes rejects the argument " that what the owner of wealth desires is not a given prospective yield but the best available prospective yield ", on the ground " that there is always an alternative to the ownership of real capital assets, namely, the ownership of money and debts ; so that the prospective yield with which the producers of new investment have to be content cannot fall below the standard set by the current rate of interest. And the current rate of interest depends, as we have seen, not on the strength of the desire to hold wealth, but on the strengths of the desires to hold it in liquid and illiquid forms respectively " (pp. 212-13).

Surely this is no answer.   For the theory that the rate of interest depends on liquidity preference *presupposes* that the owner of wealth will *not* be content with the best available prospective yield, but will hold his money idle rather than accept a yield too far below the " fairly safe rate ".

Very few owners of wealth are in a position to form an opinion at all about the future rate of interest ; in general the tendency is to accept the judgment of the market in the matter.   If this tendency were dominant, and no one speculated on a rise in the rate of interest, $L_2(r)$ would be invariably zero, and Keynes's theory would become merged in the classical theory.   Perhaps this is not very far from a true description of the facts.

Nevertheless, there is a class of people who make it their business to take future changes in the rate of interest into account, that is to say, the traders who place the free capital accumulated from their depreciation funds and reinvested profits in securities.   They have to look forward to a future sale or maturity of the securities to raise funds for replacements or extensions of plant, and they will do what seems prudent to avoid a capital loss.

Like the dealers in the investment market, they buy securities with a view to subsequent sale, and like them they assume something of the role of speculators who endeavour to make reasoned forecasts of future market conditions.

For them, securities are a substitute for cash, preferable only because they yield interest.   If the yield of interest seems to be outweighed by a prospect of capital loss, securities lose their relative advantage, and the trader holds cash.   Here is Keynes's speculative motive visibly at work.   The true speculator would become a forward seller of securities or " bear ", but the trader simply abstains from buying.

Keynes seems to limit the scope of the idle balances $L_2(r)$ to an *individual* disposing of savings (current or past) out of income.   He does not specifically refer to the case of the trader whose cash is part of his capital, previously raised from the savings of individuals and from the reinvestment of profits.   Yet the latter seems to illustrate the operation of the speculative motive better than the former.

LONG-TERM AND SHORT-TERM INTEREST

Keynes's theory of interest is concerned with the long-term rate. It is true that he warns us more than once that " the " rate of interest must be taken to mean the complex of rates for varying maturities (pp. 137, 168-9, 205-6). But the prospective yield of an investment [1] is described as " a series of annuities ". Expectations of prospective yields are based partly on existing facts and partly on future events which are the subject of " long-term expectation " (pp. 147-8). A liquidity preference for money as a means of holding wealth exists, because " there is a risk of loss being incurred in purchasing a long-term debt and subsequently turning it into cash, as compared with holding cash " (p. 169).

Keynes does indeed refer to the short-term rate of interest as being easily controlled, partly because " the possible loss is small compared with the running yield " (p. 203), as if the difference in this respect between long-term and short-term investments were one of degree only. But the risk of capital loss on a short-term investment (not exceeding twelve months) is different in kind.

In the nineteenth century it was usual for sellers of goods to draw bills on the buyers, and to hold the bills till maturity unless they needed cash. A trader who needed cash would offer a selection of his bills to his bankers or to a bill broker to be discounted. If the rate of discount were higher than when the bills were drawn, there would be a loss. Calculated for a period of a few months or weeks the loss would be too minute to be reckoned as a " capital loss " at all.

It was, no doubt, the business of the discount houses to speculate on prospective movements in the discount rate. That was part of the process of arriving at a competitive rate. But their speculations were from hour to hour, and did not involve the accumulation of idle cash.

In the present century these trade bills have dropped out of use (except in international trade). Traders' short-term investments are usually confined to time deposits. As to other forms, the banks are the creditors and the traders are the debtors.

The significant distinction is not between an investment and the holding of cash, but between a long-term investment on the one hand and cash or a short-term investment on the other. A medium-term investment occupies the doubtful ground between the two ; when it extends to somewhere about ten years, it begins to involve a perceptible capital risk ; when it extends to less than five, it approximates to the short-term class.

It is not liquidity, but the absence of any appreciable risk of capital loss, that requires not only time deposits but all forms of

---

[1] It will be remembered that " an " investment is not the same thing as investment.

short-term investment to be classified with cash for the purposes of the speculative motive.

Whatever the applicability of Keynes's theory of the speculative motive to the long-term rate of interest may be, it cannot offer any explanation at all of the short-term rate. The short-term rate cannot be determined by the function $L_2(r)$, because the speculative motive does not distinguish between short-term investments and cash. At the same time, the short-term rate of interest may quite properly be described as the price of *liquidity*. While the long-term rate affects M_2, the short-term rate affects M_1. Temporary borrowing is the means of procuring cash, and facilities for short-term borrowing allow of a smaller cash balance : less provision is necessary for contingencies or even for future commitments. Interest on time deposits is the price of giving up so much liquidity as is lost by the condition that notice of withdrawal be given.

If money is withheld from the investment market on the ground of uncertainty of the future rate of interest, Keynes's position that a low long-term rate of interest may have a deflationary effect follows. But it is still a *high* short-term rate that has a deflationary effect.

There is of course a relation between the long-term and short-term rates. To the banks and other short-term lenders, a long-term investment is to some extent an alternative, and they tend to hold the balance between the two. But though thereby the average short-term rate is prevented from diverging too far from the long-term rate, there may be very wide fluctuations about that average. Those fluctuations are not directly related to the variations in idle balances which, according to Keynes's theory, determine the long-term rate ; they have to be accounted for on quite different lines.

COMMODITIES' " OWN-RATES " OF INTEREST

Nevertheless, in a chapter on the Essential Properties of Interest and Money, the whole theory is assumed to be applicable to short-term rates of interest. This chapter is remarkable for the originality of the ideas and trains of thought contained in it. Yet it is open to criticism in certain respects.

The starting-point is the principle that any commodity which may be held over a period of time has a rate of interest reckoned in *terms of itself*, which Keynes calls its " own-rate " of interest. If x units of a commodity in hand now exchange for y units to be

delivered twelve months hence, the commodity's own-rate of interest
is $\dfrac{y\quad x}{x}$ per unit per annum.

If the spot price of wheat is £100 for 100 quarters and the twelve
months forward price is £107, the money rate of interest being 5 per
cent, then £100 now is equivalent to £105 in twelve months, so that
100 quarters now exchange for $\frac{105}{107}$ of 100 or 98 quarters in twelve
months. The wheat rate of interest or the " own-rate " of interest
of wheat is *minus* 2 per cent (p. 223).

Keynes distinguishes three attributes which different assets
possess in different degrees (pp. 225-6):

(1) Some assets produce a yield by " assisting some process of
production or supplying services to a customer " ; that is characteristic of instrumental capital (e.g. a machine) or consumption capital
(e.g. a house).

(2) Most assets (except money) involve a carrying cost (wastage,
storage, depreciation, etc.).

(3) " The power of disposal over an asset during a period may
offer a potential convenience or security ", a " liquidity premium ",
which is especially characteristic of money.

Any commodity might possess all three attributes. If, with the
commodity itself as the unit of value, the yield is q, the carrying cost
c and the liquidity premium l, the own-rate of interest is $q - c + l$.

Suppose now that a commodity is subject to an expected rise (or
fall) of price at the rate of a per unit of time. Then the expression
$a + q - c + l$ is (very nearly) the proportionate difference between
the money value of a quantity of the commodity now and the money
value of the quantity at a future date for which it can be exchanged.
This expression Keynes calls the commodity's " own-rate of money-
interest " (p. 227). In so far as there is effective competition in the
capital market, the own-rates of money-interest of all commodities
tend to equality. In the example of wheat quoted above, Keynes
assumes q and l to be zero. The wheat-rate of money interest is
equal to $a - c$. Since the price of wheat twelve months forward is
107, a is 7 per cent per annum, while c is 2 per cent. Therefore the
wheat-rate of money-interest is 5 per cent. In the case of money
a, q and c are all zero, and the money-rate of money-interest, which
we may call r, is equal to l.

Keynes applies his theory of own-rates of interest to instrumental
goods and houses. Taking a house as an illustration, he assumes
c and l to be zero, and q, the yield, has apparently to be expressed as
so many houses per hundred houses. The house-rate of money

interest is $a + q$, and this must tend to be equal to r. It would be nearer reality to make c equal to the cost of maintenance and depreciation, but this is not necessary, for we can treat q as the net yield.

If the own-rates of money interest of houses, of wheat and of money are respectively $a_1 + q_1$, $a_2 - c_2$ and l_3, " the demand of wealth-owners will be directed to houses, to wheat or to money, according as $a_1 + q_1$ or $a_2 - c_2$ or l_3 is greatest ". In equilibrium they will be equally attractive, and " $a_1 + q_1$, $a_2 - c_2$ and l_3 will be equal ". Capital assets are deemed to include all kinds of stock-held products as well as instrumental goods. For each commodity, $a + q - c + l$ will be equal to the liquidity-premium of money—that is to-say, to the money-rate of money interest, *the* rate of interest. In fact, the expression $a + q - c + l$ is the prospective yield on which the definition of the marginal efficiency of capital was based (above, pp. 166-7), and-marginal efficiency, which was defined in terms of a " series of annuities ", is now expressly taken to include the prospective yield of stock-held products.

MARGINAL EFFICIENCY AND STOCK-HELD PRODUCTS

" Those assets of which the normal supply-price is less than the demand-price will be newly produced ; and these will be those assets of which the marginal efficiency would be greater (on the basis of their normal supply-price) than the rate of interest. . . . As the stock of the assets, which begin by having a marginal efficiency at least equal to the rate of interest, is increased, their marginal efficiency . . . tends to fall. Thus a point will come at which it no longer pays to produce them, *unless the rate of interest falls* pari passu. When there is *no* asset of which the marginal efficiency reaches the rate of interest, the further production of capital assets will come to a standstill " (p. 228).

How does this apply to wheat or other stock-held products ? When the supply of houses is being added to in excess of demand, rents tend to fall. If rents no longer cover interest, the production of houses will cease. Does interest play so essential a part in the production of wheat ?

Keynes's argument requires the expression $a_2 - c_2$ for wheat to be always positive. But that cannot mean that the price of wheat is always rising. Evidently for a stock-held product, if the yield is zero, a cannot mean an anticipated *rise* of price ; it must be interpreted to be a *difference* between traders' buying and selling prices.

When no change of price is anticipated, the buying price and the selling price are both alike expected to be the same in the future as in the present, but they remain different from one another.

The price difference has to cover not only the carrying cost and interest, but all the other costs of buying and selling, and to provide a margin of profit for the trader. Nor are these other costs all comprised under overhead costs. The direct expenses or prime costs of buying and selling are substantial, and in retailing they are heavy.

Keynes would identify the advantage of holding a stock, regarded separately, as a liquidity premium; the liquidity premium is " usually negligible as soon as stocks exceed a moderate level, though capable of being significant in special circumstances ".

A liquidity premium is described as the potential convenience or security offered by the power of disposal over a commodity. This does not seem altogether appropriate to a stock, like the weaver's yarn or the baker's flour, which is acquired and held for a specific purpose. If it is counted as part of the holder's liquid assets, that is not because he could sell it as it is for money, but because it is destined to be quickly used in the production of something for sale. It is true that what he holds above an essential minimum stock is for convenience of handling and for security against an unforeseen failure of supply, but the significant part of the definition is the *power of disposal*. A balance of money can be applied to any purpose, a stock of a commodity can only be used in the ways proper to it. A producer does not sell off stocks of materials to raise money, unless he has been misled in buying more than he is going to use within a reasonable period of time.

A dealer's stock is destined to be turned into money. But to turn it prematurely into money might involve a forced sale on unfavourable terms. It would be an unattractive alternative to the usual method of raising cash by borrowing from a bank, and cannot be regarded as one of the primary purposes of holding a stock.

When Keynes said that, for a stock-held product, the liquidity premium is *usually* negligible, he meant that the advantage of holding a stock only becomes substantial when the stock is at the minimum or a little above it. " In the case of an ordinary commodity the inelasticity of the demand for liquid stocks of it would enable small changes on the demand side to bring its rate of interest up or down with a rush " (p. 235). Its " rate of interest " here means its " own-rate ", $l - c$. If the stock is near the essential minimum, a small change in the requirements may result in the existing stock being just below instead of just above the minimum, and the own-rate will jump up : there will be a premium on immediate supplies.

The assumption is that between the state where stocks are near the minimum and the liquidity premium, l, is very high, and that where they are above the minimum, and l is negligible, there is no twilight in which l may be of the same order of magnitude as the rate of interest. Keynes is reverting here to his contention in the *Treatise on Money* that the holding of stocks of goods is not sensitive to the short-term rate of interest. In the *General Theory* that assumption becomes a fundamental postulate. There is no need to repeat what has been said above on the subject (pp. 108-12). The fact is that fluctuations in stocks above the minimum are regularly permitted on grounds of convenience in buying and delivery. The demand for stocks is inelastic when they are down to the minimum, but becomes very *elastic* when they are well above it. If there were absolutely no advantage in holding stocks above the minimum, interest and carrying costs would prevent any excess being held at all.

Keynes in the passage just quoted identifies the advantage of holding a minimum stock with a liquidity premium. But a stock is as necessary to the trader's business as any other part of his equipment, and it would really be more logical to reckon the advantage as " yield ". If so, we no longer say that a stock incurs a carrying cost " without any yield to set off against it " (p. 226). The yield, it may be said, is not the yield of the stock but of the trader's enterprise, the buying and selling. But marginal efficiency is defined in terms of the selling of output, and is only attributable to an enterprise.

If the expression $a + q - c + l$ is to represent the marginal efficiency of a trader's stock of goods, we must interpret the terms afresh. If q, the yield, is to be the trader's turn between buying and selling prices, a will be confined to a true rise (or fall) of price. But if, as Keynes apparently intended (above, pp. 169-72), the trader's normal profit is to be included in running expenses, then an appropriate amount ought to be included on that account in c. Normal profit is presumably, like carrying costs and interest, a ratio to outstanding capital value, per unit of time. If we neglect l, and suppose no anticipated change of price, we are left with the simple expression $q - c$ for marginal efficiency. Marginal efficiency is simply the excess of the trader's turn or price difference over carrying costs *plus* normal profit.

If now we say that production will not continue unless $q - c$ exceeds r, we are giving a quite undeserved prominence to the rate

of interest.   The condition of the continuance of orders to producers
is that the trader's price difference exceeds carrying costs *plus*
interest by an amount calculated to yield at least a normal ratio of
profit to outstanding capital.   The rate r in the formula does not
even include all the interest that the trader pays.   He will presumably have some fixed capital, the interest on which is not included in
r, for r is merely the interest on the value of goods held in stock.

It is quite fanciful to suppose r ever to be of such magnitude as
to extinguish the margin of profit p, or even to be a very serious item
in total costs.   We have seen (above, p. 105) how Wicksell's argument was seriously vitiated by his assumption that the influence of
the rate of interest depended on its importance as an item of total
costs.   The interest r is proportional to the average stock, or, in
other words, to the average time the goods are held in stock.   Profit
on the other hand is proportional to *sales*.   To the sales corresponds
a minimum or essential stock, but the average stock will be much
above the minimum.   The ratio of the average stock to the sales is
the period of turnover.

The reason why r and c can usefully be shown separately in the
formula is that they can be varied independently of sales by varying
the period of turnover.

The supposition that interest on the value of a stock of commodities is so important a consideration that the continuance of
production depends on whether $a + q - c + l$ exceeds r is not
easily reconcilable with Keynes's postulate that interest will never
be economised by reducing the stock held.   Perhaps we ought not
to take the extension of the concept of marginal efficiency to stock-
held products as anything more than a generalisation designed
rather for elegance of form than for realistic application.

AN EXPECTED CHANGE IN PRICE LEVEL

In dealing with the marginal efficiency of capital Keynes criticises
Irving Fisher's " distinction between the money rate of interest and
the real rate of interest, where the latter is equal to the former after
correction for changes in the value of money " (p. 142).

" The mistake ", he says, " lies in supposing that it is the rate of
interest on which prospective changes in the value of money will
directly react, instead of the marginal efficiency of capital.   The
prices of *existing* assets will always adjust themselves to changes in
expectation concerning the prospective value of money.   The
significance of such changes in expectation lies in their effect on the

readiness to produce *new* assets through their reaction on the marginal efficiency of capital. . . . *If* the rate of interest were to rise *pari passu* with the marginal efficiency of capital, there would be *no* stimulating effect from the expectation of rising prices. For the stimulus to output depends on the marginal efficiency of a given stock of capital rising relatively to the rate of interest " (p. 142).

Keynes has in some respects misconceived Irving Fisher's position. If the expectation of a rise of prices occurs at a time when industry is under-employed, it has the same effect as a fall in the rate of interest. Marginal efficiency is raised from $q - c + l$ to $a + q - c + l$, and the same stimulus is given to production as if the rate of interest had fallen from r to $r - a$. Fisher expresses this by saying that the expected " real " rate of interest has fallen from r to $r - a$. If the rise of prices were not foreseen, there would be no stimulus to production, but on the other hand, when it occurred, people who borrowed money would have the same advantages as if they had paid a rate of only $r - a$. In this sense the real rate of interest would be $r - a$.

If industry is fully employed when a rise of prices is foreseen, the stimulus to production cannot be operative. But there will be a tendency to hold goods off the market, thereby raising the price level, and so diminishing the extent of the gap between present and future price levels. But this rise in the present price level can be controlled by the banking system. If the banks restrict credit, they can prevent it. If previously a state of equilibrium has existed in which $r = q - c + l$ for all commodities, and there appears the expectation of a rise of the price level at the rate of a per unit of time, then the existing price level can be maintained unchanged if the rate of interest is raised forthwith to $r + a$.

In view of Keynes's own theory that the rate of investment is always pushed to the point at which marginal efficiency is equal to the rate of interest, his criticism on the ground that it is marginal efficiency and not the rate of interest that is affected by an expected rise of prices seems to be misplaced.

YIELD AND PROFIT

All this applies to stock-held goods. What then of instrumental goods ? First we may follow Keynes by taking houses as an example. A speculative builder may realise his profit by himself selling or letting the houses he produces. Or a landowner may contract with a builder to put up houses, and may keep the disposal of them in his own hands. Either way the selling or letting must yield a margin over and above costs (including commissions payable to any house agents who may intervene).

Anyone who buys house property with a view to selling it, may either be an intermediary taking over from the seller the function of marketing, or be a speculator reckoning upon a rise of price. But anyhow here, as in the case of stock-held products, there is a distinction between a price difference and a rise of price.

If profit and outgoings are set off against the rent of a house, the residue is simply the rate of interest. If all the outgoings are c, and profit is p, then q is the rent, and

$$q - c = r + p.$$

If, following Keynes's own interpretation, we include normal profit in c as a part of running costs, p is the difference of profit from normal. We may suppose the yield, q, to include all the price differences by which dealers and agents are remunerated. so that the term a, inserted in respect of a rise or fall of price, will correspond to a true change of price—it must be a forecast of the state of prices over the series of years covered by the life of the house. The forecast is unlikely to go beyond a broad judgment whether *present* prices, costs and rents are in any way exceptional. No one would attempt to make an estimate of precisely what prices would be two or three years in the future.

In applying the formula $a + q - c + l$ to the capital equipment of a productive enterprise, the same considerations apply to the term a as in the case of a house, and we can leave it on one side. It is quite right too to exclude l. But what is the significance of c ? Yield for the purposes of marginal efficiency is the yield of an enterprise. A house is both an instrument and an enterprise, but the plant of a productive undertaking is not. If q is to represent in some sense the yield of the capital equipment of the enterprise, the yield of the other factors of production must be excluded. Therefore the cost of labour and materials must be deducted from the proceeds of sale of the product, and excluded from the carrying costs c, except that c must include the upkeep and depreciation of the equipment. With this interpretation, we put $q - c = r + p$. But it is quite wrong to attribute the whole of the profit to the equipment. No acceptable principle exists for apportioning the profit among the factors of production. A house is a capital asset, and the prospect of at least normal profit is a condition of its being produced. And likewise the prospect of at least normal profit is a condition of a productive enterprise being undertaken and equipped. But, for any particular piece of equipment to be produced, the condition is that its cost-saving capacity be sufficient to offset the interest charge. But interest is only one of the items of cost, and there is no justification for singling it out as the decisive one.

Surely it is much nearer reality to treat the *margin of profit* as determining the action of the entrepreneur than to single out one item of cost. Interest or any other item of cost is only relevant to the decision to start or to extend an enterprise in that it affects the margin of profit to be obtained from the selling price anticipated. The special importance of interest lies in its being proportional to capital, so that when it is relatively high the amount of capital used to produce a given output tends to be restricted.

INTEREST AND THE LIQUIDITY PREMIUM

Keynes makes the rate of interest equal to the liquidity premium of *money*. The liquidity premium is of course different for different people and for the same person at different times.

He who contemplates spending on anything asks himself two questions : Can I afford it ? Can I pay for it ? The answer to the first depends on the commensurability of the object of expenditure with his income and standard of living, in fact, with his propensity to consume. The answer to the second depends on his cash resources. If his cash resources are low, he may have to postpone spending on something which he can afford and which it may be very inconvenient to do without, or he may lose an opportunity of getting something which he very much desires to possess.

For him the liquidity premium is then very high. If facilities for temporary borrowing are open to him, he can pay for whatever he can afford to buy. The interest he pays may be far below the equivalent of the advantage to him of being able to do so, but may be deemed to be just equal to his liquidity premium as modified by the borrowing.

The man who is saving will be accumulating surplus cash ; except at those times when he has drawn down his cash to a low level to make an investment,[1] the surplus will enable him to pay for anything he can afford to buy. His liquidity premium is very low.

Only temporarily low, it may be said, for the surplus will be needed for his next investment operation when the time comes.

[1] The reader will remember the distinction between " investment " and " an investment " (see above, p. 160).

But unless his saving takes a contractual form (a life insurance premium or repayment of a mortgage by instalments), his investment operations are within his own discretion ; he can time them to suit his convenience ; and need never reduce his cash balance so low as to make his liquidity premium considerable.   It is when he invests that he has to weigh the advantages of his investment against the loss of liquidity involved.

A distinction has to be made between short-term and long-term liquidity.   Short-term liquidity is concerned with the active cash balance, and the receipts and payments of the near future.   For an individual with given borrowing facilities, the short-term rate of interest may be equated to the marginal short-term liquidity premium.

It is not possible for a man to make any useful forecast of his net cash position over a period of more than a few weeks or months. Long-term liquidity is concerned with payments in a more distant future, which, though neither the exact amount nor the exact time can be predicted, are too large to be left to the expedients of the moment to provide for.

A trader accumulating free capital looks forward to spending it on replacements and extensions, and may regard these outlays as commitments, though the amounts to be spent and the dates can only be approximately estimated.   When he places part of his free capital in securities, it is with the definite intention to realise them after a few years.

If he regards the future capital outlay as imperative, he does not reckon the need for liquidity as measurable at all : the question is not *whether* cash is to be available, but *how* it can be most conveniently and economically made available.   The securities must ensure the liquidity no less than the cash itself.   The cost of the liquidity they provide is the risk of capital loss.   If the risk is too heavy or the uncertainty too distasteful, he will prefer to retain the cash, and the loss of interest is then the price he pays for the liquidity.

But we cannot therefore say that the *rate* of interest is equal to the liquidity premium of money.   The liquidity aimed at is the provision of the required amount of cash at a future time, and the cost of it is the loss of interest *for the intervening period*.   The amount of interest lost depends on the length of that period.   If the long-term rate of interest is 4 per cent, and the interval before the capital outlay is to be incurred is three years, the cost of preserving liquidity by forgoing interest is 12 per cent.   But we cannot say that the liquidity premium is 4 per cent *per annum*, for it is not being paid for liquidity during the intervening years at all.   The liquidity aimed at is only at the end of the period, and the premium paid for it is the 12 per cent as a whole.

The speculative motive, as conceived by Keynes, is directed not so much to the future need of cash for definite projects or commitments, as to the possibility of making a more favourable investment by waiting, and meanwhile holding an idle cash balance. There may be a variety of reasons for delaying or hastening the moment of the investment, usually the selection of a favourable moment for acquiring a particular share or property, which the investor finds attractive. Among the possible motives for delay there may, no doubt, be a belief that the prices of securities throughout the market are too high. But surely it is a mistake to identify this motive with a liquidity preference. The money is held unspent, not because it is needed for any prospective disbursements, but because no desirable disbursement is in view. Spending on consumption is limited by what the holder can afford, and spending on securities is for the time unattractive. The purchase of securities is only in suspense, and the cash may be needed at any time should a change occur either in the market or in the investor's views. But the amount to be placed is not fixed; it is within the investor's discretion, so that in the interval before the money is needed there is a surplus balance available for all purposes, and liquidity preference is probably zero. His spending will be limited only by what he can afford, not by what he can pay for.

PAST EXPERIENCE OF THE SPECULATIVE MOTIVE

For a company which accumulates a large free capital, and invests a part of it in Government securities, it is worth while to study the market. The company will in any case be both buying and selling at intervals, and, by choosing the moments wisely, it may not merely avoid loss but realise gains. Once equipped with this special knowledge, it may extend its buying and selling beyond what is strictly necessary, and obtain the profits of a regular dealer in the investment market. In the nineteen-thirties, when the banks were large holders of Government securities, Keynes once described the Midland Bank as " the biggest jobber in the gilt-edged market ". It was open to any big company with a large free capital to make profits by dealing in Government securities, though on a more moderate scale than the big banks. That is beyond the sphere of the private investor. If he studies the market, it will be in order to speculate in shares, not in Government securities.

And it should not be forgotten that with some investors the risk to be guarded against is a loss of *income* rather than a loss of capital ; uncertainty would lead them to seek the longest-dated securities, or funded stock with no due date. It is that risk which Keynes had in mind when he wrote : " in the case of the most important class of very long-term investments, namely, buildings, the risk can be frequently transferred from the investor to the occupier, or at least shared between them, by means of long-term contracts, the risk being outweighed in the mind of the occupier by the advantages of continuity and security of tenure " (p. 163). The risk which the lessor gets rid of and the occupier consents to assume is *the direct contrary* of that risk of a rise in the rate of interest to which Keynes attributed the holding of idle balances. Individuals who save large sums usually do so for the purpose of securing incomes for themselves and their families. A definite expectation that the long-term rate of interest is going to rise would induce one with this purpose in view to postpone investing in securities. But in doing so he would be taking on himself the responsibility of preferring his own judgment to that of the market. In general, investors accept the judgment of the market, and mere uncertainty, without any expectation as to a future movement of the rate of interest, would lead one who seeks fixity of income to invest without delay.

Uncertainty therefore acts in opposite directions for different people. On the other hand, if the market and the investors alike believe in a *conventional* rate of interest, a fall of the market rate below the conventional rate would cause a general distrust of *all* securities at the same time. An investor who believed that the risk of capital loss definitely outweighed the gain from interest, would keep the whole of his resources in the form of idle balances. If there were a real glut of capital that might be the rule. And Keynes's theory would seem to imply that, if the market rate of interest fell appreciably below the conventional rate, it might still be the rule, even if the conventional rate were relatively high.

The importance of the theory depends very much on the *magnitude* of the idle balances, and upon this we are given very little guidance. To take Great Britain as an example, if many people kept a considerable proportion (say a fourth) of their capital idle, the total of idle balances would run to many thousands of millions of pounds and might greatly exceed the total of active balances.

But apparently nothing of the kind has happened yet. " During the nineteenth century, the growth of population and of invention,

13

the opening up of new lands, the state of confidence and the frequency of war " kept the marginal efficiency of capital sufficiently high, and " there is evidence that for a period of almost one hundred and fifty years the long-run typical rate of interest in the leading financial centres was about 5 per cent and the gilt-edged rate between 3 and $3\frac{1}{2}$ per cent; and that these rates of interest were modest enough to encourage a rate of investment consistent with an average of employment that was not intolerably low " (pp. 307-8). Since " the tendency of the wage unit was, as usual, steadily upwards on the whole ", it follows that the supply of money was *more* than keeping pace with needs (including idle balances).

" To-day and presumably for the future ", Keynes proceeded, " the schedule of the marginal efficiency of capital is for a variety of reasons much lower than it was in the nineteenth century."

All that the monetary system could do would be to provide a supply of money consistent with " the minimum rate of interest acceptable to the generality of wealth-owners " (p. 309), and, if that rate proved too high relatively to the marginal efficiency of capital, chronic unemployment would result.

Keynes wrote in the midst of the depression of the nineteen-thirties, when the marginal efficiency of capital had indeed fallen very low. But the low rate of interest at a time of depression is not to be interpreted as a sign of an approaching glut of capital. The low rate is one of the symptoms of a shrinkage of general demand, which retards the widening of capital and lets loose a superfluity of money from the liquidation of working capital. The investment market is burdened with a surplus of funds seeking investment and the prices of fixed-interest securities rise.

And in 1935 the recent past had vividly illustrated Keynes's admission that the conventional rate of interest will not be resistant to change (above, p. 178). " Public opinion ", he wrote, " can be fairly rapidly accustomed to a modest fall in the rate of interest and the conventional expectation of the future may be modified accordingly." After the departure of Great Britain from the gold standard in 1931, the major movements of the long-term rate of interest " were effected by a series of discontinuous jumps, as the liquidity function of the public, having become accustomed to each successive reduction, became ready to respond to some new incentive in the news or in the policy of the authorities " (p. 204).

If the liquidity function is thus liable to be modified on empirical grounds several times in the course of four years, it is not likely to be a very serious obstacle to the restoration of equilibrium.

And in the preceding period, since 1918, the gilt-edged rate in Great Britain had reached 6 per cent in 1920, fell rapidly in 1921-2, and remained about $4\frac{1}{2}$ per cent till 1932. By the time Keynes wrote the discontinuous jumps had brought up the price of $2\frac{1}{2}$ per cent Consols from 54 in 1931 to 92 in January 1935.

If the conventional rate of interest is so readily adaptable to the market rate of the recent past, Keynes's theory that marginal efficiency is adjusted to the rate of interest, and not the rate of interest to marginal efficiency is true only of the very short period. The assumption made in the classical theory that the rate of interest is adapted to the marginal yield of capital equipment is true, subject to no more than a moderate lag.

THE SPECULATIVE MOTIVE AND THE CLASSICAL THEORY

Keynes thought that Marshall's account of how the rate of interest is determined by marginal yield involved a circular argument (pp. 140 and 184). And with his own definition of investment as identically equal to saving, it was obvious that the rate of interest could not perform the function of equating them. But of course it is *active* investment which has to be equated to saving. The classical theory so understood is not open to Keynes's criticism.

At the same time he did indicate the need for an important modification in the theory when he maintained that the amount which people would choose to place in the investment market *would differ from their savings*, and that the difference would depend on the rate of interest. He did not regard the difference as exclusively reflected in idle balances ; it might be partly a matter of temporary borrowing.

" The individual who believes that future rates of interest will be above the rates assumed by the market has a reason for keeping actual liquid cash, whilst the individual who differs from the market in the other direction will have a motive for borrowing money for short periods in order to purchase debts of longer term. The market price will be fixed at the point at which the sales of the ' bears ' and the purchases of the ' bulls ' are balanced " (p. 170).

Keynes here fully recognised the *balancing* function of the investment market in equalising the inflow and outflow of funds. Those who withhold funds from the investment market, and absorb cash, reduce the inflow below current savings ; those who borrow money to buy securities raise the inflow above current savings. The classical doctrine recognised that the rate of interest, in equating active investment to the resources of the investment market, might influence the latter as well as the former. But it assumed that it would do so by affecting the amount of current saving, and left out of account the possibility of money being accumulated and yet withheld from the market.

It is this possibility that Keynes especially brought out. But it is not to be concluded that the inflow of funds into the investment market can diverge to an unlimited extent from current saving. An indefinite extension of short-term borrowing for long-term capital outlay would be unattractive to borrowers as well as to lenders.

Active investment is limited in amount because the current resources of the investment market are limited in amount. " Capital has to be kept scarce enough in the long-period to have a marginal efficiency which is at least equal to the rate of interest for a period equal to the life of the capital " (p. 218).

Capital is scarce because savings are limited. The speculative motive may intervene at times to make capital still more scarce. If liquidity preference imposes its own view of what the rate of interest ought to be, and withholds resources from any projects dependent on a lower rate, liquidity preference then becomes the operative determinant of the rate of interest. But it is not the *sole* determinant. Marginal efficiency and liquidity preference put separate lower limits to the rate of interest, and the limit put by liquidity preference becomes operative when it happens to be the higher.

When marginal efficiency is high, the rate of interest " cannot be in equilibrium at a level below the rate which corresponds to full employment, because at such a level a state of true inflation will be produced, with the result that M_1 will absorb ever-increasing quantities of cash " (p. 202). If the total quantity of money, M, is limited, the increase in M_1 will eventually reduce M_2 to zero, and can then go no further. Keynes points out that when " no one feels any uncertainty about the future rates of interest, the Liquidity Function L_2 . . . will always be zero in equilibrium " (pp. 208-9). This would seem equally to be the case when the full-employment rate of interest determined by marginal efficiency is above the conventional or " fairly safe " rate of interest.

THE SPECULATIVE MOTIVE AND THE RAISING OF CAPITAL

To the trader who is investing his free capital, long-term liquidity is a reality. Likewise to the private investor who is looking forward to buying a house on retirement from business, or who is concerned to prepare for the payment of bequests, duties and expenses from his estate on his own demise.

We have seen that the risk of capital loss can be eliminated or greatly reduced by investing in securities repayable at a due date. So long as there is an ample supply of such securities, it is difficult to believe that the effect of the speculative motive is considerable.

Repayable securities, long or medium dated, have come into fashion since 1914. They were becoming common before that date, but in the nineteenth century it was not so easy as it is now to place money in marketable securities which were free from capital risk. But mortgages were common, and a mortgage which can be called up on six months' notice at any time is safeguarded against capital depreciation.

Keynes reckoned time deposits as " money ", and regarded the delimitation of the line between " money " and " debts " as a matter of convenience (p. 167). In England we think of time deposits mainly as balances subject to a week's notice (and in practice available on demand) and yielding interest $1\frac{1}{2}$ or 2 per cent below bank rate. But in most countries deposits at three months or more, yielding interest within a fraction of a fully remunerative rate, are a favourite form of investment. Such deposits require neither a fully liquid backing nor any considerable cash reserve. It is consistent with prudent banking to hold against them the same kind of repayable securities as form a suitable investment for the free capital of an industrial concern.

We have seen that the speculative motive is operative mainly among those who look forward to occasions for substantial capital outlays in the future, and especially therefore among traders disposing of their accumulated depreciation funds and reinvested profits. And the traders who are concerned with the future rate of interest in deciding between holding cash and acquiring securities, are similarly concerned when they have to decide the favourable moment to *raise* capital for necessary outlays. The same view of the market which leads one trader to refrain from putting his free capital into securities, will lead another to sell securities for the purpose of engaging in capital extensions or replacements.

When Keynes wrote that the rate of interest " may fluctuate for decades about a level which is chronically too high for full employment " (p. 204), he meant that the rate might fail to fall as fast as a declining marginal efficiency of capital would require. He was assuming the effect of the rate of interest on active investment to work through a direct comparison of interest to be paid with expected yield. But a direct comparison is beset with uncertainty, and the variations in the long-term rate of interest which actually occur are too small to have any great effect in the calculations on which projects of capital outlay are based.

The investment market may put a limit to flotations by flatly refusing them. On the other hand, the trader who holds a reserve of securities, and can raise capital by selling them, is not dependent on a new flotation. Nevertheless, he is not indifferent to the state of the market; he will not sell in what he believes to be an unfavourable market if, by waiting for a few weeks or months, he can sell at a substantially better price. The deterrent effect is not in the rate of interest but in the *capital loss* attaching to an immediate sale, that very capital loss the prospect of which forms the subject of the speculative motive.

The idea of a long-term rate of interest below the " conventional " rate being high enough to be *deterrent* is therefore unreal. The rate of interest as conceived by sellers of securities is likely to be no less conventional than that assumed by buyers. The state of the market which leads the latter to withhold their money and to refuse to buy, will relieve the former of all hesitation in selling to raise money for capital outlay.

In fact, so " conventional " is the rate of interest that the equilibrium of the investment market can hardly be said to be maintained, as both the classical theory and Keynes's theory say, by the direct relation between the rate of interest and the yield of capital projects. The divergence from the conventional or " fairly safe " rate enters as much into the calculations of the projectors of capital outlay as into those of purchasers of securities.

We have here an explanation of how the rate of interest comes to be " conventional ". Not only is the liquidity function, $L_2(r)$, concerned rather with the divergence of r from a " fairly safe " rate, but it is the divergence of the rate from a normal or conventional rate, rather than the absolute rate, that influences the volume of capital outlay.

In the *Treatise on Money* (Vol. I, p. 203), Keynes showed the effect of a temporary rise in the short-term rate of interest on the investment market. The prices of securities would fall, but the fall would correspond to an insignificant rise in the long-term rate of interest, and he recognised that the principal effect on capital outlay would be felt in the postponement of enterprises. Had he generalised this principle, and looked for the effect of any fall of the prices

of securities, which is regarded as temporary, in the postponement
of enterprises rather than in their abandonment, he might have
modified his view of the close relation between marginal efficiency
and the long-term rate of interest.

Within fairly wide limits, it matters little what the prevalent
long-term rate of interest is ; whether it be high or low, a *departure*
of the market rate from it will hasten or retard the inflow of money
into the market, and retard or hasten the outflow.   An apparently
high rate might persist for a long time without appreciably discouraging the deepening of capital, provided it were generally
regarded not as high but as normal.

Likewise, it may be said, an apparently low rate, if regarded as
normal, would not retard the placing of money in the investment
market.   But that does not altogether dispose of the speculative
motive.   One who is faced with the prospect of a capital disbursement in a few years, and who makes no forecast of future rates of
interest, but is simply uncertain about them, may make the calculation referred to above (pp. 173-7), setting the gain in interest against
a possible capital loss on the sale of securities, and may decide that
the investment is not worth while.   Without pressing the argument
that he could avoid the uncertainty by investing in repayable
securities maturing at a not too distant date, we turn once more to
Keynes's formulae.

LIQUIDITY PREFERENCE AND MONETARY POLICY

He had little to say of the part played by the mechanism of the
investment market in determining the long-term rate of interest.
In his eyes the rate was the rate at which people were willing to place
their money in the market.   They would go on placing it till the
marginal efficiency of capital fell so low that the rate of interest
became unattractive, and then they would place no more.

" As a rule, we can suppose ", he wrote (p. 171), " that the
schedule of liquidity preference, relating the quantity of money to
the rate of interest, is given by a smooth curve which shows the rate
of interest falling as the quantity of money is increased."   The
smooth curve is expressed by the function $L_2(r)$.   It would conform
better with Keynes's approach here to express the rate of interest, r,
as a function of the idle balances, M_2, the inverse of L_2.

But in practice it is dealers in the investment market who quote
a rate of interest.   The market lowers the rate when the inflow of
money from buyers of securities exceeds the outflow to sellers, and

it is through this process that the quantity of money affects the rate of interest.

Consider now the case where the quantity of money, M_1, does not change, but marginal efficiency declines. The decline in marginal efficiency first makes itself felt in a falling off of active investment, I. Incomes, Y, are then reduced in accordance with the principle of the multiplier, $Y = kI$, and M_1 is reduced in accordance with the function, $M_1 = L_1(Y)$.

So long as r remains unchanged, M_2, or $L_2(r)$ remains unchanged. If M_1 is reduced by an amount m, $M = M_1 + M_2 + m$, and people find themselves with surplus money, m, which they do not need for their active balances, and which the speculative motive does not induce them to hold; that is to say, at the existing rate of interest, r, they are willing to place all their money in excess of $M_1 + M_2$ in the investment market.

If, as Keynes supposes, M_1 is determined by Y, not Y by M_1, surplus money cannot find an outlet by increasing Y. It therefore passes into the investment market, which parts with an equivalent amount of securities. It is at that stage that the rate of interest is affected. The investment market finds that the inflow of money from buyers of securities exceeds the outflow from sellers, and proceeds to raise prices of securities with a view to balancing buyers and sellers, or bulls and bears. In other words, the market reduces the long-term rate of interest.

Keynes never brought the cash balances of dealers in the investment market specifically under his classification. Evidently the dealers, no less than other people, will be subject to the transactions motive and the precautionary motive. Some of them may dispense with cash balances, and carry on business with bank advances, but so do some traders in commodities, and even some consumers.

In general, fluctuations in their cash, representing disparities between purchases and sales of securities in the course of their business, ought to be included in M_1. Under what conditions then will the speculative motive operate among them ? If the inflow of cash into the market exceeds the outflow, that means that the prices of securities are too low to elicit a sufficient outflow. If the dealers deliberately keep prices down, because they hope later on to replace the securities they are selling at still lower prices, they are speculating on a rise in the rate of interest. But even then their speculation is not attributable to liquidity preference : they are not having regard to future contingencies requiring the spending of the money. And the speculation is for a short period, within which the loss on account of forgoing interest will be a negligible amount.

In the particular case we are considering, when capital outlay falls off owing to the decline in marginal efficiency, it is extremely improbable that dealers will be found to speculate on a fall in the prices of securities just when the market cannot find sufficient sellers.

The appearance of the additional cash, m, in the investment market will evidently be the signal for a rise in the prices of securities. As the market rate of interest declines, the speculative motive comes into play, and M_2 increases. Consequently, when the investment market is relieved of its surplus cash, M_2 is greater than before, and M_1 is less. The market cannot then reduce the rate of interest any further, and fails to raise I and Y above the level corresponding to the reduced M_1.

In short, if M is fixed, and r falls, M_2 increases and M_1 decreases, and Y falls in proportion to M_1.

If the fall in Y has been brought about by diminished production and a fall in real incomes, there will be a diminished volume of saving. But this is not an essential condition of a new equilibrium. The fall in Y may be brought about by a fall in the price level and wage level, with undiminished production and employment, and with saving diminished only in terms of money units, provided the increase in M_2 is such that the rate of interest will be low enough to induce active investment equal to the undiminished saving. " A reduction of the wage-unit will release cash from the other uses for the satisfaction of the liquidity-motive " (p. 232).

Alternatively, the condition that M is constant might be removed, and M might be supposed to be enlarged by such amount as must be added to M_2 to maintain the desired rate of interest, M_1 remaining unchanged.

Either way the required ratios of M_1 and M_2 to Y are reached to produce full employment. The deadlock which Keynes attributes to liquidity preference is broken.

Keynes felt the need to meet this objection. He was prepared to argue that neither an increase in the supply of money nor a reduction of wages could be relied on to prevent chronic unemployment.

As to an increase in the supply of money, he argued that " a large increase in the quantity of money may cause so much uncertainty about the future that liquidity-preferences due to the security-motive may be strengthened ; whilst opinion about the future of the rate of interest may be so unanimous that a small change in present rates may cause a mass movement into cash " (p. 172). What is the " security motive "? The speculative motive is concerned with " security " of capital values, and if strengthened would contribute to the " mass movement into cash ".

Surely " a mass movement into cash " is an exceptional contingency (see below, pp. 204-6). But, perhaps security motive means precautionary motive. When the idle balances increase, they become available for all purposes. " The amount of cash which an individual decides to hold to satisfy the transactions motive and the precautionary motive is not entirely independent of what he is holding to satisfy the speculative-motive " (p. 199). The assumption that M_1 and M_2 are " largely independent of one another " is only a " safe first approximation ".

Surely not a very safe one ! For anyone who has been led by the speculative motive to accumulate a big idle balance, any further provision for the precautionary-motive becomes unnecessary. There will be individuals with no savings, who if the increase is going to cause a rise of prices, will need bigger cash balances when the rise occurs. But, when prices are expected to rise, people will reduce their balances rather than increase them ; they will hasten to buy things before the rise occurs. That is a matter in which experience amply confirms common sense. And what we are now concerned with is a creation of additional money just sufficient to maintain full employment at the existing price level and wage level.

It may be difficult to estimate exactly the right amount of additional money. Keynes gave a warning : liquidity preferences may be increasing more than the quantity of money ; the marginal efficiency of capital may be falling more rapidly than the rate of interest ; the propensity to consume may be falling off ; or prices may rise, so that the quantity of money necessary to maintain a given rate of interest is increased (p. 173).

In other words, the functions L_1, L_2 and the multiplier, k, may change, and the amount of money needed may, for that or any other reason, be miscalculated.

If the functions themselves are supposed to *change*, that means that they do not adequately represent the position ; the analysis on which the theory is based is vitiated. That is a question to which I shall return (below, pp. 211-13).

A creation of new money may be by some process, such as the coining of gold or the printing of paper money to meet current Government expenditure, through which it " accrues as someone's income " (p. 200). But, even if that is so in the first instance, the new level of income, Keynes says, will not suffice to absorb the whole in an addition to M_1. There will be a residue to be dealt with through a fall in the rate of interest. In general, new money is issued " by a relaxation of the conditions of credit by the banking system, so as to induce someone to sell the banks a debt or a bond in exchange for the new cash ".

Thus, " a change in M can be assumed to operate by changing r, and a change in r will lead to a new equilibrium partly by changing M_2 and partly by changing Y and therefore M_1 ".

" Perhaps ", Keynes concludes, " a complex offer by the central bank to buy and sell at stated prices gilt-edged bonds of all maturities, in place of the single bank rate for short-term bills, is the most important practical improvement which can be made in the technique of monetary management " (p. 206).

If the consumers' income can only be increased through a reduction of the rate of interest, and the rate of interest can only be reduced through the issue of new money, the authority which creates money can best discharge its responsibility by itself quoting the rate of interest. Then " the relationship between the complex of rates of interest and the quantity of money would be direct " (p. 205).

The central bank would still have to discover the rate of interest which in the circumstances of the moment corresponds to full employment. The new feature of the technique would be the inclusion of the long-term rate, and that is really the essential point. Underlying the whole of Keynes's *General Theory* is his postulate that borrowing for the holding of goods in stock is impervious to the influence of the short-term rate of interest. Borrowing is for the purpose of spending, and the postulate excludes from the operation of credit policy spending on the production or purchase of goods to be held for sale. Therefore the spending affected must be on something else—securities or capital assets, to be retained not for sale but for the yield of income or for use.

The postulate does not deny the creation of money for the production or purchase of goods, but only the possibility of *modifying* the amount of money so created by varying the terms on which it is lent. When money is lent for the production of goods, it " accrues as someone's income ", no less than new money created by the coining of gold or the printing of paper money, and, if the banks can induce traders to borrow more for that purpose, the increase in M_1 is accompanied by an immediate increase in Y. The postulate excludes that possibility, and allows the banks no other channel than the investment market; they can only bring about any increase in Y by increasing the inflow of money into the investment market, so that the resulting fall in r encourages capital outlay and so eventuates in a rise in Y through the operation of the multiplier. Hence results the special importance Keynes attached to the speculative motive. If the speculative motive causes M_2 to increase as the rate of interest falls, so much of the new money as is absorbed in M_2 fails of its purpose. But that only means that more money has to be created than would otherwise be necessary. The banks can take the place of their customers in buying securities and feeding the investment market with funds.

In a community where the accumulation of idle balances in consequence of the speculative motive is a phenomenon of long standing, which has been dealt with in the past by credit expansions, and where it is destined to continue on the same scale, no sudden or large increase in the quantity of money need ever be caused.

In the days of the gold standard the expansion of bank deposits was governed by the gold reserves. For stability the growth of the stock of currency and of the credit superstructure had just to keep pace with needs, and if the speculative motive was then at work, causing idle balances to accumulate, the needs to be covered included their growth as well as that of the active balances. Experience shows that the growth of a credit system based on a metallic standard is sometimes too slow, but sometimes also too fast. Even when it has been too slow, the idle balances can only have been one among the various causes of reduced activity.

A monetary policy directed expressly to stabilising the purchasing power of the money unit would create whatever amount of credit might be required to counteract any contraction of the flow of money. It would allow for the accumulation of idle balances *automatically*. The necessary expansion would proceed continuously and gradually, and there is no reason why it should have any special reaction on liquidity preferences.

Even if idle balances have been manageable in the past, it cannot be assumed that they always will be so in the future. " There is the possibility ", Keynes wrote (p. 207), " that after the rate of interest has fallen to a certain level, liquidity preference may become virtually absolute in the sense that almost everyone prefers cash to holding a debt which yields so low a rate of interest."

" If such a situation were to arise, it would mean that the public authority itself could borrow through the banking system on an unlimited scale at a nominal rate of interest."

The public authority (presumably the central bank with Government backing) would have to absorb an unlimited amount of securities, and provide in exchange suitable assets to be held by the commercial banks against the ever swelling idle balances. The assets would have to be for the most part short and medium dated.

That would be a precarious position. For when idle balances had expanded to a very large total, a change of conditions might cause them to contract again. A crop of new inventions, for example, might revive the deepening process and create a demand for capital in excess of current savings. The rate of interest rises, the idle balances are tempted back into securities, and an unlimited fund becomes available for capital enterprise. The public authority could of course start reselling the securities bought. But they might have to be sold at a very heavy sacrifice of price to compete with the new openings. An inordinate inflation would be only too likely to result.

This problem would arise in any case in the event of a glut of capital, but Keynes rendered a service to economics in pointing out that it may occur at a stage when the long-term rate of interest is still some way above zero.

It is, I think, clear, that if a true glut of capital occurred, that is to say, if the opportunities of deepening came to an end, and widening failed to absorb current savings, the long-term rate would not fall to zero. Anyone with an accumulation of savings in the form of idle money would not be prepared to tie it up for a term of years without some inducement. There might still be long-term borrowers, especially the Government, and the Government would have to pay some interest, if only a fraction of 1 per cent. The interest would be a genuine liquidity premium, though the advantages of the liquidity surrendered by the lenders would be very slight. Even when there is a true glut of capital, the rate paid on a long-term loan may vary, for the more the Government has to borrow the greater the concessions the lenders can exact from it.

The minimum rate of interest, however, is quite distinct from the conventional rate. The conventional rate may be relatively high, and is likely to change as people's opinions and forecasts are adapted to the apparent trend of the market rate and to the effect of passing events on prospects. But in general the minimum rate will be a mere potentiality, far below the market rate, the conventional rate and the marginal yield of instrumental goods alike.

Keynes had in mind a minimum rate not far below 2 per cent, or perhaps above it (p. 219). But one at any rate of his grounds for so thinking would not bear examination. The cost of bringing borrowers and lenders together is not a considerable item when reflected in yield. Big gains are made by promoters and issuing houses who undertake industrial and commercial flotations. But the promoters are the creators of the goodwill or opportunities for profit, which they sell. An issuing house, it is true, is an inter-mediary : it has to persuade intending investors of the merits of the particular enterprise which it is recommending. But their charges represent a small fraction in terms of *yield*. Moreover, if the Government were floating a loan at a minimum rate of interest at a time of glut, it would no doubt relieve the lenders of all charges and bear the costs of issue itself.

" A bank ", Keynes says, on another aspect of the question, " may have to charge its customers $1\frac{1}{2}$ to 2 per cent even if the pure rate of interest is nil " (p. 208). That is, on the assumption that the interest which the bank charges is the only source from which it can cover its expenses and provide its own profit. But of course banks can make charges directly on their depositors for the services they render, and the British banks have been doing so in recent years, when a great part of their assets has been yielding only $\frac{1}{2}$ or 1 per cent.

A man with an accumulation of money might find it worth while to deposit it in a bank, even if he had to pay a small charge, for the sake of safe-keeping. The carrying charge may thus exceed the liquidity value of the money.

A true glut of capital is a special case, and would undoubtedly require special measures. If a true glut be left on one side, it seems quite clear that the idle balances can be prevented from causing chronic unemployment by a suitable monetary expansion. In the contingency of the vicious circle of contraction being allowed to gain too firm a hold, a resort to fiscal measures, such as a big budget deficit, is by no means to be ruled out ; the deficit is in effect a monetary measure, in that its purpose is to expand the flow of money.

THE WAGE LEVEL

We have seen (above, p. 201) that, as a corrective of the chronic unemployment threatened by the speculative motive, an alternative to a monetary expansion would be a reduction of wages. At the beginning of his book Keynes challenged the " assumption that the general level of real wages depends on the money-wage bargains between the employers and the workers " (p. 12). " There may exist no expedient by which labour as a whole can reduce its *real* wage to a given figure by making revised *money* bargains with the entrepreneurs " (p. 13).

The question of changes in wages is resumed in Keynes's nineteenth chapter. He contests the generally accepted argument " that a reduction in money-wages will, *caeteris paribus*, stimulate demand by diminishing the price of the finished product, and will therefore increase output and employment . . ." (p. 257).

" In its crudest form this is tantamount to assuming that the reduction of money-wages will leave demand unaffected." Some economists, we are told, would defend this on the ground that demand depends on the quantity of money and its income velocity, but it would be " more usual to agree that the reduction of money-wages may have *some* effect " in reducing the purchasing power of the workers, even if there is an increase in other directions through increased employment and the undiminished incomes of other factors.

Keynes argues that a reduction of wages can only increase employment through its effects upon the propensity to consume, the marginal efficiency of capital or the rate of interest, and he proceeds to trace these effects.

With regard to the propensity to consume, he points out that there will be some redistribution of income. " The transfer from wage-earners to other factors is likely to diminish the propensity to consume." Some other changes may tell in the contrary direction, but on balance the effect is likely to be adverse to the propensity to consume.

This may well be so, but what it comes to is that, if full employment is preserved by means of a reduction of wages, the reduction in the volume of saving which the high wage level would have brought about does not occur.

Keynes proceeds to point out that the effect of a reduction of money wages on the marginal efficiency of capital will depend in some degree on whether wages are *expected* to continue to fall or to rise again. An expectation of a further fall will have a depressing effect on business, whereas an expectation of a rise will have a stimulating effect. Undoubtedly the reaction of the reduction of wages upon expectations may have complicating effects. But that is a matter appropriate to a dynamic theory. We may confine ourselves, in the first instance, to a static treatment. Given the propensity to consume and the liquidity preference function, $L_2(r)$, can a reduction of wages attain equilibrium ? Keynes goes to the root of the matter (on his own assumptions) when he indicates

(p. 263) that the reduction in money incomes " will diminish the need for cash for income and business purposes; and it will therefore reduce *pro tanto* the schedule of liquidity-preference for the community as a whole. *Caeteris paribus*, this will reduce the rate of interest and thus prove favourable to investment " (that is, of course, to *active* investment).

In fact, when Y falls, M_1 or $L_1(Y)$ falls, and, if M is supposed given, then, as M_1 diminishes, M_2 increases.

According to Keynes's theory this is the indispensable condition of full employment. If M_2 does not increase relatively to the wage level and therefore to Y, the old rate of interest must recur, and if at the outset that rate of interest was inconsistent with full employment, it will be equally so at the end, when wages, prices and the total of incomes have all been reduced in proportion.

There is, it may be said, also an increase in the marginal efficiency of capital. But that increase is only by comparison with marginal efficiency under conditions of under-employment. For when the total of incomes is reduced, and wages remain unchanged, there results, along with unemployment, a shrinkage of profits, and therefore of marginal efficiency. If thereupon wages are reduced in the proportion in which the total of incomes has already been reduced, profits are restored to normal and marginal efficiency likewise recovers. But the marginal efficiency corresponding to full employment and the relation of the rate of interest to full employment remain the same as before. Therefore M_2 must be such as to be consistent with that rate.

" It is therefore ", Keynes concludes, " on the effect of falling wage and price level on the demand for money that those who believe in the self-adjusting quality of the economic system must rest the weight of their argument, though I am not aware that they have done so " (p. 266). " If the quantity of money is virtually fixed, it is evident that its quantity in terms of wage-units can be indefinitely increased by a sufficient reduction of money wages. . . . We can, therefore, theoretically at least, produce precisely the same effects on the rate of interest by reducing wages, whilst leaving the quantity of money unchanged, that we can produce by increasing the quantity of money whilst leaving the level of wages unchanged."

This seems to concede the case of those economists who say that demand will be relatively unaffected because it depends on the quantity of money and its income velocity.

Nevertheless, " while a flexible wage policy and a flexible money policy come, analytically, to the same thing, inasmuch as they are alternative means of changing the quantity of money in terms of wage-units, in other respects there is, of course, a world of difference between them ".

Uniform wage reductions for every class of labour cannot be secured. The reductions will be obtained irregularly and at the cost of disputes. Relativities between wage earners on the one hand and recipients of incomes which are fixed by contract or custom will be disturbed. The burden of debts will be increased.

But while such reasons may afford very good *practical* grounds for not relying on changes of wages to attain equilibrium, they do not alter the theoretical efficacy of a reduction of wages to attain equilibrium. Keynes, it is true, says that " the same reasons which limit the efficacy of increases in the quantity of money as a means of increasing investment to the optimum figure apply *mutatis mutandis* to wage reductions " (p. 266). A moderate reduction " may prove inadequate, whilst an immoderate reduction might shatter confidence " (p. 267). It has already been suggested above (pp. 202-4) that an immoderate increase in the quantity of money would not be called for, and in the case of wages the reduction required would be no more than that which would just suffice to restore equilibrium between prices and costs with the reduced consumers' income.

All the same Keynes seems to favour an " immoderate " reduction of wages. " A sudden large reduction of money-wages to a level so low that no one believes in its indefinite continuance would be the event most favourable to a strengthening of effective demand " (p. 265). No " shattering of confidence " here ! What he deprecates is " that depressions should be accompanied by a gradual downward tendency of money-wages, a further moderate wage reduction being expected to signalise each increase of, say, 1 per cent in the amount of unemployment " (p. 265).

Keynes was inclined to assume a perpetual fall in marginal efficiency, which would require a corresponding fall in the rate of interest and presumably also in wages. If the supply of money, M, is held fixed, and the rate of interest has to go on falling, then M_2 must be continually increasing and M_1 decreasing. Chronic unemployment can hardly be cured by a chronic state of falling wages, for the expectation of a further fall of wages would always have a paralysing effect on production.

But the perpetual fall in marginal efficiency is itself an unwarrantable assumption. It is based on Keynes's assumption of unchanging technique, an assumption which ought to be abandoned as soon as any realistic application has to be made.

14

Under practical conditions, it is true, saving is likely (but not certain) to exceed what is essential to the widening of capital, and the deepening of capital will tend to lower marginal efficiency, but on the other hand invention (to say nothing of war) will be tending to raise marginal efficiency, and, whatever the net effect of these tendencies may be, profits (and therefore marginal efficiency) will be subject to fluctuations. Consequently a system of maintaining full employment by adjusting wages would not mean a perpetual fall of wages; sometimes a fall would be required, sometimes a rise.

That is not to say that such a system is *desirable*. Keynes comes, with very good reason, to the conclusion that " the maintenance of a stable general level of money wages is, on a balance of considerations, the most advisable policy for a closed system; whilst the same conclusion will hold good for an open system, provided that equilibrium with the rest of the world can be secured by means of fluctuating exchanges ". But that is a totally different thing from the thesis with which Keynes stated that it may be *impossible* to reduce real wages by reducing money wages.

In fact, Keynes's conclusion is a particular application of the general principle that stable money is best interpreted to mean a monetary policy which is consistent with an unchanging wage-level in terms of money. Stability so understood is not only the most equitable policy as between pecuniary rights and obligations, but it is best calculated to avoid the fluctuations in economic activity due to monetary causes. The introduction of Keynes's speculative motive does not affect its advantages.

In the passage quoted above a stable wage level is recommended not only for a closed system, but for an open system, provided the exchanges are allowed to fluctuate. When that condition is not fulfilled, that is to say, when there is an international monetary standard like the gold standard, a reduction of wages " will be favourable to investment, since it will tend to increase the balance of trade ", but it will " worsen the terms of trade " (pp. 262-3). The latter tendency will not be unfavourable to increased employment and may even be favourable, since " a reduction in real incomes . . . may tend to increase the propensity to consume ".

This case (which has in the past been the practically important one and may be so in the future) is similar to that where demand is kept unchanged through the quantity of money and velocity of circulation being unchanged. In practice it is usually through fixed foreign exchanges that a monetary policy of that type operates.

THE FUNCTIONS L_1 AND L_2

In the two preceding sections we have been accepting Keynes's functions L_1 and L_2 as determining the active and the idle balances, but we have already seen reason to reject the rigid division he made between the two. Is it not analytically legitimate, it may be asked, to isolate the speculative motive, and to define L_2 (r) as the difference that the long-term rate of interest makes in the quantity of money people desire to hold ? Perhaps it would be, if the effects of a change in r were independent of the manner in which the change is brought about. If that is not so, the elements which compose the function L_2 are themselves liable to be changed. At any moment L_2 depends on the prevailing view of a " fairly safe level of r ", and on " uncertainty " as to its future course (p. 201). If there were no uncertainty, L_2 would " always be zero in equilibrium ".

The function L_2 may be modified through " a change in the news which causes a revision of expectations " (p. 198). We have seen how a change in marginal efficiency will cause a change in r, even if the quantity of money be supposed unchanged (above, pp. 200-1). But r may change in response to an increase or decrease in the amount of borrowing or of debt redemption by the Government or other public authorities. That will be a totally different kind of news, and may have a different kind of effect on the liquidity function. Intervention by the central bank in the investment market would affect people's expectations in a different way again.

It will be remembered that r denotes not simply the long-term rate of interest, but the complex of rates for different maturities. The effects of a change are likely to depend materially on the manner in which it appears among the several rates. It might, for example, appear in the first instance as a change made by the banks in the short-term rates, and then react on the prices of investment securities ; or contrariwise, it might be transmitted from the investment market to the banking system.

Savings are in general first accumulated in the form of money. When one who is saving can spare a suitable amount from his growing balance, he will place it in investments. If the speculative motive intervenes, and he prefers to hold cash, the moment of placing is delayed, and the money continues to accumulate. But the speculative motive is only one of several motives that may prolong or shorten the interval before the accruing savings are placed. Intending investors will often be much more concerned with the prices and prospects of particular shares or with the attractions of particular pieces of property than with the general level of yield. So long as the speculative motive is absent, the accruing balance is all included in M_1. When placing is delayed specifically on the ground that the yield of securities in general is too low, so much as would otherwise have been placed counts as part of M_2. If M_2 is the difference that the long-term rate of interest makes in the amount of money held, then when placing is hastened because the yield of securities in general is exceptionally attractive, the resulting reduction of balances ought to enter into M_2 as a minus quantity. Keynes alluded to the case of the bull speculator who obtains bank advances to buy securities, but I do not think he intended to take account of such indebtedness as well as of the actual reduction of balances in reckoning M_2. But, even without that complication, M_2 must be assumed to be capable of becoming a minus quantity.

When an economic quantity which is in fact the resultant of several determinants is expressed as a function of only one, as M_1 is of Y and M_2 of r, the consequence is that the function itself has to be supposed to change. It is no real simplification to say that $M_1 = L_1(Y)$ and $M_2 = L_2(r)$, if the functions L_1 and L_2 are themselves subject to material changes at any time—possibly from hour to hour.

Keynes adopts a modified income velocity of money, V, relating income not to the total quantity of money, M, but to the active balances M_1. V is $\dfrac{Y}{L_1(Y)}$ and is thus a function of Y only. Yet the value of V depends " on the character of banking and industrial organisation, on social habits, on the distribution of income between different classes and on the effective cost of holding idle cash " (p. 201). Surely then it is quite wrong to make V a function of income alone.

In fact V is not a function of income at all. It is true that a change in Y may sometimes be associated with a change in V. That occurs when for a time the change in Y is not accompanied by a corresponding change in M_1. If there is a discontinuous change in the price level or in productive activity, the adjustment of M_1 will take time. In the interval before the function L_1 reasserts itself, V reflects the change in Y only because M_1 does not.

In fact M_1 can plausibly be represented as a function of Y only because, *if V is given*, M_1 is proportional to Y. As to V itself, any of the factors which influence V may happen to change when income changes, but none can properly be expressed as a function of income.

We may put the function $L_1(Y)$ in the form of $\frac{Y}{V}$, where V is *not* a function of Y.

How then is V to be expressed ? V sums up the motives which link together all the individual incomes and individual active balances. About the motives determining any kind of economic behaviour it is possible to make generalisations, when some definite bias makes itself felt, and fortuitous movements can be assumed to average out. But the standard of what is to be neglected as fortuitous can be varied within wide limits, and as a more and more refined standard is introduced, the tendencies taken into account acquire greater complexity.

V is a function of all those variables which are not neglected as fortuitous. Keynes's assumption that M_1 is determined by Y, not Y by M_1, is untenable. For M_1 is only determined by Y in so far as V is given, and, when V is given, it is equally true that Y is determined by M_1.

When Y or M_1 varies, V is likely to be modified but not in general in the simple way that can be expressed by making it a function of either of them.

EXTERNAL INVESTMENT

Keynes has little to say about international trade till near the end of his book. He deals with it in his penultimate chapter mainly from a historical standpoint with special reference to Mercantilism, the policy of securing a favourable balance of trade.

Where a country is troubled by an insufficiency of the inducement to new investment, foreign investment (including the accumulation of the precious metals) may help to fill the gap (p. 335). This is subject to the drawback that the advantage which one country gains from a favourable balance is liable to involve an equal disadvantage to some other country (p. 338).

" In an economy subject to money contracts and customs more or less fixed over an appreciable period of time, where the quantity of the domestic circulation and the domestic rate of interest are primarily determined by the balance of payments, as they were in Great Britain before the war, there is no orthodox means open to the authorities at home for countering unemployment at home except by struggling for an export surplus and an import of the monetary metal at the expense of their neighbours. Never in history was there a method devised of such efficacy for setting each country's advantage at variance with its neighbours' as the international gold (or formerly silver) standard " (pp. 348-9).

That may have been true of mediæval conditions, when the mercantilist aim could only be satisfied by acquisitions of the precious metals, but it hardly seems applicable to external investment properly so called.   In general, when one country invests in another, the rate of interest in the latter is relatively high.   That is a sign that remunerative openings for investment are waiting to be filled.   It is unlikely that the people of a country which is importing foreign capital would ever be led to accumulate idle balances on the ground that they think the rate of interest unduly low, or that the country would suffer from unemployment on account of active investment falling short of savings.   That being so, the gain to the investing country is not offset by any corresponding injury to the other.

The fault which Keynes finds with external investment is in fact of a different kind ; it is rather that " excessive facilities for foreign lending and the purchase of properties abroad frequently stood in the way of the decline of the domestic rate of interest which was required to ensure full employment at home " (p. 337).   How can this occur ?   The restriction of investment at home does not cause unemployment when the gap is filled by the production of goods for export equivalent to the external investment.   If idle balances depend on the rate of interest then the higher the rate of interest the smaller will the idle balances be, however investment at home may be reduced.   In fact external investment, so long as the economic conditions favour it, offers a method of reconciling a rate of interest high enough to prevent the accumulation of idle balances with a total of active investment sufficient to use up all the available savings.   Nevertheless Keynes does not seem to have reconsidered his previous views adverse to external investment.

REMEDIAL PROPOSALS

Keynes's concluding chapter has something to say of the remedies and safeguards which his theory would suggest.

In the past the policy of heavy direct taxation, through income tax, surtax and death duties, had been restrained by the fear of encroaching on savings, but in reality " measures for the redistribution of incomes in a way likely to raise the propensity to consume may prove positively favourable to the growth of capital " (p. 373) since an increase in the propensity to consume will (except in conditions of full employment) increase the inducement to invest. He therefore favoured a scheme of direct taxation for the express purpose (provided a sufficient incentive to enterprise were left) of diminishing the proportion of the national income applied to saving. Thereby the proportion of saving to consumption would be diminished, and full employment could be maintained with a smaller volume of active investment and a higher rate of interest.

If the rate of interest is high enough for M_2 to be zero, full employment is attained. It is attained, however, at the cost of limiting the accumulation of capital. Far from a high rate of interest being needed as an inducement to save, saving is determined by investment, and " the scale of investment is promoted by a *low* rate of interest, provided that we do not attempt to stimulate it in this way beyond the point which corresponds to full employment. Thus it is to our best advantage to reduce the rate of interest to that point relatively to the schedule of marginal efficiency of capital at which there is full employment " (p. 375).

If the rate of interest is to fall, that, according to Keynes's theory, can only be because sufficient surplus money is created to cause an increase in idle balances.

" There can be no doubt ", Keynes proceeds (p. 375), " that this criterion will lead to a much lower rate of interest than has ruled hitherto. . . . I feel sure that the demand for capital is strictly limited, in the sense that it would not be difficult to increase the stock of capital up to a point where its marginal efficiency had fallen to a very low figure." This would mean " the euthanasia of the rentier ".

" The owner of capital can obtain interest because capital is scarce ", but " there are no intrinsic reasons for the scarcity of capital " (p. 376), *unless* the individual propensity to consume is such " that net saving in conditions of full employment comes to an end before capital has become sufficiently abundant. But even so it will still be possible for communal saving through the agency of the State to be maintained at a level which will allow the growth of capital up to a point where it ceases to be scarce."

" Communal saving" here is not to be identified with public works as a device for maintaining full employment. It is just the reverse.[1] Public works constitute active investment by the State, calculated to offset an *excess* of saving. Communal saving offsets

---

[1] I have to confess that in the first edition of this book I misunderstood this passage. I supposed that if additional saving can only be brought about by additional investment then communal saving must take that form.

a *deficiency* of saving. It presumably takes the form of a budget surplus—and of course a surplus obtained otherwise than by the direct taxation which is intended to *reduce* saving.

Keynes recognised two methods of maintaining full employment : taxation which keeps down saving; and a low rate of interest which stimulates active investment. He preferred the latter. But he did not discard the former, for he favoured on its merits the removal of very great disparities of wealth and income. Communal saving he proposed as a device for hastening progress towards zero interest, and he was not against a combination of taxation calculated to reduce saving with communal saving to compensate the reduction.

As it seemed " unlikely that the influence of banking policy on the rate of interest would be sufficient by itself to determine an optimum rate of investment ", he thought " a somewhat comprehensive socialisation of investment " would be necessary, but not " a system of State Socialism which would embrace most of the economic life of the community " (p. 378).

I think what he meant here was that banking policy could do no more than reduce the long-term rate of interest to the minimum, at which " liquidity preference would become virtually absolute ", and no amount of idle money would reduce the rate any further. Industry would be unable to raise capital at a rate of interest lower than the minimum ; and unless the State intervened, and became the sole long-term lender, further progress towards the euthanasia of the rentier would be stopped.

If that is right, the " somewhat comprehensive socialisation of investment " would not become due till the minimum rate of long-term interest was reached.

This vision is governed by the assumption of a progressive fall in the marginal efficiency of capital. Even if marginal efficiency fell so low that interest sank to zero, there would have to be " some margin to cover risk and the exercise of skill and judgment " (p. 375). Profit, in fact, would survive.

It is the marginal yield of instrumental goods that tends towards zero. But marginal yield only tends towards zero if the openings for the deepening of capital come to an end. Accumulation, left to itself, might or might not bring that about at some future time. The prospect of its doing so would depend on the progress of new invention, to say nothing of the set-back to accumulation caused by war. Even at the end, Keynes does not abandon his hypothesis of unchanging technique. His " communal saving " would be expressly intended to exhaust the openings for deepening, and so to bring about the euthanasia of the rentier. Whether that consummation would be desirable would be an interesting speculation. But it is possible that it will be found not only not to be inevitable but not to be attainable. It may be that the greatest attainable amount of saving, communal and private, will fail to keep pace with the opportunities for the deepening of capital.

Since 1945 the world has seen some measures which accord with Keynes's views of policy. The scales of direct taxation have not been restricted by any fear that the sources of saving would be encroached on. By December 1946, the long-term rate of interest in the London market had been brought down almost to $2\frac{1}{2}$ per cent. There was at the time a superfluity of money, an inheritance from wartime inflation, and it would be easy to claim that idle balances were the cause of the low rate of interest.

But that would be a misconception. For in the circumstances of the time the rate of interest had no relation to the marginal yield of capital goods. Marginal yield was very *high*, but controls and restraints on capital outlay prevented it from having the effect on the rate of interest which a free market would have ensured. There was no systematic co-ordination of the amount of capital outlay permitted by the controls with the amount of resources available for it ; in 1947 the restraints proved insufficient, and the rate of interest rose.

In the United States the long-term rate of interest was kept down by a cruder method. Keynes had recommended a " complex offer by the central bank to buy and sell at stated prices gilt-edged bonds of all maturities in place of the single bank rate for short-term bills " (p. 206). The Federal Reserve Banks pegged the rate of interest at $2\frac{1}{2}$ per cent by a standing offer to buy Government securities at a price corresponding to that yield. The American authorities ignored Keynes's warning that the rate of interest " cannot be in equilibrium at a level *below* the rate which corresponds to full employment, because at such a level a state of true inflation will be produced " (p. 202). A state of true inflation was produced.

The General Theory of Employment, Interest and Money was completed in 1935 in the midst of the most severe trade depression that the world had ever known. Governments seemed to be completely at a loss for a remedy. In the United States, notwithstanding a fall of 35 per cent in the national income since 1929, bank deposits were undiminished, and Keynes saw a " crisis of liquidation, when scarcely anyone could be induced to part with holdings of money on any reasonable terms " (pp. 207-8). In Great Britain bank deposits had risen, despite the heavy fall in commodity prices, from £1,800 million in 1929 to £2,000 million in 1935.

The accumulation of idle money is a regular concomitant of trade depression, and I have explained above (pp. 71-2) how it is caused by the liquidation of working capital. The liquidation of working capital enlarges traders' free capital. And resources which may be required for a future reconstruction of working capital are even more amenable to the speculative motive than those destined for future replacements and extensions of plant. When the former are placed in securities, the securities chosen must be such as can be readily turned back into money as soon as the need for working capital revives.

But when the proceeds of the liquidation of working capital are held in cash, that does not constitute an excess of saving over active investment. There is no new saving, for the liquidation transforms what was already capital from one form into another. In fact, when the proceeds are placed in securities, they supplement the inflow of savings into the investment market, and increase its current resources.

And it is not very plausible to argue that a period of four years in which the price of Consols rose from 54 to 92 was one in which people shrank from investing in gilt-edged securities for fear of a capital loss. Perhaps 92 was thought too high; the price did in fact begin to fall, and reached 84 in November 1935. But that was a time when unemployment, though still heavy, was diminishing, and the price level was beginning to recover.

Unemployment in Great Britain seemed at the time to be chronic: the number of unemployed had never fallen below a million since 1921. Keynes was looking for an explanation of chronic unemployment, but it was hardly plausible to attribute it to the low long-term rate of interest. The yield of Government securities had been exceptionally high till the Conversion of 1932.

And in reality there is no school of thought for which the explanation of chronic unemployment presents any difficulty. If wages are too high for full employment, and resist reduction, unemployment is bound to result. Adam Smith held that for a growing population a corresponding growth of capital was essential to maintain wages at or above subsistence level; the penalty for the failure of capital to grow was unemployment as well as starvation. For his successors it was self-evident that the employment afforded by the " wage fund " was inversely proportional to the rate of wages, and, when the theory of the wage fund was superseded by that of the marginal yield of labour, it was no less self-evident that a wage-level held above marginal yield would prevent full employment. Say's *loi des débouchés* declared that production generated its own demand; but if for any reason production was below capacity and there was unemployment, the demand generated would be no more than sufficient to absorb output at that level.

Keynes made many noteworthy contributions to economic science. He introduced the concepts of liquidity preference and a liquidity premium into the theory of the capital market and the rate of interest. He showed that the long-term rate of interest is a " highly psychological ", or rather " a highly conventional phenomenon ". He generalised the theory of the multiplier, and that of commodities' " own-rates of interest ".

But his conclusions, as formulated in the *General Theory*, are subject to narrowing assumptions. Of these, the most fundamental is the postulate excluding short-term borrowing for the purchase or production of stock-held goods from the influence of the rate of interest. Viewed theoretically, the postulate is an extravagant paradox ; on the practical side, it discards the assumptions made by the bankers throughout the gold-standard period, when they avowedly regulated money through credit.

In glaring contrast with the postulate is the assumption that the amount of capital outlay reacts directly to the rate of interest, and that, whereas the speculative motive responds to the deviation of the rate of interest from a conventional or fairly safe rate, capital outlay is determined not by the deviation but by the absolute level of the rate.

Along with these assumptions, is the fiction that the idle balances, M_2, can be separated from the active balances, M_1. And the functions L_1 and L_2 carry abstraction and simplification beyond what is consistent with any useful practical application.

Keynes's analysis is expressly subject throughout to the hypothesis that technique remains unchanged, upon which depends the assumption that marginal efficiency always tends downwards.

CHAPTER VIII

PROFESSOR HAYEK'S " PRICES AND PRODUCTION "

STAGES OF PRODUCTION

In this book Professor Hayek set out to provide " an explanation of how it comes about at certain times that some of the existing resources cannot be used, and how, in such circumstances, it is impossible to sell them at all—or, in the case of durable goods, only to sell them at a very great loss " (p. 96).[1] That is to say, he offers an explanation of trade depression in its twofold aspects, under-employment of productive resources, and deficiency of demand.

Professor Hayek is a supporter and exponent of Boehm-Bawerk's theory of capital, the Continental counterpart of Jevons's theory, and his explanation of trade depression is an application of that theory : he conceives capital in the form of the period of production, and looks for the working of causes affecting capital in the lengthening or shortening of the period of production.

He adopts the device of supposing production to take place in a series of " stages ", such that " goods move intermittently in equal intervals from one stage of production to the next " (p. 43), till the final stage is reached in the delivery of the consumable products to the consumers.

Professor Hayek prefers diagrams to algebraical expressions as a means of exposition, but the following analysis (based on the notation he uses in a footnote—p. 41) will help to make his system clear.

Let r be the total length of the process of production, that is, the whole length of time from the first operation to the last (not to be confused with the period of production, which is an *average*). Then at time x the first steps are taken towards producing the output which will eventually be disposed of to the consumer at time $x + r$. At any intermediate time, t, the total activities of the original means of production (land and labour) up to date, so far as they are directed to producing the output at time, $x + r$, will be embodied in an aggregate of producers' goods (instruments, materials, intermediate products, etc.) forming a part of the capital equipment of the com-

---

[1] References, except where otherwise indicated, are to *Prices and Production* (second edition).

munity at time *t*. Let this aggregate be $f(t)$. Then the output of consumable goods at time $x + r$ is simply $f(x + r)$, for the aggregate of goods embodying the past activities of the original means of production is then disposed of to the consumers and becomes the output.

By the method of " stages " the time is divided up into a series of equal intervals, and the function $f(t)$, instead of being continuous, takes the form of a discontinuous series, $f(x + 1)$, $f(x + 2) \ldots f(x + r)$, each term representing the aggregate of producers' goods accumulated to the end of the corresponding interval, and the last term, $f(x + r)$, being the output.

At any moment of time the capital equipment of the community is composed of the accumulations of producers' goods contributing to the output of *all* future times. If the structure of production were rigidly stereotyped, output being constant, and the series of terms, $f(x + 1)$, $f(x + 2) \ldots f(x + r)$, leading up to the output $f(x + r)$, the same for every value of $x + r$, then the total capital of the community would be a fixed quantity and would be

$$\sum_{t=x}^{t=x+r} f(t).$$

Without the simplifying assumption of stages, this would be (p. 41) :

$$\int_{x}^{x+r} f(t)dt$$

The expression $\sum\limits_{x}^{x+r} f(t)$ " shows the totality of the successive stages through which the several units of original means of production pass before they become ripe for consumption. It also shows the total amount of producers' goods which must exist at any moment of time in order to secure a continuous output of consumers' goods " (p. 40). This is only true if the word " continuous " can be interpreted to mean that output is constant and the structure of production stereotyped. Professor Hayek might with advantage have been more explicit in regard to this condition.

PRICE MARGINS

Professor Hayek's theory of interest is an elaboration of certain ideas employed by Professor Mises in his *Theory of Money and Credit* (Part III, Chapter V). The following passages from *Prices and Production* indicate the line of thought :

" Temporary differences between the prices offered in the different stages of production are the only means of bringing about a shift of producers' goods from one stage to another. . . .

" If we neglect the possibility of changes in technical knowledge, which may change the usefulness of any particular producers' goods, it is obvious that the immediate cause of a change in the return obtained from producers' goods of a certain kind used in different stages of production must be a change in the price of the product of the stage of production in question " (pp. 72-3). There are " price margins " between the products of successive stages of production. " In a state of equilibrium these margins are entirely absorbed by interest " (p. 73). But " the fact that in a state of equilibrium those price margins and the amounts paid as interest coincide does *not* prove that the same will also be true in a period of transition from one state of equilibrium to another " (p. 74).

These propositions may be restated as follows in terms of the notation used above. If a_s be the " input " in the sth interval after x, that is to say, the value of the original means of production applied in that interval towards the ultimate output in the rth interval, $f(x + r)$, then the growth in the value of the producers' goods, $f(x + s) - f(x + s - 1)$, will *exceed* a_s by a margin q_s. The existence of this margin is the motive for preferring a longer or more roundabout method of production to the use of the means of production, a_s, for immediate fruition. In equilibrium the margin will be equal to the interest earned. If the rate of interest for the period of one stage is i per unit, then the condition of equilibrium is $q_s = if(x + s - 1)$. If at any stage the margin exceeds this limit, there will be a tendency for more of the original means of production to be applied at that stage, and, if the margin falls short of the limit, for less.

By way of illustration, rather than as a part of his main thesis, Professor Hayek proceeds to examine the effects which follow when " consumers decide to save and invest a larger proportion of their income. The immediate effect of the increase in the demand for producers' goods and the decrease in demand for consumers' goods will be that there will be a relative rise in the prices of the former and a relative fall in the prices of the latter. But the prices of producers' goods will not rise equally nor will they rise without exception " (p. 75), for the decline in demand for consumers' goods will affect the prices of those producers' goods which belong to the later stages, and, in the latest stages of all, will more than counteract the increase in demand for producers' goods in general.

In the penultimate stage, for example, the price of the product will fall less than the prices of consumers' goods. " This means a narrowing of the price margin between the last two stages ", which " will make the employment of funds in the last stage less profitable relatively to the earlier stages, and therefore some of the funds which had been used there will tend to be shifted to the earlier stages " (pp. 75-6). " The final effect will be that, through the fall of prices in the later stages of production and the rise of prices in the earlier stages of production, price margins between the different stages of production will have decreased all round. This change of relative prices in the different stages of production must inevitably tend to affect the prospects of profits in the different stages, and this in turn will tend to cause changes in the use made of the available producers' goods " (p. 76).

Professor Hayek adds (in his second edition) the qualification that, whereas for the sake of simplicity he speaks of actual changes in relative prices, " it would be more correct to speak of tendencies towards such a change, or of changes in the demand function for the particular commodity ", the actual effect on price depending on the elasticity of supply (p. 80).

The result of the change of the relative demand for consumers' goods and producers' goods will be a change in the rate of interest, and (if the entrepreneurs entertain correct views about the price changes which are to be expected as a result of the changes in the methods of production), the new rate of interest " should correspond to the system of price margins which will ultimately be established " (p. 84).

PRODUCERS' GOODS AND DIMINISHED CONSUMPTION

The proposition put forward is that when, through the consumers' decision to save more and consume less, the demand for consumers' goods shrinks, the demand for producers' goods will shrink, but in a *less* degree, and that the shrinkage in demand gets *less* marked the earlier the stage, that is, the longer the interval destined to elapse before the producers' goods reach fruition. What ground is there for such a supposition ? If we consider the decreased demand for consumers' goods by itself, in isolation from the increased demand for producers' goods, the truth is precisely the opposite. As Professor Hayek puts it in his *Monetary Theory and the Trade Cycle* (pp. 63-4), " every change in demand, from the moment of its appearance, propagates itself cumulatively through all the grades of

production from the lowest [latest] to the highest [earliest].   This
cumulative effect arises because at each stage, besides the change
which would be appropriate to the actual shift in demand, another
change arises from the adjustment of stocks and of productive
apparatus to the alteration in market conditions.   An increase in
the demand for consumption goods will not merely call forth a
proportional increase in the demand for goods of higher order
[earlier stages]; the latter will also be increased by the amount
needed to raise current stocks to a proportional level, and, finally by
the further amount by which the requirements for producing new
means of production exceed those for keeping the existing means of
production intact."

This passage (which is as applicable to the case of a decrease in
demand as to that of an increase) is put forward, it is true, not as a
theory of Professor Hayek's own, but as forming part of certain
non-monetary theories of the trade cycle.   But his criticism of them
is not that they are untrue, but that they do not supply an adequate
explanation of the trade cycle.   Indeed he says (*Monetary Theory
and the Trade Cycle*, p. 65), " there is virtually no doubt that all these
interconnections . . . do actually exist ; and any Trade Cycle theory
which claims to be comprehensively worked out must take them into
consideration ".

Thus, when the demand for consumers' goods declines, the
contraction of demand for producers' goods is *greater* the longer the
interval destined to elapse up to fruition.   In terms of price margins
(the changes in which, it will be remembered, are not actual but
potential) the effect is not to widen the price margins but to narrow
them.

It is therefore a mistake to say that " a greater proportion of
these producers' goods which can be used in different stages of
production . . . will now be attracted to the earlier stages, where,
since the change in the rate of saving, relatively higher prices are to
be obtained " (p. 76).   On the contrary a *smaller* proportion of these
goods will be attracted to the earlier stages, and if any change of
price ensues it will be downwards.

It must be understood that the foregoing propositions relate only
to the effects of the decline in the demand for consumers' goods, and
do not take into consideration the effects of the increased demand
for producers' goods arising directly from the increased savings.

SPECIFIC AND NON-SPECIFIC GOODS

Professor Hayek makes a distinction between " non-specific " goods, which can be used in all or many stages of production, and " specific " goods, which can be used only in one, or at the most a few (pp. 71-2). " To the first class belong not only almost all original means of production, but also most raw materials and even a great many implements of a not very specialised kind—knives, hammers, tongs, and so on. To the second class belong most highly specialised kinds of machinery or complete manufacturing establishments, and also those kinds of semi-manufactured goods which can be turned into finished goods only by passing a definite number of further stages of production " (p. 71).

This distinction acquires a very special importance as the argument develops. For if the lengthening or shortening of the period of production involves the displacement of existing processes by new ones, any specific goods used in the displaced processes will yield a diminished profit and may cease to be produced altogether. It is in the more extensive displacements which would occur in the case of a shortening of the period of production that Professor Hayek believes the cause of the under-employment of productive resources to lie.

The distinction between specific and non-specific goods is a real one, but it ought not to be expressed in terms of stages. If, in consequence of easy credit, or a prospect of increased demand, retailers decide to stock a greater quantity of some commodity, so that they hold two months' supply instead of one, the effect is to put every prior process involved in the production of that commodity a stage of one month further back. And what assumption are we to make in regard to the period for which goods are held in stock, in deciding how the stages in the production of different commodities correspond ? Is tanning an earlier or a later stage than spinning ? When we go behind the period of process, how are we going to assign stages to the manufacture of instruments ? " Any given capital good ", we are told (p. 142, *footnote*), " need not and usually will not belong to any one given ' stage ' of production only. If it is used to produce other capital goods employed in different stages, and still more if it helps to produce durable goods or is itself durable, it belongs to as many different ' stages ' as different periods of time elapse from the moment in which we consider it to the moments when the different final products which it has helped to produce are consumed."

15

And it is rarely, if ever, possible to assign a definite " stage " to any instrument. The life of an instrument is subject to many uncertainties ; it can neither be predicted for the individual instrument nor yield a significant average for any class of instrument.

When a shortening of the period of production is said to displace specific goods, the meaning is that instruments of marginal yield which become unremunerative, cannot be employed in any alternative manner. That contingency has nothing to do with the stage or stages in which an instrument is employed, but solely with its yield or cost-saving capacity.

" PRICE MARGINS " DO NOT EXIST

The term " stage " is misleading; it suggests a distinct process, as weaving is distinct from spinning, finishing cloth from weaving, and making garments from finishing cloth. But the *only* distinguishing characteristic of a " stage ", as Professor Hayek defines it, is the interval of time destined to elapse before fruition. Every commodity belongs to a variety of different stages, and every stage contains a variety of different commodities, and it is quite impossible even in theory to say what commodities belong to what stages.

What then is the meaning of a " price margin " between one stage and another ? In so far as the same products appear in the two stages, they will have the *same* price; in so far as products appear in one stage which do not appear in the other, comparison will be impossible. Indeed, Professor Hayek, faithful to his general condemnation of the use of price averages in monetary theory (below, p. 239), expressly disavows any explanation in terms of changes in the " price levels " of the goods of different stages of production (p. 70). As we have seen, he further explains (in his second edition, though not in his first) that there would not be an actual change in relative prices, but only " tendencies towards such a change ", or " changes in the demand function ".

But it is not merely the changes in price margins that are a fiction ; the price margins themselves are equally illusory. When we say that in any stage the increment of value, $f(x + s) - f(x + s - 1)$, exceeds the input, a_s, by a margin, q_s, we are not defining the margin to be a *price* margin at all. It is not a difference between two price levels, nor is it a complex composed of a number of separate price differences. The fundamental proposition that in a state of equilibrium the price margins " are entirely absorbed by interest " is a fallacy, because the price margins do not exist. Interest is not a price difference, but a *cost*.

To the traders who make the decision to produce or not to produce, to buy or not to buy, it is *profit* that appears as a price difference. Profit is arrived at by setting off all costs, including interest, against the proceeds of sale. We cannot express it in terms of stages, for the beginning and end of a stage are determined solely by the lapse of time, without reference to the moment at which the proceeds of sale are realised, and at any intermediate time selling value is a matter of hypothesis. If we take a manufacturing process and suppose the producers' goods used (including a depreciation allowance in respect of an instrument) to be $f(s)$, and the proceeds of sale of the product to be $f(t)$, then the increment of value $f(t) - f(s)$ is composed of the cost of labour and rent, of interest and of profit.[1] If for any reason the price of the product $f(t)$ rises or falls, the effect is to increase or decrease profit. But the " price difference " so created has no special relation to interest. It induces an increase or decrease of production, and a consequent increase or decrease in the activity of *all* the factors of production. If supply is sufficiently elastic, an increase or decrease in demand for the product may induce the increase or decrease in activity without any rise or fall of price.

The rate of interest determines the allocation between labour and instruments of the costs incurred to meet a given demand. It also influences the amount of capital employed in another way. A rise or fall in the rate of interest increases or decreases the cost and therefore ultimately the price to the consumer of those goods which require more capital relatively to those which require less, and the resulting transfer of productive resources from or to the former results on balance in a decrease or an increase in the total capital requirements. If an excess or deficiency of profits arises *solely* from a divergence of the rate of interest from its equilibrium level, then the readjustments which follow will presumably result in just that change in the rate which will extinguish the excess or deficiency. But that is a purely abstract assumption, which is far from identifying the rate of interest with a price margin.

We have seen (above, p. 12) that, if profit be included in cost, price is invariably equal to cost, and that if, while profit is included, interest is excluded from cost, then interest is equal to the excess of

---

[1] The original means of production are defined to mean " land and labour " (p. 36). To fit into the analysis, labour must include enterprise remunerated by profit.

price over cost and may thus be called a price margin. But surely no more sterile principle than that could be imagined.

INCREASED SAVING AND DECREASED CONSUMPTION

We may next return to the hypothesis of an increase in saving and a decrease in consumption. As we have seen, so far as the effects of the decline of consumption are concerned, the tendency would be to drive away productive resources from the earlier stages of production, and not to attract them.

We have now to take into consideration the increase in saving, which forms part of the hypothesis. If we make use of the distinction between the " widening " and " deepening " of capital, the former being the flotation of new enterprises, and the extension of existing enterprises, and the latter being the use of an increased amount of capital for a given output, we may say that the decline of consumption checks the widening process of capital. Even if this were not so, the increased savings would have to find openings in the deepening process, and, if the widening process is retarded, the deepening process must be all the more stimulated. It will be remembered that we are neglecting the possibility of changes in technical knowledge (p. 72, see above, p. 221). Consequently the deepening process can be stimulated only by a reduction in the rate of interest.

To set out to explain this stimulation through the medium of stages of production and price margins (even when these latter are transmuted into " tendencies ") is to introduce unnecessary difficulties into the subject. By way of simplifying his exposition, Professor Hayek introduces the assumption that " the original means of production are applied at a constant rate throughout the whole process of production ". That is to say, $f(s + 1) - f(s)$, the input in any past unit of time contributing to the present output, is a constant, a, and $f(s)$ the accumulation of producers' goods at the sth interval, is simply sa. The total accumulation of producers' goods in all stages at one instant of time is $\sum_{o}^{n} sa$ or $\frac{1}{2}n(n + 1)a$.

With these assumptions the period of production can only be extended by *adding earlier stages*. And Professor Hayek takes for granted that the extension must take this form. " A greater proportion of . . . the non-specific goods will now be attracted to earlier stages " (p. 76). The use of specific goods will become less profitable in the later stages and more profitable in the earlier stages (pp. 77-8).

It is quite likely that the additional investment will be predominantly in the earlier stages, but it is not necessarily so. It might happen that the next most remunerative openings for investment are mainly or exclusively among the later stages. There is no necessary connexion between the margin of investment and the stages, and the introduction of the stages into the exposition of the extension of investment serves no useful purpose. Thus we see that when savings are increased at the expense of consumption, the decline of demand for consumable goods checks the widening process of capital and tends to make producers'. goods redundant, and the earlier the stage they belong to the more redundant they are. The increase of savings has to find an outlet in an intensified deepening process, intensified all the more to make up for the check to the widening process. And in the absence, as assumed, of technical improvements, the deepening process can only be intensified by a lowering of the rate of interest and a consequent extension of the margin of investment to include appliances previously unremunerative.

INJECTION OF ADDITIONAL MONEY

The hypothesis of a diversion of incomes from consumption to saving is adopted by Professor Hayek for purposes of illustration. From it he proceeds next to consider " what happens if the ' natural ' movement of prices is disturbed by movements in the supply of money ". He distinguishes the two cases " of additional money used first to buy producers' goods ", and " of additional money used first to buy consumers' goods " (p. 85).

If " additional money is injected by way of credits to producers ", then, in order " to secure borrowers for this additional amount of money, the rate of interest must be kept sufficiently below the equilibrium rate to make profitable the employment of just this sum and no more. Now the borrowers can only use the borrowed sums for buying producers' goods, and will only be able to obtain such goods (assuming a state of equilibrium in which there are no unused resources) by outbidding the entrepreneurs who used them before " (pp. 85-6). There will be an " application of the original means of production and non-specific intermediate products to longer processes of production ", which " will be effected without any preceding reduction of consumption " (pp. 87-8). The existing input will be destined to reach fruition at a later date than would otherwise have obtained, and in an intervening period the output of consumable goods will be reduced. " A scarcity of consumers' goods will make itself felt and the prices of those goods will rise."

This " comes at the very moment when a great many entrepreneurs know themselves to be in command—at least nominally—of greater resources and expect greater profits. At the same time incomes of wage-earners will be rising in consequence of the increased amount of money available for investment by entrepreneurs." There will result " a new and reversed change of the proportion between the demand for consumers' goods and the demand for producers' goods in favour of the former ", and consequently " a return to shorter or less roundabout methods of production if the increase in the demand for consumers' goods is not compensated by a further proportional injection of bank money by new bank loans granted to producers " (p. 89).

" The banks cannot continue indefinitely to extend credits ; and even if they could, the other effects of a rapid and continuous rise of prices would, after a while, make it necessary to stop this process of inflation " (p. 90).

A RELATIVE INCREASE IN DEMAND FOR CONSUMERS' GOODS

So long as the extension of credits does continue, it induces a demand for producers' goods, which may keep pace with the growing demand for consumers' goods, so that on balance there is no excess demand for the latter. But when the extension of credits ceases, this compensatory action is withdrawn, and there supervenes " a relative increase in the demand for consumers' goods " (p. 91). The effects will be " similar to what would happen in the second case we have to consider, the case of an increase of money by consumers' credits ". If there is a relative rise in the prices of consumers' goods, " the spread between them and the prices of goods of the preceding stage becomes greater than the price margins in the higher [earlier] stages of production ".

" Very soon the relative rise of the prices of the original factors [means of production] and the more mobile intermediate products will make the longer processes unprofitable " (p. 92).

The shortening of the period of production means an alteration of the structure of production ; " non-specific " goods are attracted away from the longer to the shorter process, and those " specific " goods which are not adapted to the new structure become either useless or only of a reduced value in use. Goods in the later stages of production, though generally of a highly specific character, will be finished off. But the specific goods used in the earlier stages (presumably instruments) will fall in price, and their production will become unprofitable. There will be " a fairly sudden stoppage of work in at least all the earlier stages of the longer processes " (p. 92).

In conformity with his theory of price margins, Professor Hayek attributes this to the rise of prices of non-specific goods (including labour). He then proceeds to argue that the new shorter processes " will have to be started at the very beginning and will only *gradually* absorb all the available producers' goods as the product progresses towards consumption and as the necessary intermediate products come forward " (p. 93). It is not very clear why this should be so, but, if it is, then the rise in the prices of non-specific goods will be postponed, and with it the transference of those goods, to which the failure of the demand for specific goods is attributed.

Professor Hayek argues that " when the growing demand for finished consumers' goods has taken away part of the non-specific producers' goods required, those remaining are no longer sufficient for the long processes, and the particular kinds of specific goods required for the processes which would just be long enough to employ the total quantity of those non-specific producers' goods do not yet exist " (p. 94).

This does not carry us very far. The disuse of the specific goods in the long processes is due to the rise in the price of the non-specific (including labour), and, if there is an interval in which this rise does not take place, the long processes will continue to be employed. It is only when some rise in the prices of non-specific goods occurs that any disadvantage is felt in the use of the specific goods. There is no reason why the transference of non-specific goods should not be gradual. The specific goods in conjunction with which they have been functioning do not form a unit such that the whole must be in operation or none. They are a number of separate instruments each of which can continue or stop working independently of the rest.

We have already seen that the price margins do not exist. We have also seen that the reaction upon producers' goods from any change in demand for consumers' goods is not less but greater as the stage to which the producers' goods belong gets earlier, so that, if the price margins did exist, they would move in a manner precisely opposite to that assumed by Professor Hayek.

If he had contented himself with an exposition of a more conventional kind in terms of the rate of interest, the analysis might have been comparatively straightforward.   Given a relative increase in consumption and a diminution in saving, the widening of capital will be accelerated in response to the demand for an increased output of consumable goods, and on both counts there will be less left for the deepening process.   To preserve equilibrium, the rate of interest must be raised high enough to check the deepening process to the requisite extent.

PRODUCERS' GOODS AND WORKING CAPITAL

But Professor Hayek's theory is open to even more far-reaching objections in some other respects.   At the outset he says that, when credit is extended, the producers who borrow " can only use the borrowed sums for buying producers' goods ".   But *all* goods are producers' goods till they actually reach the hands of the consumer. The " longer processes of production " need not involve recourse to new instruments or the application of the original means of production to " earlier stages ".

The assumption is that the banks grant additional credits to producers.   Presumably the reduction of the rate of interest by which borrowers have to be attracted is a reduction of the short-term rate.   By " credits to producers " cannot be meant flotations of shares or debentures in the investment market.   The effect on the long-term rate and through it on the demand for instruments and fixed capital is indirect, and is likely to be gradual and in the first instance slight.   On the other hand, in so far as the effect works through short-term borrowing for the purchase and holding of stocks of commodities, it will be rapid.

Now if the effect of a reduction of the short-term rate of interest is manifested in an additional accumulation of stocks of commodities, the period of production is lengthened without any modification of any productive process.   There need not be in any other respect a transition to " more capitalistic methods ".

But it is a paradox of credit regulation that, whereas credit relaxation operates by giving an inducement to hold greater stocks of commodities, there actually results little or no increase in stocks. If unemployed productive resources are available, additional supplies can be produced to meet the additional wholesale .demand, but the increased productive activity generates additional incomes and additional consumer demand, which reduces stocks almost as fast as they are increased.   It may well be that the *proportion* of stocks to output actually falls, so that the period of production is reduced. If, as Professor Hayek postulates, productive resources are already fully employed, there can be no additional supplies. The increased wholesale demand will result in accumulating increased orders to producers and there will be a rise in wholesale prices. This rise in prices will be reflected in a rise in incomes and so in consumers' demand. If, as is likely, retail prices lag behind wholesale prices, consumption will exceed production, stocks will be diminished, and the period of production in this case also will be reduced. A reduction of stocks of commodities is a familiar feature of periods of inflation.

This stimulus to the purchase of goods with borrowed money will not exhaust the effects of the reduction of the short-term rate of interest. There will be a tendency to borrow for other purposes, and more particularly by dealers and speculators in the investment market, who will tend to buy and hold securities with borrowed money. This will tend to cause a rise in the prices of securities and to favour new flotations. But the effect is likely to be both slow and slight. The changes in the long-term rate of interest directly attributable to changes in the short-term rate are small, and it takes time for any change in the long-term rate to result in the production of new capital, and in an extension of the period of production.

Professor Hayek does not share the highly paradoxical view of Keynes that the volume of borrowing for the purchase and holding of commodities is insensitive to the rate of interest. Indeed at one stage of his argument he actually finds it desirable " to abstract from the existence of durable goods ", and to adopt the hypothesis that all capital is circulating or working capital. He apologises in the Preface to the Second Edition of *Prices and Production* for not having made a more explicit reference to this hypothesis in the First Edition, urging in partial justification of it that he was " under the impression that the rôle which circulating capital played was rather neglected and accordingly wanted to stress it as compared with that of fixed capital " (p. xii).

We may take it that, in his view, circulating capital *is* sensitive to the short-term rate of interest and to facilities for borrowing. But, if it is sensitive at all, its response is bound to be very much *more prompt* than that of fixed capital. New capital flotations require protracted preparations, including both technical and financial planning, and may be not merely months but even years in responding to a favourable investment market. Working capital, on the other hand, begins to respond from the moment any trader who finances his working capital with bank advances or bills, orders a fresh consignment of goods. Within a very few months practically all traders will have turned over their stocks at least once (except stocks of seasonal goods, which in any case do not react easily on productive activity), and the direct effect is completed.

The effects of a creation of credit are further explained in the following passage. When entrepreneurs are " enabled to attract factors of production from later to earlier stages . . . by additional money handed to them, . . . they will bid up the prices of these factors without there being a corresponding fall in the prices of other factors. Total money income will therefore increase, and this increase will in turn lead to an increase in the amount of money expended on consumers' goods. This increase in the expenditure on consumers' goods will necessarily follow in time upon the increase in the demand for factors. This lag will mean that for some time after the demand for factors (or producers' goods) has ceased to increase (or when its rate of increase begins to slow down) the demand for consumers' goods will continue to increase at a faster rate " (p. 148). In this passage the assumption is that the creation of credit in favour of producers first causes an excess demand for producers' goods, and then after an interval an excess demand for consumers' goods, the whole trouble being due to this change in the relative demand for the two kinds of goods. But we now see that the producers' goods for which the excess demand is created in the first instance are, more or less, *all* goods. The stimulus is given to all industries. It will not be felt to an exactly equal extent by all, but there is no reason why at the outset it should affect instrumental industries more than others. Indeed, owing to the preparatory delays already referred to, the demand for the finished products of the instrumental industries may at first be actually less stimulated than the demand for consumable goods.

There may be a lag of retail prices behind wholesale. But that does not mean that retailing will be an exception to the general tendency. In so far as prices fail to rise, the volume of sales will be greater. Increased activity in industry is precluded by Professor Hayek's postulate of full employment, but increased activity in retailing is always possible. If it were not, and the numbers engaged in retailing could not cope with increased business, the retailers would be forced to put up prices and the lag would not occur.

It is in virtue of the lag of retail prices that the volume of sales to consumers exceeds output, and working capital is diminished. What Professor Hayek is referring to in the passage quoted above is not a lag in the response of retail prices to retail demand, but a lag of retail demand itself behind the increase in total money income. This arises from the tendency of consumers to accumulate a part of their increased income in balances, thereby in some degree compensating the reduction of working capital caused by the lag of retail prices. Professor Hayek's "time lag between the first expenditure of the additional money on the factors of production and the re-expenditure of the income so created on consumers' goods" (p. 150), presupposes that the accumulation of additional balances comes at the beginning and the expenditure on consumption only after the accumulation is completed. In practice, however, the accumulation of balances is gradual. Increased expenditure on consumption starts simultaneously with the increased incomes, and in consequence of the lag of retail prices it is likely that the increased expenditure means an increased volume of consumption from the outset. Professor Hayek is considering the case of a *continuing* expansion of credit, not a single discontinuous increase to which after an interval things will be adjusted in a new equilibrium. So long as the expansion of credit is in progress, the gradual accumulation of cash balances will go on. On the other hand, the reduction of stocks of commodities will reach a limit, and retail prices will be forced up to the extent necessary to protect stocks. It is not possible to give any general theoretical answer to the question what the state of balances and stocks of goods will eventually be when the decision to stop the expansion of credit is taken.

FORCED SAVING

But meanwhile developments will have taken place in the long-term investment market. It is there that the adoption of longer processes of production is brought about, for on balance the effect of the relaxation of credit on short-term borrowing and working capital is likely to be a shortening rather than a lengthening of the period of production.[1]

Professor Hayek employs the expression "forced saving" for the process by which money is made available for investment through the grant of credit to producers, instead of through voluntary savings out of income. The expression (though many respectable authorities can be quoted for it) is not very happily chosen. The underlying idea is that, when additional resources are obtained by producers by means of bank advances, it must be at someone's expense. The credit can be created out of nothing, but the resources

[1] See above, pp. 232-3.

cannot be.   The resources, it is argued, are obtained at the expense
of those who suffer from the consequent rise of prices.   What is
certainly not " saving " to them, and might more appropriately be
called a forced " contribution ", might yet be described as saving
by the community, if it constituted a real net addition to wealth.

But in reality the resources used by the producers are in general
obtained *before* the rise in the price level ; they are derived from the
stocks of goods already in existence, the outcome of past savings,
and are not additional wealth.   That is so, whether the credit
created in favour of producers is used for the purchase of goods,
which may be supplied from stocks, or for new production.   For
the money spent on new production passes as income into the hands
of consumers, and, in so far as it is not saved by them, is spent on
goods which may be supplied from stocks.   If there is any net
addition to wealth, it is because the recipients of this money do not
spend the whole of it.   But that is *voluntary* not forced saving.

The rise of the price of any commodity is a sign that this process
is reducing the stocks of it too far.   Such rises of price bring losses
to some sections of the community and gains to others, and it would
not be possible among these losses and gains to identify a forced
contribution to be linked up with the resources originally secured by
producers through the credit granted to them.

The reconstitution of the stocks of goods that have been drawn
upon is effected by the rise of prices of consumable goods and the
consequent decline in consumption.   This rise of prices confers
excess profits on traders at the expense of consumers, and in so far
as the traders sell less goods and add more to stock, they are in effect
saving in the form of reinvested profits.   The addition thus made to
the wealth of the community is brought about by voluntary saving.
The traders who raise prices above replacement level, that is to say,
above the level which yields the retailer a normal profit, may in a
sense be regarded as levying a forced contribution upon the consumer.   But (apart from the manœuvres of monopolists) it may be
presumed that their action is the result of producers being unable to
replenish stocks as fast as they are sold.   The rise of price comes
when the productive capacity of the industry begins to be strained.
And, when that stage has been reached in industry generally, the
profits of producers will have risen above normal as well as those of
retailers, and the amount of voluntary savings will have been
increased all round.   To the extent that consumption is restricted
by a relatively larger growth of savings, the raising of prices to
consumers above the replacement level becomes unnecessary.   Thus

the forced contribution merges in the general increase of savings arising out of the increase in profits.

There is no such thing as forced saving in the sense attributed to it by Professor Hayek.

FLUCTUATIONS OF SAVINGS

It is strange that Professor Hayek leaves entirely out of account the tendency for inflation to induce increased savings out of income. When prices rise, profits rise more than in proportion and savings still more. This is likely to be far more potent as a source of increased capital outlay than the credits granted to traders. It must be admitted, however, that these increased savings, if due to abnormal profits, are precarious. If profits are abnormal, that must be because the rise of wages lags behind the rise of prices. When the rise of prices stops (even if it is not reversed), wages will begin to catch up, and (since savings out of wages are proportionately much less than savings out of profits) savings will then fall off, and consumption will increase. Thus, even though forced savings do not exist, Professor Hayek's thesis, that inflation will cause a temporary expansion of investment which will subside again when inflation ceases, even though there is no deflation, and the price level remains undiminished, is not without foundation.

But a decline of savings and of investment to the normal level does not necessarily or even probably mean a *shortening* of the period of production. That would only be so if the normal level of savings were insufficient to provide for the widening of capital. Under modern conditions it is only likely to be so in a new country where undeveloped natural resources are in course of being exploited by the efforts of an immigrant population and with the assistance of imports of capital. In all highly industrialised countries, the widening process is insufficient to use up normal savings,[1] and the deepening process is at work. This is on balance true of the world as a unit, and there would be a progressive fall in the rate of interest if new inventions were not continually revealing profitable openings for investment above the marginal yield.

So long as the amount of savings, even though diminished, exceeds what the widening process requires, there will be no shortening of the period of production ; it will continue to be *lengthened*,

---

[1] After a big war effort there may be accumulated arrears of widening, such as to absorb all available savings for years.

even if it be not so rapidly as before. If the lengthening process is retarded, that actually makes the industrial dislocation less; if the lengthening process were just suspended, and there were no shortening, no change of character would be involved in the capital-producing industries.

Professor Hayek argues that, when a start has been made with the installation of a new process, further investment is required over a long period if the original investment is not to be wasted, and he draws the conclusion that a dislocation may be caused though savings do not become a negative quantity (nor even sink to zero).

" Any lengthening of the process of production ", he says, " can only be completed over a period of time corresponding to the interval between the moment when the factors which are being shifted to an earlier stage are being invested and the moment when their product matures " (p. 136).

The principle so stated is not quite correct, but there is some foundation for it. If a new labour-saving appliance is to be introduced into an industry, the first step is to arrange for the production of the appliance. That may be possible with existing plant with very little adaptation (that is to say, the plant used in its production may be non-specific). If so, though the appliance itself may be specific, its production can be suspended at any time without dislocation.[1]

If, however, the new appliance requires expensive specialised plant for its production, this will only be provided in the expectation that it will be continuously used. The introduction of the new appliance will probably take place gradually, as those engaged in the industry which is to use it learn its advantages. If the plant is installed with a view to equipping the entire industry with the new appliances over a period of years and thereafter supplying renewals, a change of circumstances which results in the further installation of the appliance being abandoned, when the equipment of the industry with it is still incomplete, will leave the plant installed for producing the appliance insufficiently employed. Now the resources to be employed in equipping the industry with the appliance must be derived from new savings, and, if new savings fall off heavily (even though they do not fall to zero) there may be a shortage of these resources. The sign of the shortage will be a rise in the rate of interest. So long as the rate of interest is no higher than it was when the appliance was introduced, the equipment of the industry

---

[1] The appliance will go on being *used* where it is already installed, till it is worn out.

with it will continue. Only if the rate rises will this process be interrupted.

At a time of depression savings undoubtedly shrink to a very low level. But that does not mean that the rate of interest must rise. Depression starts with a decline of the consumers' income. The shrinkage of savings is accompanied by a shrinkage of demand for consumable goods, and this shrinkage of demand causes a check to the widening of capital. Not only does this check to the widening of capital compensate the falling off of savings, but the liquidation of working capital provides additional investible resources (above, pp. 71-2) so that the deepening process, far from having to be checked, actually has to be intensified. Low rates of interest, both short-term and long-term, are characteristic of periods of depression.

The decline of savings during depression is much more than a mere return to normal from the high level of the preceding activity. Professor Hayek takes the view that, apart from the creation of credit, the total demand for new capital goods is governed by the supply of savings (pp. 139 and 144). If that is correct, surely the fluctuations in savings due to periods of depression and activity are enormously more important causes of dislocation in the capital-producing industries than any change in the character of the capital goods to be produced owing to the shortening of the period of production.

DEFLATION

Professor Hayek is very insistent that monetary theory ought not to be preoccupied with changes in the general price level. He even objects to the proposition [1] that " monetary theory is constantly concerned with tendencies which affect *all* prices equally, or at any rate impartially, at the same time and in the same direction " (p. 5). But that does not prevent him from recognising the possibility of " deflation and a rapid general fall of prices " being associated with a " situation where unemployed factors and unused lending capacity of all banks exist " (p. 148). And he further recognises that the changes in the relative demand for consumers' goods and producers' goods, which form the foundation of his theory, may be counteracted or offset by changes in the quantity of money, and that " this will be particularly true if a change in relative demand is accompanied by an absolute reduction in demand and if at the same time

---

[1] Which he quotes from my paper on *Money and Index Numbers*, read before the Royal Statistical Society in 1929 (republished in my *Art of Central Banking*, p. 304).

costs (i.e. prices of the original factors of production) are rigid. In this case ", he continues, " deflationary tendencies are likely to set in, which may more than counterbalance the effect of the changed relative demand " (p. 156).

These passages seem to recognise the operation of a falling price level (or a contracting demand) as an *independent* cause of depression and unemployment. It might be contended that, even so, the changes in relative demand for consumers' goods and for producers' goods at the various stages are the sole or perhaps the predominant cause of such a contracting demand. But this is not a tenable position.

It has been pointed out above that the deepening of capital, far from being reversed in a time of depression, is actually intensified. But even if a shortening of the period of production ever occurs, the consequent unemployment is merely a particular case of displacement of one industry by another, and is far from being the most important case. The specific goods concerned are *instruments*. As Professor Hayek points out, goods in process and in stock, which are at a sufficiently advanced stage of manufacture to have become specific, will anyhow be finished off.

MARGINAL INSTRUMENTS

The importance of the class of specific instruments depends *inter alia* on " the degree to which the concrete capital equipment in earlier stages is specialised to the production of equipment for a particular industry, or whether it can be more generally used ". On this question of fact Professor Hayek draws from a recent article by Mr. Seltzer the conclusion that " the mobility of capital in this sense is far greater than is commonly supposed " (p. 141). He is referring here, it is true, to the adaptability of capital to different industries and not necessarily to different stages, but the latter is really only a particular case of the former.

It has already been mentioned that the marginal instruments are not to be identified with those required in the earliest *stages*. The period of production may be lengthened by an increased use of capital in intermediate stages, for example, by the introduction of a labour-saving instrument for a process applied near the completion of the product. The characteristic of the marginal instruments is that their yield or cost-saving capacity is only just sufficient to be remunerative at the existing rate of interest, and that characteristic is independent both of the length of life of the instrument and of the stage, early or late, at which it is to be used. In the absence of technological improvements the lengthening of the period of pro-duction is carried into effect simply by producing and using instru-ments of the marginal group. The determining condition in the minds of those who have to make the decisions is the rate of interest, and the shortening of the period of production is brought about by the rise of the rate making the marginal instruments unremunerative. For any probable variation of the rate of interest the group is likely to be a very small one.

And it is not to be taken for granted that even a considerable rise in the rate of interest will throw out of use instruments which have already been adopted. In the case of an appliance requiring no specialised plant for its production, if circumstances arise (such as a rise in the rate of interest) which make it no longer remunerative, it can be abandoned without causing any dislocation. On the other hand an appliance requiring specialised plant cannot be abandoned without loss once the specialised plant has been installed. The plant will have been installed in the expectation of making a profit. If the rate of interest rises, so that the use of the appliance no longer pays, a sufficient reduction in the price asked for the appliance will com-pensate this and will ensure its continued use. The producers of the appliance will be willing to make the requisite concession so long as they receive something in excess of their prime costs, even though their profit has become a negative quantity, that is to say, the gross margin is insufficient to provide interest on their capital. In all cases of the displacement of existing industries by new ones the gross profits of the former provide a margin for price concessions, in virtue of which they may remain in being for a long period and the dis-location due to their sudden extinction may be avoided. And in the special instance of industries displaced through the shortening of the period of production there is another margin to be reckoned with. A new appliance is not likely to be adopted in an industry unless it promises some actual surplus over and above an exact balance of its cost-saving capacity against the rate of interest. In consequence of the uncertainty attending the adoption of a new process, this surplus is usually quite considerable. But, once it is adopted, the appliance will be retained unless the rate of interest rises so high as to wipe out the surplus. A moderate rise in the rate of interest may be sufficient to stop the deepening of capital, but a very much greater rise will be necessary to cause the abandonment of instruments already in use, which count as marginal, but which in reality yield substantially more than the current rate of interest.

16

Thus a big rise in the long-term rate of interest is necessary to cause the abandonment of apparently marginal instruments. And it is open to doubt whether such abandonment *ever occurs at all*. Professor Hayek has neglected to offer any evidence whatever that it does, or to mention any instance where it has.

TECHNOLOGICAL IMPROVEMENTS

A further complication is introduced by technological improvements. In the great majority of cases the new instruments installed are not strictly marginal, in the sense that they would have been installed at an earlier date had the rate of interest been lower. They usually embody improvements which may raise their yield substantially above the margin.

Professor Hayek's argument is subject all through to the condition (repeated on p. 93) that " technical knowledge remains the same ", and that there is no change in the structure of production through technical progress. This condition removes the whole treatment from the plane of practical affairs. Whatever may be the magnitude of the industries under-employed in consequence of a rise of the rate of interest making the use of marginal instruments unprofitable, they cannot be considerable compared to the regular and steady supersession of a considerable part of the existing plant through new inventions. If the displacement of existing industries by new ones is a cause of unemployment, then technological unemployment will quite overshadow any unemployment due to the displacement of marginal instruments.

THE ORIGINATING CAUSES OF DEPRESSION

Now *any* cause adversely affecting productive activity may be the starting-point of a depression. Once activity has fallen off and output has declined, not only does demand contract in proportion to activity, but existing working capital and fixed capital become relatively redundant, a *further* slackening of activity and of demand is thereby involved, and a vicious circle of depression is set up. The originating cause *might* be the displacement of marginal instruments. This is not formally inconsistent with the statistical evidence, for a period of activity is ordinarily brought to an end by a rise in the rate of interest (though it is primarily in the short-term rate, and the long-term rate, except perhaps for a few weeks of acute financial

crisis, is relatively little affected). The period of low interest rates,
which invariably ensues, is due to the subsequent operation of the
vicious circle. But any such explanation of the onset of depression
assigns a disproportionate and fictitious importance to the particular
phenomenon of the displacement of marginal instruments. The
displacement of industries by technological progress is constantly
occurring, and often in a much more serious form, without starting
a depression.

The rise in the rate of interest which brings a period of activity
to an end is essentially a banking measure. Its immediate effects
are felt in the region of working capital, and the effects upon fixed
capital and instrumental goods can only be felt much later, when the
rise in the short-term rate has adversely affected the long-term
investment market, and the discouragement of new flotations has
had time to react upon actual capital outlay. But long before that
has happened, the vicious circle of deflation will have been set up,
and the depression will be in full swing.

Even if the displacement of marginal instruments did operate as
an originating cause of depression, it could only develop into a
serious depression through the vicious circle, the " repercussions "
by which the effects either of credit expansion or of credit contraction
tend to be indefinitely amplified. And it is the banks which decide
whether the vicious circle is to work itself out or to be summarily
cut. Adverse conditions, which would lead to a severe depression
at a time of credit restriction, miss fire at a time of credit relaxation
and expansion.

Professor Hayek attributes the turning-point to the banks being
unable to extend credits indefinitely. " And even if they could ",
he adds, " the other effects of a rapid and continuous rise of prices
would, after a while, make it necessary to stop this process of
inflation " (p. 90). (So here also we find that " changes in the
general price level " are not so utterly alien to the subject matter of
monetary theory.) His contention is that, when they take steps to
stop the inflation, an incidental effect will be a check to the production of marginal instruments, owing to the cessation of forced
savings, and this will tend to start a deflation, even if the action taken
is in other respects no more than is needed to maintain demand and
the price level unchanged. But, if the check to the production of
marginal instruments is an important factor, why should not the
banks take it into account ? In past experience we constantly find
periods of activity followed by depressions, but that is because the
credit expansion has invariably been allowed to go too far, and the

aim of the banks has not been to maintain the flow of money unchanged, but to compress it.

If after a period of inflation the banks did try to stabilise conditions, that is to say, to maintain consumers' income unchanged, then any loss of income in one group of industries must be balanced by an equivalent gain in the rest. The latter will enjoy excess profits, and will tend to expand. They will need additional labour, and will provide opportunities for employment (direct or indirect) for the men displaced from the declining group of industries. This process is always at work tending to remedy technological unemployment and similar disorders, so long as there is no contraction of the consumers' income and outlay. The transfer of labour to the new and the expanding industries may be delayed by imperfect adaptability of the workpeople displaced from the declining industries. But, provided there is an active demand for labour in the former, the delay is not likely to be long. It is not strictly necessary that the consumers' income should be undiminished, that is to say, that the *whole* of the loss of income in the declining industries should appear as excess profits in the others, provided the excess profits are substantial enough to cause as rapid an expansion as is practicable.

It is often assumed that labour displaced from declining industries cannot easily be absorbed elsewhere. That view is founded on the experience of periods of depression when few even of the most prosperous industries can absorb additional labour. When the price level is such as to yield good profits in the bulk of industries and high profits in the most active, unemployment is never a serious problem.

MONETARY POLICY

Professor Hayek leads up to certain conclusions in regard to monetary policy. He advocates keeping the volume of payments made per unit of time constant, subject to a correction for any change in what he calls the coefficient of money transactions, that is to say, the proportion between the total flow of goods and that part of it which is effected by money.

Does this mean keeping the money value of the total flow of goods constant? Probably it does. To apply the coefficient to the " total volume of payments " taken literally, of which far the greater part depends on the vagaries of short loans, of the stock market and other financial operations, would surely be an absurdity.

The total flow of goods means all the transactions in commodities on the way to the consumer. At the beginning we are asked to make the simplifying assumption that " goods moving towards consumption change hands against money in equal intervals which correspond to our unit production periods ", or stages (p. 46).

If $f(s)$ be the total producers' goods at time, s, contributing to the output of consumable goods, the production of which extends from time x to time $x + r$, the output of consumable goods at time $x + r$ will be $f(x + r)$ and the total quantity of producers' goods or capital in existence (on the assumption that the structure of production is unvarying) is $\sum_{x}^{x+r} f(s)$.

With the assumption that at every stage the goods are exchanged for money once and once only, this will also be the total flow of money and the coefficient of money transactions will be unity. If concerns engaged in successive stages are amalgamated, so that payment between the stages becomes unnecessary, the effect is to reduce the coefficient of money transactions. If goods are handled by more than one concern within the limits of a stage, the resulting payments tend to increase the coefficient.

The monetary policy advocated by Professor Hayek is therefore such as to keep the money value of the expression $\sum_{x}^{x+r} f(s)$ constant.

Thus every increase in the total of products constituting this expression must be offset by a corresponding fall of the price level. Such an increase may arise either from an increase of the output, $f(x + r)$, or from an increase in the ratio of the total expression to that output. Professor Hayek argues that " the fall of price proportionate to the increase in productivity, which necessarily follows when, the amount of money remaining the same, production increases, is not only entirely harmless, but is in fact the only means of avoiding misdirection of production " (p. 105). Provided this proposition is limited (as I think it is intended to be) to the case where the *productivity of given factors* increases, it is quite correct. But when production is increased not by improved productivity of given factors but by an increase of the factors employed, a proportionate fall in the price level means a fall in the remuneration of the factors. " A reduction of money income " would be, " in view of the notorious rigidity of wages, certainly very undesirable " (p. 106). But that is precisely what the fixation of the money value of the total flow of goods must involve in any growing community, whether the growth is in population or in accumulated wealth.

Why then does Professor Hayek recommend it? The trouble could only be avoided " if it were possible to inject the required

additional quantities of money in such a way into the economic
system that the proportion between the demand for consumers'
goods and the demand for producers' goods would not be affected ",
and this, he says, " is no doubt a task which cannot be solved in
practice ".

We have found reason to say that the fear of the injection of
money disturbing this proportion in the way suggested is quite
baseless. The measures by which the banking system modifies the
flow of money take effect in the first instance through working
capital, the effects upon long-term investment and instrumental
goods being relatively remote. And Professor Hayek himself has
since modified his position. In his *Profits, Interest and Investment*
(p. 48) he writes : " the cases of an increase of productivity of a given
supply of factors and of an increase in the supply of those factors
are not, as I then thought, similar but fundamentally different ".

The ideal policy would be to stabilise the consumers' income, not
keeping it absolutely fixed, but adjusting it to the growth of the
factors of production in such a way that equilibrium requires the
level of wages to remain unchanged. The consumers' income must
then expand (or contract) in conformity with any change in the
number of wage-earners, in the proportion of wages and salaries
above the normal wage level, in interest, in rent and in profits.
There is no more practical difficulty in applying this criterion than in
applying that of the fixed money value of the total flow of goods.
Indeed there is *far less*. For any failure to attain the stabilisation of
the consumers' income gives rise to the symptoms either of undue
activity or of depression as the case may be, and can be forthwith
corrected. If the monetary authorities aim at fixing the money
value of the total flow of goods, they have no direct statistical test of
their success ; they know that in any case the policy will involve a
state of chronic depression, the extent of which cannot be foreseen
or measured, and it is impossible to say in any given circumstances
whether the state of depression is more or less than sufficient.

The fixation of the price level, which Professor Hayek condemns,
is no doubt a less perfect policy than the stabilisation of the consumers' income. Nevertheless it is a reasonable approximation to
a sound policy. It has the advantage of a direct statistical test of
its aim. And if it results in a chronic slight tendency to inflation, as
technological progress increases productivity, that is, even from
Professor Hayek's point of view, quite innocuous. What he fears
is a reversal of the policy of granting credits to producers, a reversal
which would occur because " a rapid and continuous rise of prices

would, after a while, make it necessary to stop this process of inflation ". Against that the price stabilisation policy would be a complete safeguard.

The real objection to a crude price stabilisation policy is that in certain circumstances, where an important group of commodities rises in price owing to non-monetary causes (e.g. deficient crops), it involves a measure of deflation which is inappropriate to the monetary conditions. But even so, provided the deflation is not carried too far and does not develop into a vicious circle of depression, the harm done is quite limited.

The whole of the reasoning in the four lectures which comprise the main body of the book is governed by the hypothesis that at the outset the productive forces of the community are fully employed. In the article from *Econometrica* which is appended to the second edition a tentative effort is made to consider the consequences of removing that hypothesis, and to examine " the effect of an expansion of consumers' demand at a time when the productive forces are not fully employed and banks are in a position to expand credits to producers " (p. 154).

" If it be assumed ", Professor Hayek proceeds, " that these two conditions exist as a consequence of a preceding crisis . . . and if the explanation of the crisis which I have just discussed is accepted, it is difficult to see how the same phenomenon which has brought about the crisis, i.e. the rise in the relative demand for consumers' goods, should also be the cure for it. The scarcity of capital which of course is nothing else but the relatively high price of consumers' goods, could only be enhanced by giving the consumers more money to spend on final products " (p. 154).

Here lurks the whole fallacy of price margins. An increased demand for consumers' goods induces a *more* than proportionally increased demand for capital goods. The characteristic of a depression is a reduced demand for consumers' goods and producers' goods alike.

To assume that a depression has been caused by a " rise in the relative demand for consumers' goods " is to beg the question. We have seen reason to dissent from the view that a depression is caused in that way at all. But even if it *can* be so caused, that does not dispose of the possibility of its also being caused in other ways.

If an injection of money has the effects described, culminating in an all round rise of prices and inflation, what is the effect of a curtailment of the supply of money? If we follow in the latter case an exact parallel to Professor Hayek's reasoning in the former, we find a reduced demand for producers' goods, a curtailment of incomes and then, after an interval, a reduced demand for consumers' goods, which might, more or less, restore the former proportion between the demand for consumers' goods and the demand for producers' goods. An initial shortening of the period of production would thus make way for a subsequent lengthening.

But the parallel is not complete. It is mainly the shortening of the period of production that causes the displacement of specific goods, and this operates *at the beginning ;* the subsequent lengthening would presumably appear as a measure of relief, restoring activity to the producers of these specific goods, unless the interval has been so long that they have given up business.

And, what is far more important, whereas the hypothesis of full employment precludes any increase in the total demand for consumers' and producers' goods together, there is nothing to prevent a *decrease* in total demand. Such a decrease is evidently involved, for the reduced demand for consumers' goods follows on the reduced demand for producers' goods.

The examination of the effects of an injection of additional money is introduced with the remark: " the corresponding cases of a diminution of the amount of money we may neglect because a diminution of the demand for consumers' goods would have essentially the same effects as a proportional increase of the demand for producers' goods, and *vice versa* " (p 85).

If Professor Hayek really thinks that the difference between an increase and a decrease in general demand can be neglected, no wonder he regards the preoccupation of monetary theorists with the general price level as misguided!

THE RICARDO EFFECT

Professor Hayek's book, *Profits, Interest and Investment*, which appeared in 1939, is a collection of essays designed to improve and develop his theory of industrial fluctuations.[1] One of these in particular, that which gives its name to the book, modifies some of the positions which have been criticised in the foregoing pages.

In the revised version it is " a rate of profit, rather than a rate of interest in the strict sense, which is the dominating factor " (p. 3). If the price differences between stages are equated not to interest but to profit, that is a move towards reality. But unfortunately profit

---

[1] It is to this book that page references in the rest of this chapter relate.

and interest are still confused, in that the rate of interest is assumed
to tend to equality with the rate of profit.

Professor Hayek starts with " the familiar Ricardian proposition
that a rise in wages will encourage capitalists to substitute machinery
for labour and *vice versa* " (p. 8). And he deduces that, when a
cyclical rise of prices reduces real wages, the inducement to deepening
is diminished. Substantially the rise or fall of real wages is reflected
in a narrower or wider margin of profit. So he regards the inducement to deepening as varying inversely with the margin of profit.

Ricardo's proposition, however, has a twofold application. On
the one hand, a rise or fall of real wages affects the substitution of
machinery for labour, that is to say, the deepening of capital,
because a change in the cost of labour modifies the labour-saving
capacity of the machinery. On the other, since profit provides the
motive for the widening of capital, and widening and deepening
compete with one another for the available capital resources, an
improvement in the prospects of profit tends to divert resources from
deepening to widening, while a deterioration of the prospects of
profit discourages widening and releases resources for deepening.

In fact, there is not a single Ricardo effect, but there are two
quite distinct effects on deepening : the former may be called the
cost-effect, the latter the profit-effect. But to attribute either simply
to a change in " real wages " is an over-simplification. A change in
real wages means a rise or fall of money wages relative to prices
in general, whether the change be in wages or in prices or in both.
It is true that a change in real wages (unless it merely reflects a
contrary change in real costs), causes a change in profit margins, and
thereby tends to induce the profit-effect. But what stimulates the
widening of capital is not the increased profit margin in itself but
the *increased demand*, of which the profit margin is a symptom. If
the widening leads quickly to an increased supply, the profit effect
may occur without any actual rise of price or of profit margin at all.
And in the cost-effect, the relevant rise or fall of wages is not relative
to prices in general, but relative to the prices of the machinery or
instrumental goods by which labour is to be saved. And here it
cannot be assumed that the prevailing rate of wages measures
accurately the value of labour to the employer. Low rates of wages
would only discourage the deepening of capital if there were *an
adequate supply of labour* at the prevailing rates. There is an inducement to instal new labour-saving appliances, not only when they
yield a net saving of costs, but when the necessary labour for a
desired expansion of output is not procurable. The low level of

real wages at a time of high activity is deceptive. *Both* end phases of the trade cycle favour deepening : the climax of depression because the cost of labour is excessive, the climax of activity because there is a shortage of labour.

Professor Hayek does not distinguish sufficiently between the two applications of Ricardo's principle. He looks for the effect of an increased or decreased margin of profit on deepening, not in the reaction to the resulting increase or decrease of widening, but in the direct yield of the deepening process, as if each piece of plant could be regarded as separately contributing a share of the profit.

He has elaborated the point in an article on " The Ricardo Effect " (*Economica*, May 1942—reprinted in *Individualism and the Economic Order*, 1948). Each part of the capital equipment has its own " rate of turnover ". For example, the sums invested in current wages may be turned over six times a year, those invested in machine tools once a year, those invested in more permanent plant once in ten years. Suppose that the yield of capital has previously been 6 per cent per annum, and that the price of the product is increased 5 per cent. Then, according to Professor Hayek's reckoning, the yield of the first kind of capital rises to 36 per cent per annum, of the second to 11, and of the third to $6\frac{1}{2}$.[1]

The assumption here is that each portion of capital earns a share of profit. But that is not so. The profit is earned by the *output as a whole*, and shares in it cannot be separately imputed to the several factors contributing to the output. The mere occurrence of an exceptional margin of profit does not in itself offer an inducement to resort to less highly capitalised processes. But it does offer an inducement to resort to short-period expedients and makeshifts *to increase output* while the exceptional price margins last. That is how Ricardo's principle works through the profit-effect. To secure a given productive power, the capital outlay may be greater or less according to the kind of plant used. If the plant is less durable, the provision for depreciation must be correspondingly greater. The choice is presumably among two or more kinds of plant which call for substantially the same current charge to cover interest, maintenance and depreciation. Any kind for which the charge was appreciably greater would ordinarily be excluded from choice.

When expanding demand for a product outruns existing productive capacity, and the price rises, producers will seek to extend capacity at the least immediate cost and with the least delay that they can. They will tend to prefer the less durable plant, and their

[1] That is, $6 + 5 \times 6$, $6 + 5$ and $6 + 5 \times \frac{1}{10}$.

preference may outweigh some disadvantage in net yield. In so far as they do so, the widening process is associated with an actual reversal of the deepening process, an undeepening or enshallowing of capital.

As soon as the extension of capacity takes full effect, and the demand is met by a corresponding output, the exceptional profit margin disappears. So, even if the expansion of demand is permanent, the exceptional profit margin is transitory. The producers who are first in the field with their extended capacity will get the major share of it before their tardier competitors come into production. But for an early extension of capacity they need plant which can be quickly produced, and the short-lived plant, costing less, will usually (though not invariably) be more quickly produced than the long-lived.

If the expansion of demand is permanent, and the short-lived plant has to be regularly replaced in the future, no less than the long-lived, the permanent disadvantage of yield has to be set against the transitory gain in profit. If the short-lived plant is merely a cheaper version of the long-lived, and can be replaced when it wears out by the latter without any change in methods of production, the loss of yield will only last till the first replacement. But if this change cannot be easily made, the disadvantages of the short-lived plant may have to be reckoned as a permanency.

On the other hand, an expansion of demand which is expected to be transitory is best met by an improvised extension of capacity at relatively low capital cost, provided that the price of the product will cover the cost of writing off the capital cost by the time the exceptional demand ceases.

Nor need the improvised extension take the form of an installation of new plant. In the article on " The Ricardo Effect " Professor Hayek instances various short-run devices. Renewals and replacements may be postponed. Plant may be kept in use after it would normally be scrapped, or even, after it has been discarded, may be bought second-hand for further use. Against the saving in capital outlay so effected, there is sure to be additional expense on the maintenance and repairs of the worn-out plant. The substitution of current expense for capital outlay is an undeepening.

At the same time it is important to remember that the widening process presupposes a surplus supply of labour needing additional equipment. The profit-effect is, as Professor Hayek points out (pp. 18-20), closely related to " the acceleration principle of derived demand " (Mr. Harrod's " Relation "—below, pp. 276-7). It " will not begin to operate so long as there are unused resources of *all* kinds available " (p. 41). More precisely it begins to operate only if there is a supply of labour available, but capital fails to keep pace with it. When full employment is reached, and there are no longer unused resources of labour, it ceases to operate ; there is no further scope for widening (except by way of anticipation of future growth). Cheap labour does not of itself promote widening at the expense of deepening, even though there be expanding demand and high profits ; in order to do so, labour must be not only cheap, but in surplus supply.

The special acceleration of widening characteristic of a time of expanding demand is thus after all limited to the phase of under-employment. When full employment is reached, widening subsides to its normal rate of progress. But its rate of progress is not limited to a growth of capital equipment in proportion to employed population. For if accumulation exceeds widening and provides something for deepening, the deepening results in a saving of labour, and a further measure of widening is called for to provide the capital equipment with which the labour released can be engaged in production.

So long as demand continues to expand, traders will desire an immediate increase of output. When full employment is reached and they encounter a scarcity of labour, the deepening process itself may be modified, and may be hastened by a resort to makeshift forms of labour-saving equipment.

STAGES REVISED

Professor Hayek's theory demands that the labour and equipment employed on producing different kinds of capital goods be " not homogeneous, but often very specific to particular purposes ", so that " an increase in the demand for one kind of labour of which there is no more available can in no way offset a decrease in the demand for other kinds of labour of which there is still an unemployed reserve " (p. 12). But it does not seem likely that the labour and equipment by which the short-lived plant and long-lived plant applicable to the same labour-saving purposes are respectively produced would be " specific " in this sense.

Professor Hayek resorts again to the concept of " stages of production " as the basis of the distinction between more and less capitalistic methods. But the stages are no longer defined by the lapse of *time* between process and fruition. Each stage supplies the next with its means of production.

Stage I produces consumers' goods. Stage II supplies Stage I with raw materials and the simplest tools. Stage III supplies equipment of little durability and machinery of the least automatic type. Each stage is supplied by all the higher stages. The classification is not very clear, and Professor Hayek admits that the relations between the stages may be in some respects circular rather than linear. But, he says, " it shows that while some industries will be more or less directly and predominantly dependent on the demand for capital goods by the consumers' goods industries, others will be designed mainly to serve other capital goods industries, and still others will be suited almost exclusively to assist all other industries in the transition to more capitalistic, more labour-saving methods of production " (p. 23).

And the argument " turns largely . . . on the specificity of large parts of industry to comparatively ' early ' stages of production ".

" While there may be no single industry whose equipment is so completely specific to the production of particular kinds of capital goods that it can be used only for that and for no other purpose, nevertheless, there is no doubt that many industries are largely ' specific to the early stages '."

As industries a large part of the output of which " can be used only in that very indirect manner ", he instances " railroads and shipbuilding and a large section of the engineering industries ". And " the iron and steel industry in turn is still a stage further removed from consumption (though perhaps to a smaller extent now than before the rise of the motor-car industry) ".

Stages as here defined seem to be the " generations " in the " family tree " by which the structure of the period of production was illustrated in Chapter II (above, p. 14) except that the products of one industry may belong to many different generations.

Not only the motor-car industry, but all means of transport, including railways and ships, are in part employed in supplying consumers direct.

The engineering industries are mainly engaged in producing plant. The plant is for use not only in other industries but in the engineering industries themselves. What is the effect upon them of an expansion of demand for the products of other industries? Professor Hayek's contention is that some kinds of plant will be dispensed with because their first cost is too high in proportion to their immediate yield. But is it not likely that any less costly equipment substituted for them and designed for the same processes can be produced by the same industries?

Moreover, if there are some branches of the instrumental industries which specialise in the more costly or long-lived equipment, and are too " specific " to participate in the high demand for the widening of capital, these branches will not enjoy the rise of prices accruing to the rest. Their prices will not be high relatively to the wage level. So the cost-effect will not operate. Whatever undeepening occurs will not be due to the cost of labour being too low.

UNDEEPENING AND WORKING CAPITAL

For an industry subject to a long-range growth, underlying the fluctuations of the trade cycle, there must be times at which a normal widening process is at work. At the time of low demand for consumers' goods, widening is slackened or suspended. The cost-effect then operates; deepening is encouraged by the high real wages, but is designed to displace labour, not to increase capacity. Widening is resumed when general demand begins to outstrip productive capacity. But that is the moment when prices begin to rise relatively to wages and the profit-effect comes into play. The tendency to undeepen by substituting cheap, or makeshift or short-lived plant for the normal kinds of equipment arises so long as there is a surplus of unemployed labour needing equipment to get to work.

It would seem that the effects of undeepening on the activity of the instrumental industries is likely to be slight, and that, far from being concentrated at the turning point of the cycle, they would actually be diminished on full employment being reached.

On the other hand, in the sphere of working capital undeepening may be important. Expanding demand can be met from stocks. Pending their replenishment, traders make do with a diminished working capital. Professor Hayek (p. 22) defines Stage I as the production of consumers' goods, and presumably the holding of the finished consumers' goods in stock is a part of it. Stocks of materials are held at all stages of production, and are drawn upon when an increase of productive activity calls for immediate supplies. Therefore this form of undeepening runs through all stages. But it involves no change in the structure of production. The stocks are provided by all industries, and all industries are called upon to replenish them.

Besides the materials used up in industry, there will be instrumental goods, plant and parts, which wear out quickly or are subject to breakages, and stocks of which are held by those who use them.

The instrumental goods actually in use are a part of capital equipment, but those in stock are part of working capital.

When stocks at any stage are drawn upon, there is an undeepening in the sense that the capital actually being employed is diminished. But the standard period of production as defined in Chapter II (above, pp. 20-4) is not altered. Traders may be assumed still to regard the same relation of stocks to output or sales as acceptable, and it is in that sense that the structure of production is unchanged.

Undeepening can be said, in a more pertinent sense, to occur when traders *aim* at lower stocks. There is then diminished activity in the industries which replenish the stocks ; a negative intermediate demand, such as a rise in the short-term rate of interest is intended to cause. Undeepening of working capital does not furnish an exact parallel to undeepening of instrumental capital. The resort to makeshifts, on which Professor Hayek lays so much stress, is not available to reduce the goods held in stock. So long as stocks are above the minimum, they can be reduced without ado. If they fall near the minimum, possibly something may be done to economise them, e.g. by hastening transport from places of production to places of consumption, but the principal response to an excessive depletion of stocks is a rise of price. The depletion of stocks is in fact the process by which an expansion of demand takes effect in a rise of price.

CHAPTER IX

"THE THEORY OF UNEMPLOYMENT" BY
PROFESSOR A. C. PIGOU

ELASTICITY OF DEMAND FOR LABOUR

IT was long a reproach to what may be called the classical school of economists that they ignored unemployment. They did so for two reasons: first that they contented themselves with a static theory, dealing only with equilibrium conditions, and they regarded unemployment as a symptom of disequilibrium; secondly that they were unwilling to admit that money could ever enter in a substantial way into the chain of economic causation. The second reason might be regarded as derived from the first, for the equilibrium conditions assumed in their static theory included monetary equilibrium. But the classical view that money was a matter of the form and not of the substance had independent roots in Adam Smith's assault on mercantilism.

Professor Pigou's *Theory of Unemployment*, which appeared in 1933, was a notable new departure in that the analytical apparatus which has been evolved by the modern representatives of the classical school is utilised in a dynamic treatment. Nevertheless he remains under the influence of the classical antipathy to the recognition of monetary causes.

" It is possible ", he says, " to study the problem of unemployment either from the money end or from what I shall call in contrast the real end. The two studies, if made complete and carried through correctly, must necessarily come to the same thing, their analyses meeting in the middle." He has chosen to start from the " real " end, and " to bring in the monetary factor only at a fairly late stage ".

After some preliminary chapters, Professor Pigou embarks upon the development of his subject in Part II, the Short-Period Elasticity of the Real Demand for Labour. Here he investigates " the differences or variations, in quantity of labour demanded that are associated with given differences, or variations, in the rates of real wages for which workpeople stipulate, *when the relevant demand functions for labour are given* " (p. 33).

The starting point of the investigation (p. 41) is the principle that at any centre (apart from monopoly conditions) " the quantity of labour demanded there at any given rate of real wage is such that the value in terms of wage-goods of its marginal net product (i.e. of the difference made to the total physical yield by the marginal man with the help of existing equipment) approximates to that rate of wage " (wage being defined to include employers' contributions to social services).

In the case of an industry which buys materials, applies a process to them, and sells the finished product, we may suppose that x units of labour yield y units of processing. If $\psi(y)$ be the demand function for the finished product and $f(y)$ be the supply function of the raw material, $\dfrac{d\psi}{dy}$ will be the demand price of the finished product (" at works ") and $\dfrac{df}{dy}$ the supply price of the raw material.

Then the demand price of labour " in terms of wage-goods " will be :

$$w = \left(\frac{d\psi}{dy} - \frac{df}{dy}\right)\frac{dy}{dx} = \frac{d\psi}{dx} - \frac{df}{dx}.$$

The elasticity of the demand for labour will be :

$$\frac{w}{x\dfrac{dw}{dx}}.$$

Expanded, this yields what Professor Pigou calls an ungainly formula. But an elegant and ingenious transformation finds a significance for all the second differential coefficients contained in it in terms of elasticity of demand for the finished product, and for units of processing, and of elasticity of supply of raw material, etc. (pp. 43-4).

PROFIT AND THE MARGINAL UNIT

The assumption that the rate of wage is equal to the marginal net product is only true if the employer asks for no contribution whatever towards the net profit and overhead expenses from the output of the marginal man. Professor Pigou's assumption is that it will be worth while to employ additional labour, dx, at a cost of wdx, so long as the selling value, $\dfrac{d\psi}{dy}dy$, of the additional output exceeds the cost of materials, $\dfrac{df}{dy}dy$, by at least wdx. The limit at which no more

17

labour will be engaged is therefore reached when

$$wdx = \frac{d\psi}{dy}dy - \frac{df}{dy}dy, \text{ or } w = \frac{d\psi}{dx} - \frac{df}{dx}.$$

But, in practice, the limit will be reached earlier. The employer will not increase his output beyond the point at which $\frac{d\psi}{dy}dy - \frac{df}{dy}dy$ exceeds wdx by an appropriate margin of gross profit, Kdy. Gross profit here means excess of proceeds over prime costs.

Thus the formula should be:

$$w = \frac{d\psi}{dx} - \frac{df}{dx} - K\frac{dy}{dx}.$$

K is not simply a function of y, the output; it depends on various circumstances, and particularly upon the prospects of future business.

In Professor Pigou's formula, K is zero. That does not mean that the margin between costs and the proceeds of sale is zero. This margin, in fact, is equal to $y\left(\frac{d\psi}{dy} - \frac{df}{dy}\right) - wx$. But it is a quasi-rent, different in character from profit, whether gross or net. Indeed, if $\frac{dy}{dx}$ is greater than $\frac{y}{x}$, it will be a negative quantity.

If gross profits were assumed to be a constant proportion of the wages bill, Professor Pigou's equations could be employed with very little alteration. We should have $Kdy = kwdx$, where k is a constant, and

$$(1 + k)w = \frac{d\psi}{dx} - \frac{df}{dx}.$$

In fact $(1 + k)w$ could take the place of w wherever it occurs.

But Professor Pigou does not suggest such a formula. And it would in reality be no improvement, except in its formal recognition, that gross profits exist. For the fundamental importance of gross profits in the theory of the demand for labour arises from the very fact that the proportion of profit on the marginal output is *not* constant.

In introducing his formula, Professor Pigou says that the variation in output is to be " with existing equipment ", and that " the differences in the quantity of wear-and-tear suffered by equipment and in the costs of non-manual labour employed, that are associated with differences in output, are ignored as being, in general, of secondary importance " (p. 42).

It is quite legitimate to assume that in the short period an increase in employment involves no increase in overhead expenses. But even when that is so, it is quite unwarrantable to assume that the employer will be content to receive *no contribution* towards overhead expenses from an increment of output. When his concern is employed much below capacity, he will be content with an inadequate contribution; he will reduce the margin of gross profit below the usual percentage, and he may in an extreme case reduce it to nothing. As the concern becomes more fully employed, he will increase the percentage. When the industry as a whole is very active, the percentage will rise above normal. But it is not solely on the actual output that the percentage depends. Even when underemployed, a producer will be reluctant to make big price concessions if he thinks that the orders so obtained will prevent him from taking more remunerative orders in the near future.

Professor Pigou takes account of " monopolistic policy, whether in the guise of formal agreement or of tacit understanding or of a general refusal without any understanding, to sell down to prime cost " (p. 135). But he supposes these " shifts towards monopoly ", securing a margin above prime cost, to take place " predominantly in times of low demand for the commodity ", and the shifts towards competition, securing no such margin, to be characteristic of good times. That is the direct contrary of the facts.

Marshall devised an illustrative example in which the marginal shepherd " adds to the total produce a net value just equal to his own wages ". But that example was carefully framed as one in which " nothing has to be allowed for earnings of management ". In the general case the net product of a marginal agent of production is to be reckoned " after deducting for any extra expenses that may be indirectly caused by the change ". Earnings of management must presumably be included in expenses. Marshall would very likely have demurred to adding on a more or less arbitrary overhead proportion, but *in practice* that is what we have to do.

It may be that some industrial concern which is unusually full up with orders will expand its output above its normal capacity either by working overtime or by taking on hands in excess of the number conveniently equipped and accommodated. If the pressure is likely to continue, so that the resulting output is really additional, it will be worth while to carry these measures up to the limit at which an additional increment of labour power is marginal, in that the excess of its contribution to output over its cost falls to nothing. But it is not to be taken for granted that the approach to this limit is physically possible at all. Probably little can be done in the way of straining the limits of accommodation and equipment, and when no more labour can be fitted in it may well be that the last increment of labour is still far above the margin. Such devices for extending capacity beyond its normal limit are likely to be of a merely subsidiary character, except in the particular cases of double shifts and overtime. These, however, are not often resorted to except when prices and profits are abnormally high, and there is a substantial margin even over the increased prime costs involved.

Thus it is only in unimportant special cases that the gross profit vanishes and the rate of wage becomes equal to the entire marginal net product.

Gross profits interpose a cushion between variations in the proceeds of sale of the product and variations in costs. They profoundly modify the demand for labour and greatly reduce its elasticity. Professor Pigou recognises that " normal capacity for any occupation means the rate of output [at] which the equipment is designed to yield at least average supplementary *plus* prime cost per unit " (p. 50). But even if, when he points out that in a highly capitalised industry the marginal output is relatively high, he means that marginal output *exceeds the rate of wages*, that does not lead him to correct his mathematical formula.

From time to time in the course of his book, he refers to the effects of booms and depressions on elasticity. " In times of boom, owing to the limitation of fixed capital equipment, it is not, in general, feasible to push employment further except at the cost of sharply decreasing physical returns. . . . It is impossible for the real demand for labour in terms of wage goods to be other than highly inelastic. In times of depression, however, when the bulk of a country's capital equipment is working much below capacity this is not so " (p. 89).

The point here is not that the state of activity or depression affects the gross profit aimed at by the employer, but simply that at a time of activity labour cannot profitably be engaged in excess of the numbers to which the capital equipment is adapted. In that case there will, no doubt, be an increased gross profit, owing to the failure of output to keep pace with demand. But the admission of this exception to the marginal productivity formula is very far from a recognition of the vital importance of gross profit to the general theory.

The equation $w = \left(\dfrac{d\psi}{dy} - \dfrac{df}{dy}\right)\dfrac{dy}{dx}$ deals with the labour employed in " processing ", to the exclusion of that employed either in marketing and transporting the finished product, or in producing the materials. Thus $\dfrac{d\psi}{dy}$ is the price of the finished product " at works ". With regard to the subsequent operations of marketing and transport, " for purposes of a rough approximation we may postulate that the proportion of the total value contributed by the cost of these services remains constant " (p. 46). But commerce and transport are themselves sources of employment. Even in countries where they are much less important than " processing ", they are far from negligible.

Marketing and transport should more properly be regarded as *subsequent processes*. And the production of materials and intermediate products are likewise sources of employment, and should be regarded as *prior* processes. Professor Pigou treats materials as affecting employment in the industries which use them, and seems to have forgotten the labour employed in producing them (p. 122). He does indeed mention them as examples of complementary industries, " wherever one industry produces something that is used as material or machinery for the work of another, an element of complementariness is present " (p. 67), but he does not pursue the matter further.

We should be closer to the facts if we regarded any finished product as the outcome of a series of economic activities, each stage buying the output of the one before. If the cost of the output of the rth stage, bought by the $r + 1$th stage, be $f_r(y)$, and the labour employed at the rth stage be x_r and the rate of wage w_r, Professor Pigou's formula could be generalised into :

$$w_r \frac{dx_r}{dy} = \frac{df_r}{dy} - \frac{df_{r-1}}{dy}.$$

Here y must be interpreted to mean the number of units of output in progress, a factor common to all stages.

If we insert a term K_r for gross profit on the marginal product, the formula becomes :

$$w_r \frac{dx_r}{dy} + K_r = \frac{df_r}{dy} - \frac{df_{r-1}}{dy}.$$

At the *first* stage, where a primary product (whether organic or mineral) is derived direct from the soil, we have $f_0 = 0$.[1] At the last stage, where the finished product is sold to the final purchaser,

$$\frac{df_r}{dy} = \frac{d\psi}{dy} = \text{the price to the final purchaser.}$$

If we sum all stages from first to last in a single equation, we get simply :

$$\Sigma \, w_r \frac{dx_r}{dy} + \Sigma \, K_r = \frac{d\psi}{dy}.$$

Price is reduced to the sum of the cost of labour and the gross profit for all stages, without the cost of materials appearing explicitly anywhere.

It might not be easy to evolve from this formula a convenient mathematical expression for the elasticity of demand for labour. We can assume either a general increase of wages or an increase at one particular stage. The immediate effect will be an increase in costs and an equal diminution in gross profits. There may follow a rise in the price charged to the final purchaser and a consequent contraction of demand and of output. Much might be said of the repercussions arising throughout the several stages, but it can, I think, be much more intelligibly and adequately expressed in terms of the human motives involved than in terms of mathematical symbols.

Professor Pigou expresses elasticity in terms of the calculus, as the relation between an infinitesimal change in wages and the consequent infinitesimal change in employment. This does not represent any practical problem. The changes in wages that actually take place are always discontinuous and finite, and nothing is gained by assuming them to be continuous and indefinitely small. That, however, is a criticism which applies to the concept of elasticity as generally interpreted by economists, and not merely to Professor Pigou or to the elasticity of demand for labour.

WAGE GOODS

When Professor Pigou reaches his formula for the demand price of labour, he states it to be " in terms of wage-goods ". And throughout the book " wage-goods " are employed as a standard for the comparison of real wages with other values.

Wage-goods are the goods on which wages are spent, and therefore compose the real remuneration of the workpeople. It is

---

[1] This is not literally correct. There will probably still be some purchases of materials (such as seed and fertilisers, or explosives or pit-props).

very natural, when approaching the subject from the " real " end, to assume all values to take the form of " prices " expressed in wage-goods as a standard.

It is explained in Part I, Chapter IV, how the measurement of an aggregate of wage-goods depends on a system of weighting in an index number. The upshot is that " changes of real wage-rates are incapable of exact measurement ".

" When, between two dates, there has occurred any sensible change in the proportions in which the representative wage-earner buys different sorts of wage-goods, the term, a unit of wage-goods, has no exact meaning " (p. 20).

It would seem to be a distinct drawback to the approach of the subject of unemployment from the " real " end, that all values have to be expressed in terms of units which have " no exact meaning ". In reality, however, Professor Pigou need not have complicated his formula for a particular industry by bringing wage-goods into it at all. The employer is not concerned with the real remuneration of his workmen, but only with the relation between the exchange value of the wages and the exchange value of his own product. If " reality " necessarily means barter conditions, and we have to imagine that the employer undertakes to supply his workmen with the goods they want to consume, then the employer will, of course, be very directly interested in wage-goods. But for the purposes of an analysis of the demand for labour, it is sufficient to assume that the functioning of markets results, directly or indirectly, in the establishment of a definite ratio between wages and the exchange value of the product in each industry. We need take no account of any medium to serve as a common unit for them. When we have expressed the value of wages in wage-goods, and the value of the product in wage-goods, we proceed to calculate the value of wages in terms of the product, and then the wage-goods drop out. We could equally well make the calculation in terms of *anything possessing a market value* provided it is independent of *y*. It might be sealing-wax or tame lizards, or (if that were not too extravagant a departure from reality) it might be money.

On the other hand when we turn from a particular industry to examine the elasticity of demand for labour as a whole, we do need some unit of measurement with reference to which we can say that the general level of wages has risen or fallen and by how much.

Each industry separately has its formula, $w = \dfrac{d\psi}{dx} - \dfrac{df}{dx}$, which can be interpreted as relating w, a rate of wages, directly with $\dfrac{d\psi}{dy}$, the

value of the product, $\dfrac{df}{dy}$ the value of the materials, and $\dfrac{dy}{dx}$ the

marginal productivity of labour. But how are we to arrive at an average wage for *all* industries, and to measure its increase or decrease?

The real facts are those relating to particular industries; each wage rate is linked to its own product by the appropriate productivity function, and the demand for the product is governed by the appropriate demand function. We might assume the wage rates in the several industries all to change independently of one another. But that would not suit Professor Pigou's purpose. He wants to investigate the elasticity of demand for labour in response to a change in wages applying to all industries alike. The supposition of a uniform change in the purchasing power of wages in terms of wage-goods supplies what is required.

This supposition involves him in a distinction between those industries which are themselves engaged in producing wage-goods, and the others.

He divides the labour employed in the community into x men engaged in producing wage-goods and y men engaged otherwise, and infers that if $F(x)$ is the output of the former, the general rate of

wage will be $\dfrac{dF}{dx}$ for *both* classes of labour (pp. 89-90). That rate

being applied to the non-wage-good industries, y may be regarded as a function of x.

But it is a mistake to suppose that the real wages of those engaged in producing wage-goods can be thus simply equated to their marginal output. For the weighting of the different kinds of

wage-goods in the marginal output, $\dfrac{dF}{dx}$, is quite different from the

weighting required to compute real wages. Professor Pigou avoids this difficulty by assuming in the first instance that there is only a single sort of wage-good. But he does not face the problem that arises when that assumption is withdrawn.

Wage-goods include some products which are predominantly consumed by the working classes, but they must include others of which the proportion so consumed is very small. And every graduation will be found between those for which the proportion is

80 or 90 per cent and those for which it is 1 or 2 per cent. Little is to be gained by segregating the products for which the proportion is *nil*, and excluding them from the marginal productivity function which determines the general rate of wages.

The boundary line between wage-goods and non-wage-goods is not a very significant one. By adopting a more minute subdivision of products, so that the differences of quality constitute different products, we can extend the list of non-wage-goods. Cigars, wireless sets, seats at the theatre, are wage-goods, but the more expensive qualities in each case might be separated off and classed as non-wage-goods. In making the classification, what we have to discover in the case of each product is whether any part of the output, however small, is ever consumed by the wage-earners. But for a product of which we know that the working-class consumption in any case does not exceed a very small proportion, the question whether that proportion is, or is not, absolutely nothing is quite unimportant. We might neglect such cases and count as non-wage-goods all those for which the proportion is below an arbitrary limit, say 5 per cent, but we should still find that the difference between 80 per cent and 5 per cent is much more significant than the difference between 5 per cent and *nil*.

In fact, if we wish to explore the reaction upon real wages of a change in the productivity of any industry or group of industries, what we want to know is not whether these industries are wage-good industries or not, but what proportion of the output of each enters into wage-earners' consumption, and what proportion of that consumption it represents.

Part III deals with movements of the real demand for labour. In order to isolate the effects of changes in demand, we have to suppose that wages do not change, and here again Professor Pigou has recourse to the standard of wage-goods. He postulates that the real rate of wage is given. This involves once again all the complications of the distinction between wage-good and non-wage-good industries.

At that stage it is a mere effort of abstraction made for the purposes of analysis, but when at the end we turn to the causes of unemployment (Part V) we need some measure which will enable us to say whether wages are or are not " changing " or " resisting change ". That is essential, because it is only through *the resistance of wages to change* that a variation in the demand for labour affects employment at all. " With perfectly free competition among workpeople and labour perfectly mobile . . . there will always be at work a strong tendency for wage-rates to be so related to demand

that everybody is employed. The implication is that such unemployment as exists at any time is wholly due to the fact that
changes in demand conditions are continually taking place, and
that frictional resistances prevent the appropriate wage adjustments
from being made instantaneously" (p. 252). Professor Pigou
points out that in practice this implication requires to be qualified,
for wage-policy may be aiming at wage-rates which are not consistent, even in stable conditions, with full employment. Whenever
that is so, wage-policy is itself a cause of unemployment.

The " frictional resistances ", however, are themselves a part of
wage-policy. The system of demand functions is always in process
of change. " Wage policy, even though its general tendency and
intention is constant, cannot adjust itself instantaneously to each
momentary state of this process " (p. 272).

Throughout Part III, Movements of Real Demand, Professor
Pigou assumes that real wages, that is to say, wages in terms of
wage-goods, remain unchanged. Implicitly that means that the
inertia of wage policy is directed to keeping real wages unchanged.

Any such assumption is quite out of accord with the facts. In
Part V, The Causation of Unemployment, Professor Pigou discusses
the factors of inertia that interfere with the appropriate adjustments
of wages, and proceeds :

" These factors of inertia, which, in an economy where wage-
rates were always contracted for in kind, would tend to keep real
wages stable in the face of changing demand, in a money economy
tend to keep money wages stable. To a great extent people—
employers and employed alike—think in money. . . . If the conditions of real demand were stationary, and known to be stationary,
and the only variable factor was the quantity of money available for
expenditure, the custom of basing wage contracts for long terms on a
cost-of-living sliding scale might, after a time, win wide acceptance."
But as things are, there are obstacles to this practice, and " thus,
except in periods of very violent price oscillations, employers in
general fight strongly against upward movements in money rates
of wages and workpeople against downward movements. Money
wage-rates show themselves in practice highly resistant to change "
(pp. 294-5).

In fact, wage agreements relate to money wages, and the resistance which causes unemployment in case of a change in the demand
for labour is a resistance to a change in money wages.

Wage-goods are introduced into the analysis because Professor
Pigou, having chosen to approach his subject from the " real " end

and not from the " money " end, is precluded from attaching the
inertia of wage-policy to money wages, and he therefore attaches
it to real wages. But the result is to vitiate all the reasoning based
on that assumption in its practical application to a monetary
economy. In this respect it is not true to say that the two methods
of approach " must necessarily come to the same thing, their
analyses meeting in the middle ". The investigator approaching
the subject from the " real " end, who proceeds on these lines, will
find that he must retrace his steps.

Wage-goods are relevant to wages as *incomes*. An investigation
of unemployment or of the demand for labour is concerned with
wages as *costs*.

Wage-policy is a link between the two. Wages as costs may be
determined by a wage-policy which is influenced by wages as
incomes. But, as we have seen, wage-policy is not, for the most
part, guided by real wages.

Professor Pigou builds his theory on wage-goods from the
foundation. " When the real rate of wage stipulated for is given,
the quantity of labour demanded in the aggregate of all industries
varies, and can only vary, in precise proportion to the quantity of
wage-goods available for, and devoted to, the payment of wages "
(p. 143). At the beginning of the book he elaborates a formula, in
which he reckons out the wage-goods available, whether from new
production, from importation or from stocks, and deducts the wage-
goods consumed by non-wage-earners, and the net amount transferred by non-wage-earners to the wage-earning classes otherwise
than in wage-payments (old age pensions, etc.). If the quantity so
arrived at be divided by the average rate of real wages, the result is
the amount of employment. This is a proposition " not of economics, but of arithmetic " (p. 24). And a proposition of arithmetic
it must remain in any world in which employers do not remunerate
their workmen with wage-goods, and workmen do not formulate
wage-policy in terms of wage-goods.

The manner in which wage-goods enter into the analysis throughout the book may be illustrated by the following passage, relating to
the effects of an improvement in productivity in a particular wage-
good industry :

" If the demand in terms of wage-good units for the product of
that industry has, over the relevant range, an elasticity greater than
unity, an improvement in productivity will increase the quantity of
labour demanded in the industry, and will also increase the output
of this particular wage-good item. This item consequently becomes

cheaper in terms of other wage-good items. That fact, since it implies an increase in the value of every other wage-good item in terms of wage-good units, will make it worth while for employers, at a given real wage-rate, to engage more men in other wage-good industries. The quantity of labour demanded there will, therefore, increase. Moreover, there being a larger total of wage-good units in being, and, therefore, a larger surplus available to non-wage-earners, these persons will, in general, devote more wage-goods than before to setting labour to work in non-wage-good industries. . . .

" It is possible, however, that the non-wage-earners' attitude towards the particular item of wage-goods is such that the demand for it in terms of wage-good units has an elasticity less than unity. In this case the quantity of labour employed upon it will decrease in consequence of an improvement. . . . None the less, however, the output of the commodity must be increased " (p. 167).

All this would be very important if the condition that the real wage-rate is given were fulfilled. It is only within twenty pages of the end of the book that the reader encounters the fatal disclosure that it is money wages and not real wages that resist change. How much of the ingenuity devoted by Professor Pigou to his investigation, before that final stage, has been misdirected!

In any theory of movements in the real demand for labour it might be supposed that international trade and international competition would be given great prominence. Professor Pigou has something to say of the interdependence of the demand for labour in different centres, and refers very cursorily to the tendency of wage reductions in any centre to spread to competing centres (pp. 69-70), and to the increased demand for labour likely to result from the improved efficiency of export industries (pp. 169-71). But he never deals with the adverse effect on employment of the improved efficiency of foreign competitors in the export market.

He is chiefly interested in international trade as a means of exchanging non-wage-goods for wage-goods :

" In so far as additions to exports consequential upon a reduction in wage-rates are offset by additions to imports of foreign securities or of non-wage-goods that do not compete with native products, the industries that make them are, from the present standpoint, on a par with industries that make non-wage goods for home consumption. But in so far as they are offset by additions to imports of wage-goods or of raw materials, the industries that make them are on a par with home wage-good industries. An expansion in them indirectly promotes an expansion in the demand for labour in home non-wage-good industries. *Per contra*, in so far as additions to exports involve additions to imports that compete with the products of home non-wage-good industries, the demand for labour in those industries is affected adversely " (p. 76).

THE STANDARD MONETARY SYSTEM

Part IV brings Professor Pigou to the consideration of monetary factors. Their exclusion from the earlier parts " does not mean that our analysis has assumed the monetary mechanism to be non-existent and so [has been] relevant, not to the actual world, but only to an abstract and unreal simulacrum of it. On the contrary, everything that has been said has been relevant to the actual world " (p. 185).

Professor Pigou builds the monetary section of his theory of unemployment on a " standard monetary system ". This supplies a norm, somewhat like that which some economists find in " neutral " money, though Professor Pigou disavows any purpose of finding a system " under which economic life will proceed as it would do if there were no money at all " (p. 188).

He defines " the standard monetary system as one so constructed that, for all sorts of movements in the real demand function for labour or in real rates of wages, whether they last for a long time or a short, the aggregate money income is increased or diminished by precisely the difference made to the number of workpeople (or other factors of production) at work multiplied by the original rate of money wages " (pp. 205-6).

The standard monetary system is thus defined in terms of the aggregate money income. Its essential characteristic would seem to be that, whenever employment is increased or diminished by a non-monetary cause, the aggregate money income will be increased or diminished in proportion to the factors of production at work. The definition presupposes some relation between the rate of wages paid to the workpeople and the rates of remuneration of the other factors of production, profit, salaries, interest and rent. Such a relation is definite enough under equilibrium conditions, when, on the average, normal profits accrue after all the appropriate overhead expenses have been duly met. But when equilibrium is disturbed, and the margin increases or diminishes, how is the appropriate rate of remuneration of the profit-makers to be reckoned? When employment is increased or diminished, how are we to measure the increase or decrease in the amount of services rendered by the profit-makers, regarded as a factor of production?

Even at this stage of his subject Professor Pigou cannot resist the allurements of wage-goods. He proceeds to a further explanation of the standard monetary system: " In order that money income shall vary in correct accord with variations in the quantity of factors of production at work, industrialists in times of boom must only obtain money for engaging more labour to the extent that they and the people from whom they borrow abstain from spending money on wage-goods and imported non-wage-goods, and in like manner in times of depression, in so far as industrialists invest less money in hiring labour, they or other people must spend correspondingly more money upon wage-goods and imported non-wage-goods " (p. 211).

What is the relation between this explanation and the original definition of the standard monetary system? The clue is to be found in an illustration which precedes the definition (pp. 204-5). For the sake of simplicity, we may neglect the imported non-wage-goods, which are introduced only because they are regarded as taking the place of a potential supply of wage-goods.

In this illustration Professor Pigou supposes a certain quantity of wage-goods to be diverted from consumption by non-wage-earners, and to be applied to hiring labour for the production of non-wage-goods. " The money concomitants of the real movement work themselves out as follows. Non-wage-earners . . . pay out to new wage-earners an amount of money, withdrawn from purchasing wage-goods . . . sufficient to enable them to buy the wage-goods that represent their real wages ; money wage-rates and prices remaining the same as before. If W is the real rate of wage, K the number of additional workers employed, and P the money price per unit of wage-goods, . . . the aggregate money income of the community is increased by KWP."

But under actual monetary systems the course of events is usually different, " in that the extra money handed to wage-earners is not balanced against an equal contraction in the expenditure of non-wage-earners upon wage-goods for their personal consumption ". When there is an upward movement, total money income is increased by substantially more than KWP ; and when there is a downward movement, it is decreased by substantially more than this.

The definition of the standard monetary system is intended to represent it as the system which avoids these disproportionate movements of money incomes. The definition is generalised so as to take account not merely of additional workmen, but of additional " factors of production ".

Where, then, is the significance of wage-goods? The additional incomes are of all kinds, and may be spent on all kinds of goods. The money obtained for engaging more factors of production will have to be offset by a reduction of expenditure not on " wage-goods and imported non-wage-goods " but on *any* goods.

The principle that emerges seems to be that the additional working capital required should be provided *out of income*, and therefore not by a creation of bank credit or by drawing on existing cash balances.

Of his illustration, which I have quoted above, Professor Pigou says : " Nothing has occurred to alter the size of the stock of money, M. Therefore, since income per unit of time has increased from I to $(I + KWP)$, . . . it follows that v, the former income velocity of the total money stock, has increased to v_2, where $v_2 = \dfrac{I + KWP}{I} v$ " (p. 205).

Nevertheless, when he has reached his general definition, he points out that the new wage-earners will accumulate cash balances out of their increased incomes, and " in order that this may happen, it is necessary that the stock of active money shall be, in some measure, increased ". We may apply the same reasoning to the other factors of production, and conclude that they will likewise need additional cash balances.

Thus the standard monetary system requires that, in case of increased economic activity, there be a monetary expansion to provide the desired increase of cash balances.

But that means that the additional working capital will *not* be found exclusively out of income. In order that the appropriate expansion of money incomes may be effected, a part must be provided by credit creation, and not by any abstention from expenditure on the part of non-wage-earners.

The standard monetary system is not put forward as the embodiment of an ideal monetary policy. Rather it is intended to be used as a *criterion* to distinguish monetary from non-monetary disturbances, monetary disturbances being those involving a departure from the standard monetary system.

Still, Professor Pigou does regard the departures from the standard monetary system as on the whole harmful. What the standard monetary system implies is that " if the real demand function [for labour] varies, money income will vary with it in a certain specified way and not otherwise. With monetary systems not of standard type, money income does vary otherwise than in this specified way. In consequence . . . disturbances of the real demand function for labour take place that would not take place with a standard monetary system, and disturbances which would have taken place in any event, though in certain circumstances they may be damped down, are, in general, aggravated " (p. 210).

This is further explained on page 216. In case of an extension of demand for some product, industrialists will seek to borrow to extend their working capital. Unless the rate of bank interest is put up to the " proper " rate (that which just satisfies the needs of the standard monetary system) they will do so.

" But the banking system, so long as it acts on current principles and does not follow a deliberate policy of stabilisation, will not push up the actual rate of bank interest so high as this. For it is to its interest to lend more than usual when borrowers are offering better terms than usual. Hence, in the face of an upward movement in the demand for labour initiated on the real side, banking systems, as currently operated, always allow the actual rate of bank interest to rise less than the *proper* rate. In like manner, in the face of a downward movement, the banking system always allows the actual rate of bank interest to fall less than the *proper* rate."

This passage betrays a misconception of the working of banking systems " on current principles ". Banks do not " lend more than usual when borrowers are offering better terms than usual ". Their lending is regulated by their cash reserves. At a time when the pressure from borrowers is greater than usual, the banks will both lend more than usual in proportion to their reserves and also charge higher rates. But they charge higher rates *because* their loans exceed the appropriate proportion. And they will continue to take these and other measures to deter borrowers till they have reduced their loans to the required extent. The competitive banks can, of course, rectify their cash proportions when there is a central bank from which they can borrow. But they merely pass on the pressure to the central bank. So long as the central bank is subjected to excessive pressure from the competitive banks, it will maintain a high bank rate and other deterrent measures.

It is, therefore, the reserve position of the central bank that is the governing condition. If its gold reserve is deficient, credit restriction will be maintained, and any disturbance tending towards increased activity will be checked, while any disturbance tending towards diminished activity will be reinforced. If, on the other hand, the gold reserve is redundant, the central bank will relax credit, with the contrary result.

If, then, " current principles " mean the working of the gold standard as hitherto understood, it is not true to say that there is any tendency to aggravate disturbances of the demand for labour arising from non-monetary causes. The action of the banking system tends rather to override these disturbances and obliterate them.

Of course, in doing so, the banking system becomes an independent source of disturbances in the demand for labour. The standard monetary system is devised not only to avoid itself causing disturbances, but also to leave the field clear for the non-monetary disturbances.

Would it not be possible to retain the overriding power by which the banking system obliterates the non-monetary disturbances, without originating monetary disturbances on its own account?

" It is conceivable ", we are told, " that for some country with a monetary system of non-standard type, events should so shape themselves that disturbances initiated on the side of money supply always exactly offset disturbances initiated on the real side, so that at every moment the *proper* rate of bank interest was actually established. In such a case a monetary system not standard in intention would be standard by accident " (pp. 221-2).

But such a system would not be standard at all. The standard system allows free scope to all non-monetary causes of unemployment. The suggested system would *counteract* them. In that respect it would be a great improvement on the standard system. Nor would it necessarily come into operation " by accident ". It might do so by design. That would mean a modification of the working of the gold standard as hitherto accepted.

The standard monetary system has to meet every shrinkage of the demand for labour with a proportionate contraction of the money income of the community, and so allows the shrinkage of demand to take full effect in unemployment. If the money income of the community were *kept unchanged* (except for what economic growth requires), then, as soon as any part of the factors of production became unemployed, the demand in terms of money for the output of the factors of production remaining employed would be intensified, and this intensified demand would tend to restore full employment. A monetary policy which aimed at stabilising the aggregate money income of the community would thus tend to eliminate unemployment altogether, except when wage-policy raised money wages.

18

MONETARY AND NON-MONETARY CAUSES

There are two distinct reasons why money should be of paramount importance in the theory of unemployment. One is that it is the rate of money wages that resists change. The other is that a monetary cause affects all branches of economic activity in the same direction at the same time, whereas a non-monetary cause only affects a particular industry or group of industries.

The non-monetary causes affecting the demand for labour are indicated in Part III, Chapter II: changes in demand for any product, changes in the productivity of labour and changes in the supply of raw materials (pp. 110-12).

The effects on employment in general of an intensification of demand in one industry are considered—from the " real " end—in Part III, Chapter IX. There Professor Pigou argues that, in so far as wage-goods are merely diverted from employing wage-earners in other industries, no additional employment will result. To increase employment, wage-goods must be withdrawn from the consumption of non-wage-earners, or from stocks, or they must be imported, or they must be diverted from unemployment benefit.

These possibilities he examines in detail.

The consumption of wage-goods by non-wage-earners is " highly stable ", and " no substantial variations in the wage-fund " are likely to come from this source.

As to stocks of wage-goods, " owing to the high cost and the risks of loss involved in holding large stocks, their absorbing capacity is also narrowly restricted ", and reactions here " are not in general important " (p. 147).

Imports may make a big contribution *to any one country*, but " booms and slumps are largely international in character, so that the whole world, rather than a single country, is the proper object of study. For the whole world, however, the item . . . is, as we have seen, nil " (p. 148).

As to unemployment benefit, nothing is available unless employment is *already assumed to be increased*. " For an employment-making policy that, if the unemployment fund does not help, will fail, that fund contributes nothing; but for a policy that, without its help, would succeed in some measure, it will provide the means of enlarging that success " (p. 151).

How limited, then, must the effect of a non-monetary disturbance of the demand for labour be! [1]

---

[1] It may be mentioned that the passages quoted above apply to the stimulation of the demand for labour through public works.

In reality Professor Pigou is led by his pre-occupation with wage-goods to understate the effects of a non-monetary cause. Such a cause acting in a monetary economy will not be limited in its effect by the amount of wage-goods diverted. The workmen drawn into employment are paid with *money*, and if they cannot be supplied with wage-goods from stocks or from increased output, then the prices of wage-goods will rise, and real wages will fall. Or, if fewer workmen are employed and the demand for wage-goods falls off, prices will fall and real wages will rise.

The effect on employment will thus be greater in each case than if real wages were prevented from varying. But even so, the effect of non-monetary causes remains far less important than that of monetary causes.

It is not that the monetary cause necessarily has an immediate effect on real wages. The change in real wages may be delayed, and, when it comes, may be limited. The monetary cause modifies the relation in every industry between the price of the product and wages *as costs*.

CHAPTER X

MR. HARROD ON " THE TRADE CYCLE "

THE RELATION

MR. HARROD has some common ground with Keynes, but diverges from him in several important respects. He makes use of Keynes's concepts of the propensity to consume and of the " Multiplier ", the function expressing the proportion of an increment of the consumers' income to the consequent increment of saving. The foundation of his theory is the need, as a condition of equilibrium, for saving and active investment to be equal.

Along with this, he lays stress on what is commonly called the acceleration principle. As he says in his preface, " there is a well-established relation, vouched for by experience and the laws of arithmetic, between the demand for consumable goods and the demand for durable goods, the essence of which is that the absolute amount of the latter depends primarily on the rate of increase of the former ".

Assume the conditions to be such that any quantity of output, added to or subtracted from a given level, requires an amount of extra capital goods of various kinds bearing the same proportion to the existing volume of capital goods of each kind that the increment or decrement of output bears to the given level. Then

" (i) In order to maintain output at a given level, replacements of a constant amount are necessary ;
" (ii) In order to increase the output of consumable goods, additional capital goods (net investment) are necessary.

" The amount of these latter depends on the rate at which consumption is increasing. Thus, if consumption were advancing at the rate of 2 per cent per annum, only half as much net investment would be necessary as would be required to sustain an advance of 4 per cent " (p. 55).

This is the " Relation " referred to in Mr. Harrod's preface. It expresses in arithmetical terms that relation between the widening of capital and consumption demand with which we have already become acquainted. As was pointed out above (p. 63), a trader's judgment as to the prospects of demand, and therefore as to the moment at which an extension of capacity becomes advisable, is mainly empirical. To suppose an automatic or mechanical adaptation of the widening of capital to the growth of consumption demand is pushing the assumption of empiricism too far. There is, no doubt, a certain amount of more far-sighted net investment (particularly in transport and public utilities) which assumes current fluctuations in demand to be transitory. Still, Mr. Harrod has formulated an approximation to the true relation between the widening of capital and consumption demand.

DEEPENING OF CAPITAL AND THE RATE OF INTEREST

He proceeds to introduce the deepening of capital. There may be additional net investment " because a representative parcel of consumable goods comes to require more capital for its production. This may occur either (i) owing to a fall in the rate of interest which makes capital a relatively cheaper factor of production and so stimulates its use, or (ii) owing to a fall in the relative prices of capital goods compared with those of consumable goods, or (iii) owing to improvements of productive technique " (p. 59). It follows that net investment is not rigidly limited by the Relation.

If the deepening process could always be relied on to fill the gap between saving and the widening process, the existence of the gap could never cause depression and Mr. Harrod's theory would fall to the ground. Accordingly it is essential to his argument to prove that the deepening process fails.

It is the rate of interest and the improvements of productive technique that are important ; the contingency of a fall in the prices of capital goods is a secondary matter.

Mr. Harrod points out, with some force, that a fall in the rate of interest of " a small fraction of 1 per cent is not appreciable and is not likely to have *any* effect on the technique of production or the choice of consumers. . . . Unless the safe rate of interest is thought to have fallen by at least, say, $\frac{1}{2}$ per cent, the change is likely to have no effect " (p. 112).

No doubt over any short period, the effect of a small reduction in the long-term rate of interest in stimulating capital outlay by admitting instruments of marginal yield, is likely to be insignificant. But the investment market does not rely exclusively on that effect to adjust capital raised to its available resources. It is ordinarily in the position of resisting the pressure of new flotations and sales in order to keep its holding of securities within limits.

The effect of a rise or fall of the long-term rate of interest is financial rather than economic, low prices of securities causing projects to be postponed and high prices causing them to be hastened. And an unfavourable state of the market is also made manifest in other ways : higher commissions ; a wider spread between the prices of new issues and of existing securities ; a blank refusal of the less eligible issues.

If at any time the deepening process reached complete exhaustion, these negative methods would be no remedy ; a mere relaxation or removal of pressure would not restart activity. But in practice the deepening process never gets anywhere near exhaustion. As we have seen, its occasional failure at times of severe depression is attributable to a glut of a purely temporary character. Never at a time of normal industrial activity has there been anything but pressure in the investment market. At times of activity, it is true, the widening process is in full swing, but there is no doubt that for the past century economic activity has been becoming more and more highly capitalised.

At this point the question merges in that of technological improvements. Mr. Harrod points out that such inventions are not necessarily labour saving. They may save more capital than labour. And he adduces some considerations which " suggest scepticism with regard to the view that in the normal course of progress the proportion of capital goods to the income flow would, with a constant rate of interest, tend to rise " (p. 103).

When he puts his argument this way, Mr. Harrod is, I think, forgetting that his subject is the trade cycle, a phenomenon which had been recurring for more than a century before 1914. A suggestion of scepticism as to whether invention *will* increase the proportion of capital to income in the future is quite irrelevant to the explanation of the cycle as it has existed in the past.

Nevertheless this future development would not be any the less important in itself on that account, and it deserves investigation.

Instruments enrich the community by enlarging its productive capacity. It is as if the manpower of the community were itself increased. We have shown that when the deepening process works, whether with or without technological progress, labour is displaced and becomes available for other employment. Its absorption into other employment is an application of the widening process. Here once more we see the mutual reactions of the widening and the deepening of capital. The displaced labour requires additional capital equipment with which to produce additional output. The problem of providing this additional capital merges into that of providing capital for the natural increment of working population; it involves as much uncertainty, but no more.

The additional output thus organised generates incomes equal to its own selling value. Meanwhile the industries from which the labour has been displaced continue their output quantitatively undiminished, and, if costs have been reduced, actually increased. The increase in wealth is not limited to the additional income derived in the form of interest from the additional capital. The additional output will carry with it the corresponding profit. If the growth of capital is outstripping technological progress the rate of interest will fall, and what the owners of capital lose in income on this account will accrue to the rest of the community in the cheapening of commodities. If technological progress outstrips the growth of capital and the rate of interest rises, commodities are cheapened all the more.

So long as we think of the deepening process as increasing the capital equipment of *a given output*, it appears to be subject to narrow limitations. As soon as we recognise it as increasing the capital equipment of *a given working population*, the limits begin to recede. As it proceeds, output is not only increased but it becomes more varied.

And this widening of capital offers a larger and larger field for the deepening process. New commodities are introduced which would find no consumers in a poor community, and these offer new opportunities to the inventor. Scarcely less are the opportunities offered by the penetration of new zones of demand among the masses for commodities previously enjoyed only by the rich.

This does not mean that the deepening of capital can never end. But it does suggest that the state of true glut is still a long way off.

If we appeal to statistical evidence, we find that the rate of progress of the deepening process is extremely slow and gradual. The capital equipment of a modern industrial community (valued at first cost, without any deduction for depreciation) may be estimated at, say, four times its national income. Annual saving may be estimated at one-tenth of the national income, or $2\frac{1}{2}$ per cent of the capital. A part of this is needed for the widening process. As we have seen, this part may be substantially in excess of the rate of increase of population. What is left might accumulate for many years without making much impression on the potentialities of labour-saving appliances.

The whole of Mr. Harrod's theory of the trade cycle is founded on the assumption that the deepening process will regularly fail to fill the gap which appears between savings and the widening of capital. In this respect he differs from Keynes. They both alike trace trade depressions to a deficiency of demand arising from an absorption of cash. But whereas Mr. Harrod supposes the absorption of cash to occur in the investment market through a disparity between investment (in the sense that I have defined it) and capital raised, Keynes regards this disparity as non-existent or unimportant, and traces the absorption of cash to people withholding savings from the investment market.

THE DYNAMIC DETERMINANTS

In working out his theory Mr. Harrod traces the movements of the Relation and the Multiplier to three " dynamic determinants ". Two of these, the propensity to save and the shift to profit, work through the multiplier. The propensity to save is " the relation of the proportion of the increment of a representative man's income saved to the proportion of the previous total of income that was saved " (p. 90). The shift to profit increases the relative amount of saving, even when the propensity to save remains unchanged, because " profit-earners save a larger proportion of income, especially of increases of income likely to be transitory " (p. 74). These two between them determine how much of any increment of income will be saved, and how much consumed. The third dynamic determinant, the amount of capital used in production, is simply the deepening process.

If the output of a community be supposed to increase by a constant proportion per unit of time (a geometric series), and its stock of capital to grow in the same proportion, then saving will be a constant proportion of output and net investment will be a constant proportion of the *growth* of consumption. But if the rate of growth of output and capital exceeds the rate of growth of working population, then average income per head is rising and it is likely that the proportion of saving to income is increasing. Consequently capital will be growing faster than consumption. A shift to profit would accentuate the tendency.

If the third determinant (the deepening of capital) " exactly overcomes whatever restrictive force the other two may have, a steady advance may be maintained. But it may not be maintained. We cannot rely on the three determinants to maintain it. It would be a blessed coincidence if they did. If there is any drop in the rate of advance, a recession must occur " (p. 104).

One is impelled to ask what is a market for? Is it not the special function of the investment market to equalise the supply of securities with the demand? Is it a " blessed coincidence " if the market accomplishes this purpose? That the market works imperfectly we have seen. Mr. Harrod quite rightly doubts the adequacy of the long-term rate of interest as an equalising force. But he does not take into account the more direct methods that the market can employ.

Moreover, if output per head is increasing and capital is growing at the same pace as output, it follows that capital per head is growing. That is to say, the increase of capital is not exclusively by widening but also by deepening. There is nothing to differentiate the deepening that is proceeding under those conditions from the slightly greater amount of deepening required when the proportion of output consumed falls off.

Imagine a community in which the national income in millions of currency units is 4,000 and the national capital (at cost) is 16,000. Let capital and income both increase at the rate of $2\frac{1}{2}$ per cent per annum, so that saving is 400 millions, and the national income increases in a year from 4,000 to 4,100. If the working population is increasing by 1 per cent per annum, then a proportional increase of capital requires 160 millions, so that of the 400 millions of saving, a portion amounting to 240 millions is applied to deepening.

Now suppose that equilibrium is disturbed by an increase in the proportion of the additional income saved from one-tenth to, say, one-fifth. Saving, instead of rising to 410, rises to 420, and consumption instead of rising to 3,690 rises only to 3,680. Is this a catastrophic change? Will the deepening process, which could place 246 millions, fail to place 256 millions? [1] Even if the proportion of the additional income saved rose not merely to one-fifth but to one-half, the increase in the operations of the deepening process from 246 to 286 millions would not be very formidable for a community where the total capital is 16,000 millions.

We have assumed a start from equilibrium. But of course, if it can be shown that equilibrium will not last, we ought to assume fluctuations to be already prevalent. " Suppose at a point of time the level of output to be below what is possible. . . . Suppose an increase of output actually to eventuate. After any outstanding surplus capital plant is brought back into use, the activity of the

---

[1] It may be that this accelerated accumulation of capital leads to a correspondingly accelerated increase of output. But increased output generates increased income and the position is not materially altered.

capital goods trades becomes abnormally high." For the rate of increase of consumption exceeds what is normally due to increasing population and improving technique.

" When the period of abnormal advance comes to an end, there must be some recession in the capital goods industries. . . . If the total output, and therefore the total income of the community, falls, it is highly probable that there will be some recession in consumption and therefore in the consumption goods industries. This is the depression " (pp. 56-7).

In our hypothetical example, we must suppose the widening process to be swollen by arrears to something more than 1 per cent of the existing capital. Instead of 160 millions, it may be 200 or 300 or it may even absorb the whole 400, and the margin available for deepening will be reduced to 200, 100 or nothing. When the arrears of widening are overtaken, equilibrium will require an increase of deepening to 240 millions. But it would be quite a mistake to suppose that a jump up of deepening from nothing to 240 millions a year (even if it had to be accomplished in a year or two) would put a strain on the limits of deepening. For deepening will itself have fallen into arrears. At a time of activity, when the widening process has been at its maximum, far from there being any lack of projects for new departures in capital equipment, there is rather a queue formed at the doors of the investment market eager to raise capital as fast as the resources of the market permit. The assumption of a revival from depression makes the failure of the deepening process seem even less probable as the originating cause of depression.

MONETARY ASPECTS

If, whatever the circumstances, the deepening process *did* fail there would be, as we have seen, an absorption of cash by the investment market and a deficiency of general demand. " In a short period the amount of investment which those responsible *intend* to make may not be equal to the amount which people choose to save. If the former exceeds the latter, net investment will fall below what was intended owing to a depletion of stocks below the level at which, if developments had been foreseen, they would have been maintained. If the latter exceeds the former, net investment will be above what was intended owing to an undesigned accumulation of stocks. . . .

" These short-period disequilibria, consisting of undesigned changes in the level of stocks, will lead to action intended to rectify matters. If stocks have to be replenished there is a consequent rise in the level of activity and income, and conversely " (pp. 73-4).

This is unexceptionable as a description of the effects of an absorption or release of cash. Mr. Harrod, however, is unwilling to express his theory in monetary terms. " The set of ideas ", he says, " to which the doctrines of this essay are most repugnant are those connected with the Quantity Theory of Money " (p. 125).

" The quantity of money is an observable phenomenon. . . . Velocity is also observable, but the causes which govern it are less easy to distinguish." If asked for a theory of velocity consistent with his theory of the cycle, he would answer " that perhaps there is no further and separate theory, that this doctrine of trade fluctuation is itself the theory of velocity. Those forces which have been enumerated govern the volume of output and the level of prices ; these in turn cause the velocity of circulation to be what it is " (p. 126).

His claim to have enumerated the forces which govern the level of prices as well as the volume of output is not altogether valid. His theory is embodied in four " static determinants " : (i) the rates of pay at which prime factors of production can be secured ; (ii) the efficiency of the prime factors ; (iii) the elasticity of demand for commodities ; (iv) the general price level. The fourth has to be included because the first three do not of themselves determine the price level. In order that they may determine activity, the rates of pay which form the subject of the first must be real wages. Given the relation of real wages to money wages the price level may be deduced.

We may assume given rates of money wages and a given price level at the outset, and Mr. Harrod's analysis will show what subsequent variations they will undergo. Suppose there is a falling off of activity, a shrinkage of output and of income. In virtue of the " plasticity of prime costs " there will be some fall of wages. If diminishing returns operate, there will be some rise in marginal productivity, so that prices can be reduced more than wages. If demand becomes more elastic (a topic to which we shall return below, p. 288), the effect on output of a fall of prices will be less. If the three determinants act in this manner they have a stabilising effect. A movement being assumed to originate with the dynamic determinants, the static determinants mitigate its effects. The upshot is a change in the price level.

How is this change in the price level to be reconciled with the quantity theory of money? The fall in output and in the price level constitutes a fall in the consumers' income. No positive action being assumed to alter the quantity of money, this presupposes a fall in velocity of circulation.

Mr. Harrod's explanation is based on the liquidation of redundant working capital. Consumers whose incomes fall off draw upon their cash. The recession in the consumption trades is delayed; the receipts in these trades " are maintained, but their outlay is reduced. This excess of receipts over outlay does not represent profit and cannot be distributed as dividends. The reduced outlay implies a reduction in the volume of physical circulating capital. The surplus money in hand must be reckoned as part of the firm's capital " (pp. 135-6). Some of this money may be used to reduce indebtedness to the banks, and so to bring about a decrease in the quantity of money. The rest is surplus cash.

What happens when the holders of the surplus cash try to exchange it for more remunerative assets? " The demand for remunerative capital assets by holders of money rises above the supply. This may cause a rise in the prices of remunerative capital assets." At this point Mr. Harrod resorts to Keynes's position. If the prices of fixed interest securities have been unduly raised, and if the prices of shares are only not correspondingly high because the reduction of their prospective yield more than outweighs the higher rate of capitalisation, people will prefer to hold their idle circulating capital in the form of money.

But this is to assume that investment of the idle balances *does* take place on so large a scale as to disturb the investment market in a material degree. Mr. Harrod argues that the fall in the rate of interest cannot be expected " to restimulate the system to its previous level of activity. That would only be so on the palpably false assumption that people were absolutely unwilling to hold money as a capital asset . . . and that they would bid the price of securities up and up until the consequential fall in the rate of interest and the consequent stimulus to trade took the idle money off again into active circulation."

But he started to explain, not why there cannot be a revival from the depression, but why there is a diminished velocity of circulation. Without assuming a complete restoration of activity we may yet suppose that the fall in the rate of interest induces some increase in capital outlay. This, so far as it goes, will generate incomes and start a portion of the money in active circulation. And even so much of the money invested as fails to get placed in new enterprise will reduce the bank advances to the investment market.

Thus a great part and possibly far the greater part of this idle money will either pass into active circulation or be applied to extinguish bank advances. There will be a reduction of the quantity of money.

Will the monetary authorities remain passive? Apparently Mr. Harrod's answer would be that they are powerless. He has assumed that, so far as the long-term investment market is concerned, the deepening process is completely suspended. His theory is evolved without any consideration at all of the possibility of influencing the monetary situation through lending for the purchase of commodities. His treatment of this part of the subject is sufficiently concise to be quoted *in extenso*.

The short-term rate of interest " is not likely to have a great effect either on methods of production or on consumers' choice. It affects the cost of carrying stocks. But the volume of these is influenced far more by the rate of turnover and the prospective movement of prices. And it must be remembered that the price of any particular commodity is likely to be subject to much larger possibilities of variation than the general price level " (p. 122).

I shall return to this subject below (pp. 297-301). Here I need add nothing to the detailed arguments above (pp. 76-8 and 104-12), except to recall that for very many commodities of the manufactured and partially manufactured types the individual prices will be subject to much smaller variations than the general price level, and that for any commodity of this class there will usually be long periods when there is no expectation at all of a change of price in the minds of the traders concerned. Even when such expectation exists it may be subject to so much doubt that it carries little weight.

Once the susceptibility of stocks of goods to credit regulation is granted, the action of the banks in this direction must take its place among the determinants. And it possesses decisive importance because it is subject to human control. It is therefore to be regarded primarily not as a *cause* of fluctuations but as a *corrective*.

Mr. Harrod eschews any theoretical analysis of the effects of rising or falling prices, and prefers to rely on the " empirical evidence for the proposition that rising prices are associated with increasing activity " (p. 39). " Reasons and explanations ", he says, " can indeed be found for the phenomenon. But without the brute fact to guide them it is most unlikely that theorists would ever have reached this proposition as a conclusion drawn from general reasoning " (p. 40).

But what of Hume? The explanation of the effects of an increasing or decreasing price level in Hume's essay on *Money* (which appeared in 1752) must have been based in part, like all economic principles, on experience, but was none the less a piece of theoretical reasoning.

Mr. Harrod deprecates the arguments of latter-day exponents of the theory, who " refer to the behaviour of banks and the rate of interest ", and who delude themselves " if they imagine that they could have gone through all that maze of deduction and reached this conclusion by the light of pure reason ". But in reality the argument is by no means so far fetched. Given Hume's explanation, only a slight adaptation is required to allow for the modern practice of issuing currency and creating money against discounted bills and bank advances. The rise or fall of the short-term rate of interest is merely a device for regulating that process.

The acceptance of the association of rising prices with increasing activity and of falling prices with declining activity as a merely empirical conclusion has the serious disadvantage that it does not show which is cause or which is effect. It leaves Mr. Harrod, therefore, with a very unsatisfactory kind of determinant.

Mr. Harrod devotes a passage (pp. 142-5) to arguing that banks cannot increase the amount of investment. They " are mere conduit pipes. They have no power of making the saving available for use in investment greater on any day than the amount that people are choosing to save." Of course so long as investment is taken in Keynes's sense, that is true. But when the banks create credit they may stimulate *active* investment. The occurrence of passive disinvestment will then promote activity as Mr. Harrod has shown. But this is no more than a side-issue. The main point is that the action of the banks is not limited to the channel of the investment market, but influences production through working capital.

Mr. Harrod is a supporter of stable money, stable, that is, in terms of purchasing power. But it is not surprising to find that he is sceptical as to its practicability.

PROFIT

Mr. Harrod bases his theory of profit on the theory of imperfect competition, according to which the price received by the individual producer will not be rigidly governed by outside market conditions, but will be free to vary to some extent relatively to competitors' prices ; it will thus be a function of the producers' own output. The marginal revenue is the increase in receipts derived from an increment of output, account being taken not only of the price of the increment but of the fall of price of the rest of the output.

The producer will make his net gain a maximum if he adjusts his output to the point at which marginal revenue is equal to marginal cost. Marginal revenue is less than price, and therefore marginal cost will be less than price. Mr. Harrod would identify the difference with profit.

He is here, I think, putting a greater strain on the theory of imperfect competition than it will bear. That there is room for some variation of any trader's price from that of his competitors is an important practical principle which has gained recognition from economists in recent years. But it is not to be inferred that traders will be at all ready to exploit this possibility. Even one who has some substantial advantage, such as a local monopoly or a reputation for some special quality of product, which his rivals cannot imitate, will often prefer to keep his advantages secure by charging no more than the equivalent of his competitors' prices. Where a trader's advantage is confined to a goodwill based on custom and inertia, he will be careful never to endanger it by giving his customers the slightest reason for leaving him. Thus in the great majority of cases the difference between marginal revenue and price is a mere potentiality. Where that is so, Mr. Harrod's formula would allow no profit unless marginal cost follows a law of diminishing returns, and in the common case of increasing returns profit would be a negative quantity.[1]

An enterprise is started with the intention that the proceeds of sale of a unit of output shall yield a sufficient margin over prime cost to cover overhead costs and to yield at least a normal profit. The prime cost of the last unit when it is employed up to capacity is probably assumed to be the same as when it is under-employed, and every unit is intended to carry the appropriate margin. If in some concerns employment to capacity involves the use of reserve plant of inferior efficiency or working under some disadvantage of organisation, that does not mean that the marginal unit of output yields nothing for profit or overhead charges. If such a marginal unit exists anywhere, that is a mere accident, and does not modify

---

[1] Marginal cost for this purpose must include marketing costs (see Mr. Harrod's article on "The Law of Decreasing Costs", in the *Economic Journal* for December 1931), so the case of negative profit would not be so likely to occur as appears at first sight.

the general principle that goods produced or dealt in should yield a margin for overhead charges and profit. When an industry is under-employed, on account either of a general depression, or of causes specially affecting the industry, the traders concerned will sacrifice some or all of their profit, and they may sacrifice a part of their overhead charges and work at a loss. And even when an industry is active and prosperous, particular concerns in it may through adversity find their profit reduced below normal or turned into a loss. That is only to say that profits are subject to big variations according to circumstances, not that a trader ever *plans* to receive no profit on his marginal unit of output.

Mr. Harrod attaches importance to what he calls the Law of Diminishing Elasticity of Demand. This is closely related to his theory of profit and to the prevalence of imperfect competition. As depression grows, people become more calculating and careful in their expenditure and more ready to break the intangible ties upon which goodwill depends, and traders are under greater pressure to make price concessions to retain customers. On the other hand, with growing prosperity, people are less calculating and careful, and the trader can raise his prices with less risk. In so far as this law operates, there will be greater shifts to profit in times of prosperity and greater shifts away from profit in times of depression than would otherwise occur. The effect of higher prices in times of prosperity would be to restrain activity, and that of lower prices in times of depression to maintain activity. The law would thus have a stabilising effect.

The argument is very ingenious, but how much substance there is in it is difficult to judge. So far as producers are concerned, they will undoubtedly cut prices at a time of shrinking demand in the hope of keeping their plant as nearly as possible fully employed. At such a time the ties of business goodwill may well give way before the strain of intensified competition. But Mr. Harrod goes beyond this. Since he restricts profit rigidly to what the excess of price over marginal revenue permits, he excludes any sacrifice of profit beyond what is consistent with that formula. His law of diminishing elasticity is essential to account for the undeniable fact that sacrifices of profit beyond that limit do occur.

DYNAMIC ECONOMICS

Mr. Harrod has pursued his theory of the Relation and the Multiplier a step further in his recent work, *Towards a Dynamic*

Economics.[1] He defines dynamics as being "concerned with an economy in which the rates of output are changing" (p. 4). Professor Hicks defined economic dynamics as those parts of economic theory "where every quantity must be dated" (*Value and Capital*, p. 115). In dynamics, however, as Mr. Harrod conceives it, "dating is no more necessary than in statics" (p. 10).

No doubt Mr. Hicks's definition is too rigid. When rates of change are in progress, the relative rates of change in various factors and the order in which the successive phases of all of them occur are essential to a dynamic theory, though precise assumptions as to the measurability of the periods of time involved may be quite unnecessary.

Mr. Harrod regards Keynes's *General Theory* as "essentially static" in the formulation and handling of its subject matter. Changes in marginal efficiency "are all of a once-over character, and not continuing changes generated by the special nature of a growing economy" (p. 11). Keynes, in fact, neglects Mr. Harrod's Relation. The Relation or acceleration principle "is essentially a dynamic principle, since it regards the volume of demand for a new capital as a function of the rate of increase of the economy" (p. 12).

It is more especially in the application of the acceleration principle that the dynamic theory which follows consists.

RATES OF GROWTH

Saving, s, expressed as a fraction of income may be regarded as the product of two factors G C (p. 77).

G is the increment of total production in any unit period, expressed as a ratio to total production. It is a rate of increase per unit of time.

C is the ratio of the increment of accumulated wealth per unit of time to the increment of production per unit of time.

In the product GC the numerator of G cancels out against the denominator of C, and there emerges the ratio of the increment of wealth per unit of time to production.

But the increment of wealth is saving, and production is equal to income, so $GC = \dfrac{\text{saving}}{\text{income}} = s.$

[1] In the rest of this chapter page references refer, unless otherwise stated, to that work.

19

If income (production) is Y, the increment of production is GY. C is a *period of time ;* if the additional output requires its normal proportion of capital equipment, C is the period of production corresponding to GY. The capital required for this increment of production is CGY.[1] The ratio of this to Y is s.

With the numerical illustration used above (p. 281), production is 4,000 millions per annum, the increment of production is 100 millions per annum per annum, and G is therefore $\frac{1}{40}$ per annum. The increment of wealth is 400 millions per annum, and C is $\dfrac{400}{100 \text{ per annum}}$ or four years. GC is $\frac{1}{10}$, for $s = \frac{400}{4000}$.

The period of production, four years, represents the existing structure of production, equipped with a total capital of 16,000 millions.

But to assume that there is no change in the structure of production would give " too much emphasis to the acceleration principle " (p. 79). So Mr. Harrod deducts from the total accumulation an amount k, being " current additions to capital . . . the worth-while-ness of which is not deemed to have any relation to current require-ments ". In other words, it is " capital outlay of a long-range character, which no one expects to see justified or not justified within a fairly short period ".

" Units of equipment, etc., which are included in k must be omitted in the computation of C." A similar deduction must be made from the other side of the equation $GC = s$. With s so modified, accumulation is to be equal not to s but to $s + k$.

If s be given, there will be a certain value, G_w, of the rate of growth such that, if C_r be the value of C corresponding to it, $G_w C_r = s$.

" This equation expresses the condition in which producers will be content with what they are doing " (p. 81).

G_w is " the warranted rate of growth ", and the increment of wealth which forms the numerator of C_r is the amount of new capital required for the increment of production which forms the numerator of G_w.

The equation, $G_w C_r = s$, " expresses the equilibrium of a steady advance ". The total accumulation $s + k$ has to provide for that part of the increment of wealth, k, which is determined by long-range considerations, and for equilibrium the residue s has to be equated to the residue of the increment of wealth, which is adapted to current

---

[1] It is not accurate to say, " C is the addition to capital " (p. 80).

requirements, that is to say, is regulated by the acceleration principle, the " relation ". If the advance in production, measured by G, is to be maintained, the quantity of capital accruing, measured by C, must be what is needed (p. 85). Capital here covers both equipment and stock-in-trade. " C consists in part of consumer goods, including non-durable consumer goods. In an advancing community goods in the pipe-line, shops, warehouses, transit and producers' stores, have to increase in proportion."

" If G has a value above G_w, C will have a value below C_r. . . . On balance producers and traders find the goods in the pipe-line or the equipment insufficient to sustain existing turnover." Orders therefore for replenishment of stocks and for more equipment will be increased. Conversely, if G is below G_w, orders will be decreased. Either way " centrifugal forces are at work, causing the system to depart further and further from the required line of advance " (p. 86).

This is the principle of the vicious circle, the inherent instability of credit (above, pp. 64-8). An excess or deficiency of stocks in relation to the acceptable level is a cause of disequilibrium, in that it gives rise to an intermediate demand, negative or positive. When production is actually increasing at the rate G, the necessary plant must presumably be forthcoming, but it is possible, up to a point, to do with reduced stocks ; so it is on stocks that any deficiency of C falls. And similarly an excess of C over C_r will not usually be added to equipment, but to stocks.

For this stage in his analysis Mr. Harrod gets rid of the long-range capital outlay, k, by introducing the assumption that " on average all the various inventions and improvements accruing in a unit period are neutral, those requiring more capital per unit of output balancing the effect of those which require less " (p. 83). Also by assuming the rate of interest to be constant, he eliminates the deepening that would be brought about by a gradual lowering of the rate. Thus, while the structure of production is altered by the inventions and improvements, the period of production remains unchanged. More capital equipment may be used in proportion to the labour employed, but in proportion to output it remains the same.

" The rate of growth G ", Mr. Harrod says (p. 86), " is a quantity determined from time to time by trial and error." And " if the aggregated result of trial and error by numerous producers gives a value for G which is different from G_w, there will not be any tendency to adapt production towards G_w, but, on the contrary, a tendency to adapt production still farther away from it, whether on the higher or lower side " (p. 87).

There is a " natural " rate of growth G_n, being that which " the increase of population and technological improvements allow ". If the actual rate of growth G falls behind the natural rate G_n, G may thereafter for a time exceed G_n. In fact G_n would be the rate of growth if the productive capacity of the community were always fully employed ; it " sets a limit to the maximum average value of G over a long period ".

If the rate of growth of production is determined by trial and error, who will be making the trial and by what error will he correct it ? The error will be revealed in an excess or deficiency of stocks. But it will not be in the amount of goods *received* into stock, for that will have been determined by the traders' own orders to producers. (Delays in delivery can be neglected unless they are so serious as to bring stocks down to the essential minimum.) The excess or deficiency of stocks is a symptom of a deficiency or excess of *sales*. Sales of stock-held goods are a part of disposals, and reflect general demand.

The volume of production is determined by general demand, *plus* intermediate demand. So long as production is below capacity, G can exceed G_n ; whether it does so depends on demand.

G_w, the warranted rate of growth, is that which requires an increment of capital just equal to the rate of accumulation s. So long as production in any industry is below capacity, no increment of capital is actually required by the industry at all. There may be long-range capital outlay, such as was assumed to be included in k. And a further expansion of demand, which is expected to outstrip capacity, may induce anticipatory capital extensions. But, till capacity is reached, the limit imposed by the warranted rate of growth is not felt.

These stages will not synchronise in different industries. Some may be experiencing an expanding demand even in the depths of general depression ; some may remain under-employed at the height of activity. In the course of an expansion of demand, as industries reach capacity one after another, each in turn will need an extension of capacity if it is to accept and fulfil the orders coming to it. The capital outlay required for these extensions will grow gradually, and will have to be provided out of the available saving or accumulation, s. The maximum that can be so provided is that corresponding to the warranted rate of growth of production G_w. Any capital outlay in excess of that limit will be offset by an equivalent deficiency of goods in stock; a positive intermediate demand and a vicious circle of expansion will result.

When industry is under-employed, the formula $GC = s$ loses much of its significance. C is no longer the period of production. Only a fraction of G, say mG, needs an extension of equipment, and it is mC that is equal to the period of production. C may very greatly exceed the period of production. $C_r G_w$, being the amount of capital outlay that accumulation can provide, will allow of a value of G such that $mG = G_w$. If m were very small G might be very large. But it must be remembered that accumulation itself fluctuates. Saving may fall very low at a time of depression (p. 89), so that even the modest extensions of capacity put in train in the early stages of revival may be not less than G_w. Revival brings about an increase of saving. Saving may rise considerably above its average level, and, when revival culminates in full employment, there is a danger that G_w may rise above G_n " and, if it does so, a vicious spiral of depression is inevitable ". Widening in fact is limited to what " the increase of population and technological improvements allow ", and, if the increment of capital required for it is insufficient to use up current saving, there will be an unabsorbed residue of accumulation, and a negative intermediate demand will result.

During the process of revival, even though extensions of capacity are at a low level, there is a positive intermediate demand, for, as output expands, traders need increased stocks in proportion to their sales. It is a prerequisite condition of the continuance of revival that the capital outlay and the intermediate demand together use up at least the whole of current saving. So long as they exceed current saving, the shortage of stocks is growing. Even when they cease to do so, there will still be a positive intermediate demand till the accrued shortage of stocks is made up. And up to the moment of full employment production will still be expanding, so that the acceptable level of stocks will be becoming higher.

It is possible that before full employment is reached there may be so big an expansion of saving that, for all the demands upon it, a surplus is accruing to stocks in excess of what traders judge acceptable. If so, negative intermediate demand would supervene, and would set up the vicious circle of depression. But if not, a period would be entered upon in which output could no longer be expanded by bringing reserves of labour into employment. Orders given for products to replenish traders' stocks fail to secure the hoped for increase of supplies, and result in overburdening the producers with orders which they can only execute after growing delays. That is the stage at which prices rise, and experience of the trade cycles of the past clearly shows that that is what used to happen. There was invariably a substantial rise of prices and a state of high employment in the last year or two of the active phase.

The assumptions made in this part of Mr. Harrod's analysis exclude any deepening of capital, but they do not exclude technological progress. There may be any amount of cost-saving improvements, provided that they are capital-saving as well as labour-saving, so that on balance the period of production remains unchanged. The " natural " rate of growth G_n requires a widening of capital to absorb not only the growth of population but the labour set free by the improvements. The amount of capital employed per unit of output remains unchanged, but the amount per workman employed increases.

In withdrawing this assumption (p. 96), Mr. Harrod does not re-introduce the term k, long-range capital outlay, but a term d, " for deepening ".

$$G_w C_r = s - d.$$

where s once again extends to all accumulation.

THE RATE OF INTEREST

" If inventions are ' capital-saving ', d is negative." It may be positive, either because inventions are on balance labour-saving, or because the rate of interest is falling.   " Our aim should be to get such a progressive reduction of the rate of interest that

$$G_w C_r = s - d = G_n C_r."$$

Will there be " any natural tendency for the rate of interest to come down sufficiently? "

Keynes's theory, Mr. Harrod says, points to a negative answer. Keynes held that when the long-term rate of interest fell below the conventional rate, people would cease to place their savings and spare cash in the investment market, or would at least retain a part in idle balances. If marginal efficiency were falling, and the continuance of deepening required the rate of interest to fall below the conventional rate, the market would fail to equate capital outlay to the whole volume of savings. The market would seek to perform its equalising function by lowering the rate of interest, but the effect would be felt in a reduced influx of savings before the desired increase in capital outlay could materialise. The classical theory assumed that savings would always be invested in their entirety, because, however low the rate of interest, it would always be better to get some interest than to hold money idle in excess of current needs. Keynes challenged this assumption. The speculative motive would lead people to withhold their money, if they thought the interest to be received insufficient compensation for the risk of capital loss. " In Keynes ", Mr. Harrod says (p. 65), " interest is reduced to nothing more than a risk premium against fluctuations about which we are uncertain "—fluctuations, that is, in the rate of interest itself. To the criticism that Keynes " leaves interest suspended, so to speak, in a void, there being interest because there is interest ", his reply is ; " did Keynes anywhere say that liquidity preference was the sole and only reason why there ever had been or could be interest? Or did he not rather merely say that liquidity preference was the sole determinant of the level of the interest rate ? "

Surely the answer to the first question is Yes, and to the second No. Keynes quite definitely said that interest was the reward for parting with liquidity. But as to the level of the interest rate, he held that " the owner of capital can obtain interest because capital is scarce " (*General Theory*, pp. 213 and 376).

So long as the market rate of interest is above the conventional rate, Keynes's theory and the classical theory are the same. (The difference between Keynes's marginal efficiency of capital and Marshall's marginal yield of instruments, is not here in point.) Mr. Harrod is quite unjustified in " denying the existence of the alleged orthodox theory, and claiming that the Keynes theory ought properly to be regarded as an attempt to fill a void " (p. 67). Keynes's theory is far from giving " a negative answer " to the question whether, when the scarcity of capital is diminished and deepening requires to be stimulated, the investment market " will tend to mark the rate of interest down at an appropriate pace " (p. 97). The appropriate fall of the rate of interest will not be interrupted so long as it keeps above the conventional rate. I need not repeat the grounds I have adduced (above, pp. 194, 197 and 204) for supposing that the speculative motive has not been a serious obstacle in the way of the desirable progress of deepening.

If the speculative motive does cause an absorption of cash, either in consumers' balances, or in traders' free capital, there results an excess of production over disposals, and an accumulation of unsold goods. That is only one of the various ways in which a vicious circle of depression may be started. Mr. Harrod gives a very restrained approval to the Keynes theory ; he is not prepared to reject it as untenable (p. 67), but he does not rely on it for a solution of his problem.

" Strictly in Keynesian theory the effect of the multiplier on activity is instantaneous. But there is, no doubt, an interval in which there is a discrepancy between ex-ante and ex-post invest-ment " (p. 98). If there is an excess of saving over active investment, those holding " unwanted stocks ", will have drawn on any spare cash they may have, before coming into the capital market for the loan of funds, and " there may be an excess of the supply of funds over the demand ". The proceeds of the liquidation of working capital will be accumulating.

" Or again income may continue to be distributed after output has fallen." Consumers will release cash—possibly in part for investment.

As we have seen (above, p. 72) the free capital accumulated by traders from the liquidation of their working capital is likely to percolate into the investment market, and to depress the long-term rate of interest *below* the level at which it would merely equate capital outlay with current savings. Nevertheless, Mr. Harrod quite rightly comments that " it is not usually sufficient to prevent the onward movement of the recession ". For only a part of the proceeds of the liquidation of working capital would find its way into the investment market, and the rest would swell traders' idle cash balances. And the cash accumulated from the liquidation of working capital is no other than the counterpart of goods delivered to traders by producers in fulfilment of past orders, the very goods which remain unsold for want of demand, and set up the vicious circle of contraction.

It is not certain that the favourable tendency of the investment market will suffice to break the vicious circle.

Mr. Harrod, however, once more throws doubt on the power of any change up or down of the long-range rate of interest within the limits which the market allows itself to have any prompt effect. He goes further than in *The Trade Cycle* (above, p. 277), for he argues that to equalise the demand for new capital with the supply over short periods, " variations of at least the order of 1 or 2 per cent in the rate of interest " would be required (p. 64). " The idea ", he adds, " that the market will, in the course of a short period, mark perfectly good British Government securities now at 140, now at 70, is quite wide of the mark."

It has been pointed out (above, p. 83) that it is the postponement rather than the abandonment of projects that an unfavourable investment market causes, and that a fall in the prices of securities corresponding to a trivial rise in yield may yet be sufficient to induce postponement.

An unfavourable spell will therefore see an accumulation of postponed capital outlay, and a reversion to a favourable market will open the way for the projects previously postponed.

It is at a time of *activity* that the market is unfavourable. " Whenever G exceeds G_w there will be a tendency for a boom to develop " (p. 88). G exceeds G_w when widening outstrips saving, and that is the situation which the unfavourable investment market has to correct. If it succeeds in causing a sufficient postponement of capital projects, to keep G within the limits imposed by G_w, then, when the pressure passes, and the rate of interest is lowered in order to stimulate capital outlay, there is an accumulation of capital projects ready to take advantage of the favourable terms offered.

Therefore the investment market is a more efficient instrument for regulating capital outlay than Mr. Harrod allows. Nevertheless it does not pretend to correct an absorption or release of cash either by consumers or by traders, and fortuitous variations in its own net cash holdings are bound to occur.

Mr. Harrod's conclusion that " variations in the rate of interest will not play an important part in our contra-cyclical armoury " (p. 117), if it is confined to the long-term rate, seems to be justified. However efficient the investment market may be, long-term projects cannot be quickly adjusted to market conditions. An efficient market will keep down the disparities between savings and capital outlay to a minimum, but cannot be expected to eliminate them altogether.

CREDIT POLICY AND THE SHORT-TERM RATE OF INTEREST

In this work Mr. Harrod concedes more recognition to credit policy as an instrument for regulating fluctuations in activity than in *The Trade Cycle*. " That the short-term rate ", he says, " has been most potent in British banking history is obvious enough." About its quick effects on the short-term foreign balance of payments there is no dispute. " It has also been used to break the boom at the top. But that is a very different matter from curbing a boom or reducing a recession in the earlier stages of either " (p. 118).

Yet he cannot admit any efficacy for the short-term rate of interest except in " some useful subordinate role, e.g. in checking speculations ".

The proposition which he attributes to me, and which he would controvert, is that the short-term rate affects the volume of activity " by making it more or less profitable to hold additional stocks (whether of raw materials or semi-finished goods) ". And he reverts to his argument that the volume of stocks is influenced more by the prospective movement of prices than by the short-term rate of interest (above, p. 285).

He particularly instances the case of the speculator in an organised exchange. And of course speculators do hold large and fluctuating stocks of materials, particularly of products of the soil, and interest usually forms but a small part of their calculations. But even in the case of these products there are holders who eliminate the speculative element by hedging. The profit of the trader who has made a forward sale of his stock depends on his turn, the difference between buying and selling prices, and when the rate of interest is high it is not negligible in comparison with this difference.

But it is in manufactured goods that the impact of credit conditions on output is felt. Unlike products of the soil, they are produced in response to orders, and traders' decisions to hold small stocks are reflected directly in the orders they give. Anticipations of price changes are bound up with changes in demand, as manifested in sales.

As to that, Mr. Harrod confines himself to saying that " where the goods are less standardised and more finished, obsolescence becomes a danger ". Apart from the limited class of fashion goods, the danger of obsolescence is not material, when the choice is between buying, say, six weeks' supply or four.

" A trader or producer who cannot meet his customer's order in a line in which he specialises, for lack of stock-in-hand, must look rather a fool, and suffer loss of goodwill " (p. 119). Of course a trader cannot afford to let his stock fall below a minimum level. But in general traders hold stocks much *above* the minimum level. It is in deciding how much above that they have to balance their convenience and the economies of larger deliveries against outgoings, of which interest may be a part.

In fact, the theoretical case which Mr. Harrod makes against the sensitiveness of traders' stocks to the short-term rate of interest is very thin. But he supplements the theoretical argument by an appeal to practical evidence : " the chorus of merchants and traders and producers have testified in the negative ".

He is referring, no doubt, to the sample inquiry made in 1939 by a Research Group, of which he himself was Chairman, the results of which appeared in *Oxford Economic Papers* in March 1940. Answers to a questionnaire were obtained from 313 businesses (out of 1,308 to whom it had been sent). They were asked whether (*a*) bank rate, (*b*) discount rate, (*c*) overdraft rate, (*d*) yield on Government securities, or the facility of obtaining, (*e*) overdrafts, or (*f*) new capital from the public, ever affected (III) the size of stocks held, or the decision to make or to defer making expenditure on (I) plant extensions, or (II) maintenance and repairs. For our present purposes it is (III) that matters. And the justification for Mr. Harrod's claim of a negative chorus is that only 48 affirmative replies were obtained against 245 negative.

No one has ever maintained that all traders obtain bank advances, and evidently only those who do would answer yes. Most *manufacturers* prefer to finance their working capital from their own resources, and to be independent of their bankers. Any risk of an interruption of their supply of materials is far more serious for them than for merchants and retailers. More than three-fourths of the questionnaires were sent to manufacturers, and of the 313 replies only 20 were from retailers and 20 from merchants and wholesalers. Out of 18 retailers who answered in regard to stocks, 5 gave an affirmative answer; out of 18 merchants, 4.

The proportions may seem surprisingly small, but it should be mentioned that whereas the manufacturers were sampled from concerns of all types and sizes, the dealers (retail and wholesale) were selected exclusively from public companies. It is hardly necessary to say that a public company is much more likely to raise sufficient resources to cover its maximum requirements of working capital without borrowing than a partnership or private company.

Moreover, the time at which the inquiry was made was especially unfavourable to affirmative answers. Bank rate had remained unchanged at 2 per cent for seven years, and ineffective at that. A trader had to search his memory to find circumstances in which the question was significant, and it is clear from the comments with which the majority accompanied their answers that many, at any rate, took the inquiry to refer specifically to the circumstances of 1939.

And not only had the short-term rate of interest been extremely low, but ever since the depression started there had been a superfluity of money in traders' hands. The liquidation of working capital had evidently taken place on a great scale. From 1929 to 1938, while the wholesale price index fell on balance 12 per cent, bank deposits rose 25 per cent. So more businesses would be able to carry on without borrowing than under conditions of normal activity. And among the comments of those who answered in the negative, much the most usual reason given, was that they could finance their stocks without borrowing.

The comments are sometimes more informative than the yes or no of the answers. How many of those who answered No show by their comments that they ought to have answered Yes ! One (No. 9 of the negative answers) said, " if a company has sufficient capital for its needs, the answer is ' No '. If on the other hand, the company has not sufficient capital then the answer is in the affirmative." So that concern, if it had to borrow, *did* consider the cost and facility of borrowing. Several said they had no difficulty in borrowing, and surely, if that is worth mentioning, a difficulty in borrowing would make a difference. One (No. 74) said that " the effect of the discount rate, etc., is relatively so small in comparison with other expenses that it would have to be a very substantial movement in either direction to influence them in any way ". Another (No. 88) referred to " extreme fluctuations in interest rates ". (No. 128) : " unless the bank rate is at a very high level, the method by which the banks advance money to business is much more important than the actual rate of interest." What did " substantial movements " or " extreme fluctuations " mean when for seven years the market rate of discount on bank bills had rarely touched 1 per cent?

Some of the comments were concerned to point out how trifling is the charge on short-term borrowing in comparison with costs or profits or price movements, and showed thereby that they had missed the point of the inquiry in regard to stocks.

(No. 30) : " they do increase their stocks if they consider that the market is likely to rise, but this is more a question of price than of the rate of interest, although it is appreciated that these are closely connected ". That cannot mean that the rate of interest is altogether disregarded.

(No. 115), stocks " are controlled generally by trade prospects. Interest rates, within reasonable limits, are a relatively small factor." If " relatively small ", not to be altogether disregarded.

(No. 137) : " they always endeavour to keep stocks at a minimum, and the rate of interest would be considered only in relation to the benefit expected to be derived from the increased holding of stocks, e.g. heavier buying to obtain cheaper prices ". Could there be a more fitting illustration of the principle expounded above (p. 46)?

These instances, it may be said, are for the most part not very explicit, and hardly supply by themselves a very firm foundation for any general principle. But I have selected them entirely from the concerns that *gave a negative reply to the questionnaire*. I have not quoted anything from the comments of the 48 which gave an affirmative reply.

I cannot agree with Mr. Harrod's claim that there was a " chorus " testifying in the negative.

CHAPTER XI

MEASURES FOR FULL EMPLOYMENT[1]

A FULL EMPLOYMENT TARGET

IN 1949, at the instance of the Economic and Social Council, the Secretary-General of the United Nations appointed a group of five experts to report on national and international measures required to achieve full employment. The experts, Messrs. J. M. Clark, Arthur Smithies, Nicholas Kaldor, Pierre Uri and Ronald Walker, presented their Report on the 16 December 1949.

The Report (para. 19) distinguishes three main kinds of unemployment arising respectively from:

(1) a lack of the capital equipment or other complementary resources necessary to keep wage-earners at work;

(2) structural causes, such as " frictional unemployment ", and " declines in particular industries " ;

(3) insufficiency and instability of effective demand.

The third, the Report says, is the major cause of unemployment in industrialised countries. " In the light of present uncertainties in the world economic situation, we felt that it was this problem with which our terms of reference required us most particularly to deal. For the practical purposes of this report, full employment may be considered as a situation in which employment cannot be increased by an increase in effective demand " (para. 24).

The experts were wise to concentrate their attention on the unemployment attributable to insufficiency of effective demand. But the neglect of the other two causes makes the adoption of a statistically measured " full employment target " (para. 28) unreal.

In Italy and Western Germany for instance, unemployment has been a serious problem for the past four years, and has not been primarily due to deficient demand. In Italy there were already 2,000,000 unemployed before the deflationary measures of 1947 were started. The cause in both cases has been an insufficiency of equipment to employ a greatly increased population.

[1] This chapter reproduces (with some slight revisions) an article which appeared in Italian in the *Rivista di Politica Economica* for January 1951.

The Report assumes (paras. 144-5) that a target corresponding
to the smallest percentage of unemployment which can be maintained in the light of seasonal movements and structural changes
would be some such range as 2 to 4 per cent, or 3 to 5.   Of lack of
equipment in this connexion it says nothing.

Lack of equipment is really just one of the structural causes of
unemployment.   It may be brought about either by a sudden
influx of population (as in Germany) or by a rapid natural growth
of population at a time when circumstances do not allow a corresponding expansion of equipment as in Italy ; but it may also be due
to a decline of a staple industry making the equipment installed in
it no longer capable of giving profitable employment.

Whatever the cause, there is an excess of labour, which, when all
the active industries are employed up to capacity, cannot find
employment for the time being, except to the extent that occupations which need no equipment or no additional equipment are
on offer.

Sometimes an emergency is clearly temporary ; it may be caused
by a temporary shortage of materials, by an interruption of transport
facilities, or by a trade dispute.   Sometimes it is permanent, a new
invention supersedes an entire industry, as in the case of Chilean
nitrates after the First World War.

It will be convenient to make a two-fold division between
unemployment due to a general deficiency of demand, and that due
to other causes.   The former may be called general unemployment ;
the latter special unemployment.

The appropriate measures for dealing with special unemployment
will be different in different circumstances.   But anyhow, they will,
in general, not be identical with those appropriate to general unemployment.   A target or normal unemployment percentage does
not distinguish between special and general unemployment.

The Report is concerned with remedial measures appropriate to
general unemployment, but the target would always be liable to give
the signal for action when it is really some form of special unemployment that needs to be dealt with.   And, as the Report says, the
Government would have to reserve to itself discretion to disregard
the signal " when there is clear evidence that a rise in unemployment
is due to causes other than a fall in effective demand and cannot be
cured by a stimulation of effective demand " (para. 172).

Policy in fact cannot properly be left to the uncritical acceptance
of a statistical criterion.   Unemployment is a malady demanding
skilled diagnosis in each separate instance.   When employment rises

above a normal minimum, it is for the authorities to estimate how much, if any, of the excess is due to deficiency of demand, and how much to other causes.

DEFICIENCY OF DEMAND

The usual sign of a deficiency of demand is a shrinkage of profit margins in industry generally. Unemployment follows as producers complete outstanding orders and fail to get sufficient new orders at remunerative prices to maintain their output. Unemployment is therefore not the earliest symptom. Bankers are in a position to become aware of a slackening of business *before* an increase in unemployment supervenes, and the Central Bank ought to be in sufficiently close touch with them to have early warning of the tendency. A full employment target would be needed only if the banks were not sufficiently on the alert.

The Report recommends the target as providing an *automatic* signal for remedial measures (paras. 79-81, and 141 (iii)). It would be " an assurance that, if and when other methods for maintaining effective demand in an economy clearly fail over a definite period, effective counter-measures will be brought into operation automatically to restore the situation " (para. 81). " Automatically ", of course, subject to the discretion reserved to the Government.

The target, in fact, will become operative when unemployment has already begun to appear. By that time, however, the slackening of business will already have made great headway, and it will be *too late* to prevent quite serious unemployment developing. The signal is to be given only when unemployment has exceeded the target limit for three successive months (para. 79). It might well be several months more before any remedial measures then started could make any impression.

To depend on a target would be to accept failure : a policy of palliatives rather than of remedies. But the question of a target is one of detail. If an earlier symptom can be made the signal for action, there is no need to wait for a visible rise in unemployment.

What is material is that a state of business threatening general unemployment can be recognised. When then it is recognised and diagnosed, what measures does the Report recommend?

Part II of the Report starts with an exposition of the problem of demand.

" If the whole of the price received from the sale of goods and services were turned into income, and all the incomes were fully and regularly expended on the purchase of goods and services, . . . production in the aggregate could not be limited by an insufficiency of purchasing power, since productive activity itself would necessarily generate sufficient buying power to absorb all the goods and services produced " (para. 35).

The Report proceeds to show that a disparity between production and spending may occur through tax revenue not being equal to Government expenditure, through exports not being equal to imports, or through savings not being equal to " goods and services which are charged to capital accounts (investment expenditures) " (para. 36).

With the provisional assumption that tax revenue is equal to Government expenditure, and imports are equal to exports, the Report arrives at the conclusion (in accord with the theories now in fashion) that an excess or deficiency of spending can be identified with an excess of decisions to invest over saving or of decisions to save over investment [1] (para. 38). " There is general agreement that the primary factor responsible for cyclical fluctuations is the instability of the level of private investment, including investment in plant and equipment, business inventories and residential construction " (para. 45).

INFLUENCING INVESTMENT

When the Report comes to consider the subject of Full Employment Policies, it turns first to Stabilising the Level of Investment (paras. 68-73).

" Spontaneous tendencies to fluctuations in the level of productive investment may be regarded as inevitable so long as the decisions to invest are made by private business firms acting independently of each other " (para. 69). Controls (such as building permits, allocation of materials, etc.) can restrain an expansion of investment, but cannot remedy a contraction.

The traditional method, which " operates through the banking system ", by means of " the variation of interest rates and other conditions of credit ", is also " more effective in placing an upper limit to investment than in preventing downward movement " (para. 70).

Therefore the Report goes on to recommend devices by which " the Government can influence the rate of investment ".

[1] " Investment " is used in the Report in Keynes's sense of accumulation, and " decisions to invest " would seem to be what I call " active investment ".

20

One of these, the resort to taxes and subsidies to induce people to postpone or hasten their projects, it does not view with favour, as being complicated to administer.

So the Report reaches the familiar specific of public works, that is to say, " offsetting the fluctuation in private investment by countervailing fluctuations in public investment " (para. 71).

STOCK-HELD PRODUCTS

In paragraph 45, investment is defined to include not only capital outlay but " investment in business inventories ", that is to say, in goods in process, in transit or in stock awaiting sale.

In any discussion of the relation of investment to full employment the two kinds of investment, capital outlay and accumulation of stocks, need to be treated separately. A grave defect in what has come to be the accepted approach to the problem is the failure to make this distinction.

What is meant by investment in inventories or stocks of goods? Productive activity is applied in three ways : work may be done on capital installations, plant or structures ; or it may be done on materials destined to be converted into consumable goods ; or it may take the form of services rendered direct to consumers.

In the first case, capital outlay accrues ; in the second, consumable material products ; in the third, immaterial products or consumable services. Consumable material products have the special characteristic that they can be held in stock pending sale. Immaterial products cannot. Nor in general are capital installations. New equipment or plant is usually ordered by the industrialist who is to use it. There is no intermediary to hold it in stock pending sale. That is not true without exception, however, for materials and intermediate products and standardised appliances destined to be embodied in capital installations may be held in stock. And even houses, shops and offices, when put up by speculative builders, can be regarded as a " stock " awaiting sale.

Production culminates in the disposal of the product. In the cases of services rendered direct to consumers, and of capital equipment or other things produced to the direct order of the user or consumer, disposal coincides with the act of production. But in the case of stock-held goods it does not. A net addition to stocks is composed of goods *not* disposed of.

It is only in stock-held goods that there can be a difference between production and disposals. A deficiency of demand takes effect in a deficiency of disposals and an accumulation of stocks.

So far as stock-held products are concerned, the demand experienced by the producers and affecting employment is to be found not in the sales to consumers, but in the orders received from traders to replace their sales and to replenish their stocks. " Decisions to invest " are made when traders, in calculating their orders, aim at increased stocks, that is to say, the amounts ordered exceed their sales. The producers then experience what we have called an intermediate demand, a demand in excess of that proceeding from consumers. When traders aim at diminished stocks, and orders fall short of consumers' demand, intermediate demand becomes a negative quantity.

The statement quoted above from paragraph 35 of the Report, to the effect that, if spending were exactly equal to income, production could not be limited by an insufficiency of purchasing power, requires modification. The accumulation of unsold goods, even though it may be called " investment ", is not *spending out of income*, and cannot properly be aggregated with consumers' expenditure. Even if " all the incomes were fully and regularly expended ", there might still be an intermediate demand, positive or negative, causing an excess or deficiency of employment.

THE CAPITAL MARKET

Capital outlay and additions to stocks are the two branches of investment, and corresponding to them are the two branches of the capital market, one dealing with long-term securities and flotations, the other with short-term lending. The traditional methods of control by the banking system, " through the variations of interest rates and other conditions of credit ", belong to the latter. The banking system does not control the long-term capital market.

It is the function of the long-term capital market to adjust capital outlay to the resources made available for it from current savings. To do so, it varies the prices of securities (corresponding to the inverse of the long-term rate of interest), but it also influences the raising of capital for new projects through the direct action of the intermediaries by whose agency flotations and capital issues are made. The market cannot discharge its function of equalising savings and capital with perfect precision, and it makes up the difference with temporary borrowing. It thereby encroaches on the other branch of the capital market, that of short-term lending.

Short-term lending for long-term projects is not acceptable either to lenders or to borrowers. The principal function of the short-term capital market is lending for the purposes of working capital, including stocks of goods destined for sale.

THE FLOW OF MONEY

Now it is the banking system that creates money, and it is through *short-term* lending by the banks that the traditional methods of control through the banking system work. There has been much controversy in recent years about the methods of dealing with unemployment. But that a contraction of the flow of money causes unemployment there is no dispute. The flow of money for this purpose means the process by which incomes generate spending, spending induces production and production generates incomes. A deficiency of demand is a deficiency of the flow of money.

A deficiency of demand is not accurately defined as a deficiency relative to production; it is a deficiency relative to productive *capacity*. When industry is not working up to capacity, there is unemployment, even though " all incomes are fully and regularly expended ".

Consequently the problem of full employment, while primarily that of maintaining the flow of money stable at a level which makes production up to capacity remunerative, is secondarily that of expanding the flow of money whenever it falls below that level.

The methods recommended by the Report for regulating capital outlay (paras. 68-73, referred to above) aim essentially at expanding the flow of money. Yet capital outlay is an extremely clumsy medium to rely upon for that purpose. The experience of the nineteenth century led to reliance on the other branch of the capital market, short-term lending and the holding of stocks of goods.

Traders pay for the goods they purchase or produce out of their cash balances, and if they raise additional cash by short-term borrowing, that is because their balances are insufficient. So long as the banks lend to them on easy terms and without demur, they can determine their purchases for stock wholly by their own convenience. They will find that purchases on a large scale and therefore at considerable intervals make both for convenience and for economy.

When bankers raise their charges, and become less willing to lend, it is easy for the traders to diminish their borrowing by keeping down their stocks. They can arrange smaller and more frequent purchases at a slight cost of inconvenience and expense, without reducing their stocks at any time anywhere near the indispensable minimum. That is how business has been found readily amenable to regulation through the short-term rate of interest. Even where the immediate occasion for a manufacturer's short-term borrowing has been some capital outlay, such as an extension or improvement of plant, he can most readily reduce his indebtedness, by keeping down his stocks of materials.

A VICIOUS CIRCLE

Bank advances are the source which supplies the community with money, and the flow of money can be contracted by measures deterrent of borrowing from that source. The Report points out that past experience has shown the traditional monetary methods of control to be " more effective in placing an upper limit to investment than in preventing downward movement " (para. 70).

The past experience referred to is that of the nineteen-thirties, when a prolonged period of cheap money did fail to evoke anything like a full revival of activity either in Great Britain or in the United States. And it may properly be claimed, that a single instance suffices to sustain the conclusion that failure is *possible*. On the other hand, earlier experience does seem to show that failure *can be avoided*.

The experience of the nineteenth century showed that the flow of money could be successfully regulated through the instrumentality of the short-term rate of interest. Adherence to the gold standard did not ensure an absolutely stable flow of money. It did not prevent periodical expansions, which, when the strain began to be felt, were reversed by dear money. But, once expansion had given place to contraction, it was the invariable practice to make a prompt transition to cheap money. Dear money induces economy of borrowing by keeping down stocks of goods. A change from dear money to cheap removes the inducement, and gives rise to an intermediate demand. So long as the expansion is in progress, stocks are relatively low, and dear money, when it is imposed, tends to keep them low. If the change from dear money to cheap is made in good time, while stocks are still low, the intermediate demand is felt in an excess of orders to producers over disposals to consumers. Increased production generates increased incomes and increased demand, and the conditions for a renewed expansion are set.

But this treatment is not infallible. When there is a contraction of demand, traders seek to reduce their stocks in proportion to their sales. They give orders less than equivalent to sales. There is a negative intermediate demand. Reduced production means reduced incomes, and a further reduction in demand. A vicious circle of declining demand is started, and traders fail to secure the reduction of stocks which they aim at. The vicious circle is set up only if a contraction of the flow of money is allowed to continue too long. It is not especially characteristic of a contraction initiated by the traditional methods of dear money and credit restriction, but might be an incident of any contraction, however caused, if too severe or too prolonged. If the contraction is started by dear money, it can be ended by cheap money *promptly applied*.

If, in default of timely action, the vicious circle is joined, then no doubt other methods of breaking it than by cheap money must be resorted to.

DEFICIT FINANCE

The Report does not recommend unreservedly the devices for stimulating capital outlay (paras. 68-73). It assumes that the policy will be to *stabilise* the level of investment. To secure full employment it would presumably have to be stabilised " at levels approaching the peak periods of activity ", and, if so, " the continued high rate of investment would lead to a growing over-capacity of plant and equipment ". There would occur " an exhaustion of useful investment opportunities " (para. 73). " This, of course ", the Report adds, " does not apply to under-developed or partially developed economies, whose stock of capital is inadequate."

In a world still suffering acutely from the after effects of war, an exhaustion of useful investment opportunities is not a contingency calling urgently for consideration in any country, and it is not necessary to pursue that hypothesis further. In any case the Report regards the stabilisation of investment through a public works programme as open to the objection that " public works cannot be varied rapidly enough to fulfil the necessary criteria for such a scheme by themselves " (para. 171). It accordingly proceeds to consider other methods of stabilising aggregate demand. Its recommendations (paras. 74-81) are for various measures calculated to bring about a deficit, an excess of public expenditure over revenue.

" If the rates of taxation were lowered in times of declining demand, and raised in time of rising demand, the purchasing power in the hands of consumers could be altered sufficiently to maintain total demand at a stable level " (para. 76). For such variations in the rates of taxation, the most suitable taxes are " general sales taxes, social security contributions, or personal income taxes, which in a number of countries are now collected on a ' pay-as-you-earn basis ' " (para. 77).

Provided the deficit is financed by a creation of credit, and not by recourse to the long-term investment market, the effect is an expansion of the flow of money. The decrease of taxation is a direct increase in the taxpayers' spending power, and there is a presumption that most of it will be spent. A part of the spending may be on consumable services, causing a direct and equal increase in incomes. The major part is likely to be on stock-held products, and, if stocks are heavily redundant, this part may fail to be reflected in increased orders to producers. But even so, the additional disposals will reduce the redundancy, and the increase in sales will set a higher standard of stocks required. Progress will thus be gained towards an acceptable level of stocks.

If the deficit is met by long-term loans through the investment market, it may still induce expansion, for the loans may be subscribed out of balances which would otherwise have been held idle. If, however, the loans are subscribed out of resources which the investment market would otherwise have applied to projects of capital outlay, there is no net expansive effect.

A public works programme is a particular case of a deficit. But it is at a disadvantage, not only in being slower in operation than a reduction of taxation, but in being itself a structural change, both the start and the finish of which may cause a certain amount of dislocation.

CAUSATION

It is important to appreciate that the Report does not claim the measures proposed, whether deficit or public works, to be preventive of unemployment. They are described as " compensatory " para. 141 (iii)). The recommendations are dominated throughout by the assumption, for which " general agreement " is claimed (para 45), that the cause of fluctuations is primarily " the instability of the level of private investment ". As we saw above (p. 91), a conspicuous feature of cyclical fluctuations has been a specially marked fluctuation of the amount of capital outlay and of the activity of the industries providing it, but it is not to be inferred that the fluctuations in capital outlay were the *cause*. In fact, a contraction or expansion in the flow of money, however it might be started, would be bound to cause a more than proportional contraction or expansion in *both* saving and capital outlay.

No doubt there may be spontaneous fluctuations in capital outlay, which would tend to induce general fluctuations in economic activity—for example, the innovations on which Schumpeter built his theory of the trade cycle. But that is only one among various possible sources of disturbance.

The natural place to look for the cause of a monetary contraction is in the mechanism which supplies the community with money, the banking system. The banking system operates through short-term lending, and therefore through " decisions to invest " in stocks of goods. Spontaneous fluctuations occur in these decisions to invest, but in the days of the gold standard it was the practice of the banking system to counteract them. Bank rate was put up or down when an expansion or contraction seemed to be going too far. The periodical expansions and contractions that did occur were due to a credit policy which refrained from counteracting them so long as they were consistent with the gold reserve position.

Bank rate practice was developed empirically ; it was worked by a method of trial and error. Experience led to the rate being reconsidered at weekly intervals, and even altered at an hour's notice. The ground for such short-period adjustments was that any tendency to expansion or contraction, if not promptly checked, was liable to be amplified by the " self-generating processes " which the Report refers to (para. 45), in other words, to the vicious circle of expansion or contraction. I have already explained how prompt action is needed to prevent a vicious circle being set up.

Bank rate policy was applied to check both expansions and contractions. Expansions and contractions occurred because observance of the gold standard did not of itself ensure prompt enough action to anticipate them. The unemployment problem of the nineteenth century resulted from the necessity, from time to time, not merely to check an expansion but to reverse it by positively deflationary measures.

The essential aim of a full employment policy is to avoid deflation. The traditional banking policy failed to avoid deflation because it failed to avoid inflation. The ideal monetary policy would avoid both inflation and deflation. If inflation could be successfully avoided, it would never be necessary to impose deflation *intentionally*, though there might occur fortuitous deflationary tendencies, which would have to be counteracted when they arose.

INFLATION

If, on the other hand, there are to be recurrent bouts of inflation, and none of deflation, the resulting cumulative degradation of money will bring about social evils on which it would be superfluous to enlarge. Nor does the trouble stop there, for eventually there would grow up a distrust of money which would rob even a monetary expansion of its stimulative power.

The Report deals with the danger of inflation in paragraphs 84-9. " It is essential that steps should be taken to ensure that the stimulation of effective demand is carried only to the point required to maintain full employment, and not in excess of this amount." The vicious circle of expansion is always liable to intervene, and to amplify an excess demand to an indefinite extent. If the excess is not to get out of hand, the corrective measures taken must be *prompt*. As to the nature of those measures the Report gives no guidance. " Governments must be left free to adapt their counter-measures to the needs of particular situations " (para. 89).

A simple reversal of the fiscal measures recommended for stimulating demand could not be effectively employed for this purpose. A budget surplus of sufficient magnitude applied to extinguish bank credit may be an effective instrument of deflation, provided the credit extinguished is not replaced by an expansion of bank advances. But adjustments of the burden of taxation cannot be made promptly or at short intervals.

The Report contemplates the adjustments being made by administrative action, at any rate in the case of income tax deducted on a current basis under the pay-as-you-earn system, or social security contributions. Advance legislative authorisation could be given for varying the rates. That, no doubt, would be a step towards prompt action.

But is it to be supposed for a moment that the taxpayer will be content to accept without protest a sudden increase of burden for the apparently remote purpose of checking inflation? If action is to be taken in time to prevent an inflationary movement from getting started, the need for it will only be understood within a narrow circle of bankers and expert advisers, who cannot convey to the public the grounds on which they recommend it. Even at that stage, the increase in burden must be substantial. If, as is almost certain, the finance minister holds back and fails to take action until the progress of inflation has been such as to receive general recognition or indeed to arouse anxiety, the burden inflicted will have to be much greater, and it is only too likely that inflation will then have made such headway that it cannot be reversed without a severe deflation.

But, it may be asked, would not a rise of bank rate also arouse opposition? Perhaps it would, but a different kind of opposition. For the only objection to a rise of bank rate is that it has a deflationary effect. It imposes no serious immediate burden on anyone. To the trader the cost of short-term borrowing, even at what is regarded as a high rate, is a very minor item in his calculations. It affects his action by influencing the orders he will give for the production of goods to replenish his stocks, and it is only the producer who feels any noticeable effect.

And, if early action is taken, there need be no positively deflationary effect. There will be some slackening in the orders given, which *ex hypothesi* are becoming excessive, but, before the slackening reaches the stage of causing under-employment of capacity, the pressure will be relaxed.

By contrast, treatment of an inflationary tendency by an increase in taxation immediately affects the household affairs of three-quarters of the population.

Resort to fiscal measures to affect the monetary situation is best kept in reserve for the contingency of more prompt and flexible methods failing to work. In that event, the case for spectacular budgetary measures can be made clear.

BANK RATE

On the employment of the traditional methods of control through the banking system, the Report has practically nothing to say. The references to them are few, brief and uninformative. Had the Report been made at a time when the traditional methods were in full operation in the financial centres of the world, it might be assumed to take their continuance for granted. But ever since the fatally blundering applications of credit policy in the inter-war period, bank rate has been under a cloud. In dealing with the inflationary movements of the past five years it has been deliberately discarded, at any rate in London[1] and New York. The omission from the Report of any recommendation on the subject of bank rate and credit regulation must be interpreted in the light of this situation.

[1] This was written before the change of Government in October 1951 and the resulting modifications of policy (above, p. 123).

The problem of full employment, in so far as it means avoiding general unemployment due to deficiency of demand, is the problem of maintaining an equable flow of money. The first requisite of a solution is the suitably contrived working of the *source* of money, the banking system. In 1797, 1825 and even for a time in 1847 the Bank of England tried to check expansion by refusing to lend. The raising of bank rate was a milder and more delicate device for the same end, and it has successfully stood a long trial. The inherent instability of credit, its liability to break out into a vicious circle of expansion or contraction, makes a prompt corrective essential to ensure an equable flow. In this respect there is no rival to bank rate.

DEFLATION ABROAD

An important part of the Report is devoted to international aspects of full employment (paras. 90-140 and 183-205). A country may suffer unemployment from a deficiency of demand for its exports, resulting from an economic depression generated elsewhere.

A passage on the maintenance of over-all international equilibrium starts with the " essential condition " that " each country should individually strive to attain a balance in its international transactions " (para. 100). That is not in itself part of the problem of full employment, and the Report proceeds to consider two sources of trouble : instability of the flow of international investment ; and the spread of a deflationary tendency from one country to another.

It will be convenient to deal with the latter first. " It is eminently desirable that countries should not be placed in the position of having to restrict imports in order to offset a fall in their exports caused by deflationary pressures abroad " (para. 120). If they were supplied with the means of paying for undiminished imports, they would not need to restrict them. And the Report proposes a system under which any country whose purchases from other countries fall off as a result of its own deflation should make available through the International Monetary Fund sufficient sums in its own currency to enable the other countries to go on buying from it, notwithstanding the decline in their sales to it (paras. 124 and 205).

This plan would help to relieve the deflation at its source, because the country suffering from it would enjoy an undiminished demand for its exports. How great the relief would be would depend on the magnitude of its export industries relative to its production as a whole. It would also depend on the circumstances of the deflation.   If the deflation were intentionally imposed for the purpose of lowering the price structure of the country, any measure which weakened it would in the end prolong it.   If, on the other hand, the deflation were fortuitous, and if the creation of credit to finance imports did not cause any restriction of credit for other purposes, the effect would be favourable.

But the other countries would not be shielded from the contagion of the deflation.   They would receive undiminished imports from the country of deflation, but at the depressed prices corresponding to its diminished home demand.   And, instead of maintaining the activity of their export industries by sending their own products in return, they would draw upon the currency provided to pay for their imports.

Deflation means raising the value or purchasing power of the money unit by diminishing the flow of money.   Deflation in one country causes a disparity between the values of its money unit and of other units.   The direct way to correct the disparity would be through an alteration of rates of exchange.   If the rates were adjusted in proportion to the change in the price level in the country of deflation, the price levels in other countries could remain unchanged.   There might no doubt be some change in the relative prices of different products.   If the deflation occurred in an important industrial country, the decline in demand for raw materials might cause a fall in the price level of primary products in comparison with that of manufactured products.   But if the rest of the world successfully avoided the deflation, and maintained their demand for primary products, the disparity in the two price levels would not be very great.

It is strange that in the thirty-five pages devoted by the Report to the international aspects of full employment, the possibility of offsetting deflation abroad by a corresponding reduction of the foreign exchange value of the money unit is nowhere mentioned. There are brief allusions to the appropriateness of this expedient in the case where inflationary pressure compromises a country's ability to export and aggravates its need to import (paras. 107 and 188), but none to the case, very similar in principle, where the cause of disequilibrium is not inflation at home but deflation abroad.   So long as rates of exchange remain fixed, deflation in any important country is inevitably transmitted to the others, except in so far as contact with these latter may mitigate the deflation itself.

INTERNATIONAL INVESTMENT

Deflation restricts the demand for invisible imports as well as for visible; it diminishes or extinguishes an export of capital. A country invests abroad because it has savings to spare. Savings are derived to a great extent from profits, and deflation causes a disproportionate shrinkage of profits and of current savings. " Past experience ", says the Report (para. 112), " has shown that foreign investment, if left to private initiative, tends to be extraordinarily unstable; it tends to dry up in periods of depression—at the very time when its cessation does the greatest damage to the maintenance of world prosperity." So the Report recommends a plan for stabilising international investment " over substantial periods " (para. 111).

In consequence of political instability and national exclusiveness, the extent of private foreign investment is likely to be limited, and the solution will be " to organise a large part of long-term foreign lending through an international organisation ", such as the International Bank (para. 112).

" Lending countries should fix annual targets for long-term international investment for five-year periods " (para. 193). The target or plan would include private investment, and the amount a lending country would put at the disposal of the International Bank in successive periods of six months would be adjusted for past discrepancies between estimated and actual amounts of private investment.

I shall not embark on any detailed criticism of this proposal, but will content myself with pointing out that the proposal does not distinguish between fluctuations due to inflation or deflation in a lending country, and changes in the source or direction of external investment due to other causes. For the former, the right remedy would of course be to avoid the inflation or deflation; if they are not avoided, stabilisation would mean at one time continuing external investment when the requisite surplus of saving does not exist, whereas at another the surplus might be so swollen that a reduction of the public portion of external investment to *nil* might still fail to keep within the planned amount. And the capital-importing countries would offer diminished opportunities for investment at a time of depression, and highly attractive opportunities at a time of activity.

If monetary expansions and contractions be supposed successfully avoided, a five-year forecast of economically desirable international investment would sometimes be very conjectural, and liable to be upset by the pressure of facts. If the flow of resources were arbitrarily stabilised for five year periods instead of being allowed to adjust itself gradually to changing economic conditions, there would tend to be big discontinuities at the end of each quinquennium.

It is characteristic of the Report that throughout it concentrates on measures which take many months or a period of years to operate. The only quick-acting measures, the regulation of terms of credit and rates of exchange, by which timely action in checking inflation or deflation is possible, are practically omitted from consideration.

INDEX

Absorption of cash
and abortive saving, 117
by consumers, 56, 58, 60, 63, 91, 280, 295
defined, 59
distinct from saving, 91-2, 152
by investment market, 73-5, 80, 92, 102, 280, 282
owing to
deficiency of capital outlay, 93, 117
liquidation of working capital, 71-3, 80, 86, 218, 284, 296, 299
from reinvested profits or depreciation, 89-90, 180
and technological unemployment, 128-9
by traders, 58, 63, 71-2, 76, 89, 100-1, 295-6
Absorption or release of cash (*see also* Absorption, Release), 58-61, 140-1
by banks, 59, 76, 142, 144-5
cannot occur in the community as a whole, 59, 148
and circulating capital, 89, 107, 141, 151
defined, 59
evokes further absorption or release, 60, 149-50
by the foreign exchange market, 143-4
by investment market, 60, 63, 75, 80, 99, 103-4, 283, 297
and monetary regulation, 60, 76, 89-90
Power of banks over, 60, 76, 102-3, 118
and the quantity theory, 150
Acceleration principle (*see also* " Relation "), 6, 63, 95-6, 99, 251, 276, 289-91
Accidental destruction, 138
Accumulation, 9, 23, 55, 129-31, 160, 215-16, 290-3
of unsold goods, 161, 295
Active
balances, 159-60, 191, 193, 211, 213, 219
investment, 161-6, 172, 195, 197-8, 200-1, 208, 214-15, 276, 286, 305 *n.*
and saving, 161, 173, 195, 218
Activity, Productive
and capital outlay, 69, 92-3
Climax of, 100-1, 112-13, 254
Declining, 65-7
and demand, 62, 92, 114, 227, 292
and employment, 62, 65

Activity, Productive (*cont.*)—
encourages inventions, 75
Fluctuations in, 69, 91, 210, 248, 281, 312
generates incomes, 61, 75, 166, 232, 305, 309
Normal, 128
and orders to producers, 62, 78, 119
and passive investment, 161
and prices, 67, 285
and profit, 171
and rate of interest, 77-9, 82
and release of cash, 60
and sales, 64-8
Activity in retailing, 234
Adaptability of labour, 19, 127, 244
Advances, Bank, *see* Bank advances
Age of an instrument, 13-15, 19, 21
Agricultural products, 47, 50, 109
Prices of, 47, 109
Stocks of, 47
Algebraical notation, 5, 24, 132, 220
Amateur speculators, 124-5, 136
America, 42, 117, 121, 123, 124-5, 217
Aptitudes of workpeople, 19
Arrears
of deepening, 282
of improvements, 121
of maintenance and renewals, 120-2
of spending, 120
of widening, 63, 95-6, 237 *n.*, 297
Autonomous investment, 96

Balance of payments, 144, 210, 213, 297, 315
Balances
Active, 93, 159, 191, 211, 213, 219
Consumers', 58, 72, 132-3, 150, 155, 235, 271
of dealers in the investment market, 200
Depletion of, 102
Idle
and borrowing, 60, 150
drawn on by Government expenditure, 116, 122, 311
from liquidation of working capital, 53, 71-2, 194, 218, 284
and the speculative motive, 158-9, 173, 178-80, 193-5, 199-206, 211, 214, 217-18, 284, 294
Traders', 58-9, 89, 132-3
Working, 107

319

21*